MICROSOFT

Works 6

Introductory Concepts and Techniques

Gary B. Shelly
Thomas J. Cashman
Glenda A. Gunter
Randolph E. Gunter

Contributing Author
Victoria O. Rath

COURSE TECHNOLOGY
25 THOMSON PLACE
BOSTON MA 02210

SHELLY CASHMAN SERIES®

Australia • Canada • Denmark • Japan • Mexico • New Zealand • Philippines • Puerto Rico • Singapore
South Africa • Spain • United Kingdom • United States

Asia (excluding Japan)
Thomson Learning
60 Albert Street, #15-01
Albert Complex
Singapore 189969

Japan
Thomson Learning
Palaceside Building 5F
1-1-1 Hitotsubashi, Chiyoda-ku
Tokyo 100 0003 Japan

Australia/New Zealand
Nelson/Thomson Learning
102 Dodds Street
South Melbourne, Victoria 3205
Australia

Latin America
Thomson Learning
Seneca, 53
Colonia Polanco
11560 Mexico D.F. Mexico

South Africa
Thomson Learning
Zonnebloem Building,
Constantia Square
526 Sixteenth Road
P.O. Box 2459
Halfway House, 1685
South Africa

Canada
Nelson/Thomson Learning
1120 Birchmount Road
Scarborough, Ontario
Canada M1K 5G4

UK/Europe/Middle East
Thomson Learning
Berkshire House
168-173 High Holborn
London, WC1V 7AA United Kingdom

Spain
Thomson Learning
Calle Magallanes, 25
28015-MADRID
ESPANA

For more information, contact Course Technology, 25 Thomson Place, Boston, MA 02210.

Or visit our Internet site at www.course.com

PHOTO CREDITS: *Project 1, pages W 1.4-5* Feather and scroll, Courtesy of Image Club; *Project 2, pages W 2.2-3* Space scenes, Hubble telescope, and Albert Einstein, Courtesy of NASA; *Project 3 pages W 3.2-3* Discs, books, computers, video tapes, sunglasses, basketball, and wrench, Courtesy of PhotoDisc, Inc.

ISBN 0-7895-6306-1

1 2 3 4 5 6 7 8 9 10 BC 05 04 03 02 01

CONTENTS

PROJECT 1

Creating a Formatted Document with Clip Art

PROJECT 2

Building a Spreadsheet and Charting Data

PROJECT 3

Using Form Design to Create a Database

Preface

The Shelly Cashman Series® offers the finest textbooks in computer education. The Microsoft Works books continue with the innovation, quality, and reliability that you have come to expect from this series. We are proud that all our previous Microsoft Works books were best sellers, and we are confident that this book will join its predecessors.

Microsoft Works 6 includes two new major enhancements, the Works Portfolio tool and Works Format Gallery. The Portfolio tool allows you to collect and organize photos, graphics, text, and more, all in one convenient location. The Works Portfolio can be used with other programs and displays on the Windows desktop. With the new Format Gallery, you can browse hundreds of font and color sets and choose the combination that best suits your documents.

Works 6 has an improved Task Launcher, improved Word Processor and Spreadsheet tools, and an updated Help system. The improved Task Launcher is an easy-to-use navigation system that provides a task-oriented environment and brings all the applications and templates into one central resource. The improved Word Processor tool includes AutoCorrect, a feature that automatically corrects common errors as you type. The Word Processing tool also allows you to add Web links to your documents. Now you can jump to the Web directly from your documents. The improved Spreadsheet tool includes a new file format (.xlr) that allows users to open Works spreadsheets in Microsoft Excel. The Database tool is very similar to Microsoft Works 2000 in the way the tool looks and operates. The updated Microsoft Works suite includes extensive new clip art images, more than 250 templates, and a companion copy of Microsoft Internet Explorer, which you optionally can install.

In our Microsoft Works books, you will find an educationally sound and easy-to-follow pedagogy that combines a step-by-step approach with corresponding screens. The projects and exercises in the books are designed to take full advantage of the Microsoft Works 6 features. The popular Other Ways and More About features offer in-depth knowledge of Microsoft Works 6. The project openers provide a fascinating perspective on the subject covered in the project. The Shelly Cashman Series Microsoft Works books will make your computer applications class exciting and dynamic and one that your students will remember as one of their better educational experiences.

Objectives of This Textbook

Microsoft Works 6: Introductory Concepts and Techniques is intended for a course that covers a brief introduction to Microsoft Works. No experience with a computer is assumed and no mathematics beyond the high school freshman level is required. The objectives of this book are:

- To teach the fundamentals of Microsoft Works
- To expose students to examples of the computer as a useful tool
- To give students an overview of how to use the Word Processor, Spreadsheet, and Database tools
- To provide a knowledge base of Microsoft Works on which students can build
- To acquaint students with the proper and correct way to create documents, spreadsheets, and databases, suitable for course work, professional purposes, and personal use
- To develop an exercise-oriented approach that allows students to learn by example
- To encourage independent study and help those who are working alone in a distance education environment

When students complete the course using this textbook, they will have a basic knowledge and understanding of Microsoft Works.

The Shelly Cashman Approach

Features of the Shelly Cashman Series Works 6 books include:

- **Project Orientation:** Each project in the book presents a practical problem and complete solution in an easy-to-understand approach.
- **Screen-by-Screen, Step-by-Step Instructions:** Each of the tasks required to complete a project is identified throughout the development of the project. The steps are accompanied by full-color screens.
- **Other Ways Boxes for Reference:** Works 6 provides a wide variety of ways to carry out a given task. The Other Ways boxes displayed at the end of most of the step-by-step sequences specify the other ways to do the task completed in the steps. Thus, the steps and the Other Ways box make a comprehensive reference unit.
- **More About Feature:** These marginal annotations provide background information that complements the topics covered, adding depth and perspective to the learning process.
- **Integration of the World Wide Web:** We have integrated the World Wide Web into the students' Works 6 learning experience through More Abouts that provide students with additional information and currency on topics of importance.

Other Ways

1. Click Task Launcher button, click History tab, click desired document
2. On File menu click Open, click desired document, click Open button
3. Press CTRL+O
4. Click Open button on toolbar, click desired document, click Open button

More About

Microsoft Works 6

To receive a free quarterly Works 6 e-newsletter from Microsoft, visit the Works 6 More About Web page (www.scsite.com/works6/more.htm) and then click Newsletter.

Organization of This Textbook

Microsoft Works 6: Introductory Concepts and Techniques consists of three projects. A short description of each follows.

Project 1 – Creating a Formatted Document with Clip Art In Project 1, students are introduced to the Works Word Processor tool. Topics include starting and closing Works; entering and correcting text; centering text; creating a bulleted list; changing font, font size, and font style; inserting clip art; using print preview; opening and editing a word processing document; and using Works Help.

Project 2 – Building a Spreadsheet and Charting Data In Project 2, students are introduced to the Works Spreadsheet tool. Topics include entering text and numeric values; summing columns and rows using the AutoSum button; copying cells using the fill handle; centering text across columns; coloring text; using the AutoFormat feature; changing column widths; saving a spreadsheet; printing a spreadsheet; charting the data in the spreadsheet using a 3-D Bar chart; opening a spreadsheet file; and correcting errors.

Project 3 – Using Form Design to Create a Database In Project 3, students are introduced to the Works Database tool. Topics include an explanation of form design view; creating a form design view title using WordArt, entering fields and labels on the form; saving; formatting the database title; inserting clip art from the Clip Gallery; positioning the fields on the form by dragging; and formatting fields and labels. The form view of the database is described; data is entered into the database; list view is explained; and the data is formatted in list view. Finally, the database is saved, printed in form view, and then printed in list view using landscape orientation.

End-of-Project Student Activities

A notable strength of the Shelly Cashman Series Works applications books is the extensive student activities at the end of each project. Well-structured student activities can make the difference between students merely participating in a class and students retaining the information they learn. The activities in the Shelly Cashman Series Works 6 books include the following:

- **What You Should Know** A listing of the tasks completed within a project together with the pages where the step-by-step, screen-by-screen explanations appear. This section provides a perfect study review for students.
- **Test Your Knowledge** Four activities designed to determine students' understanding of the material in the project. Included are true/false questions, multiple-choice questions, and short-answer activities.
- **Use Help** Any user of Works applications must know how to use Help. Therefore, this book contains extensive exercises that require students to use Help. These exercises alone distinguish the Shelly Cashman Series from any other set of Works instructional materials.

- **Apply Your Knowledge** This exercise requires students to open and manipulate a file from the Data Disk for the Works 6 books. To obtain a copy of the Data Disk, follow the instructions on the inside back cover of this textbook.
- **In the Lab** Three in-depth assignments require students to apply the knowledge gained in the project to solve problems on a computer.
- **Cases and Places** Up to seven unique case studies allow students to apply their knowledge to real-world situations.

Shelly Cashman Series Teaching Tools

A comprehensive set of Teaching Tools accompanies this textbook in the form of a CD-ROM. The CD-ROM includes an Instructor's Manual and teaching and testing aids. The CD-ROM (ISBN 0-7895-6316-9) is available through your Course Technology representative or by calling one of the following telephone numbers: Colleges and Universities, 1-800-648-7450; High Schools, 1-800-824-5179; Career Colleges, 1-800-477-3692; Canada, 1-800-268-2222; and Corporations and Government Agencies, 1-800-340-7450. The contents of the CD-ROM follow.

- **Instructor's Manual** The Instructor's Manual is made up of Microsoft Works 6 files. The files include lecture notes, solutions to laboratory assignments, and a large test bank. The files allow you to modify the lecture notes or generate quizzes and exams from the test bank using your own word processing software. Where appropriate, solutions to laboratory assignments are embedded as icons in the files. When an icon appears, double-click it and the application will start and the solution will display on the screen. The Instructor's Manual includes the following for each project: project objectives; project overview; detailed lesson plans with page number references; teacher notes and activities; answers to the end-of-project exercises; test bank of 110 questions for every project (25 multiple-choice, 50 true/false, and 35 fill-in-the-blank) with page number references; and transparency references. The transparencies are available through the Figures in the Book. The test bank questions are numbered the same as in Course Test Manager. Thus, you can print a copy of the project test bank and use the printout to select your questions in Course Test Manager.

- **Figures in the Book** Illustrations of the figures and tables in the textbook are available in Figures in the Book. Use this ancillary to create a slide show from the illustrations for lecture or to print transparencies for use in lecture with an overhead projector.
- **Course Test Manager** Course Test Manager is a powerful testing and assessment package that enables instructors to create and print tests from the large test bank. Instructors with access to a networked computer lab (LAN) can administer, grade, and track tests online. Students also can take online practice tests, which generate customized study guides that indicate where in the textbook students can find more information for each question.
- **Course Syllabus** Any instructor who has been assigned a course at the last minute knows how difficult it is to come up with a course syllabus. For this reason, sample syllabi are included for each of the Microsoft Works 6 suite that can be customized easily to a course.
- **Lecture Success System** Lecture Success System files are for use with the application software, a personal computer, and projection device to explain and illustrate the step-by-step, screen-by-screen development of a project in the textbook without entering large amounts of data.
- **Instructor's Lab Solutions** Solutions and required files for all the In the Lab assignments at the end of each project are available.
- **Lab Tests/Test Outs** Tests that parallel the In the Lab assignments are supplied for the purpose of testing students in the laboratory on the material covered in the project or testing students out of the course.
- **Student Files** All the files that are required by students to complete the Apply Your Knowledge exercises are included.
- **Interactive Labs** Eighteen hands-on interactive labs that take students from ten to fifteen minutes each to step through help solidify and reinforce mouse and keyboard usage and computer concepts. Student assessment is available in each interactive lab by means of a Print button. The assessment requires students to answer questions.

MyCourse.com

MyCourse.com offers instructors and students an opportunity to supplement classroom learning with additional course content. You can use MyCourse.com to expand on traditional learning by accessing and completing reading, tests, and other assignments through the customized, comprehensive Web site. For additional information, visit mycourse.com and click the Help button.

Acknowledgments

The Shelly Cashman Series would not be the leading computer education series without the contributions of outstanding publishing professionals. First, and foremost, among them is Becky Herrington, director of production and designer. She is the heart and soul of the Shelly Cashman Series, and it is only through her leadership, dedication, and tireless efforts that superior products are made possible. Becky created and produced the award-winning Works series of books.

Under Becky's direction, the following individuals made significant contributions to these books: Doug Cowley, production manager; Ginny Harvey, series specialist and developmental editor; Ken Russo, senior Web designer; Mike Bodnar, associate production manager; Mark Norton, Web designer; Meena Moest, production editor; Michelle French, graphic artist and cover designer; Hector Arvizu, Christy Pardini, and Chris Schneider, graphic artists; Jeanne Black and Betty Hopkins, Quark experts; Lyn Markowicz, copyeditor; Kim Kosmatka, proofreader; Cristina Haley, indexer; Jenny Gunter, editing assistant, and Victoria Rath, contributing writer.

Special thanks go to Richard Keaveny, associate publisher; Lora Wade, product manager; Erin Roberts, associate product manager; Francis Schurgot, Web product manager; Marc Ouellette, associate Web product manager; Erin Runyon, editorial assistant; and Rachel VanKirk, product marketing manager.

Gary B. Shelly
Thomas J. Cashman

Glenda A. Gunter
Randolph E. Gunter

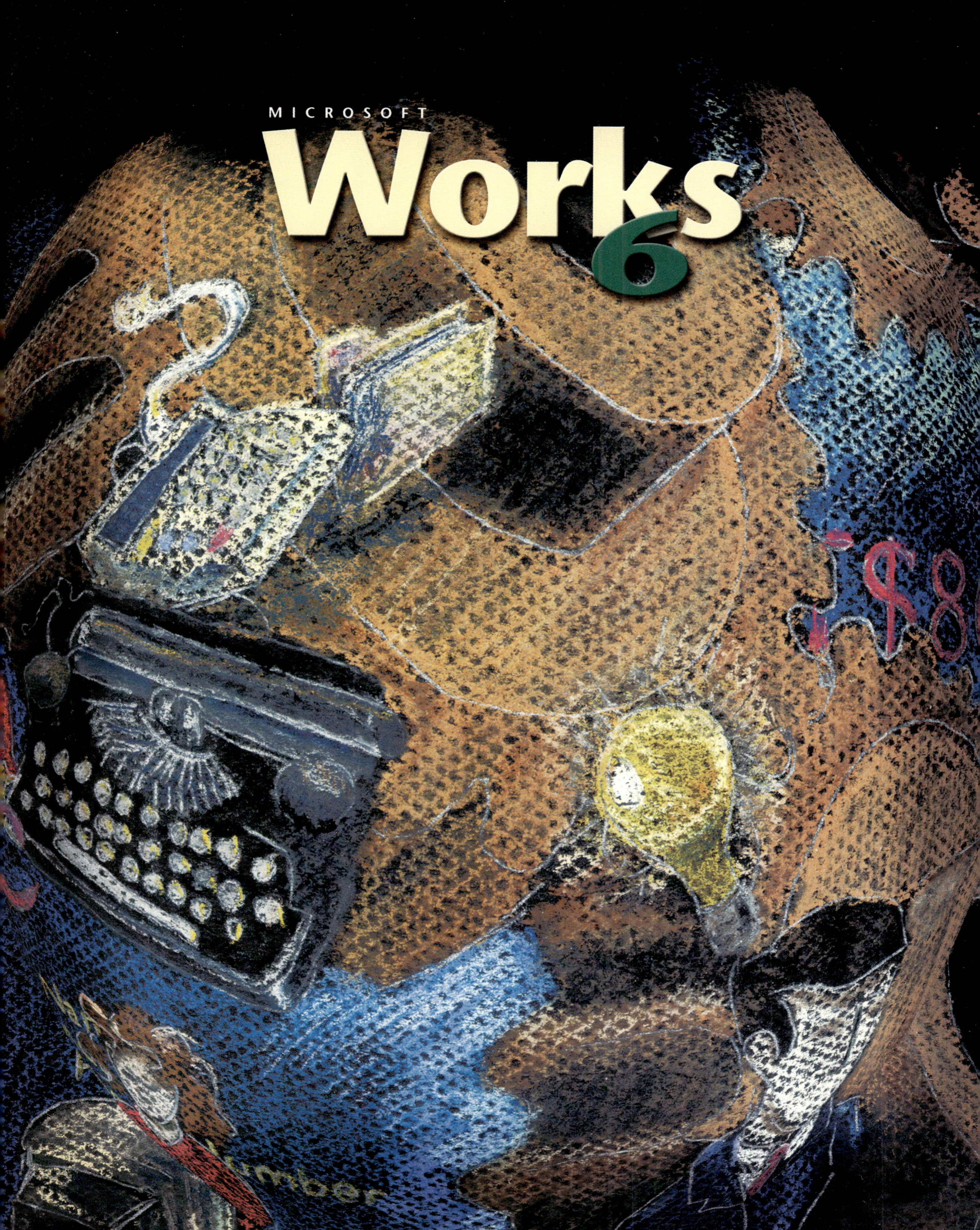
MICROSOFT
Works
6

Microsoft Works 6

Creating a Formatted Document with Clip Art

OBJECTIVES

You will have mastered the material in this project when you can:

- Start Microsoft Works
- Start the Word Processor tool
- Identify the features of the Works Word Processor window
- Enter text
- Save a document
- Select a character, word, line, or paragraph
- Center one or more words
- Change fonts, font sizes, and font styles
- Create a bulleted list
- Change the color of text
- Insert clip art in a document
- Use the Print Preview feature
- Print a document
- Close a document
- Quit Works
- Open an existing document
- Delete and insert data
- Use Help

To Be or Not To Be…

Works Word Processor Provides Options

How many words did William Shakespeare add to the English language? Guesses range from a few hundred terms to more than 10,000, with the most likely estimate approximately 1,500 words. Other English Renaissance writers also added words to the English language. The dramatist Ben Jonson is credited with coining words such as *analytic* and *antagonist.* But it is Shakespeare's inventiveness and imaginative wordplay that created words such as *puppy dog, watchdog,* and *zany.* He used them in hundreds of plays and poems to enrich the arts.

Imagine the possibilities if Shakespeare would have had Works Word Processor. In many ways, twenty-first century writers are more fortunate than Shakespeare. Even if you don't plan on writing as many literary masterpieces as he, the Works Word Processor with its built-in Task Wizards for letters, resumes, and other documents gives anyone a running start.

While in college and during virtually any career thereafter—chemist, engineer, journalist, or playwright—it is essential that you present the ideas and products of your work in clear, accurate written form. In fact, just getting a start in a chosen profession may depend on how well you are represented by your stand-in: a well-prepared resume. Making a favorable first impression is not only important, it is vital.

Once you have employment, you are likely to find that companies no longer provide secretarial assistance for creating and revising documents. Now employers expect professionals to come to the workplace prepared with these skills.

Fortunately, technology has risen to the challenge. During Shakespeare's days of quill pens and inkwells, every change and every mistake meant rewriting the entire page or sometimes the whole document. Today's innovations enable words, sentences, paragraphs, and even whole pages of text to be added, deleted, or reordered with the click of a mouse before using a single page of printer paper. The built-in spelling checker and thesaurus are included for finding spelling errors and finding hard to pin down synonyms.

Accuracy is important. The reason is simple. Consider *TIME* magazine's $100,000 missing "r." The presses had already begun rolling out the cover of the March 2, 1983 issue when someone discovered the letter r missing from the word "Control" in the headline: "A New Plan for Arms Contol." The mistake cost the publication $100,000 and a day's delay to add the letter r. Spelling checker would have spotted this.

Written errors also can become legends. In 1631, an authorized edition of the Holy Bible came off the presses in London with the "not" missing from the seventh of the Ten Commandments. The result: "Thou shalt commit adultery." The book's publishers were fined 3,000 English pounds and went down in history as the creators of the *Wicked Bible*. This illustrates that even the best tools cannot replace careful proofing.

Although the Works Word Processor is not a substitute for careful review or original thought, even Shakespeare would agree that it can remove many of the barriers that might stand in the way of getting a quality education and a quality job.

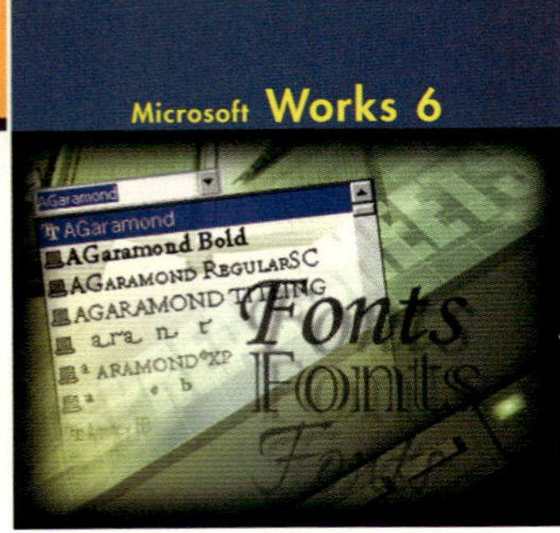

Microsoft Works 6

Creating a Formatted Document with Clip Art

CASE PERSPECTIVE

After attending a recent administration meeting, Gracie Scott, president of the Student Government Association (SGA), learned that school administrators are considering increasing Internet usage by coordinating efforts to provide all students and faculty with off-campus, high-speed Internet access. Students and faculty will be able to choose from a varitey of Internet service providers that have agreed to offer Internet access at significantly reduced rates. The technology department director stated that the reason for this new program is to enhance learning by making Internet access from home affordable for all students. Before offering this new service, however, administrators want feedback from students and have asked the SGA to help.

Gracie is enthusiastic about this initiative. To make students aware of the program, she decides to organize an Open Student Forum. After evaluating the response from the attendees, she then can provide their reactions and questions to administrators.

As a member of the SGA, you have volunteered to create an eye-catching and informative flyer that will notify students of the upcoming Open Student Forum.

Introduction to Microsoft Works 6

Microsoft Works 6 is application software that provides word processing, spreadsheet, database, calendar, address book, and portfolio capabilities in a single package. Works also provides quick access to the Microsoft Network (MSN), Internet Explorer, and Microsoft Outlook.

The applications within Microsoft Works, called **tools**, work together to help you create your documents. These tools are described briefly in the following paragraphs.

1. **Word Processor Tool** — Use the Word Processor tool to prepare all forms of personal and business communications, including letters, business and academic reports, and other types of written documents.
2. **Spreadsheet Tool** — Use the Spreadsheet tool for applications that require you to enter, calculate, manipulate, and analyze data. You also can use the Spreadsheet tool to display data graphically in the form of charts, such as bar charts and pie charts.
3. **Database Tool** — Use the Database tool for creating, sorting, retrieving, displaying, and printing data such as names and addresses of friends or customers, company inventories, employee payroll records, or other types of business or personal data. You can use the Database tool for virtually any type of record-keeping activity that requires you to create, sort, display, retrieve, and print data.
4. **Calendar Tool** — Use the Calendar tool to manage your schedule. The Calendar tracks appointments and reminders for important dates such as birthdays, tests, and upcoming school events.

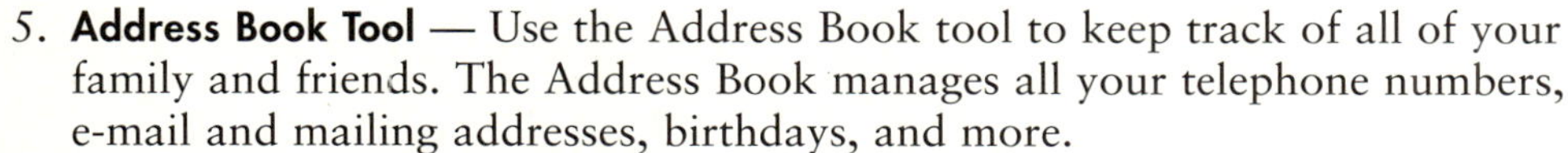

5. **Address Book Tool** — Use the Address Book tool to keep track of all of your family and friends. The Address Book manages all your telephone numbers, e-mail and mailing addresses, birthdays, and more.
6. **Portfolio Tool** — Use the Portfolio tool to collect all of the information that you find and want to keep as you work on your computer. The information is stored in a collection and can be quickly inserted into other documents or e-mail messages.

More About

Microsoft Works 6

The Word Processor, Spreadsheet, and Database tools provide fundamental business- and home-computing capabilities and integration. Although the larger and more sophisticated stand-alone products such as Microsoft Word or Excel are more refined, the Works 6 big advantage is that it offers a package that includes the most important tools of the stand-alone products at a fraction of the cost. For more information on the tools of Works 6, visit the Works 6 More About Web page (www.scsite.com/works6/more.htm) and then click Microsoft Works 6 Tools.

Microsoft Works Accessories

Additional software features, called **accessories**, are a part of the software package that helps you work more effectively with the various tools. These accessories include AutoCorrect, which automatically detects and corrects certain typographical errors, misspelled words, grammatical errors, and incorrect capitalizations; Background Spell Checking, which checks for misspelled words as you type; Spelling and Grammar, which allows you to proofread documents for errors in spelling and grammar by identifying the errors and offering corrections; Thesaurus, which provides synonyms for selected words; Microsoft Clip Gallery, which contains illustrations you can insert in documents; WordArt, which allows you to change plain text into artistically designed text; Microsoft Draw, which allows you to create and modify drawings that can be inserted into a Word Processor document or a Database form; and Microsoft Paint, which allows you to create and modify objects that can be inserted in a document. These accessories will be explained in detail as they are used throughout the book.

Tasks, Templates, and Wizards

In addition to the Microsoft Works tools and accessories, Works includes more than 250 tasks, templates, and wizards to help you create professional-looking documents. **Tasks** are activities that you can choose to create Works documents. When you start a task, Works starts the appropriate program or the program and document that you need to perform the tasks. Many tasks use resources that are available on the World Wide Web.

Templates are documents that contain all the settings, text, and formats that you can reuse. Works contains many already designed templates or you can create your own. For example, when you create a thank-you letter for a job interview, you can save it as a template and reuse it as a basis for writing other thank-you letters for interviews.

Wizards make it easy to create professional-looking documents. You can use a wizard to create a resume, letter, stationery, or school report. When the wizard is finished, you can add or remove text and make any changes you want.

More About

Templates

Works 6 comes with 250 templates. To download additional and featured templates, visit the Works 6 More About Web page (www.scsite.com/works6/more.htm) and then click Templates.

Project One — Formatted Document with Clip Art

Because word processing is widely used in both the academic and business world, the Word Processor is the first of the Works tools presented. To illustrate the use and power of the Word Processor, the steps necessary to create the document shown in Figure 1-1 are explained on the following pages. This announcement, named Off-Campus Internet Access, advertises an open forum for students.

OFF-CAMPUS INTERNET ACCESS

OPEN STUDENT FORUM

Please attend an open forum to discuss a school initiative that will provide off-campus, high-speed Internet access for all students. Your opinion counts and administrators want your feedback.

Items for discussion:

- E-mail enhancements
- Disk space allocation for personal Web page development
- Cost
- Other access options for students

Please attend

Tuesday, October 27
Kennedy Auditorium
4:00 p.m. to 5:00 p.m.

FIGURE 1-1

To create the announcement, you must type the text, center selected lines, use several different fonts and font styles, increase the font sizes, change the font styles to bold, add bullets to the list, insert an illustration into the document, and display the last three lines in red. You can accomplish these tasks easily using the Microsoft Works Word Processor.

Starting Microsoft Works

To start Works, Windows must be running and Microsoft Works must be installed on your computer. Perform the following steps to start Works.

To Start Microsoft Works

1 Click the Start button on the taskbar, point to Programs, and then point to Microsoft Works.

The Start menu displays (Figure 1-2). When you point to Programs, the Programs submenu displays numerous commands including the Microsoft Works command.

Programs command

Start menu

Start button

taskbar

Microsoft Works command

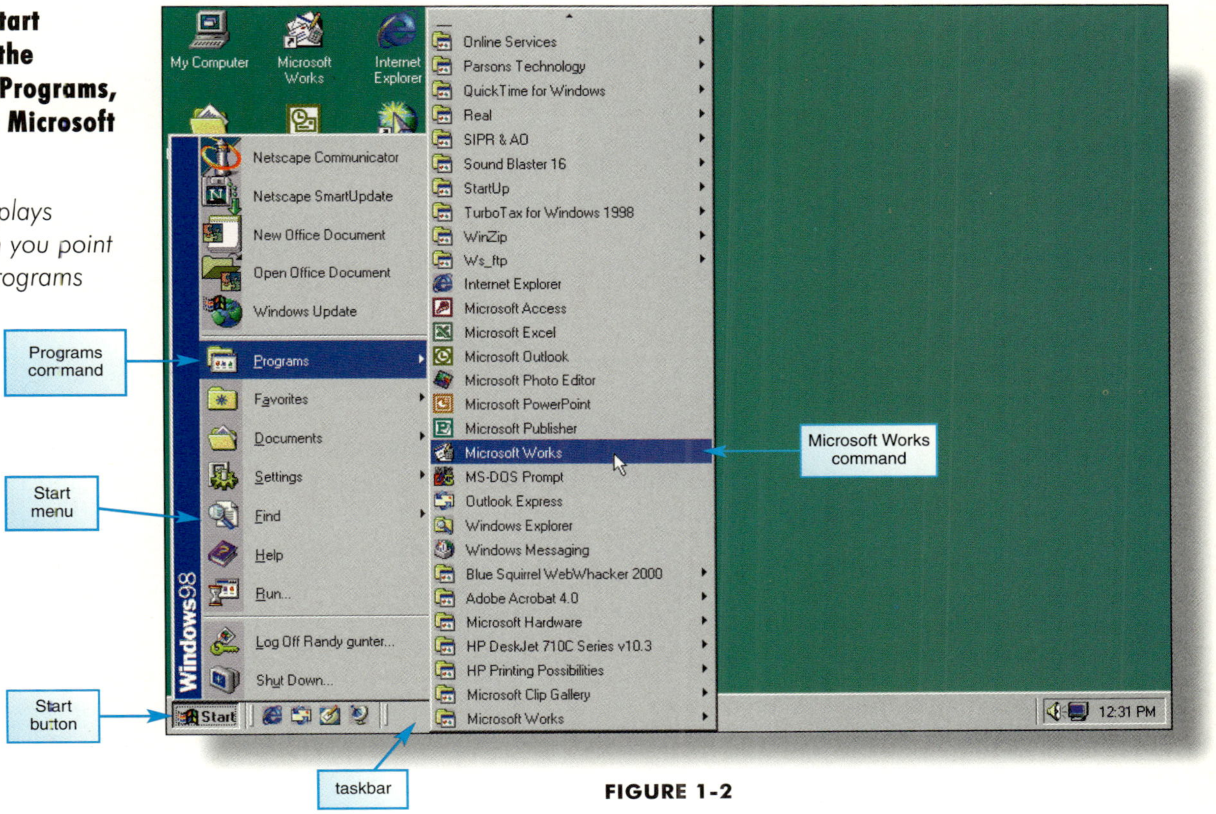

FIGURE 1-2

2 **Click Microsoft Works. If the Programs sheet does not display, click the Programs tab.**

The Works Task Launcher splash screen displays momentarily and then the Programs sheet displays in the Works Task Launcher window (Figure 1-3).

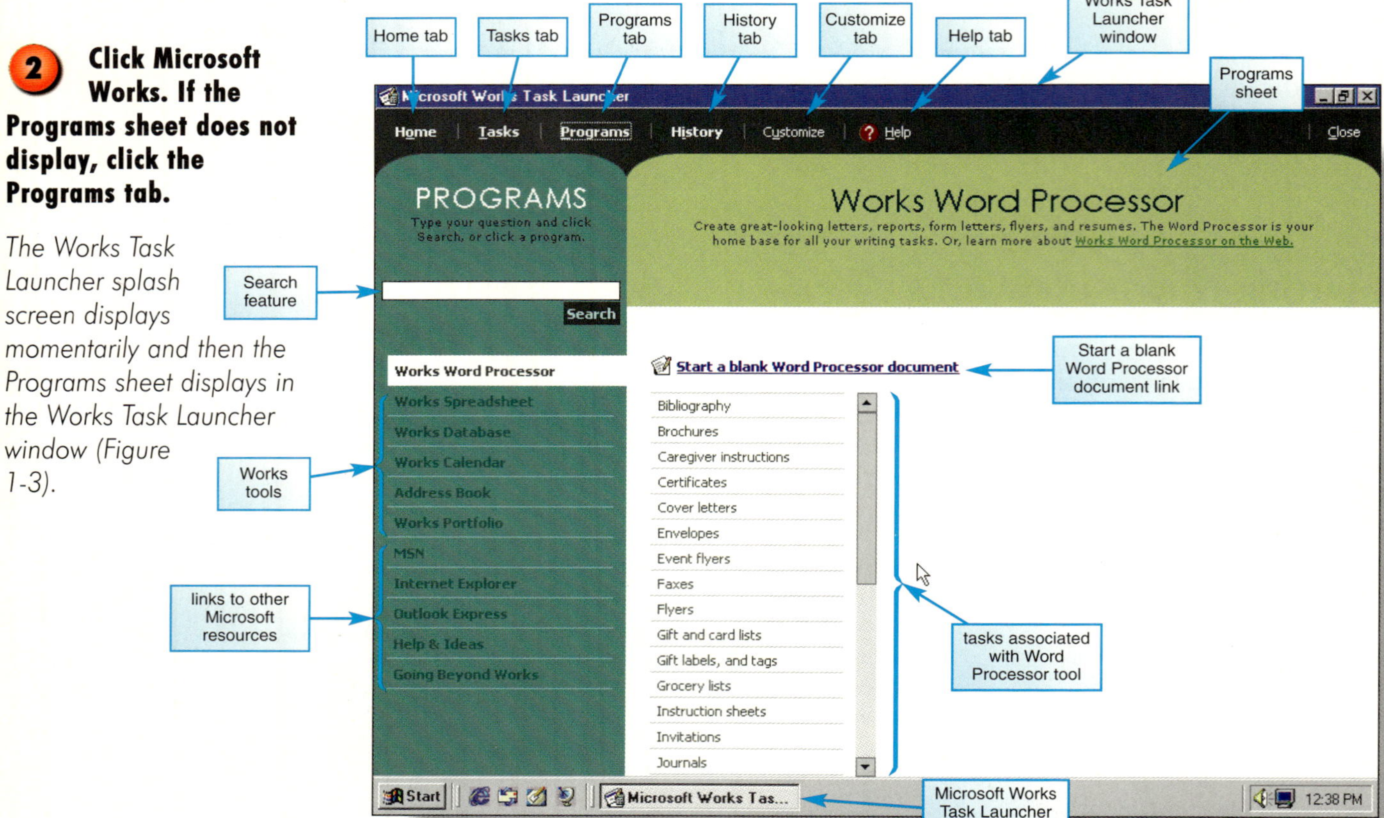

FIGURE 1-3

Other Ways

1. Double-click Microsoft Works icon on desktop

The **Works Task Launcher** window contains six tabs: Home, Tasks, Programs, History, Customize, and Help. Clicking the Programs, Tasks, and History tabs displays sheets that are explained on the following pages. Clicking the **Home tab** displays the **Home sheet**, which contains links to the Task sheet, Program sheet, History sheet, and a link to a tour of Microsoft Works. Clicking the **Customize tab** displays an Options dialog box that allows you to play sounds, clear history, and have Microsoft notify you when program updates to Works are available. Finally, clicking the **Help tab** displays the Help menu, which allows you to access various Help topics. When you start Works, the Works Task Launcher window displays the sheet that was displayed the last time Works was used, usually the Program sheet.

Programs Sheet

The **Programs sheet** (Figure 1-3) displays with information on the Works Word Processor tool. In the Programs sheet, you can access any of the Works tools, Tasks, History, Help, and more. Features of the Programs sheet include:

A **Search feature** that lets you search for Works Tasks by entering a keyword or phrase and then clicking the Search button. The **Works Spreadsheet link** that displays spreadsheet-related tasks and a link to start a blank spreadsheet. You will be using the Works Spreadsheet tool later in this book. The **Works Database link** that displays database-related tasks and a link to start a blank database. You will be using the Works Database tool later in this book. The **Works Calendar link** that opens the Calendar tool. You access the Address Book tool by clicking the **Address Book link** and start the Works Portfolio tool by clicking the **Works Portfolio link**.

If you are connected to the Internet, you can access the Microsoft Network (MSN) by clicking the **MSN link**, which will provide you with numerous online Microsoft services. You also can open Internet Explorer and Outlook Express by clicking the appropriate links.

The **Help & Ideas link** provides numerous resources to help you learn how to use the various Works tools, including the Works Getting Started Manual. The **Going Beyond Works link** provides information on Works Suite that includes Works 6 and other applications.

Tasks Sheet

Clicking the Tasks tab displays the Tasks sheet (Figure 1-4). The **Tasks sheet** contains hundreds of tasks, templates, and wizards organized by category. A categories list displays in the left pane of the window and the tasks, wizards, and templates available in the selected category display in the right pane of the window. Clicking any of the tasks will provide information on the task and provide a Start this task button for you to begin creating the task.

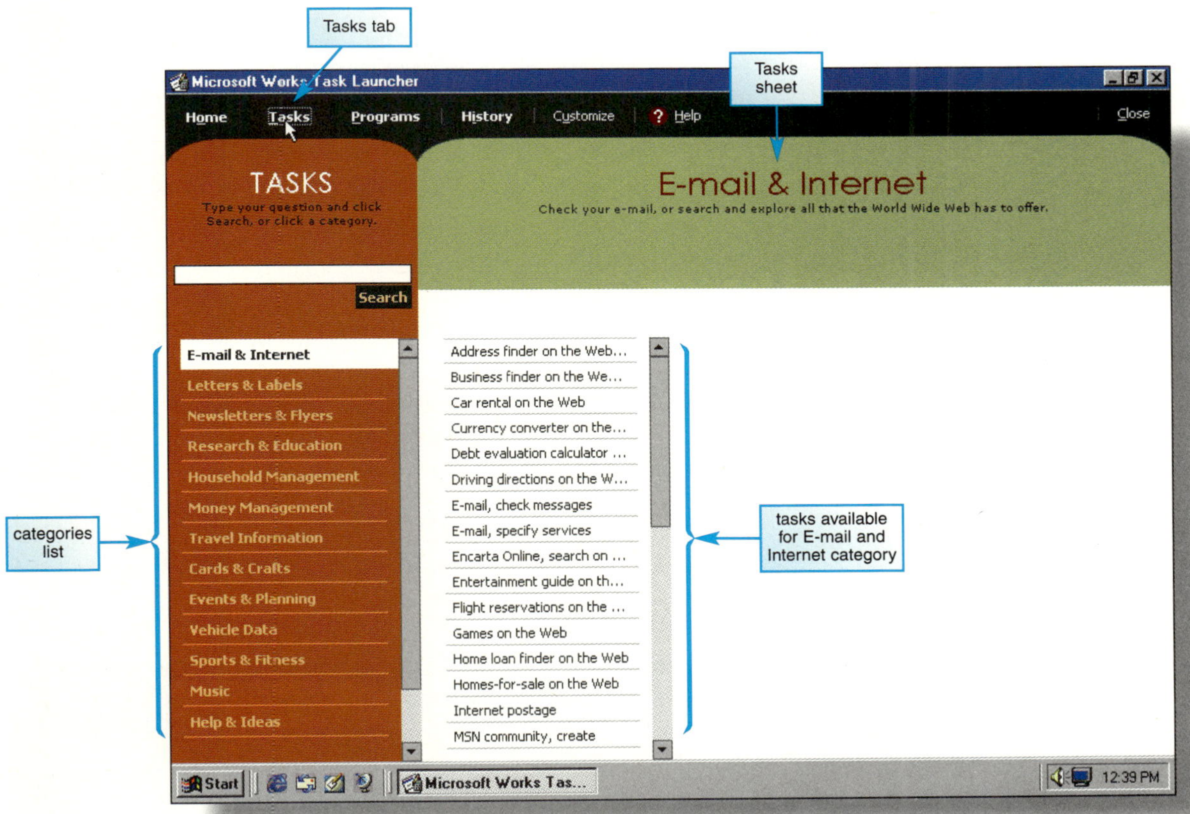

FIGURE 1-4

History Sheet

Clicking the History tab displays the History sheet (Figure 1-5 on the next page). Use the **History sheet** to open a file you worked on before. Click the appropriate file to open the document or click the **Find Files or Folders link** to access the **Find: All Files dialog box**, which can help you find files on your computer's hard disk or a floppy disk.

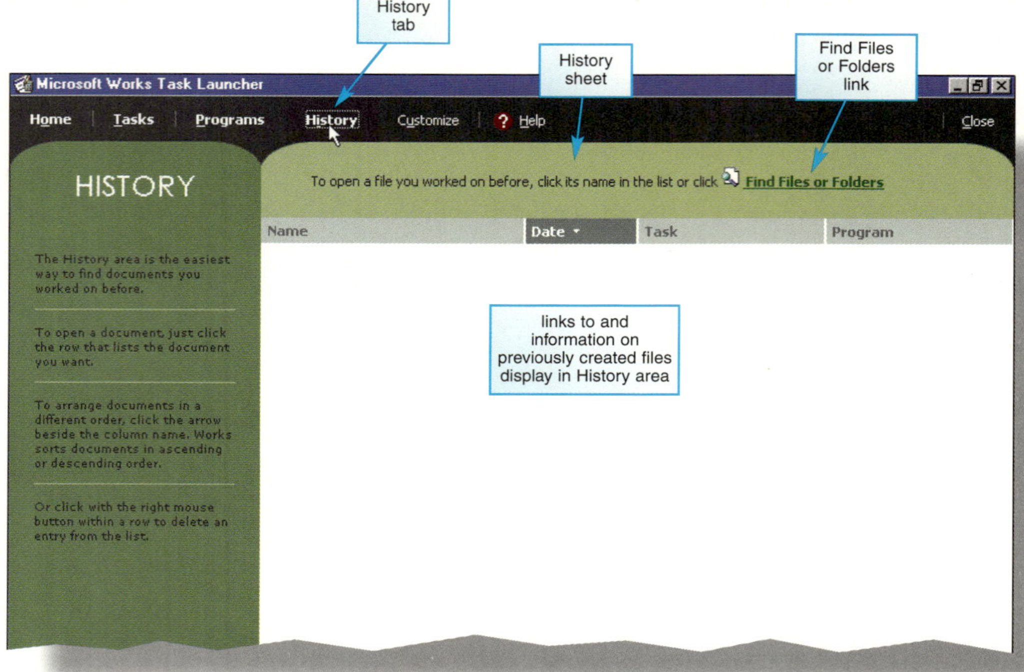

FIGURE 1-5

With Works started, you are ready to choose the tool you want to use. In this project, you will use the Word Processor tool to create the document shown in Figure 1-1 on page W 1.8.

Starting the Word Processor

To start the Word Processor, you click the appropriate link in the Programs sheet. If the Programs sheet is not displayed on your computer, click the Programs tab (see Figure 1-3 on page W 1.10). If necessary, click the Works Word Processor button in the left pane to display information on the Word Processor tool. The following steps explain this process.

To Start the Word Processor

1 Point to Start a blank Word Processor document link in the Works Task Launcher.

Start a blank Word Processor document displays light blue (Figure 1-6).

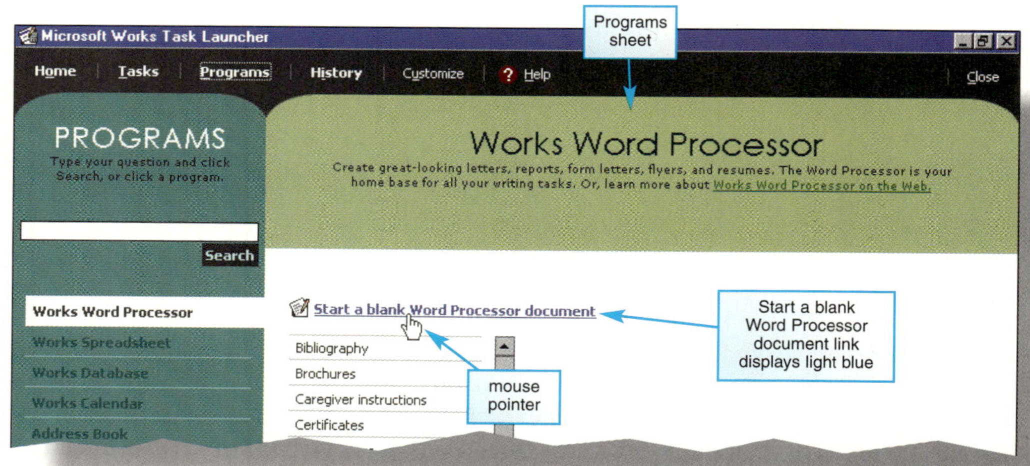

FIGURE 1-6

2 Click Start a blank Word Processor document link.

Works opens the Word Processor window containing the document name, Untitled Document (Figure 1-7). The Works Help pane displays to the right of the Word Processor window, and the Portfolio tool normally displays at the top of the window. The Start using the Word Processor topic displays in the Works Help pane because the Word Processor tool was chosen. The Works Help pane and the Portfolio tool may or may not display depending on the status of the features the last time the Word Processor tool was used.

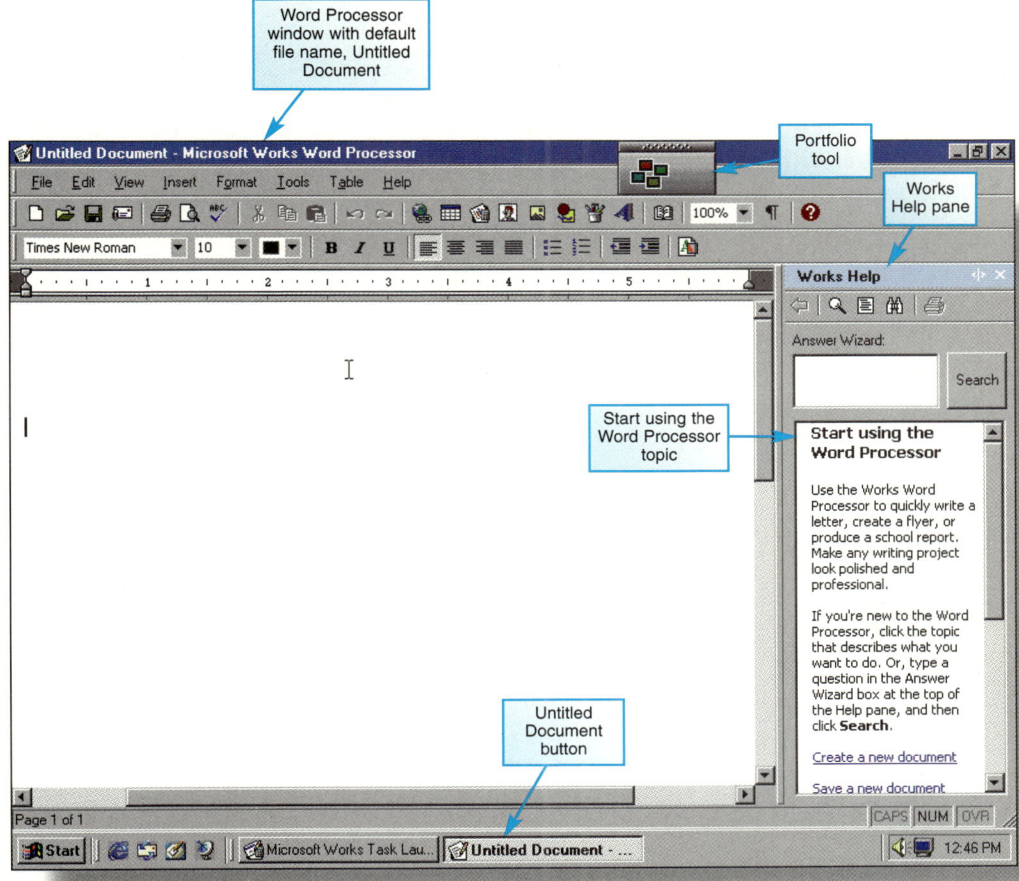

FIGURE 1-7

3 Click the Portfolio tool. When the Portfolio tool expands, click the Tasks box arrow and then point to the Close command.

Works expands the Portfolio tool in Compact view and the Tasks menu displays (Figure 1-8).

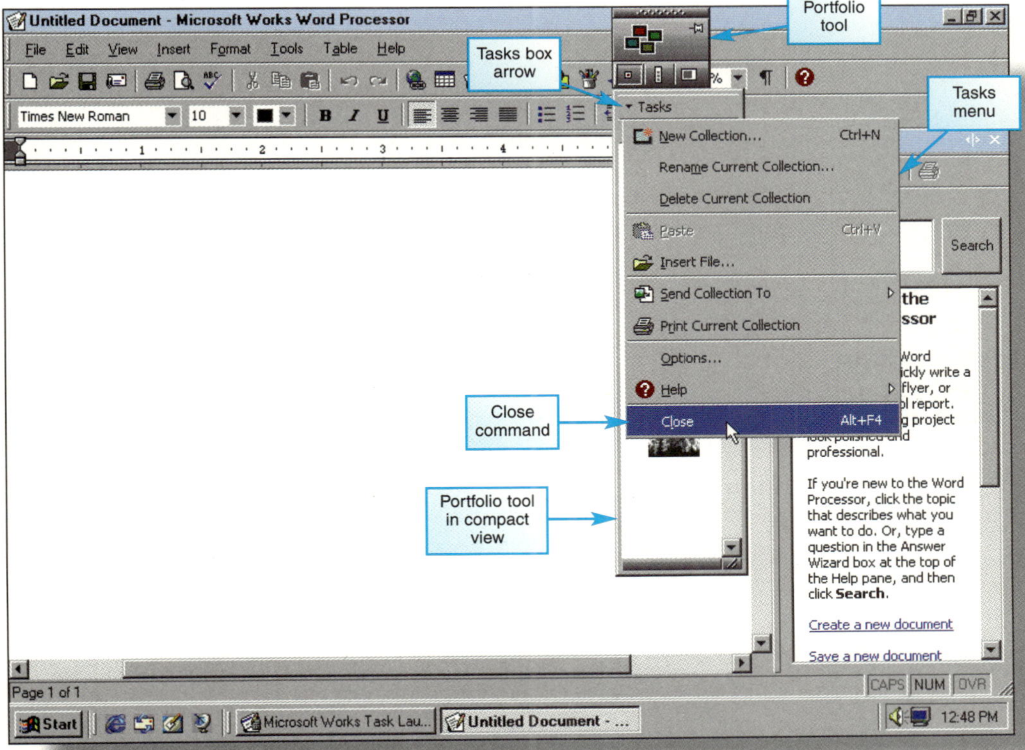

FIGURE 1-8

4 **Click Close and then point to the Close Help button located at the upper-right corner of the Works Help pane.**

Works closes the Portfolio tool (Figure 1-9).

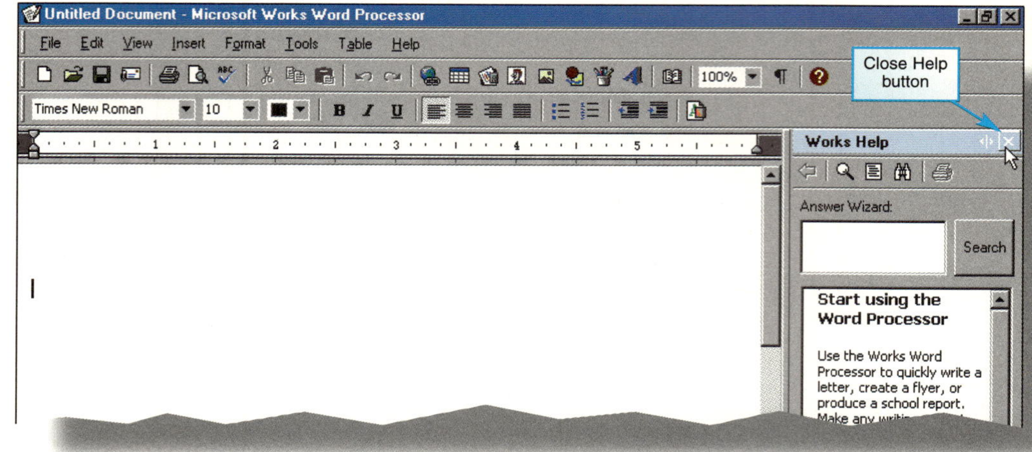

FIGURE 1-9

5 **Click the Close Help button.**

Works closes the Works Help pane and the Word Processor window expands to fill the entire screen (Figure 1-10).

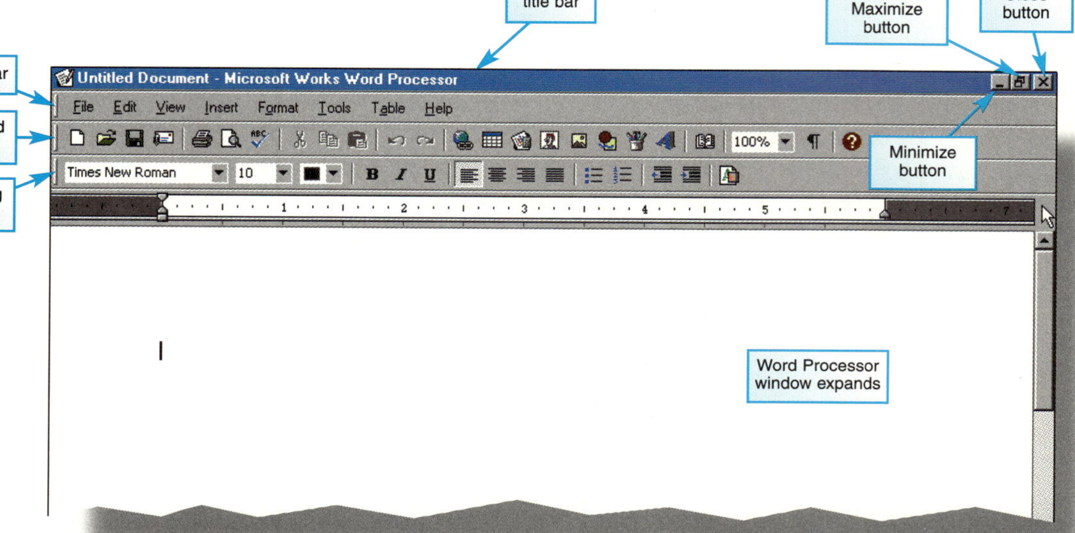

FIGURE 1-10

More About

Microsoft Works 6

To receive a free quarterly Works 6 e-newsletter from Microsoft, visit the Works 6 More About Web page (www.scsite.com/works6/more.htm) and then click Newsletter.

When you close the Works Help pane, you can see more of your document. Redisplaying Works Help pane will be covered later in this project. To redisplay the Works Portfolio tool, click the Works Portfolio link on the Programs sheet (see Figure 1-3 on page W 1.10) and then click the Start Works Portfolio link.

Works Portfolio is a powerful tool that lets you collect and organize objects, text, entire files, and much more into one location that you can use as you work on your computer. All the elements you gather are stored in a **collection**, which is an individual Portfolio storage location for information. You can create as many collections as you want, and you can give each collection a unique name. Each piece of information added to a collection is called an **item**. Once you have added items to a collection, you easily can insert one, several, or all items into other documents or an e-mail message. You also can print items from a collection.

Works includes a detailed tutorial on using the Works Portfolio tool. To access this tutorial, click the Home tab on the Works Task Launcher window and then click the Take a Tour link. When the Microsoft Works Quick Tours window displays, click the Works Portfolio link.

The Word Processor Window

The Word Processor window has many of the features common to all window screens. The following section describes these features.

Title Bar

The **title bar** (Figure 1-10) contains the title of the document, in this case, Untitled Document, and shows that you are using the Microsoft Works Word Processor. The title bar also contains the Minimize, Maximize or Restore, and Close buttons.

Formatting Toolbar

Many of the buttons on the Formatting toolbar are toggles; that is, click them once to format the selected text; and click them again to remove the format from the selected text. For example, clicking the Bold button bolds selected text; clicking the Bold button again removes the bold.

Menu Bar

The **menu bar** (Figure 1-10) displays menu names. Each menu contains a list of commands you can use to perform tasks such as open, close, save, or print documents, or otherwise manipulate data in the document you are creating.

Toolbars

Toolbars contain buttons that allow you to perform frequently required tasks more rapidly than when using the commands in the menus. Each button on a toolbar has a pictorial representation in a small square box that helps you identify its function. Two build-in toolbars are the Standard toolbar and the Formatting toolbar (Figure 1-10). Figure 1-11(a) illustrates the Standard toolbar and describes the function of each of the buttons and boxes. Figure 1-11(b) illustrates the Formatting toolbar. Each button and box is explained in detail as you use the buttons and boxes in the projects in this book.

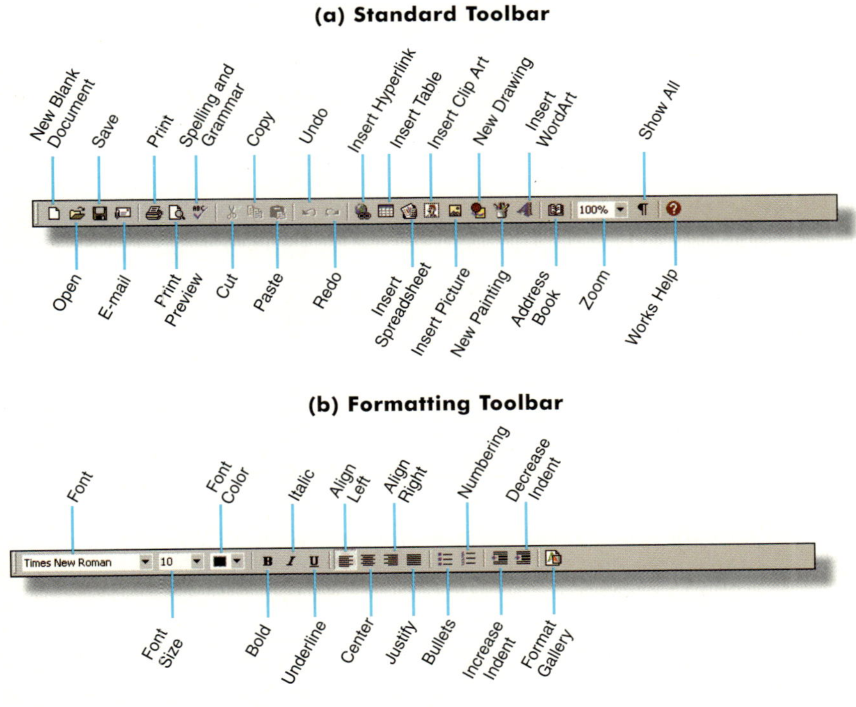

FIGURE 1-11

More About

Accessibility Features for People with Disabilities

Microsoft is committed to making its products and services easier for everyone to use. Many features, enhancements, and services in Microsoft Works and Microsoft Windows result in more accessibility for people with disabilities. To learn more about these features, click Accessibility Help on the Works Help menu. For additional information and services provided by Microsoft, visit the Works 6 More About Web page (www.scsite.com/works6/more.htm) and then click Accessibility Aids.

To choose any of these buttons, position the mouse pointer on the button and then click the button. Any button you choose appears recessed or light gray. When you position the mouse pointer on a button on the toolbar, a ScreenTip displays. A **ScreenTip** is a small rectangular box that contains a word or words describing the purpose of the button. You can control when the toolbars display by clicking the appropriate Toolbars command on the **View menu**.

Ruler

In the area below the two toolbars is a numbered bar called the **ruler** (Figure 1-12). The zero point is on the left side of the ruler and it indicates the left edge of your text. Toward the right side of the ruler is the 6-inch mark that indicates the right edge of your text. The numbers in between show the distance in inches of the document. Thus, a line approximately six inches in length is represented on the screen. As you type characters on the screen, the characters display in the document workspace below the ruler. By comparing the typed characters with the ruler, it is easy to see the number of inches occupied by the characters.

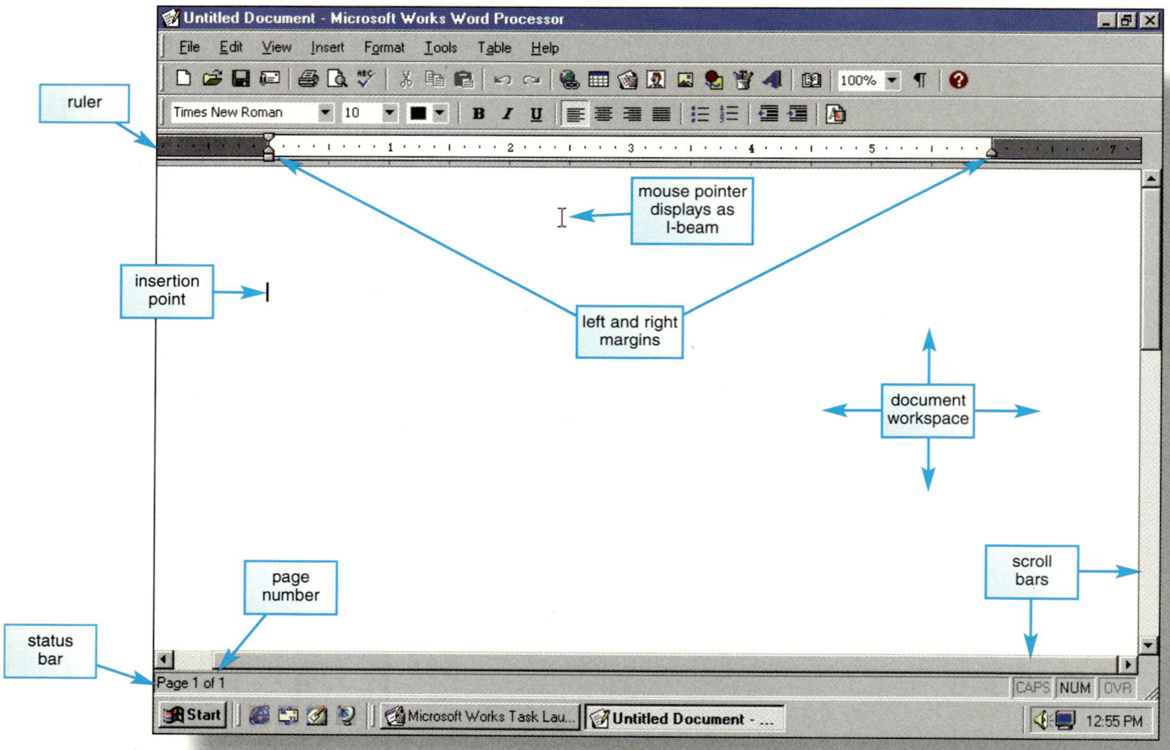

FIGURE 1-12

You can use the small triangles on the left and right sides of the ruler to control paragraph indents. When the ruler is displayed, you can change paragraph indents by dragging the small triangles. Tab stops are set by default at each half inch on the ruler and are denoted by the small vertical line on the ruler line.

Scroll Bars

When the text you enter occupies more space than you can view (for example, when the Works Help pane displays or you change margins that extend beyond the edges of the document window), you can use the **scroll bars** to move through the document (see Figure 1-12).

Status Bar

The **status bar** is located at the bottom of the Works window (see Figure 1-12). The page number and the total number of pages in a document display on the left side of the status bar. The CAPS, NUM, and OVR keyboard indicators display on the right side of the status bar. **NUM** indicates that Works will display numbers if you press the keys on the numeric keypad that is located to the right of the standard keyboard. **CAPS** displays when you want to type in all capital letters, and **OVR** displays when you want to insert text using the INSERT key.

Mouse Pointer

The **mouse pointer** is used to point to various parts of the screen and indicates which area of the screen will be affected when you click or right-click (see Figure 1-12). The mouse pointer changes shape in different parts of the screen. Within the blank area of the screen, called the **document workspace**, the mouse pointer takes the shape of an I-beam. An **I-beam** is a vertical line with short crossbars on the top and bottom.

On the menu bar, the ruler, and the scroll bar areas, the mouse pointer takes the shape of a block arrow. Other forms and uses of the mouse pointer are explained as required in the development of various documents.

Formatting Fonts

Be cautious when using multiple fonts, font styles, and colors in a document. Beginning designers usually use too many special features that make reading a document difficult. Most experts advise using no more than three fonts in a document so you do not overtax and confuse the reader. Use color to draw attention to an important fact in the document.

Insertion Point

The **insertion point** is a blinking vertical bar that indicates where the next character you type will display on the screen (see Figure 1-12). The insertion point also indicates the beginning position in a document where you can insert text, delete text, or change the appearance of text. The insertion point is controlled by the movement of the mouse or keyboard keys.

Word Processor Defaults

Before you enter the text to create a document, you should know about the predefined settings for the Word Processor, called **defaults**, that affect the way your screen displays and the way a document prints. Consider the following important defaults.

1. Margins – When printing a document, Works places a one-inch top margin and a one-inch bottom margin on each page. The right and left margins are one and one-quarter inch each.
2. Spacing – Text is single-spaced.
3. Line width – Line width is six inches.
4. Tab stops – Tab stops are set along the ruler at one-half inch intervals.
5. Default drive – Drive C, the hard disk, is the default drive for saving and retrieving documents.

You can change these defaults by using the commands from various Works menus.

Understanding Fonts, Font Styles, and Font Sizes

To create the announcement in Figure 1-1 on page W 1.8, you must format the page. **Formatting** refers to the process of controlling the appearance of the characters that display on the screen and in the printed document. With Works, you can specify the font, font size, font style, and color of one or more characters, words, sentences, or paragraphs in a document.

Fonts

A **font** is a set of characters with a specific design. Each font is identified by a name. Some of the commonly used fonts are Times New Roman, Courier New, and Arial (Figure 1-13).

Times New Roman font

Courier New font

Arial font

FIGURE 1-13

Each of the fonts in Figure 1-13 has a unique design. When using Windows, a variety of fonts become available for you to use with Works.

Most fonts fall into one of two major categories: (1) serif, or (2) sans serif. **Serif** fonts have small curved, finishing strokes in the characters. The Times New Roman and Courier New fonts are examples of a serif font. Serif fonts are considered easy to read when large blocks of text are involved and normally are used in books and magazines for the main text material.

Sans serif fonts are relatively plain, straight letter forms. The Arial font in Figure 1-13 is a sans serif font. Sans serif fonts commonly are used in headlines and short titles.

Font Style

In Works, **font style** is the term used to describe the special appearance of text and numbers. Widely used font styles include bold, italic, and underlined (Figure 1-14). You can choose bold, italic, and underlined font styles using the toolbar buttons. All three styles can be applied to a set of characters.

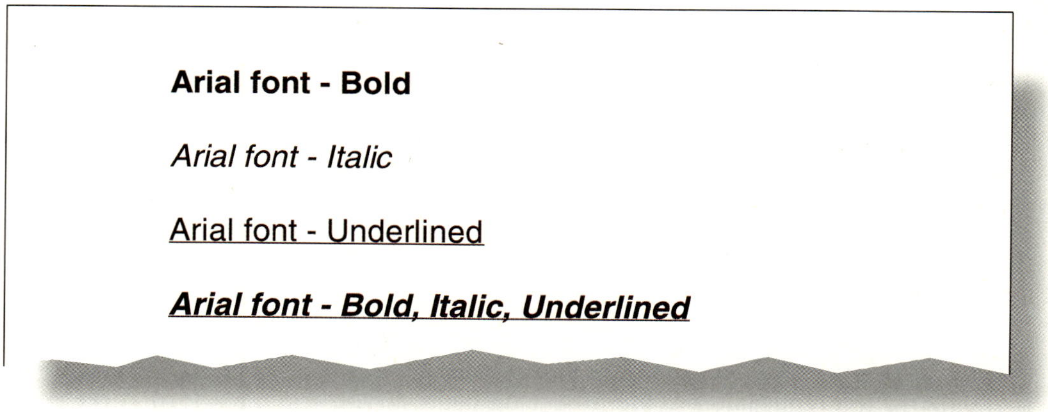

Arial font - Bold

Arial font - Italic

Arial font - Underlined

Arial font - Bold, Italic, Underlined

FIGURE 1-14

Font Sizes

Font sizes are measured in **points**. One inch consists of 72 points. Thus, a font size of 36 point is approximately one-half inch in height. The measurement is based on measuring from the top of the tallest character in a font (such as a lowercase l) to the bottom of the lowest character (such as a lowercase g). Figure 1-15 illustrates the Arial font in various sizes.

Arial font - 12 point

Arial font - 18 point

Arial font - 24 point

Arial font - 36 point

FIGURE 1-15

The fonts and font sizes you choose sometimes depend on the printer you are using and the fonts available within your software. Available fonts can vary from system to system. In the Works Word Processor, the default font is 10-point Times New Roman.

Changing the Default Font Size

Perform the following steps to increase the font size before you begin typing.

To Change the Default Font Size

1 **Click the Font Size box arrow on the Formatting toolbar.**

A list of available font sizes display in the Font Size list and the default size (10) is highlighted (Figure 1-16).

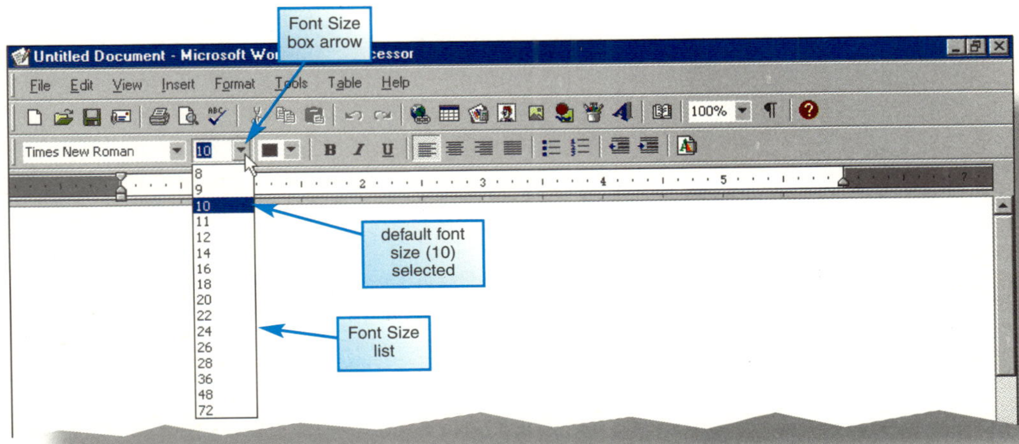

FIGURE 1-16

2 **Point to the number 12, which indicates 12-point font size (Figure 1-17).**

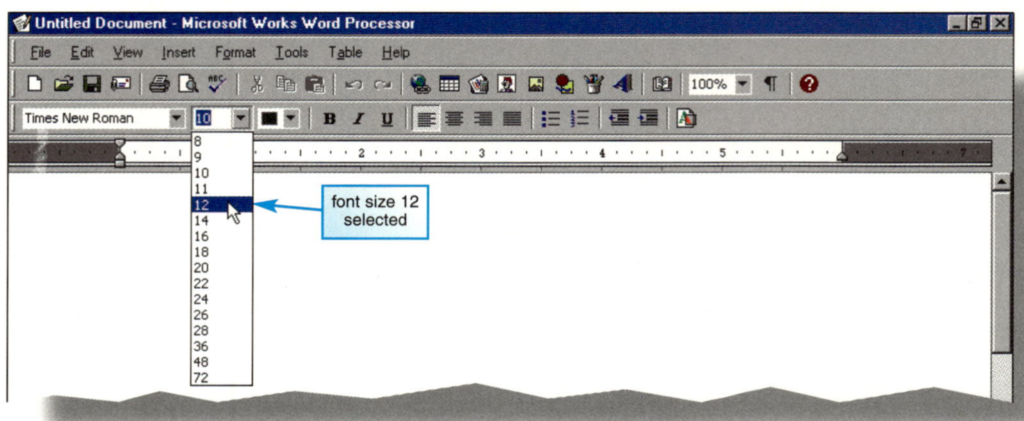

FIGURE 1-17

3 **Click 12.**

The font size for characters in this document changes to 12 (Figure 1-18). The size of the insertion point increases to reflect the new font size.

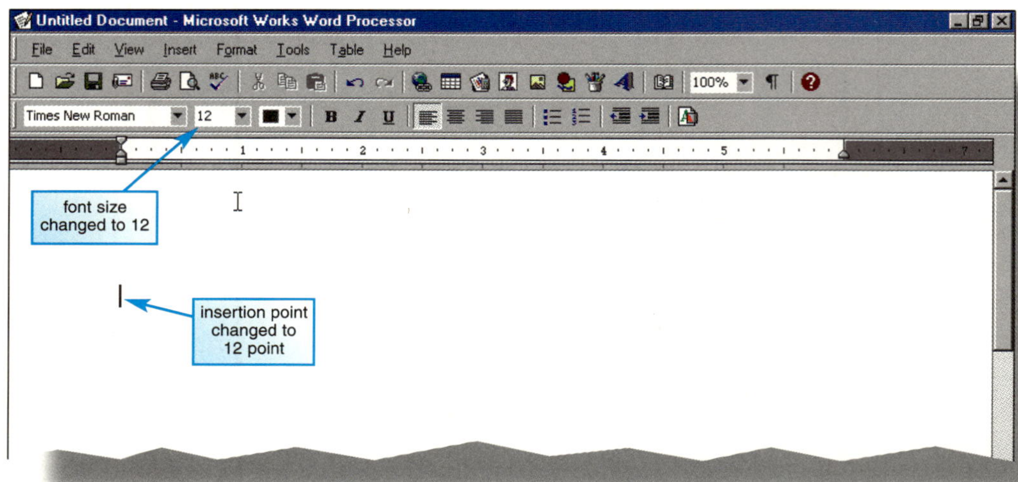

FIGURE 1-18

Formatting Requirements for Project One

The announcement used in this project is illustrated again in Figure 1-19 on the next page. Before typing the text, you must understand the fonts, font styles, font sizes, and colors you will use in creating the announcement.

In this document, the first heading displays on the first two lines of the document, is centered on the page, and displays in 36-point bold Book Antiqua font. The second heading is centered on the page and displays in 16-point bold Book Antiqua font. An illustration from the Microsoft Clip Gallery is placed after the second heading. The next three lines are single-spaced and display in 12-point Times New Roman font. These lines are followed by a blank space and then another line displays in 16-point Times New Roman font. The next four entries are indented three-quarters of one inch, contain a bullet (solid dot) before the beginning of each entry, and display in 16-point Times New Roman font. The line following the bulleted list is centered on the page and displays in 16-point Arial italic font. The last three lines in the document are centered and display in 16-point Arial red font.

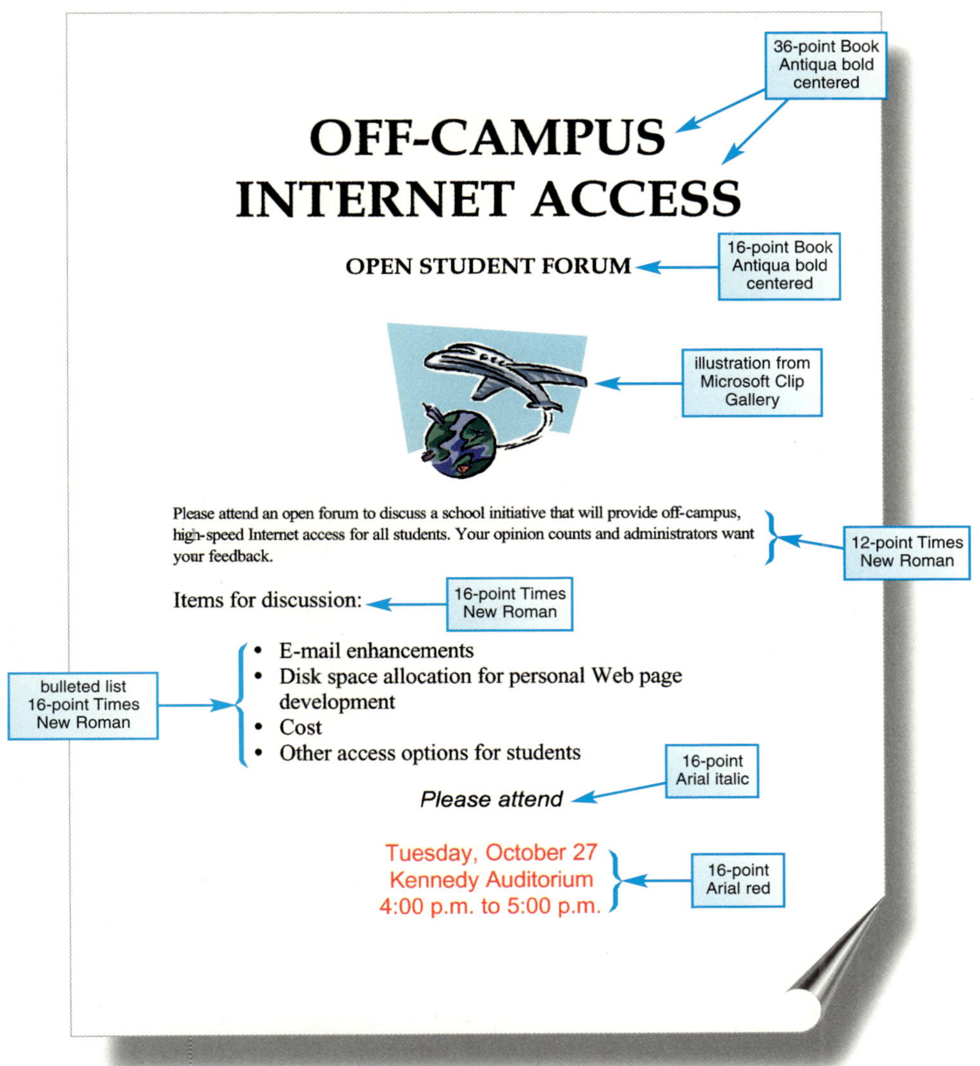

FIGURE 1-19

When you understand the format of the document, you are ready to use the Word Processor tool to create the document.

Creating a Document

Many reasons exist for creating documents. When a task in the Works Task Launcher does not match your requirements, or you simply want to create a document from scratch, you will begin entering text in the blank Word Processor window to create an original document. In this project, you are creating an announcement with clip art and formatting it according to the requirements just described. After the document is finished, you will save it and then print it.

More About

All Characters Command

The All Characters command displays all nonprinting characters on the screen, which can be useful when learning word processing or when you need to locate a problem within your document. Once you become proficient at word processing, however, you may want to toggle between Show All and Hide All.

All Characters Command

When using the Works Word Processor, each time you press a key on the keyboard, a character is entered, and each character becomes part of the document. For example, pressing the SPACEBAR between words creates a small black dot (•), called a **space mark**, in the space between the words. Pressing the ENTER key creates a character (¶) called the **paragraph mark**. These characters do not print, but it is recommended that you display these special characters as you type.

The following steps explain how to display on the screen all the characters you type.

To Display All Characters

1 Point to the Show All button on the Standard toolbar (Figure 1-20).

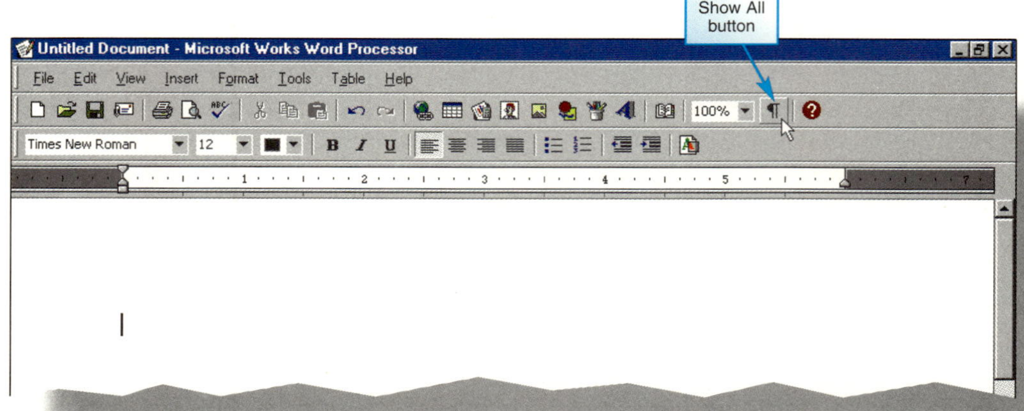

FIGURE 1-20

2 Click the Show All button.

The Show All button on the Standard toolbar is recessed and formatting marks display in the document window (Figure 1-21).

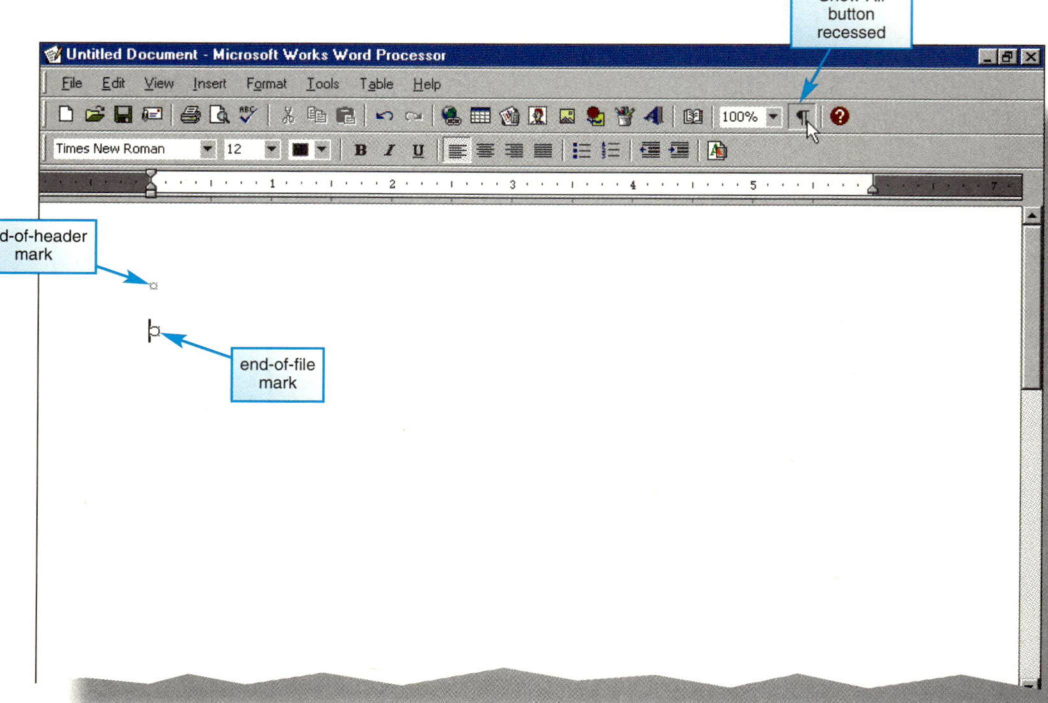

FIGURE 1-21

Works automatically inserts an **end-of-file** mark at the end of every document. This mark displays as the last character in every document and indicates where the document ends. You can move the insertion point throughout the document you create, but you cannot move it beyond the end-of-file mark. Because you have not yet entered text, an end-of-file mark appears after the insertion point because it is the end of the document at this time.

Works also inserts two other end-of-file type marks. The uppermost mark, **end-of-header**, designates the location and the end of the header. Text you type in the header will display at the top of each page of the document on the screen and will print at the top of each page when the document is printed. An **end-of-footer** mark designates the location and end of the footer at the bottom of each page. Text you type in the footer will display at the bottom of each page of the document and will print at the bottom of each page when the document is printed. Using headers and footers will be covered in later projects.

You now are ready to enter the text to create the document.

> **More About**
>
> **Entering Text**
>
> Often when you first enter a heading in a document, you have no idea how the formatting of the text will affect the display of the text. When increasing font size at a later time, the one-line heading may display on multiple lines.

Entering Text

Perform the following steps to enter the text of the document.

Steps To Enter Text

1 **Press the CAPS LOCK key on the keyboard and then type** OFF-CAMPUS INTERNET ACCESS **as the first line of text.**

As you type, the characters display in capital letters, the insertion point and end-of-file mark move to the right one character at a time, and the CAPS indicator displays on the status bar (Figure 1-22). If you make an error while typing, press the BACKSPACE key to delete the character or characters you have just typed and then type the characters correctly.

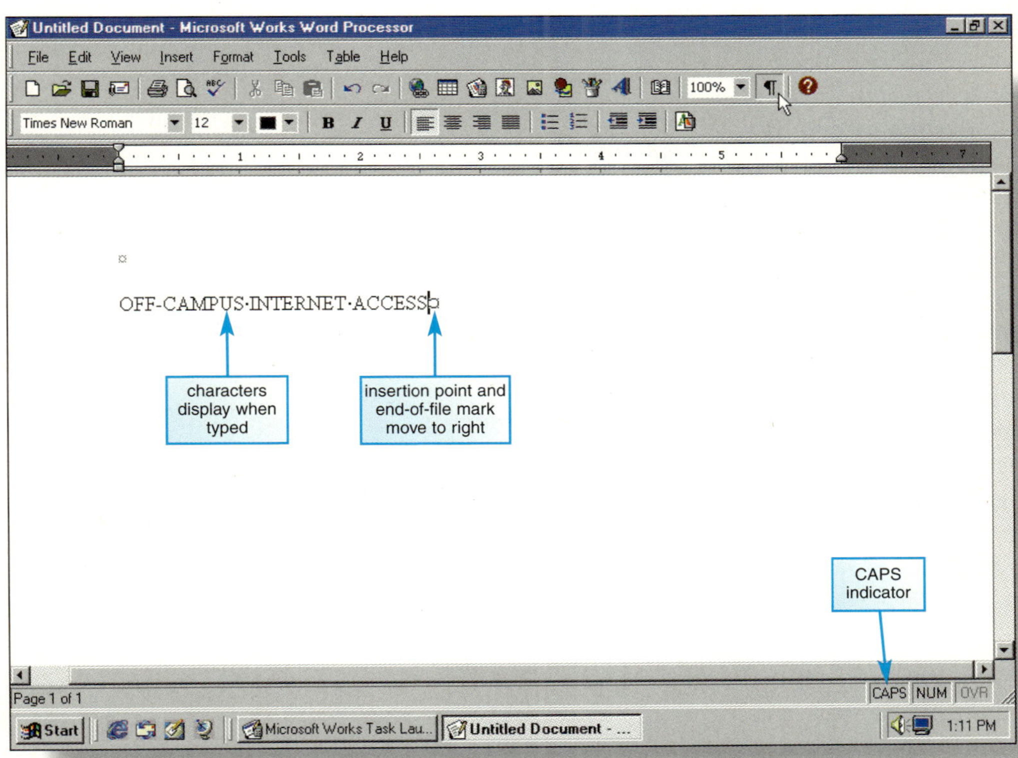

FIGURE 1-22

2 Press the ENTER key to end the first line.

When you press the ENTER key, Works inserts a paragraph mark immediately after the last character typed (Figure 1-23). The insertion point moves to the beginning of the next line followed by the end-of-file mark.

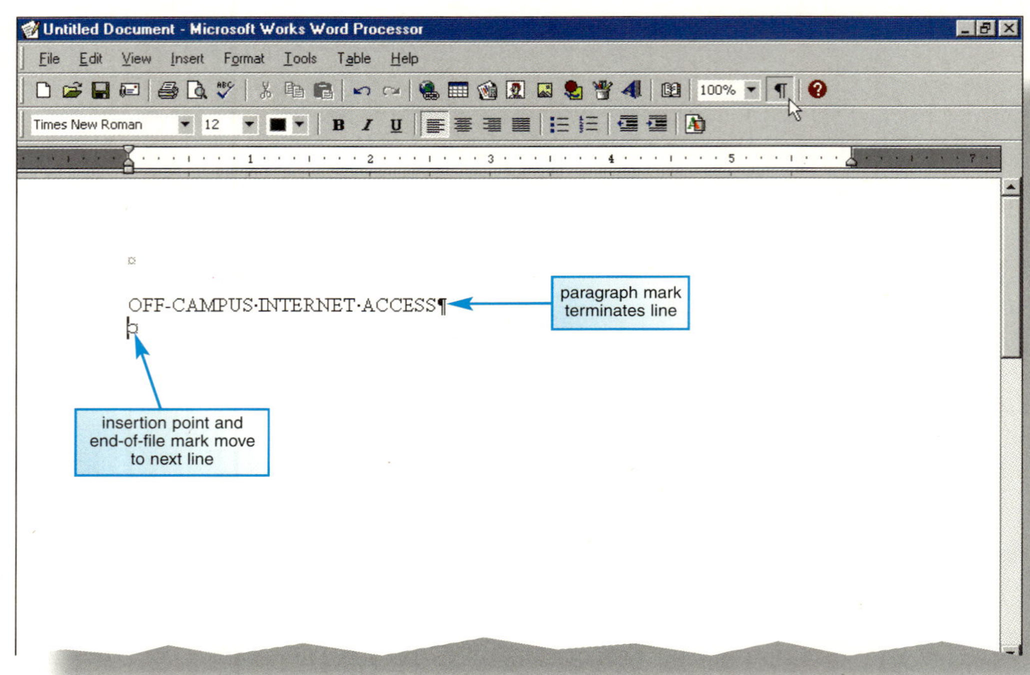

FIGURE 1-23

3 Press the ENTER key to enter a blank line. Type OPEN STUDENT FORUM **as the second line of text, and then press the ENTER key once to end the second line of text. Press the ENTER key four more times to insert two blank lines before the clip art illustration, a line for the illustration, and a blank line following the illustration. The insertion point now displays on the line where you will type the next line of text.**

Only one line needs to be allowed for the clip art illustration (Figure 1-24). When Works inserts the clip art in the document, the space is expanded to allow the clip art to be placed between the lines of text.

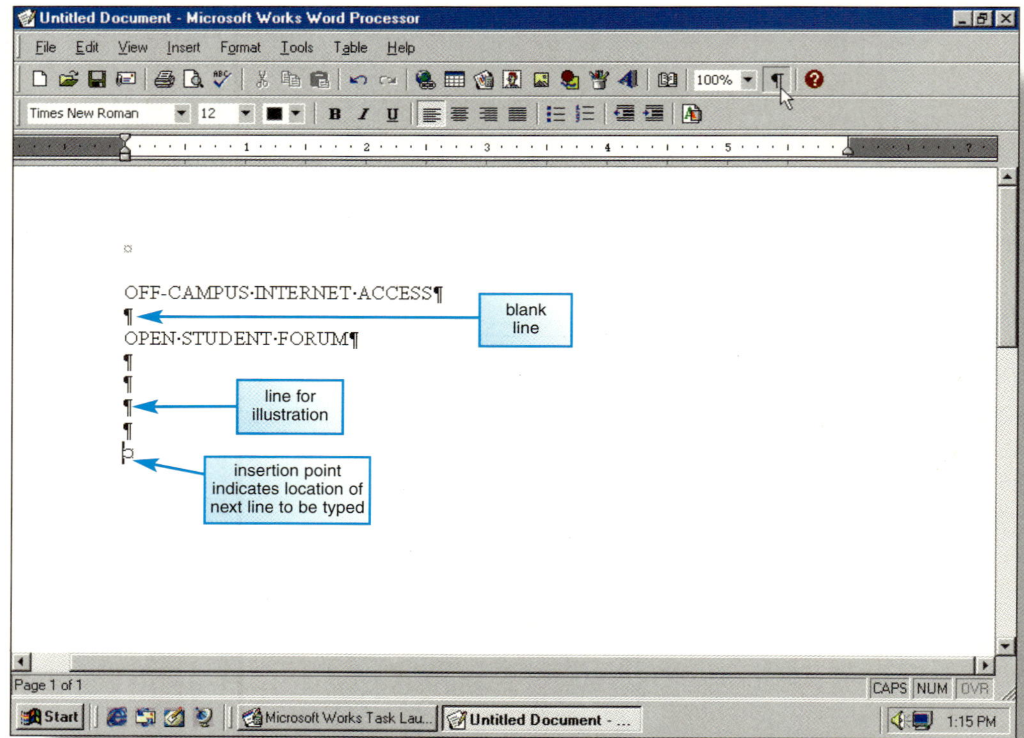

FIGURE 1-24

Paragraph Marks

It is important to understand the purpose of the paragraph mark. The term **paragraph**, when using the Works Word Processor, can mean a blank line, a single character, a word, a single line, or many sentences. You create a paragraph by pressing the ENTER key. When you are typing and then press the ENTER key, Works inserts a paragraph mark after the last character typed.

A paragraph is a section of text treated as a unified group of characters to which various types of formatting can be applied. Once you have established the characteristics of a paragraph, text you add to the paragraph will take on the characteristics of that paragraph.

Wordwrap

Your printer controls where wordwrap occurs for each line in your document. For this reason, it is possible that the same document could wordwrap on different words if printed on different printers.

Using the Wordwrap Feature

Wordwrap allows you to type multiple lines without pressing the ENTER key at the end of each line. When typing text that requires more than one line, the insertion point continues to the right margin and then automatically drops down to the beginning of the next line. In addition, when you type a line and a word extends beyond the right margin, the word automatically is placed on the next line. Thus, as you enter text, do not press the ENTER key when the insertion point reaches the right margin.

Wordwrap is an important feature of the Word Processor because it facilitates rapid entry of data and allows Works easily to rearrange characters, words, and sentences within a paragraph when you make changes.

Perform the following step to use the wordwrap feature.

To Use Wordwrap

1 If necessary, press the CAPS LOCK key to remove the all caps feature. Type `Please attend an open forum to discuss a school initiative that will provide off-campus, high-speed Internet access for all students.` **as part of the first paragraph in the body of the announcement.**

The CAPS indicator on the status bar is turned off (Figure 1-25). Works automatically wraps the words, high-speed, to the beginning of the next line because it is too long to fit on the first line. Your document may wordwrap on a different word, depending on the printer you are using.

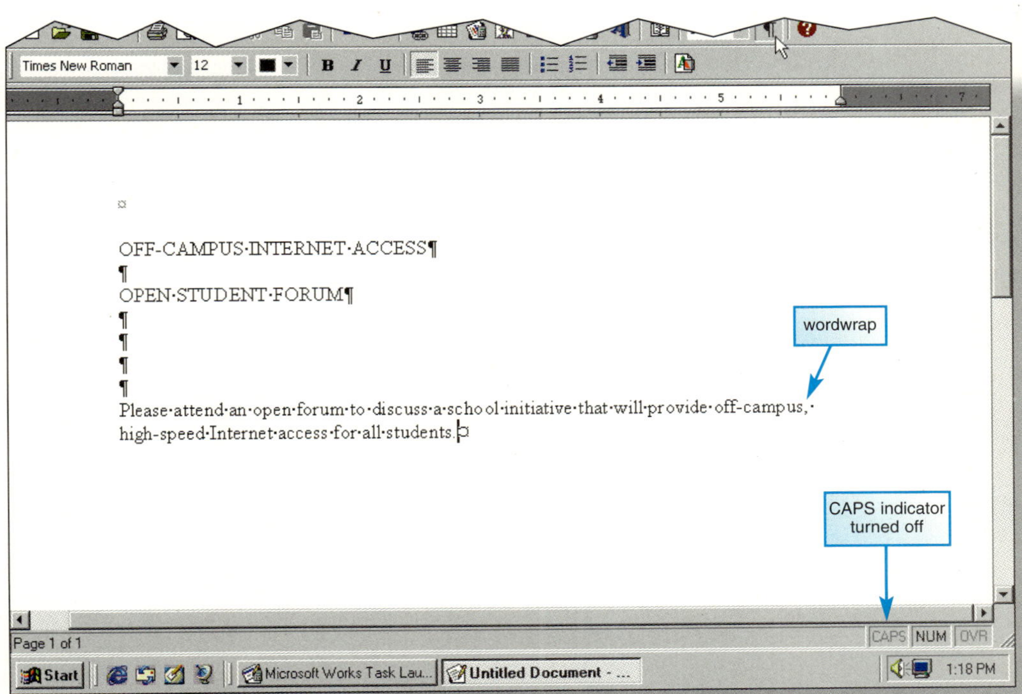

FIGURE 1-25

Using AutoCorrect and Checking Spelling as You Type

As you enter text in the Word Processor window, Works' AutoCorrect feature automatically detects and corrects certain typographical errors, misspelled words, grammatical errors, and incorrect capitalizations. For example, if you type the characters, teh and then press the SPACEBAR, AutoCorrect replaces the incorrect characters you typed with the word, the. You also can use AutoCorrect to quickly insert text, graphics, or symbols. You can view and make changes to the various AutoCorrect options by selecting AutoCorrect on the Tools menu, which displays the AutoCorrect dialog box.

As you type text, Works also checks your typing for possible spelling errors. If a word you type is not in the dictionary, a red wavy underline displays beneath it. Although you can check the entire document for spelling and grammar errors at once, this feature allows you to check spelling errors immediately.

When a word is **flagged** with a red wavy underline, it is not in the Works dictionary. A flagged word, however, is not necessarily misspelled. For example, many names, abbreviations, and specialized terms are not in the Works main dictionary. In these cases, you tell Works to ignore the flagged word. As you type, Works also detects duplicate words. For example, if your document contains the phrase, to the the store, Works places a red wavy underline beneath the second occurrence of the word, the. To display a list of suggested corrections for a flagged word, you right-click it and then choose the correct spelling on the shortcut menu.

In the following example, the word, opinion, has been misspelled intentionally to illustrate the Works check spelling as you type feature. Your announcement may contain different misspelled words, depending on the accuracy of your typing. Perform the following steps to check spelling as you type.

To Check Spelling as You Type

1 **Press the SPACEBAR once. Type** `Your opinon counts and administrators want your feedback.` **to complete the paragraph entry.**

Works flags the misspelled word, opinon, by placing a red wavy underline beneath it (Figure 1-26).

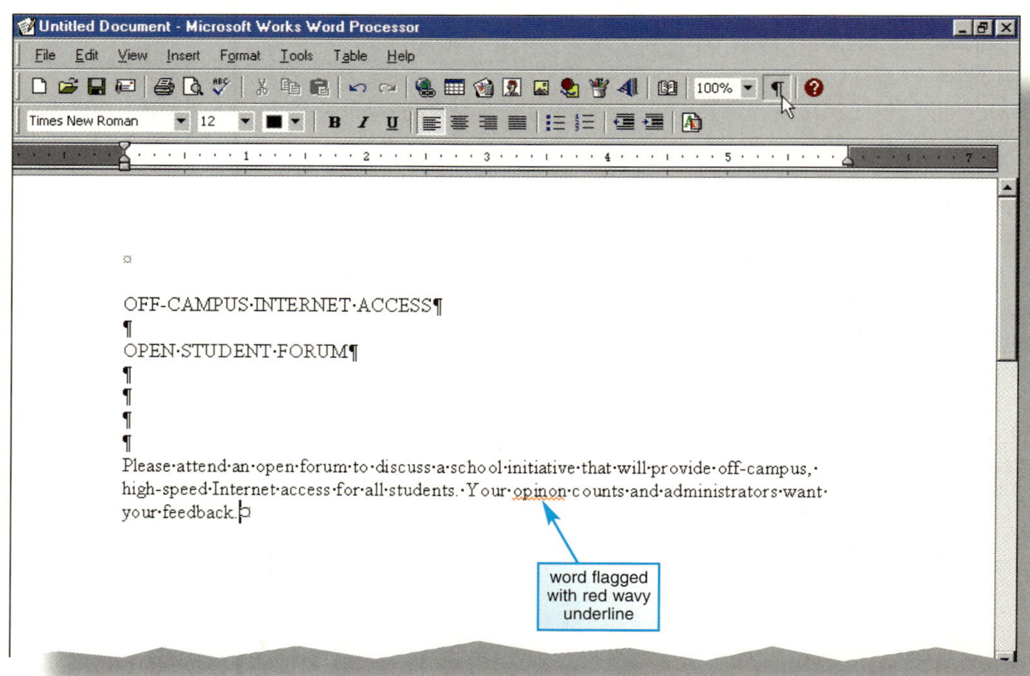

FIGURE 1-26

2 Position the mouse pointer in the flagged word (opinon, in this case).

The mouse pointer's shape is an I-beam when positioned in a word (Figure 1-27).

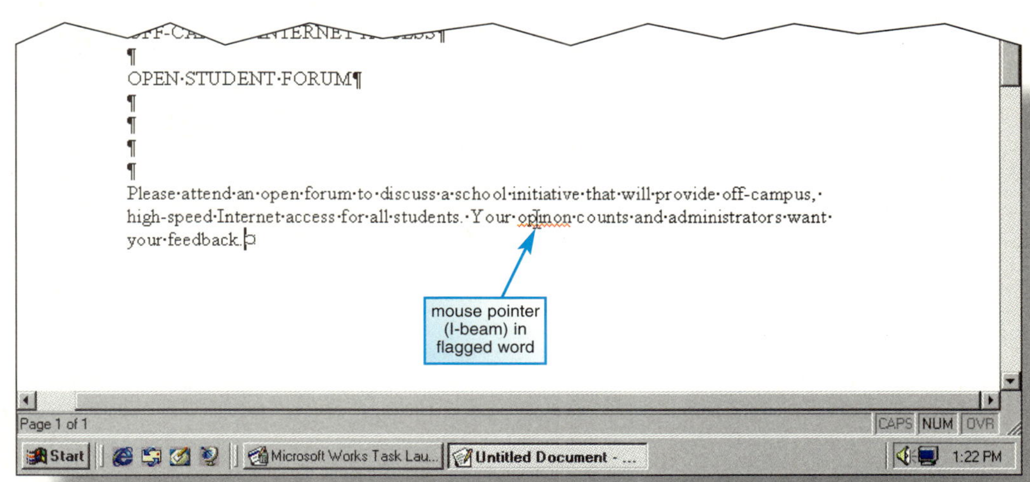

FIGURE 1-27

3 Right-click the flagged word, opinon. When the shortcut menu displays, point to opinion.

Works displays a shortcut menu that lists suggested spelling corrections for the flagged word (Figure 1-28).

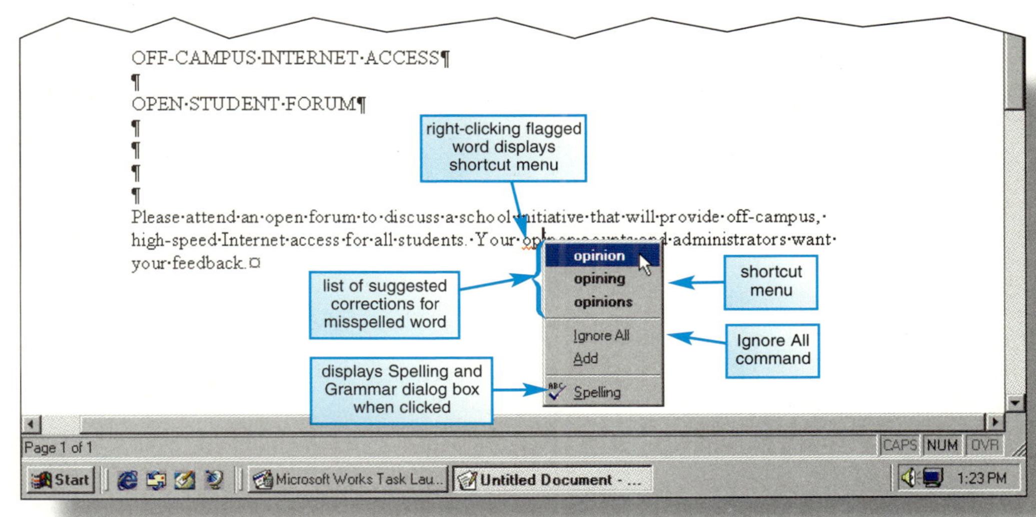

FIGURE 1-28

4 Click opinion.

Works replaces the misspelled word with the correct word chosen on the shortcut menu (Figure 1-29).

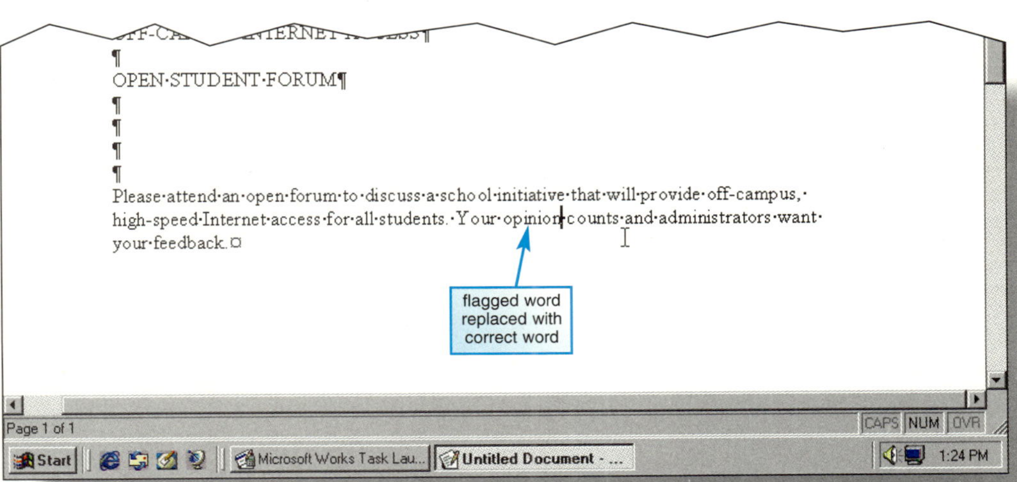

FIGURE 1-29

If the word is spelled correctly and, for example, is a proper name, you can right-click it and then click Ignore All on the shortcut menu (see Figure 1-28). If, when you right-click the misspelled word, your desired correction is not in the list on the shortcut menu, you can click outside the shortcut menu to make the menu disappear and then retype the correct word, or you can click Spelling on the shortcut menu to display the Spelling and Grammar dialog box. The Spelling and Grammar dialog box is discussed in a later project.

Entering Text that Scrolls through the Word Processor Window

As you type more lines of text than Works can display in the text area, Works **scrolls** the top portion of the document upward off of the screen. Although you cannot see the text once it scrolls off the screen, it still remains in the document.

Perform the following steps to enter text that scrolls through the Word Processor window.

To Enter Text that Scrolls through the Word Processor Window

1 Hold down the CTRL key and then press the END key to reposition the insertion point at the end of the paragraph. Press the ENTER key twice to enter a blank line. Type `Items for discussion:` **and then press the ENTER key twice (Figure 1-30).**

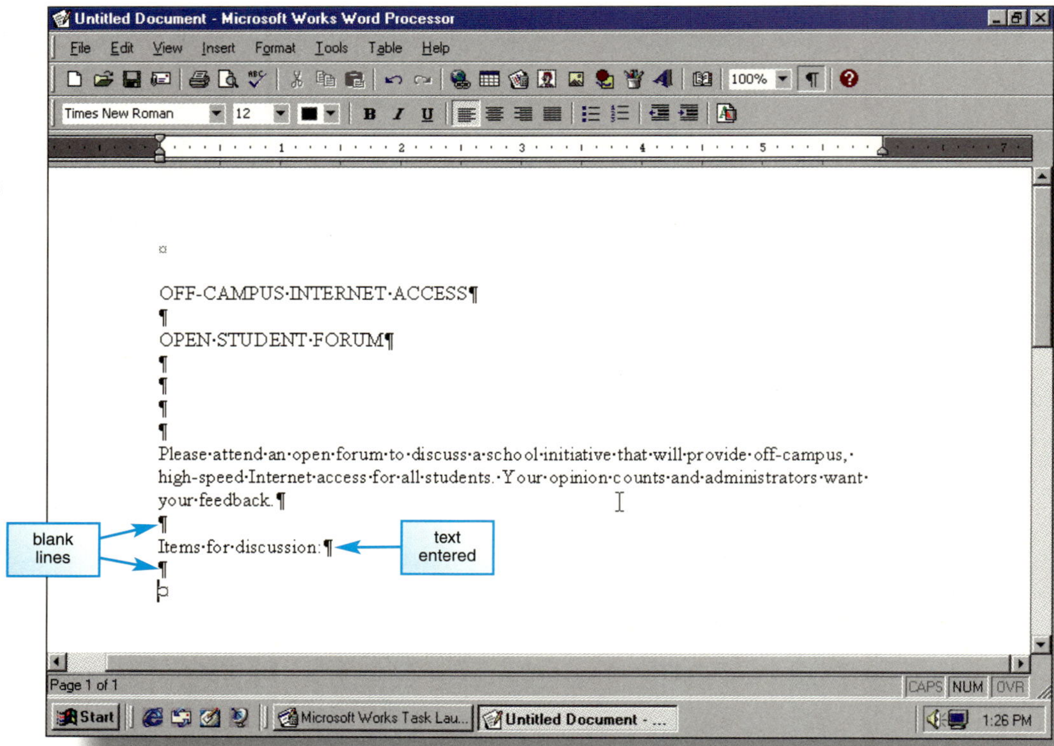

FIGURE 1-30

2 **Type the remaining lines of text as shown in Figure 1-19 on page W 1.20. Press the ENTER key to end each paragraph, except press the ENTER key twice after the paragraphs ending with students and attend.**

Works scrolls the headline off the top of the screen as you type Kennedy. Your screen may scroll differently depending on the type of monitor you are using (Figure 1-31). All of the text in the announcement has been entered.

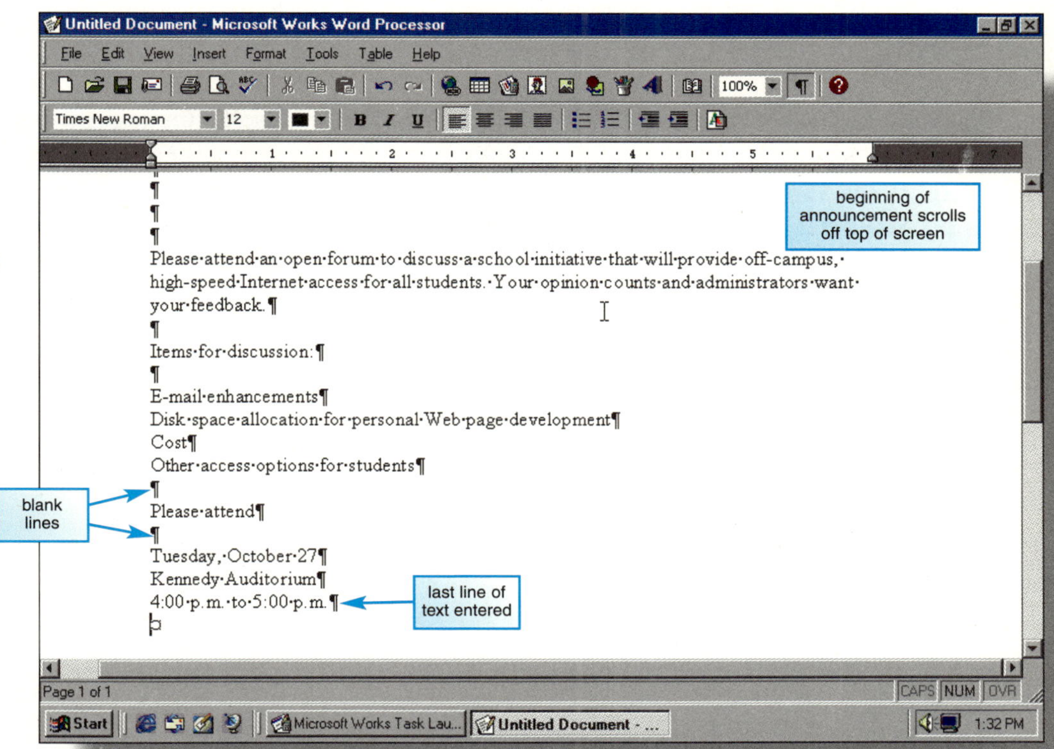

FIGURE 1-31

Saving a Document

When you create a document, the document only is stored in your computer's random access memory. If the computer is turned off or a power loss occurs before you save a document, your work will be lost. You should save all documents either on the hard disk or on a floppy disk.

When you save a Word Processor document, Works automatically adds the extension .wps to the end of the name you select. The Works extension, .wps, may not display depending on how your computer is configured. To save the document created in Project 1 on a floppy disk in drive A using the file name, Off-Campus Internet Access, perform the steps on the next page.

More About

Long File Names

One of Works features is its capability of supporting long file names. Using long file names allows you to assign meaningful names to your files. This can save you time because, appropriately named, you can identify your files even months after they have been created. A file name can contain up to 255 characters, including spaces. The only invalid characters are backslash (\), slash (/), colon (:), asterisk (*), question mark (?), quotation marks ("), less than symbol (<), greater than symbol (>), and vertical bar (|).

To Save a Document

1 **Insert a formatted floppy disk into drive A. Point to the Save button on the Standard toolbar (Figure 1-32).**

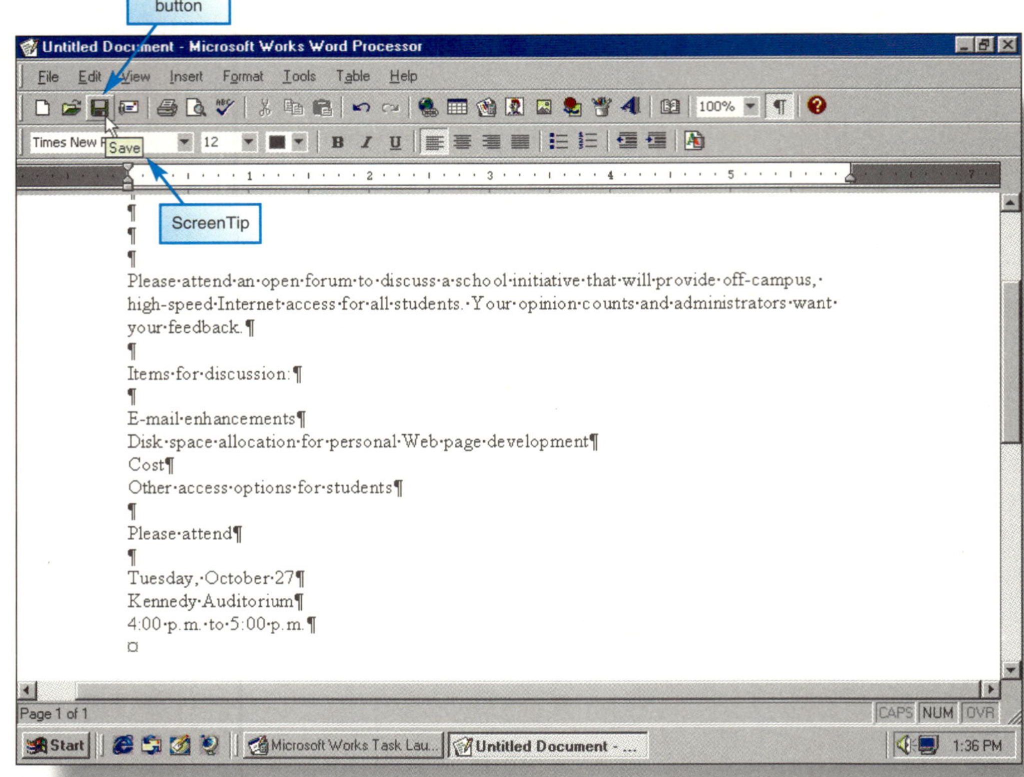

FIGURE 1-32

2 **Click the Save button on the Standard toolbar. When the Save As dialog box displays, type** `Off-Campus Internet Access` **in the File name text box. Point to the Save in box arrow.**

The Save As dialog box displays (Figure 1-33). A blinking insertion point displays in the File name text box when the Save As dialog box first displays. The file name you typed displays in the File name text box.

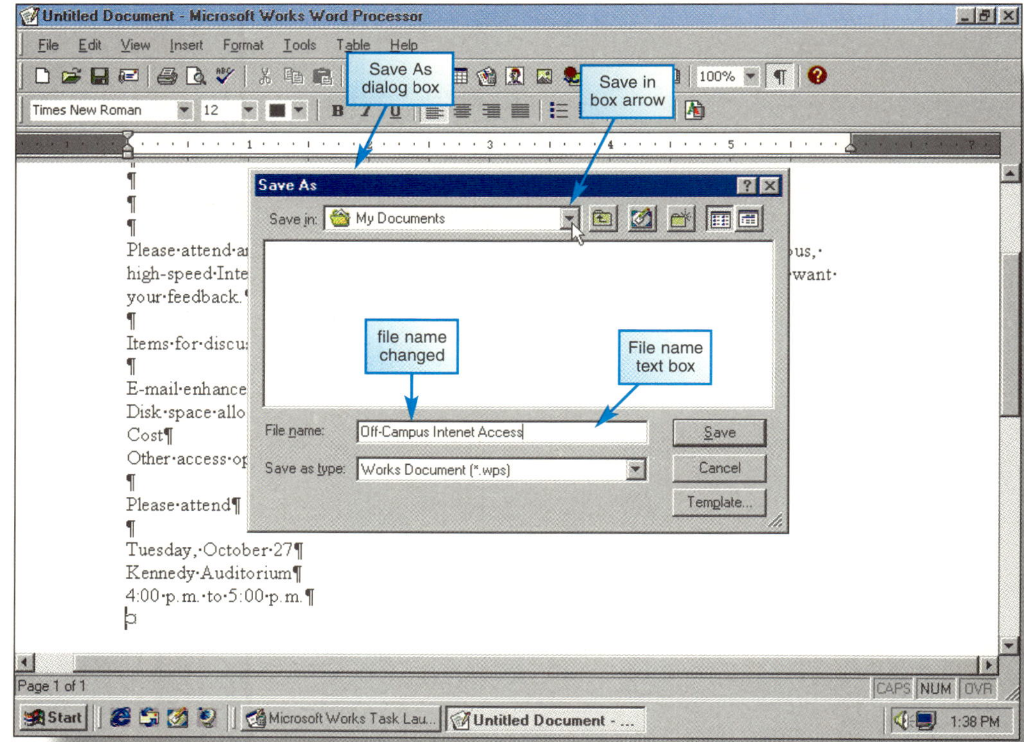

FIGURE 1-33

3 Click the Save in box arrow and then point to the 3½ Floppy (A:) icon. If necessary, scroll up to bring 3½ floppy (A:) into view.

The Save in list displays available drives and commands (Figure 1-34). The list of available drives may be different on your system.

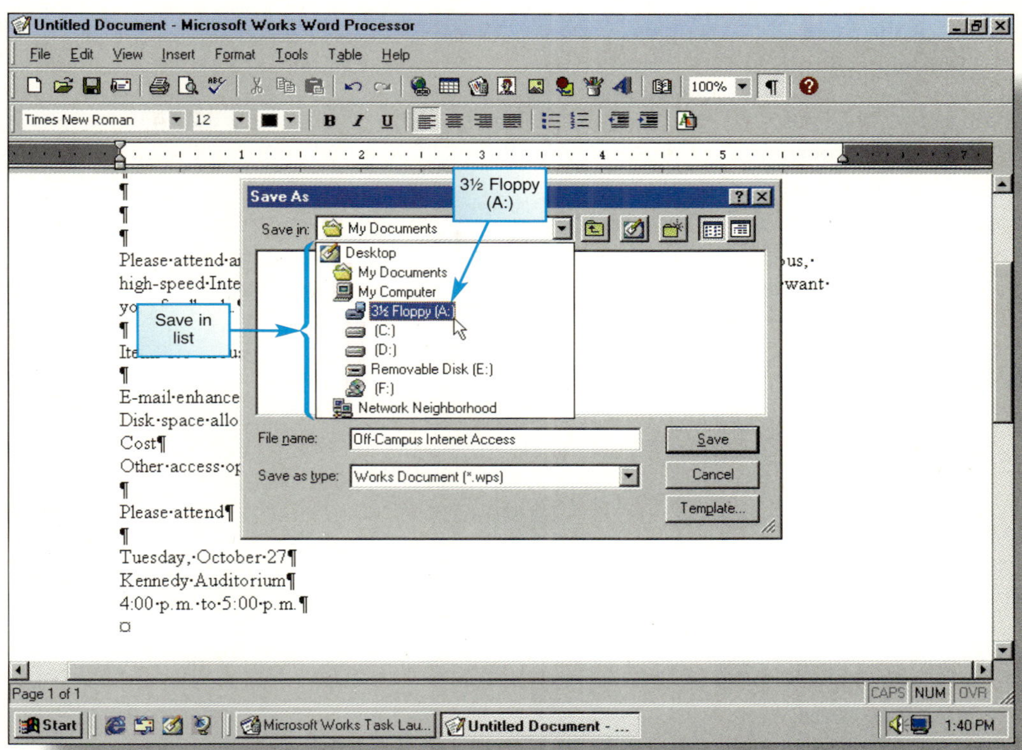

FIGURE 1-34

4 Click 3½ floppy (A:). Point to the Save button in the Save As dialog box.

Drive A becomes the selected drive (Figure 1-35).

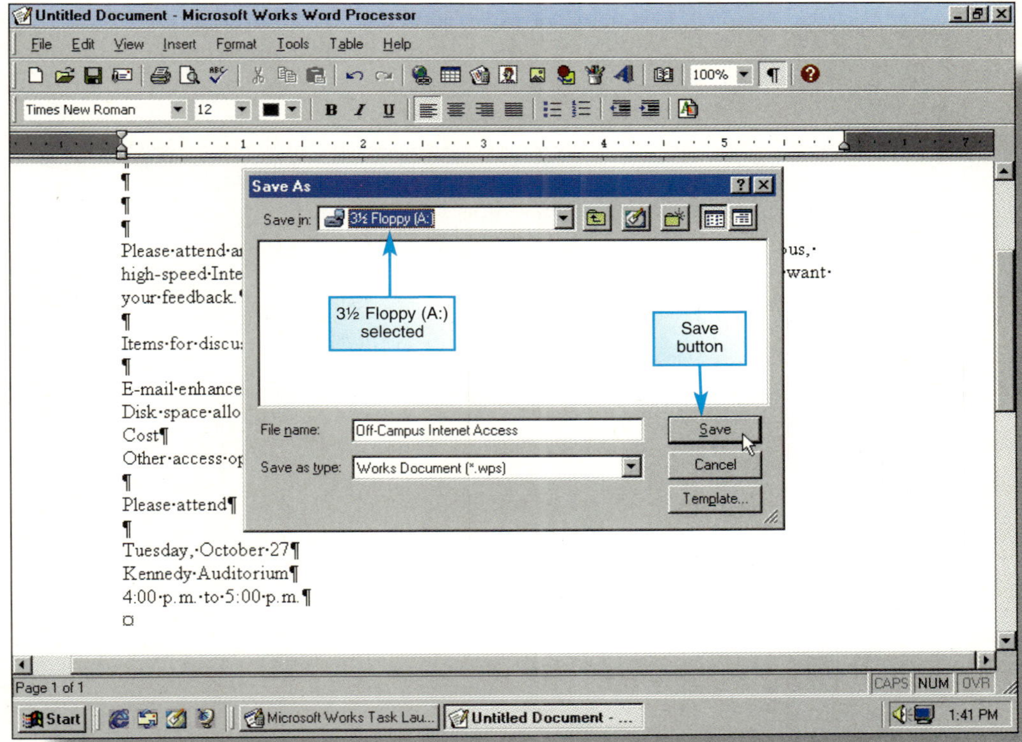

FIGURE 1-35

Click the Save button.

The dialog box disappears and the document remains displayed on the screen (Figure 1-36). Works saves the document on the floppy disk on drive A. The name changes on the title bar from Untitled Document to the name of the document saved (Off-Campus Internet Access.wps).

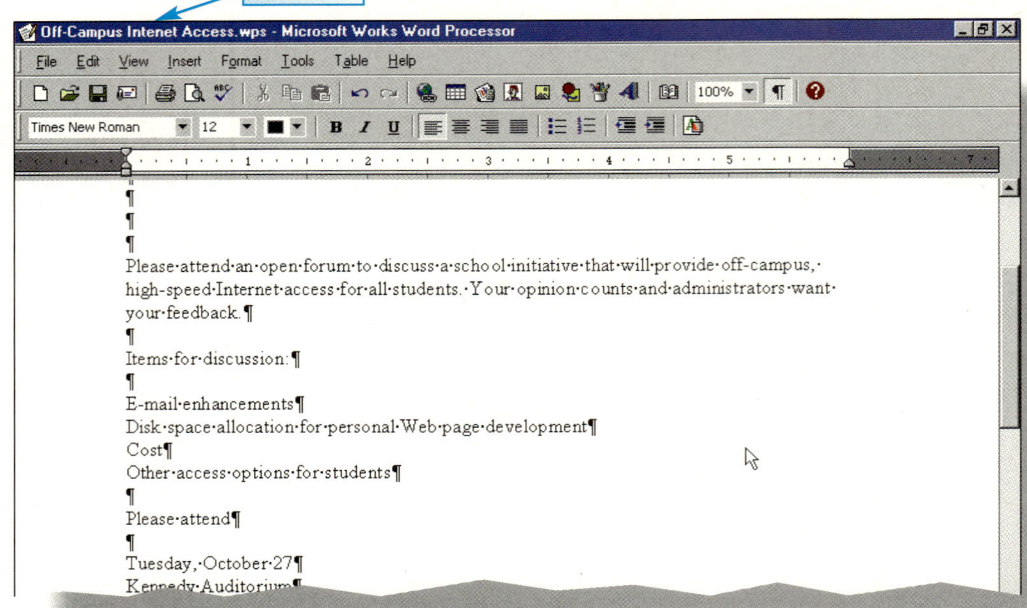

FIGURE 1-36

Other Ways

1. On File menu click Save As, type file name, click OK button
2. Press CTRL+S

Formatting the Document

The next step in preparing the announcement is to format the document, which involves centering selected lines, specifying the font and font size for each of the lines, and applying the proper font style and color to the lines.

Selecting Characters, Words, Lines, and Paragraphs

Before you can change the format of a document, you must select the text you want to change. **Selected** text displays highlighted as white text on a black background on the screen. Figure 1-37 illustrates a selected word in a sentence.

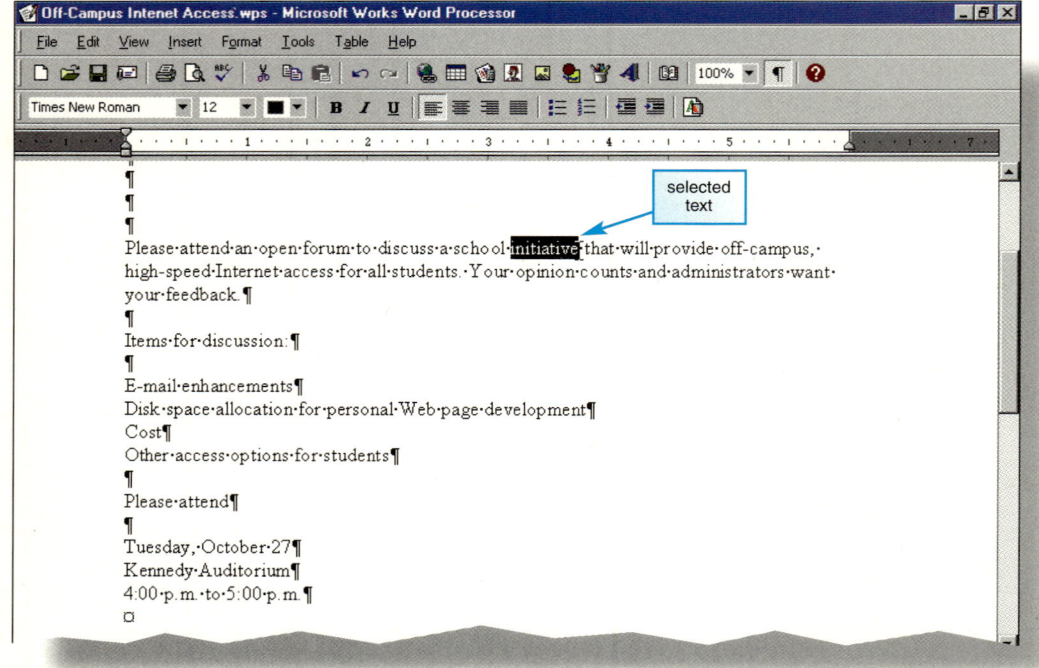

FIGURE 1-37

Works provides a variety of ways to select text. One method of selecting is to move the mouse pointer to the first character of the text to format and then drag the mouse pointer through the text you want to select.

Table 1-1 explains other techniques you can use to select text.

When selecting more than one word using the mouse, Works automatically selects all of the next word as you drag through that word. If you have selected text and want to remove the highlighting for any reason, click anywhere within the document workspace. The highlighting will be removed. You also may press any arrow key to remove highlighting.

Table 1-1 Techniques to Select Text

TO SELECT	ACTION TO BE PERFORMED
A word	Double-click when the mouse pointer is located anywhere within the word.
A line	Click in the left margin of the Word Processor window beside the line. The I-beam pointer changes to a block arrow in this area.
A sentence	Drag the mouse pointer through the sentence.
A paragraph	Double-click in the left margin of the Word Processor window beside the paragraph.
Several lines	Position the mouse pointer in the left margin of the Word Processor window and drag the pointer up or down.
An entire document	On the Edit menu, click the Select All command or press CTRL+A.

Centering Paragraphs

The first two heading lines of the announcement are centered within the margins of the document. Several approaches can be taken when centering these two lines. You can center one line at a time, or by selecting both lines, you can center both lines at once with a single click of the mouse. It is more efficient to center both lines at once, so this approach is illustrated in the following steps.

Perform the following steps to center the paragraphs.

To Center Paragraphs

1 Hold down the CTRL key and then press the HOME key to display the top portion of the document on the screen. Position the mouse pointer in the left margin of the Word Processor window next to the first line of the paragraphs you want to center.

The insertion point is moved to the beginning of the document (Figure 1-38). The mouse pointer becomes a right-pointing block arrow.

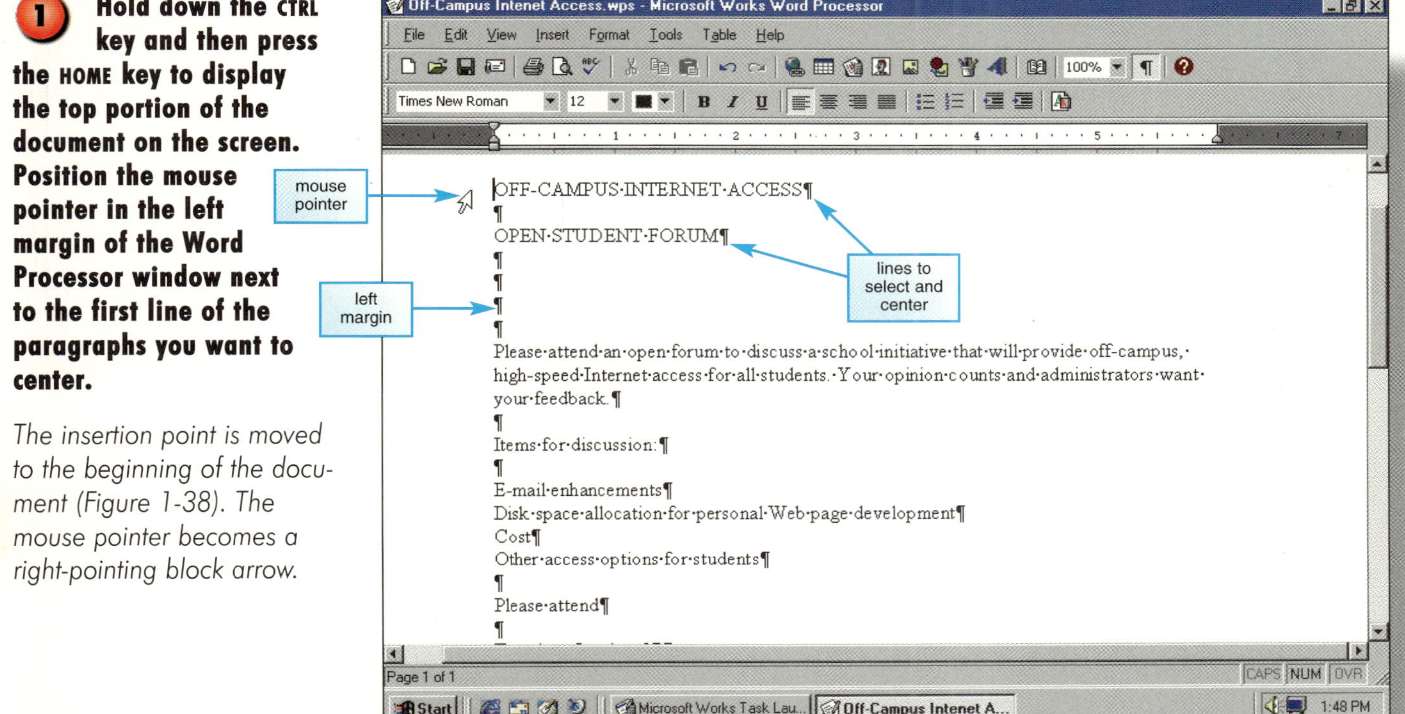

FIGURE 1-38

2 **Drag the mouse pointer through the left margin of the document window until the lines you want to center are selected. Release the left mouse button.**

The lines are selected (Figure 1-39).

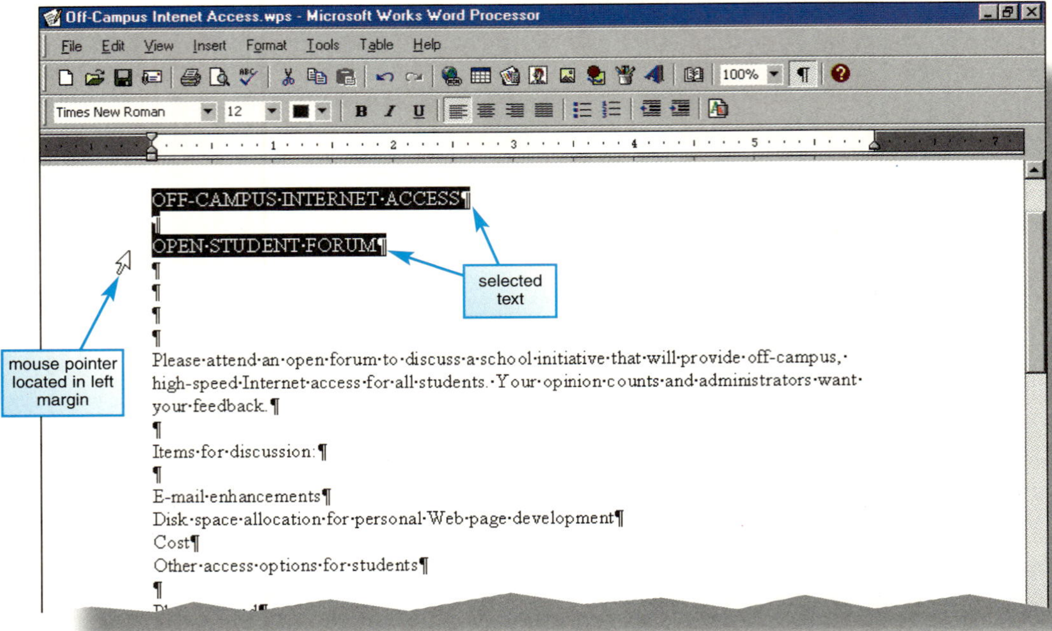

FIGURE 1-39

3 **Click the Center button on the Formatting toolbar.**

Works centers the two heading lines between the page margins (Figure 1-40). Notice the Center button on the Standard toolbar is recessed, indicating the paragraphs are centered.

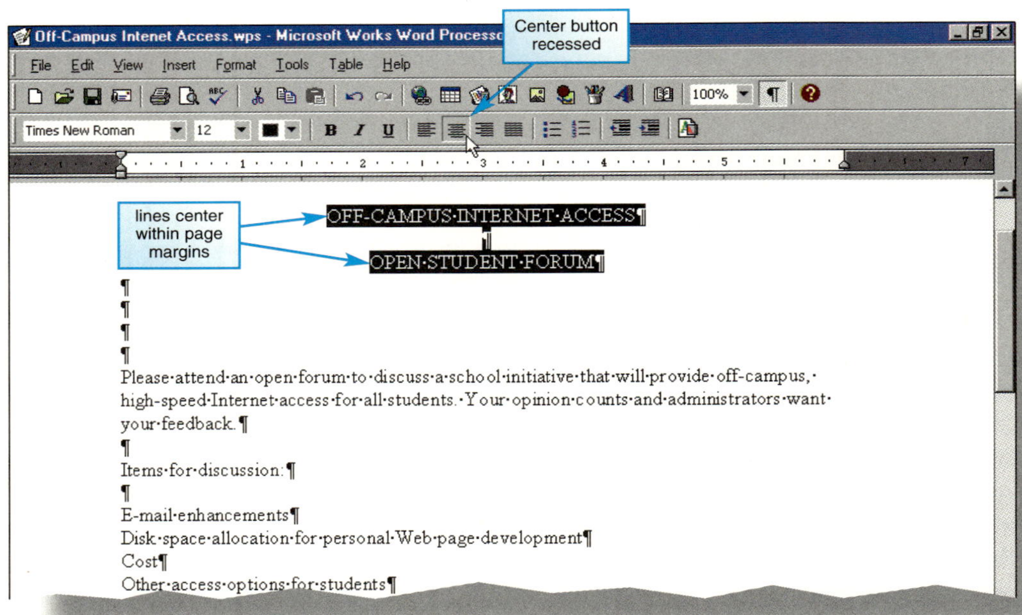

FIGURE 1-40

Other Ways

1. Right-click selected text, click Paragraph on shortcut menu, click Indents and Alignment tab, click Center, click OK button
2. On Format menu click Paragraph, click Indents and Alignment tab, click Center, click OK button
3. Press CTRL+E

Changing Fonts

When Works is started, the default font is Times New Roman. Works displays this information on the left side of the Formatting toolbar.

The text in the announcement now displays in 12-point Times New Roman font. The first two heading lines should display in Book Antiqua font. To change from Times New Roman font to Book Antiqua font, perform the following steps.

To Change Fonts

1 Select the paragraphs you want to change to Book Antiqua font and then click the Font box arrow on the Formatting toolbar.

Works displays the Font list which contains a number of font names (Figure 1-41). The font list displays the fonts the way they will look on screen. The font names on your computer may be different from the font names shown in Figure 1-41.

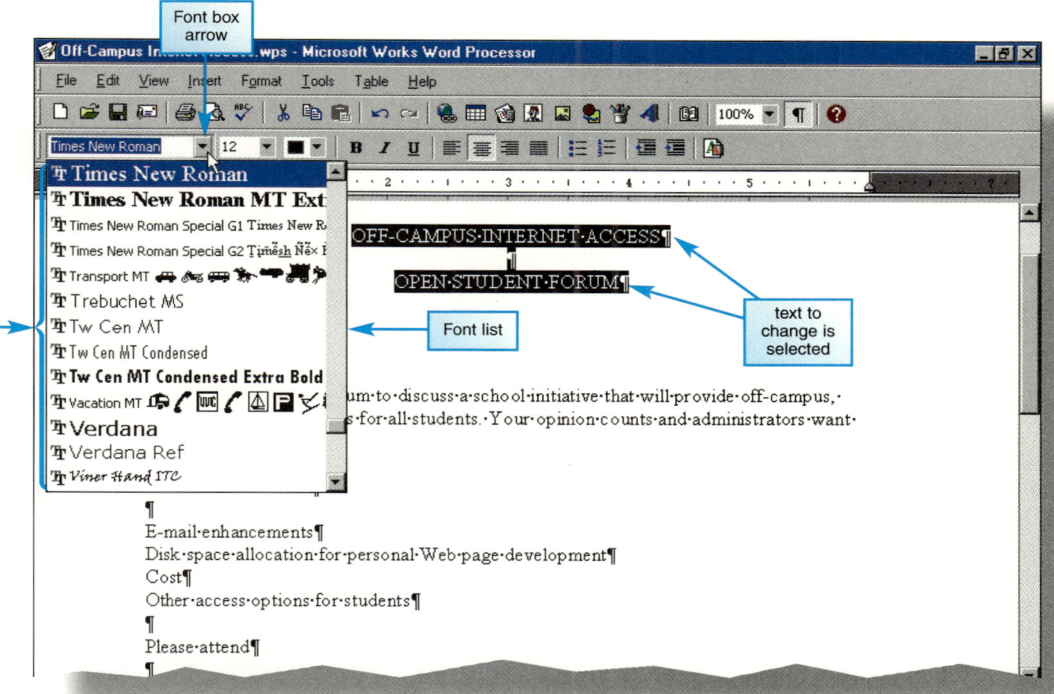

FIGURE 1-41

2 Click the up scroll arrow and scroll though the list until the Book Antiqua font name displays and then point to the Book Antiqua font name.

Additional font names display as you scroll through the Font list (Figure 1-42). The Book Antiqua font name displays near the top of the list.

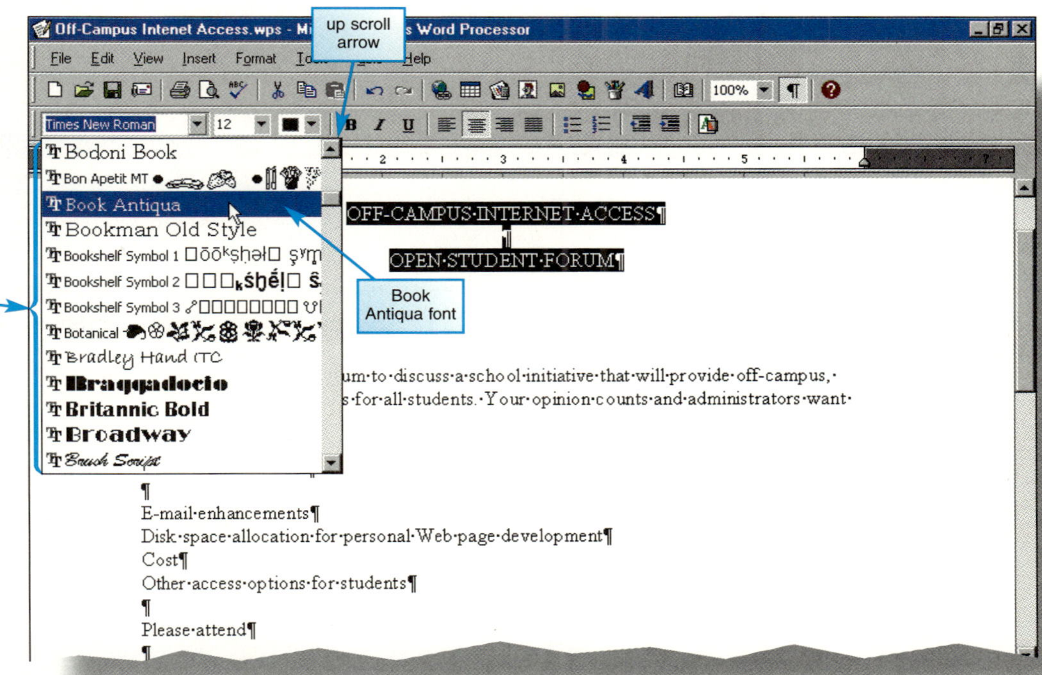

FIGURE 1-42

Click Book Antiqua.

The two heading lines display in Book Antiqua font (Figure 1-43). The Book Antiqua font name displays in the Font box on the Formatting toolbar.

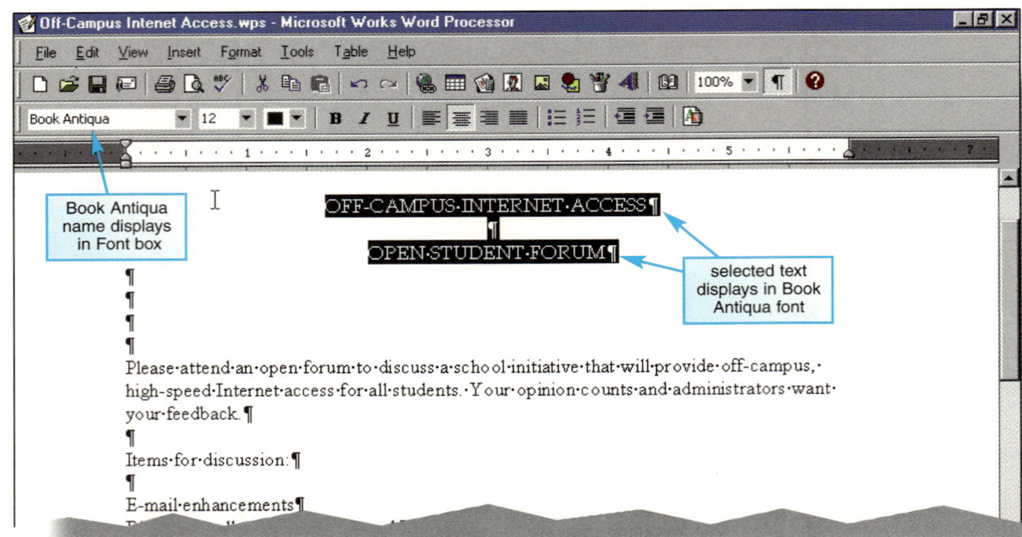

FIGURE 1-43

Other Ways

1. Right-click selected text, click Font on shortcut menu, click desired font name in Font list, click OK button
2. On Format menu click Font, click desired font name in Font list, click OK button

After choosing the font, the changed lines remain selected. To remove the highlighting, click anywhere in the document workspace.

Changing Font Size

The next step in formatting the document is to change the font size of the heading lines. The words, OFF-CAMPUS INTERNET ACCESS, should display in 36-point font size.

Perform the following steps to change the font size.

To Change Font Size

1 Select the line of text to enlarge (OFF-CAMPUS INTERNET ACCESS) by clicking in the left margin of the Word Processor window on the same line as the text.

Works highlights the words, OFF-CAMPUS INTERNET ACCESS (Figure 1-44).

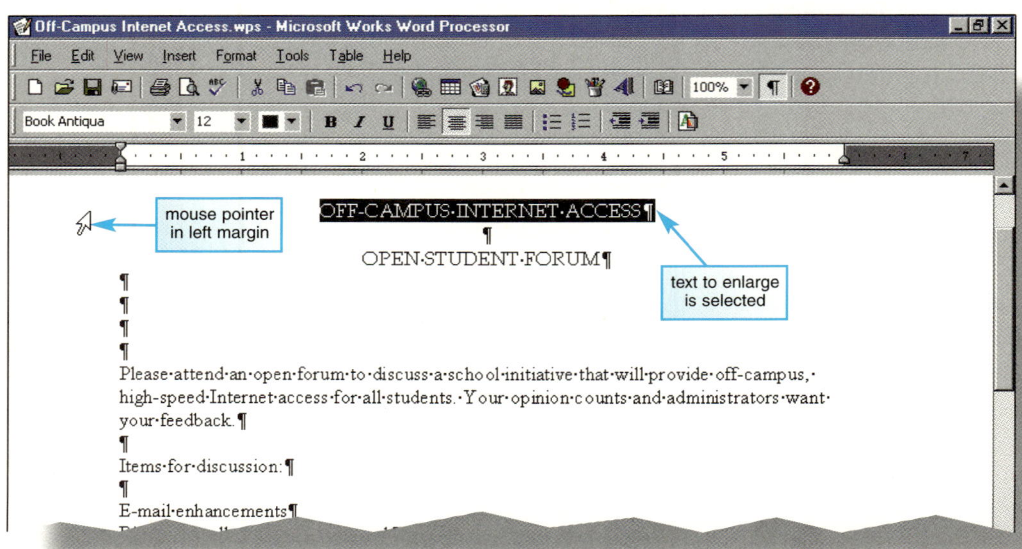

FIGURE 1-44

2 **Click the Font Size box arrow on the Formatting toolbar and point to the number 36.**

A list of font sizes displays and the number 36 is selected (Figure 1-45).

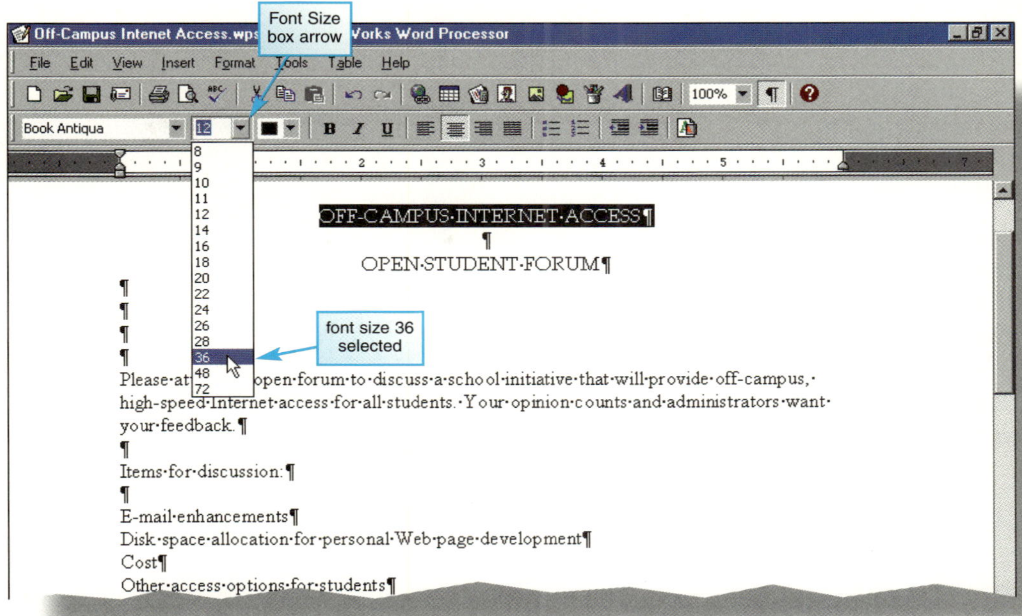

FIGURE 1-45

3 **Click 36.**

Works changes the first heading line to 36-point Book Antiqua font (Figure 1-46). The number 36 displays in the Font Size box on the Formatting toolbar. Because the heading line is increased to 36 points, Works automatically wraps the word, ACCESS, to the beginning of the next line and centers the text.

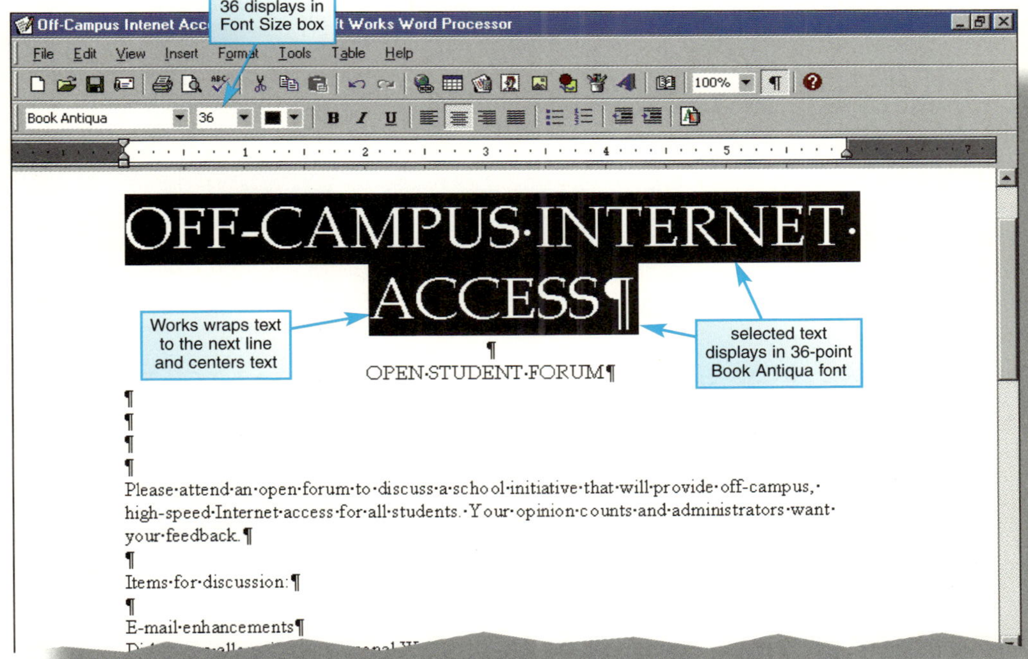

FIGURE 1-46

Other Ways

1. Right-click selected text, click Font on shortcut menu, click desired font size in Size list, click OK button
2. On Format menu click Font, click desired size in Size list, click OK button

Formatting the Remaining Heading Lines

The heading line, OPEN STUDENT FORUM, should display in 16-point Book Antiqua font. Perform the steps on the next page to accomplish this formatting.

To Change Font Size

1 Select the line of text to change (OPEN STUDENT FORUM) by clicking in the left margin of the Word Processor window on the same line as the text. Click the Font Size box arrow on the Formatting toolbar and then point to the number 16.

Works highlights the words, OPEN STUDENT FORUM, and the Font list displays (Figure 1-47). The number 16 is highlighted in the list.

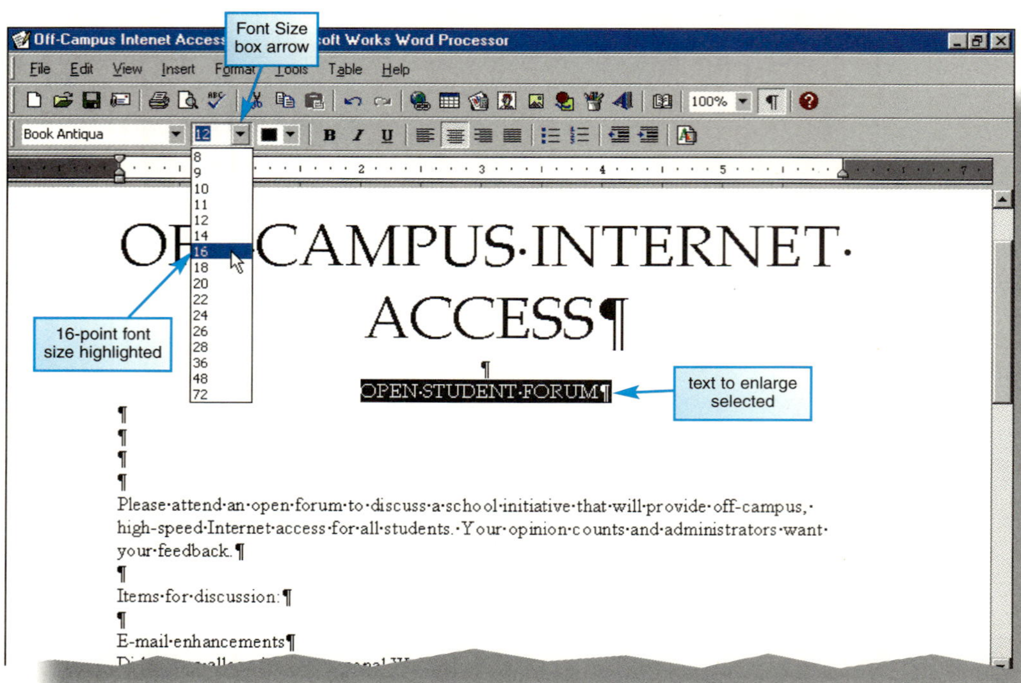

FIGURE 1-47

2 Click 16.

Works changes the second heading line to 16-point Book Antiqua font (Figure 1-48). The number 16 displays in the Font Size box on the Formatting toolbar.

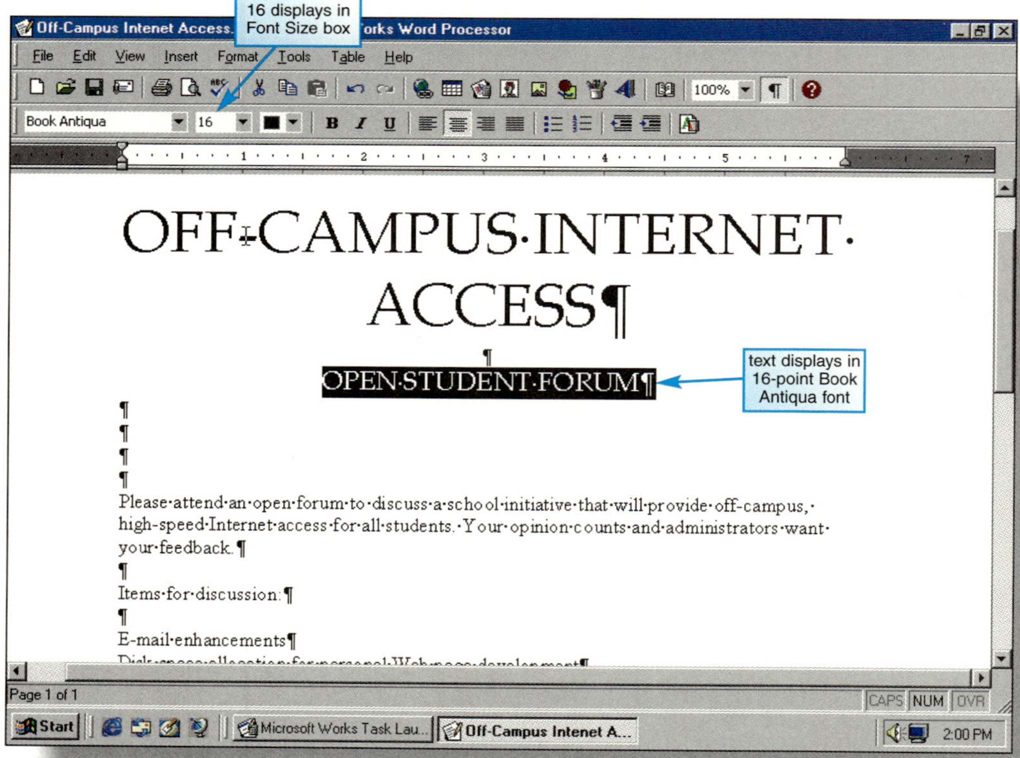

FIGURE 1-48

The heading lines now are formatted in the proper font and font size.

Formatting Additional Text

The three lines following the heading lines display in 12-point Times New Roman. Because the font and font size are 12-point Times New Roman, no additional steps are necessary. The five lines following the body of the announcement beginning with the words, Items for discussion:, are to display in 16-point Times New Roman. Because the default font and font size are 12-point Times New Roman, the only step necessary is to change the font size for the lines to 16 point. To accomplish this formatting, perform the following steps.

To Change Font Size

1 Scroll the document to view the line containing the words, Items for discussion:. Select the five lines of text to be formatted by dragging through the left margin of the Word Processor window opposite the words, Items for discussion. Click the Font Size box arrow on the Formatting toolbar and then point to the number 16.

Works highlights the five lines of text and the Font Size list displays (Figure 1-49). The number 16 is highlighted in the list.

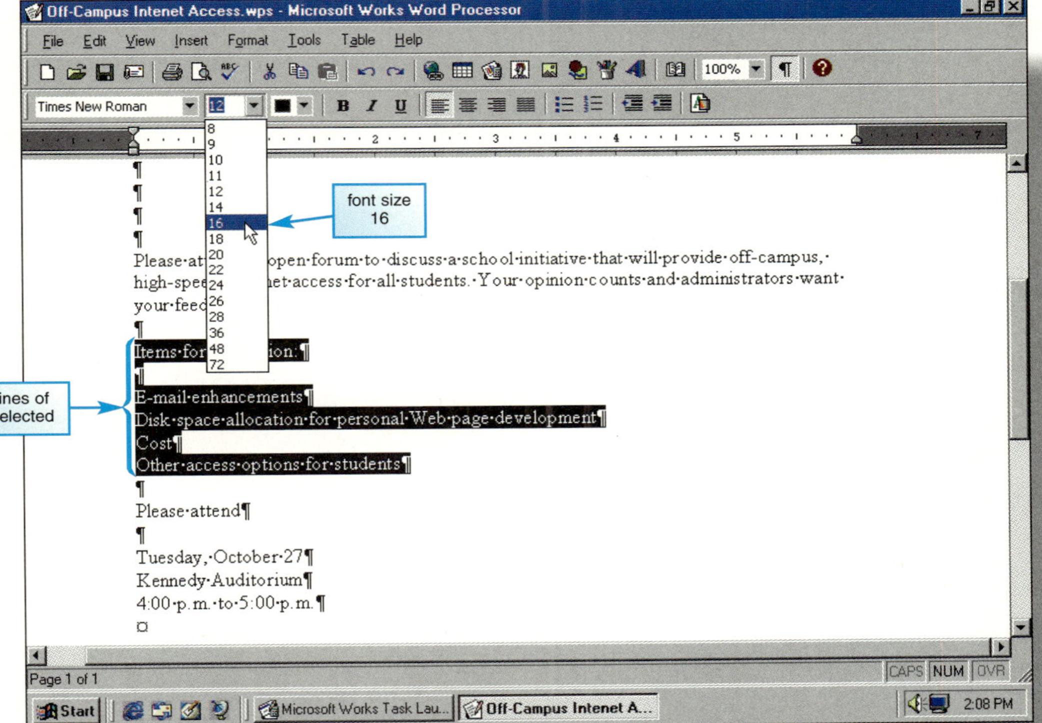

FIGURE 1-49

Click 16.

Works changes the five lines to 16-point font size. The number 16 displays in the Font Size box on the Formatting toolbar (Figure 1-50).

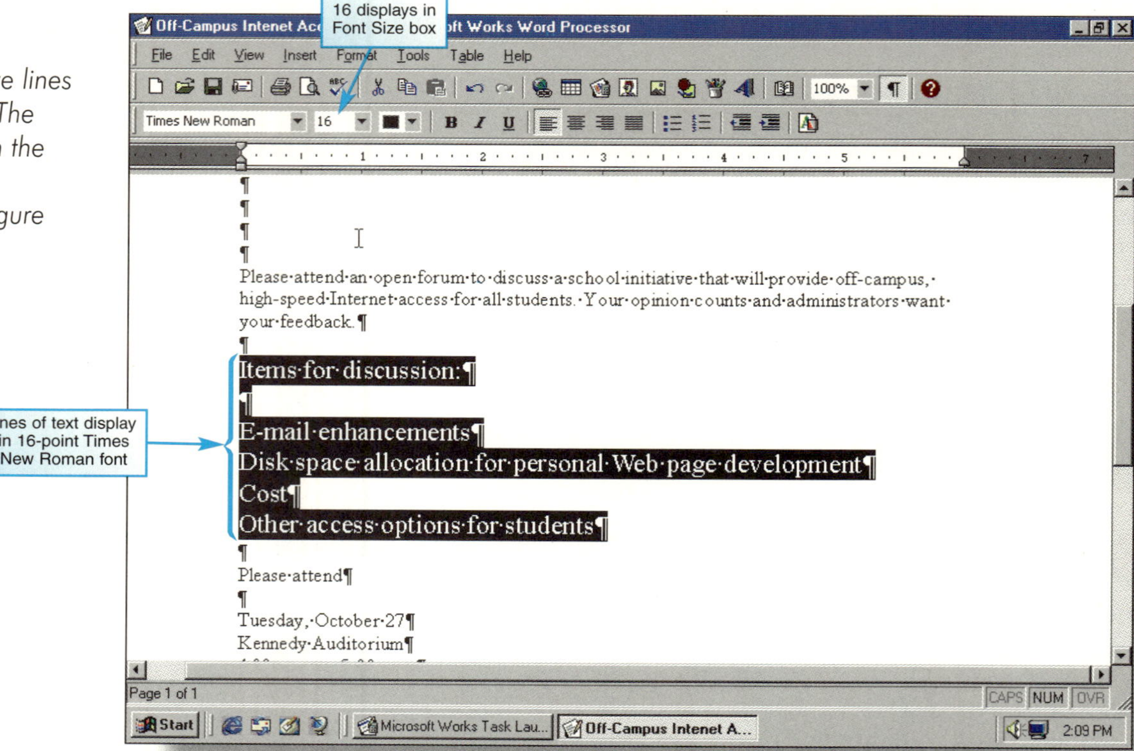

FIGURE 1-50

Shortcut Menus

Right-clicking any selection causes Works to display a shortcut menu with commands you can use specific to the operation. In addition to clicking any command on the shortcut menu, you also can right-click any command to carry out a task.

The first part of the announcement now is formatted with the proper fonts and font sizes.

Creating a Bulleted List

The four paragraphs following the words, Items for discussion:, are indented three-quarters of one inch from the left margin and display as a bulleted list (see Figure 1-19 on page W 1.20). A **bulleted list** consists of a word or words on one or more lines preceded by a special character at the beginning of the line. The purpose is to have the list stand out from the rest of the text.

You can create a bulleted list by clicking **Bullets and Numbering** on the shortcut menu. The shortcut menu contains frequently used commands to use with the current selection. You activate the shortcut menu by right-clicking the selection. To create a bulleted list using the shortcut menu, complete the following steps.

To Create a Bulleted List

1 Select the four lines that are to comprise the bulleted list, beginning with E-mail enhancements. Right-click the selected text. When the shortcut menu displays, point to Bullets and Numbering.

The four lines are selected and the shortcut menu displays (Figure 1-51).

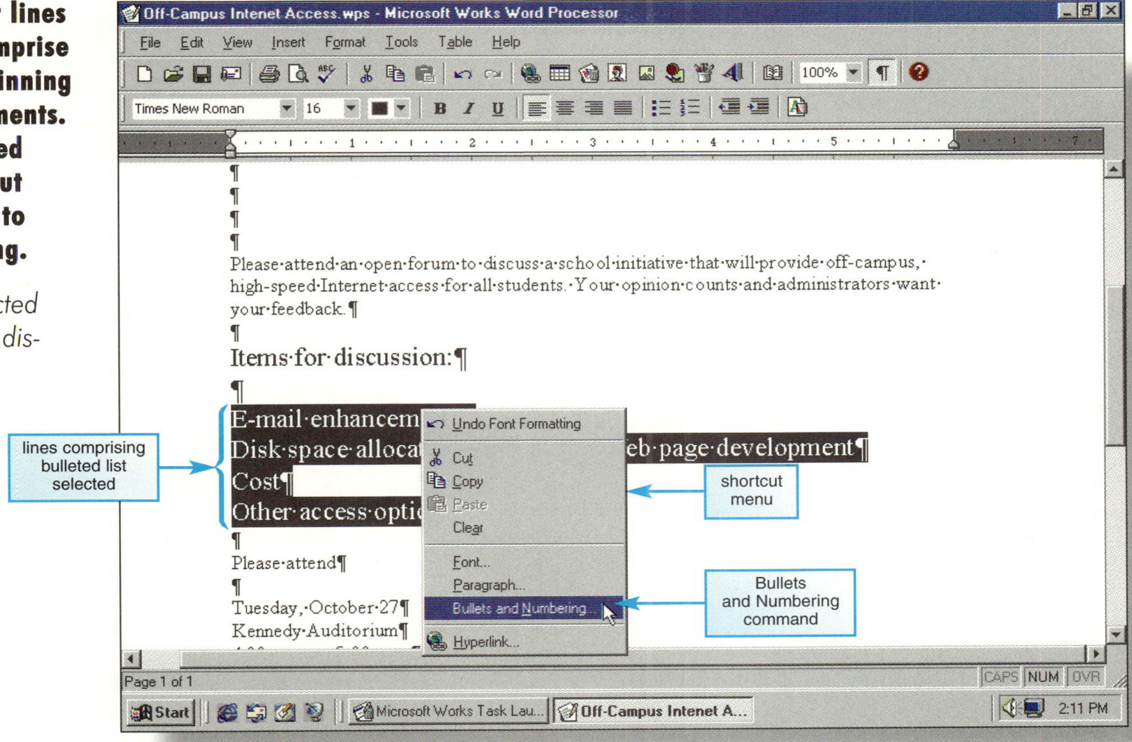

FIGURE 1-51

2 Click Bullets and Numbering. When the Bullets and Numbering dialog box displays, if necessary, click the Bulleted Tab, and then click the solid dot-shaped bullet in the Bullet style box.

Works displays the Bullets and Numbering dialog box (Figure 1-52). Twenty-eight different styles of bullets display in the Bullet style box. The solid dot-shaped bullet in the Bullet Style box displays with a blue border indicating that it is selected.

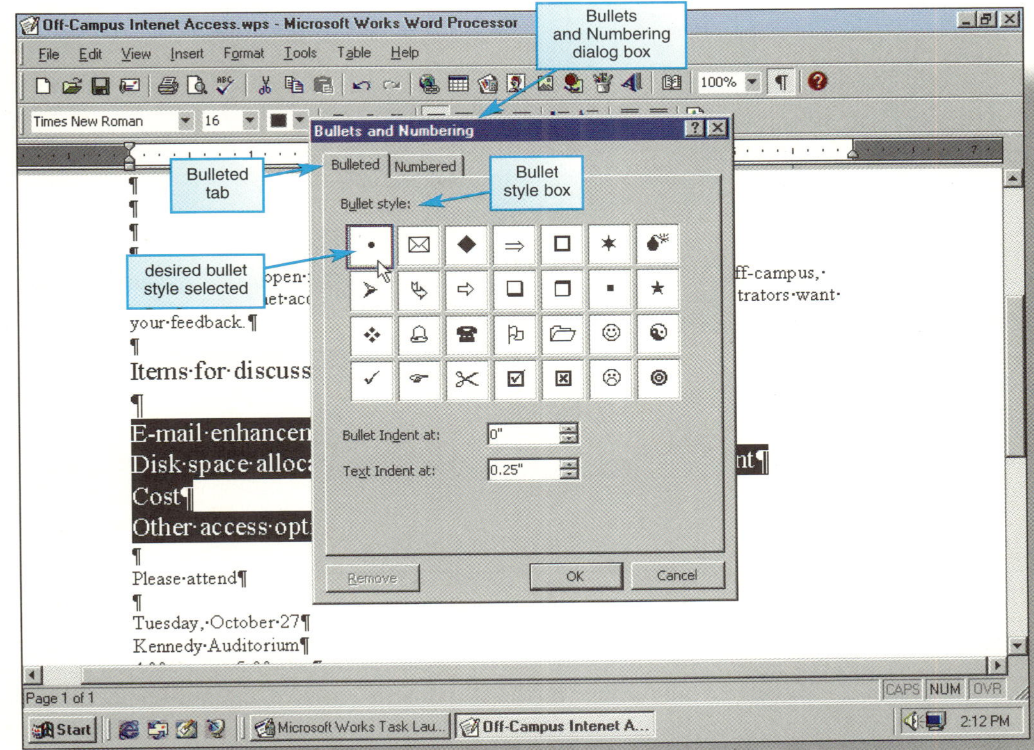

FIGURE 1-52

3 **Drag through the Bullet Indent at text box to highlight the default setting (0). Type** .75 **in the Bullet Indent at text box and then point to the OK button.**

The Bullet Indent at text box displays .75 (Figure 1-53).

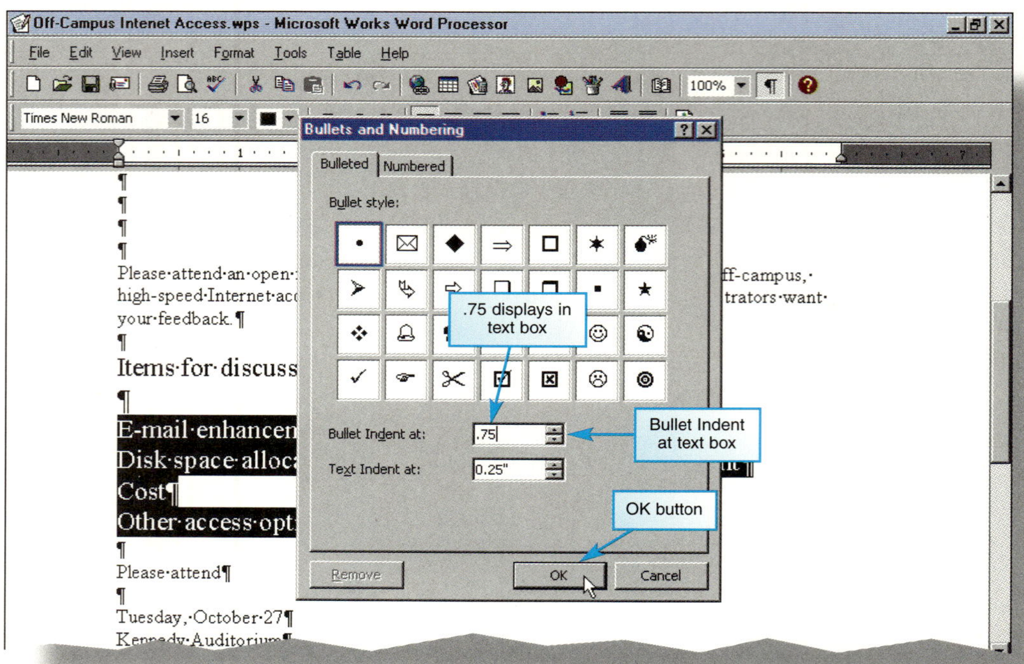

FIGURE 1-53

4 **Click the OK button.**

The bullets are indented three-quarters of one inch from the left margin and the text begins one inch from the left margin (Figure 1-54). The top triangle on the left side of the ruler, called the ***First Line Indent marker****, moves to the right three-quarters of one inch, and the bottom rectangle called the* ***Left Indent marker****, moves to the right an additional one-quarter inch. The Bullets button on the Formatting toolbar is recessed, indicating the selected text contains bullets.*

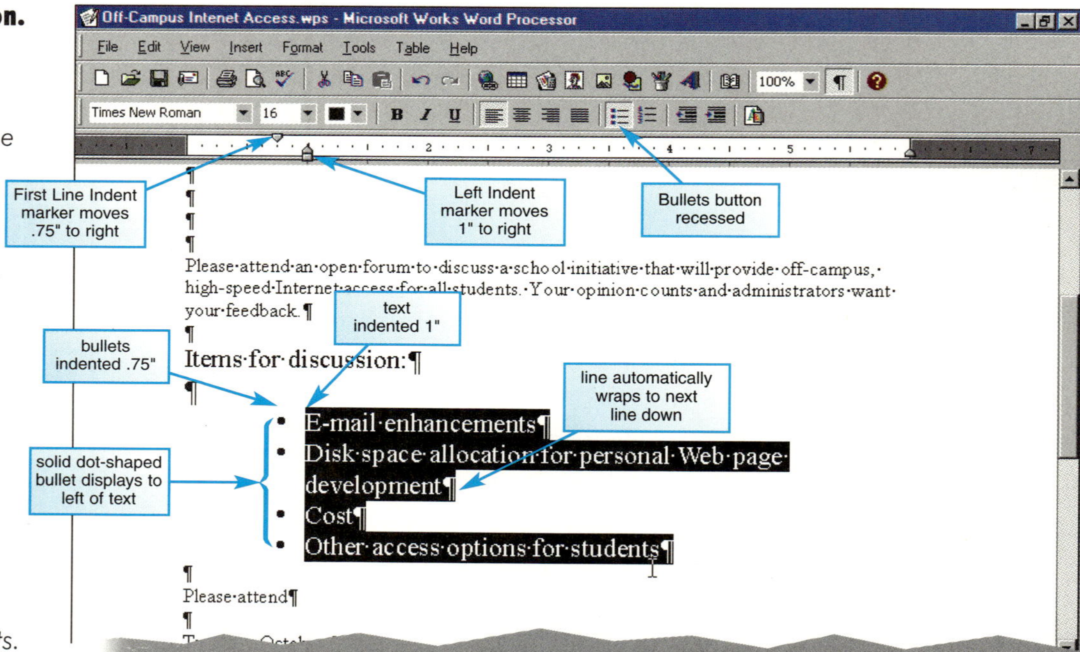

FIGURE 1-54

Other Ways

1. On Format menu click Bullets and Numbering, click desired bullet style, click OK button
2. Click Bullets button on Formatting toolbar

To remove the highlighting from the selected text, position the mouse pointer anywhere in the document workspace and click. Be aware that using the Bullets button creates a bulleted list using the special character that was chosen last in the Bullets and Numbering dialog box.

To remove the bullets from the bulleted list, select the bulleted list and then click the Bullets button on the Formatting toolbar. If you want to change the bulleted list to standard text at the left margin, select the bulleted list and then press CTRL+Q.

The document now is formatted with the proper font and font sizes except for the last four lines. The lines following the bulleted list should be centered within the margins of the document and display in 16-point Arial font. To center the last four lines and then change the font to Arial and the font size to 16, complete the following steps.

TO CENTER TEXT AND CHANGE FONT AND FONT SIZE

1. Select the last four lines in the document.
2. Click the Center button on the Formatting toolbar.
3. Click the Font box arrow on the Formatting toolbar to display the list of fonts. Scroll the list to bring the Arial font name into view.
4. Click Arial in the Font list.
5. Click the Font Size box arrow on the Formatting toolbar to display the Font Size list.
6. Click 16.

The last four lines are centered and display in 16-point Arial font (Figure 1-55)

Font Size

Many people need to wear reading classes. Thus, use a font size of at least 12 in your documents. Because an announcement usually is posted on a bulletin board, its font size should be as large as possible so that all potential readers can see and read the announcement easily.

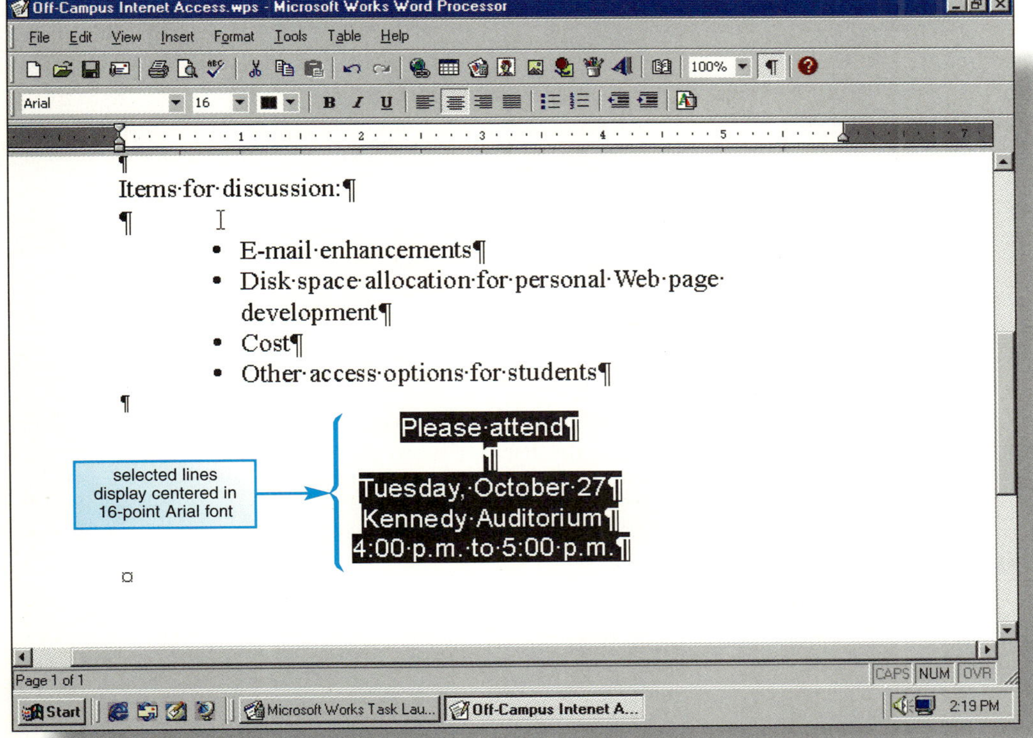

FIGURE 1-55

Displaying Text in Italics

The next step is to select the first line after the bulleted list and italicize the characters in it. Perform the following step to italicize text.

To Italicize Text

1 Select the line to be italicized, in this case, Please attend. Click the Italic button on the Formatting toolbar.

The selected text displays in italics (Figure 1-56).

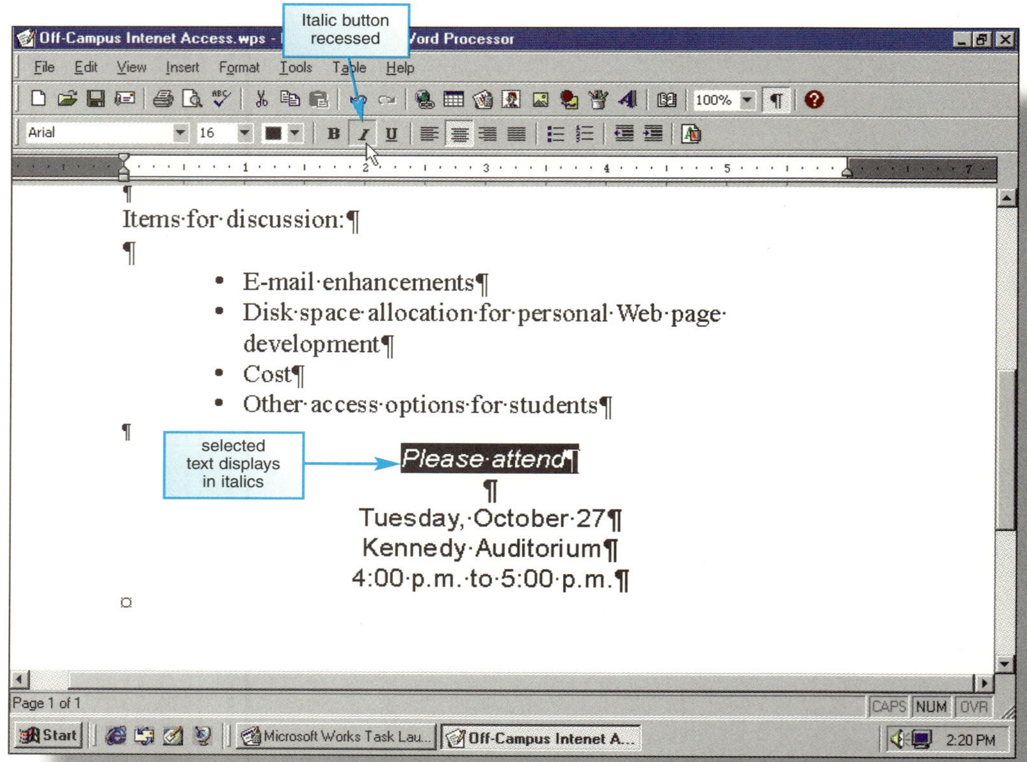

FIGURE 1-56

Other Ways

1. Right-click selected text, click Font on shortcut menu, click Italic in Font Style list, click OK button
2. On Format menu click Font, click Italic in Font Style list, click OK button
3. Press CTRL+I

When the selected text is italicized, the Italic button on the Formatting toolbar is recessed. If you want to remove the italic format from the selected text, click the Italic button a second time.

Displaying Text in Color

The last three lines are to display in red. To format these lines, use the Font Color box on the Formatting toolbar as shown in the following steps.

To Display Text In Color

1 **Select the last three lines in the document. Right-click the selected text. Point to Font on the shortcut menu.**

The last three lines in the document are selected and the shortcut menu displays (Figure 1-57).

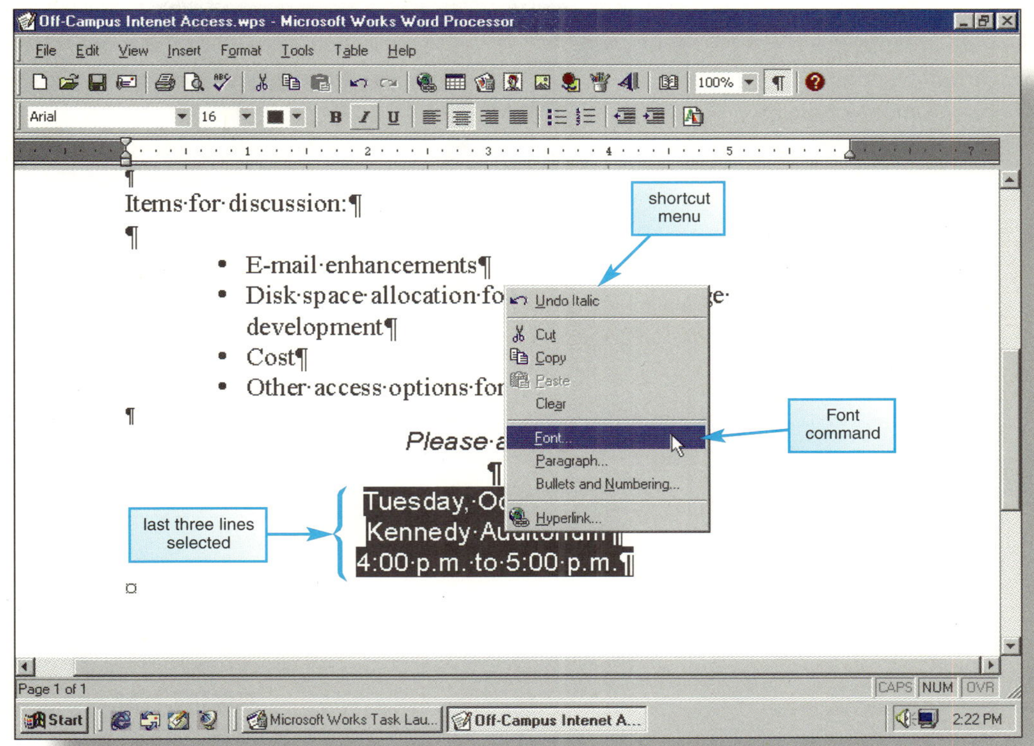

FIGURE 1-57

2 **Click Font. When the Font dialog box displays, click the Color box arrow and then point to the Red color box.**

Works displays the Font dialog box (Figure 1-58). In the Font dialog box, Arial displays in the Font box, 16 displays in the Size box, indicating the font for the selected text is 16-point Arial.

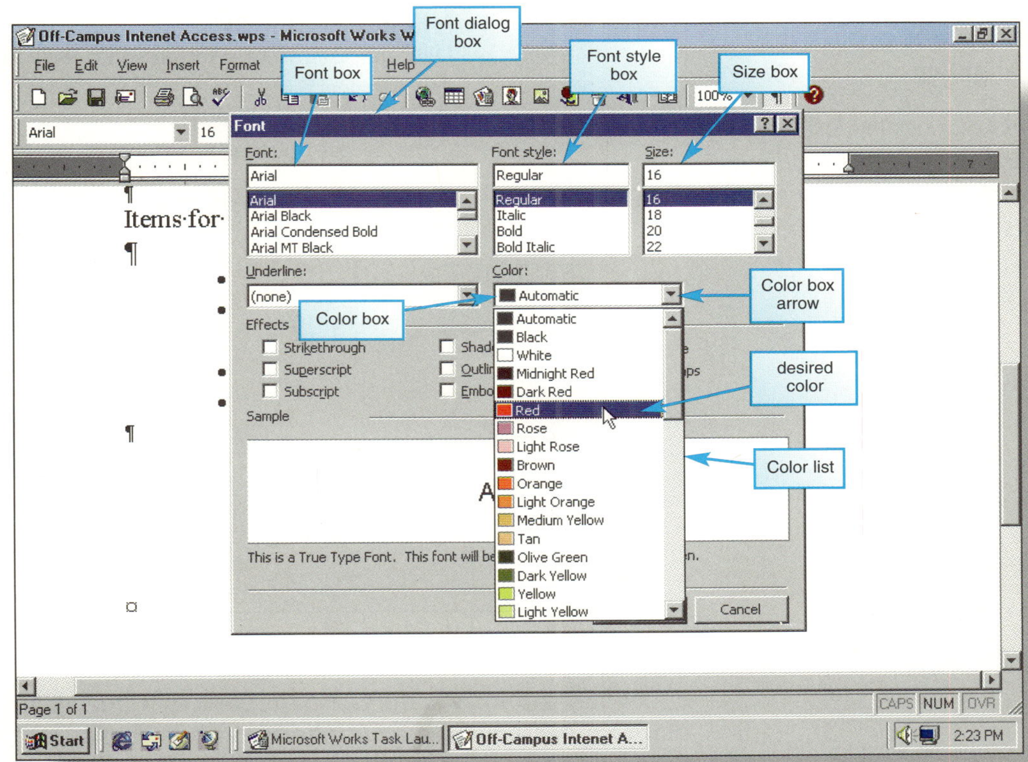

FIGURE 1-58

3 Click Red and then point to the OK button.

Text in the Sample box displays in red 16-point Arial font and the mouse pointer points to the OK button (Figure 1-59).

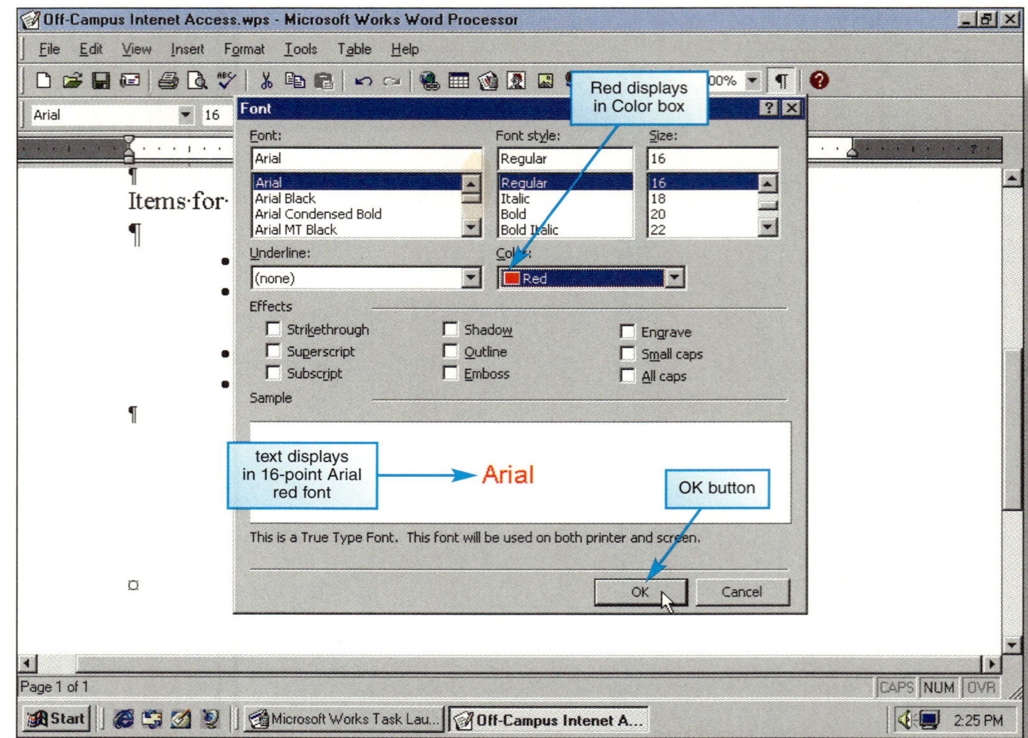

FIGURE 1-59

4 Click the OK button. Click anywhere in the blank document workspace to remove the highlighting.

Works displays the last three lines in 16-point Arial red font (Figure 1-60). The paragraph mark for the next paragraph retains the formatting from the previous paragraph.

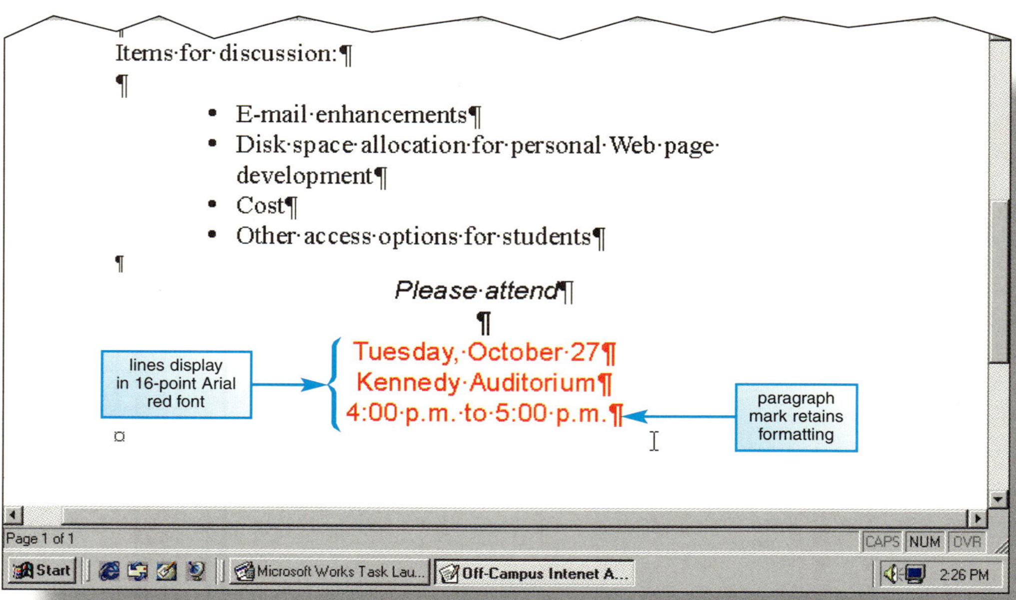

FIGURE 1-60

Other Ways

1. On Format menu click Font, click desired color in Color list, click OK button
2. Click Font Color box arrow on Formatting toolbar, click desired color

When you format the last paragraph in a document, the formatting remains in place for subsequent paragraphs unless you change it. That is the reason the paragraph mark on the last line in Figure 1-60 displays centered in red 16-point Arial font.

The Font dialog box shown in Figure 1-59 on the previous page contains check boxes. A **check box** represents options that you can turn on or off. A check in a check box indicates the option is turned on. To place a check mark in a box, click the box. In Figure 1-59, the Style box contains nine check boxes. None of the boxes contains a check mark, indicating the options are turned off. You can select more than one check box at a time.

Bold Style

To further emphasize the contents of the announcement, the headline text, OFF-CAMPUS INTERNET ACCESS and OPEN STUDENT FORUM, will be formatted to display in bold. To display the headline text in bold, perform the following steps.

To Display Text in Bold

1 Hold down the CTRL key and then press the HOME key to display the top portion of the document on the screen. Select the headline text, OFF-CAMPUS INTERNET ACCESS and OPEN STUDENT FORUM.

The headline text in the document is selected (Figure 1-61).

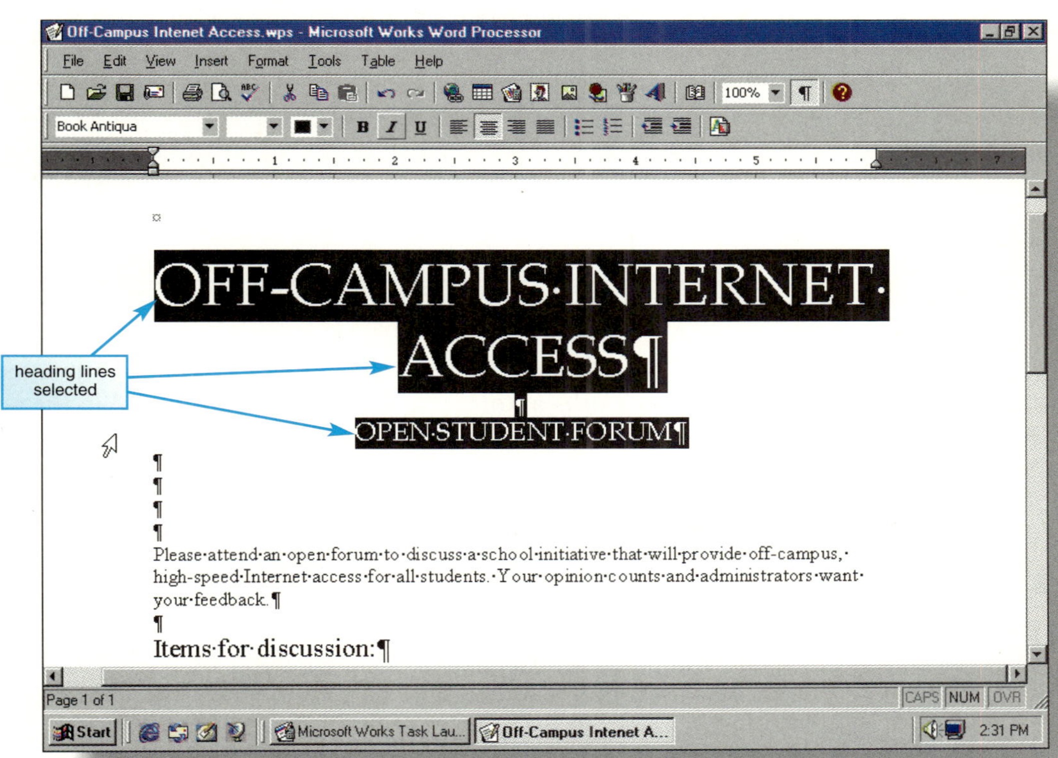

FIGURE 1-61

2 **Click the Bold button on the Formatting toolbar and then click anywhere in the document.**

Works changes the selected text to bold (Figure 1-62).

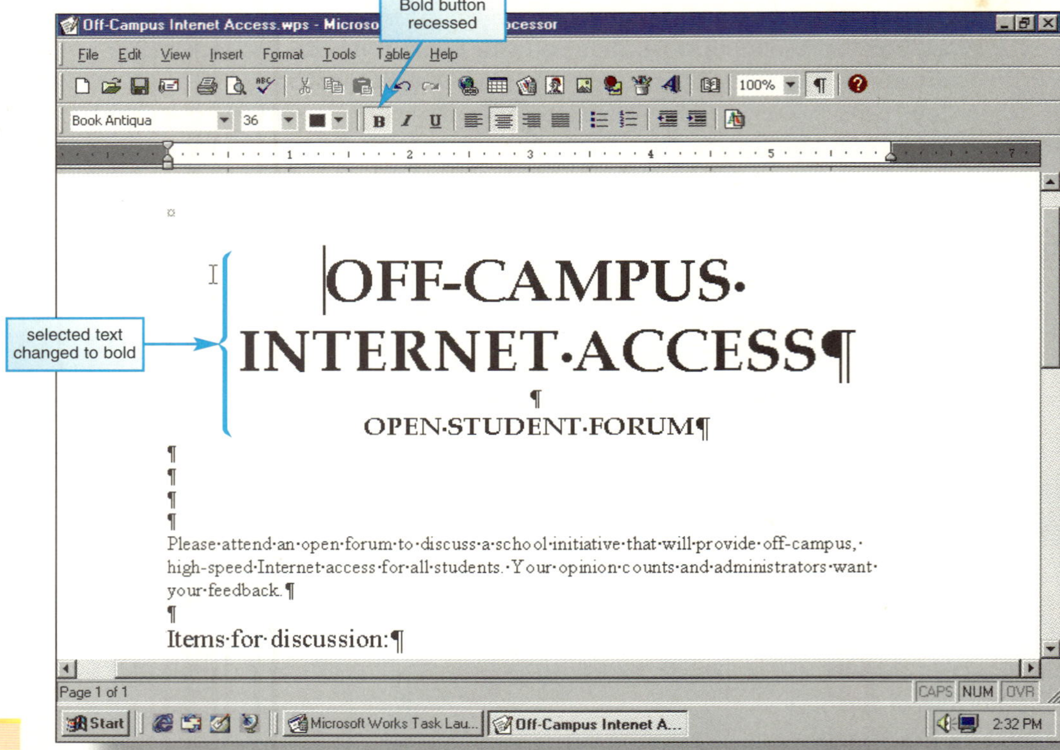

FIGURE 1-62

Other Ways

1. Right-click selected text, click Font on shortcut menu, click Bold in Font Style list, click OK button
2. On Format menu click Font, click Bold in Font Style list, click OK button
3. Press CTRL+B

When characters are bolded, they become slightly larger. Because the text is larger, Works automatically wraps the third word in the announcement title, Internet, to the beginning of the next line and centers the text. The document is formatted except for the illustration that must be inserted in the document.

More About

Clip Gallery Live

Graphics can add to your document, presentation, or Web sites and make them much more striking to the reader. Microsoft's Clip Gallery Live can help meet all your needs with over 120,000 items to choose from — including graphic images, photographs, sounds, and Web animations. At this Web site, you can download items and use them to enhance the overall look and feel of your documents. For more information on Microsoft's Clip Gallery Live, visit the Works 6 More About Web page (www.scsite.com/works6/more.htm) and then click Clip Gallery Live.

Using Clip Art in a Document

The next step in preparing the announcement is to insert an illustration related to the seminar in the document (see Figure 1-1 on page W 1.8). To accomplish this, you will use Microsoft clip art (predrawn illustrations) that is available for use as a part of the Word Processor.

Inserting Clip Art in a Word Processing Document

You insert clip art into a document by clicking the **Clip Art command** on the Insert menu. Perform the following steps to insert clip art into the announcement.

To Insert Clip Art into a Document

1 Click the line in the document where you want to place the clip art.

The insertion point is positioned on the line where you will insert the clip art (Figure 1-63).

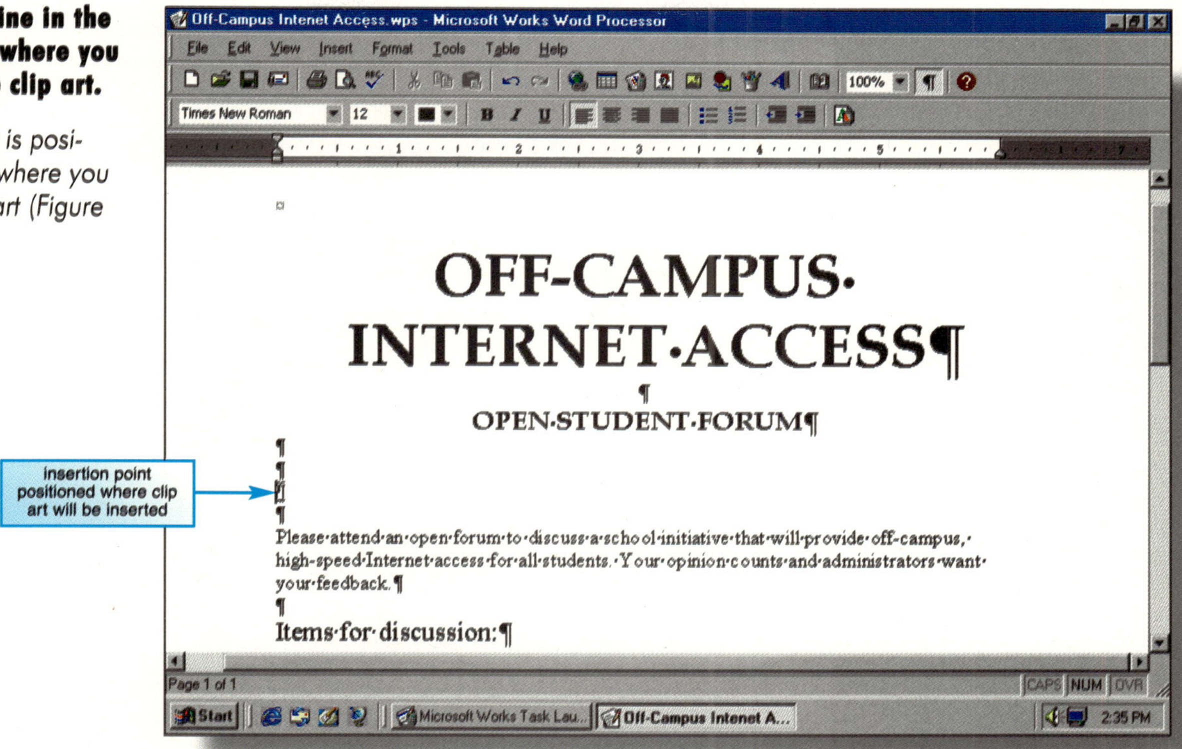

FIGURE 1-63

2 Because you want to center the clip art, click the Center button on the Formatting toolbar.

Works centers the insertion point and the paragraph mark in the document window (Figure 1-64).

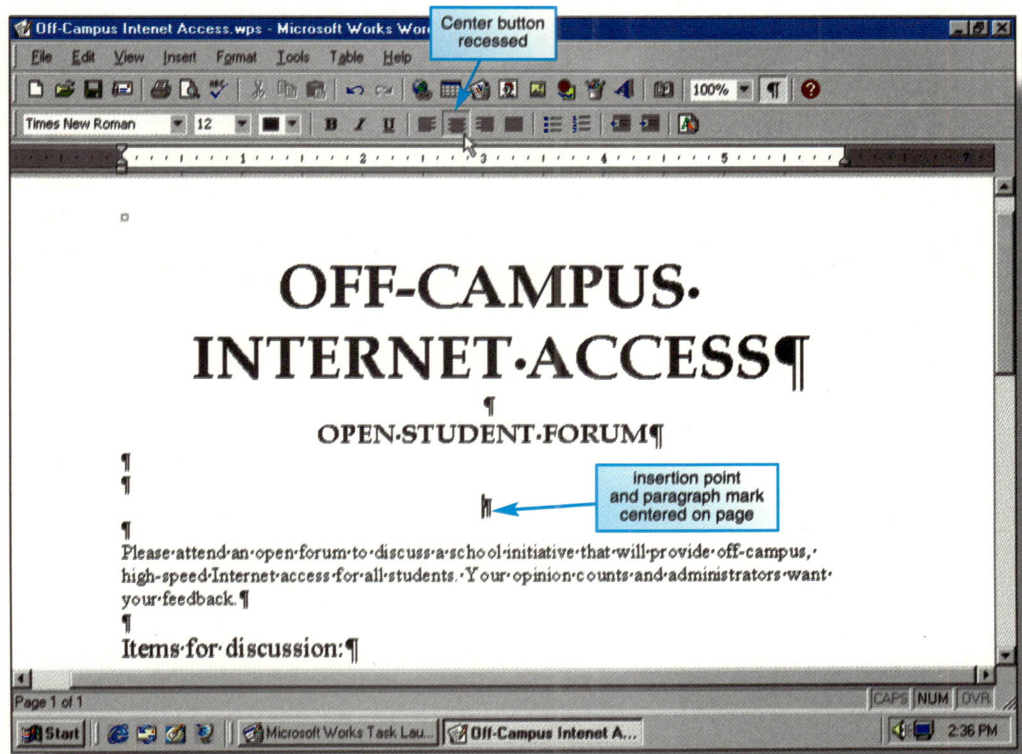

FIGURE 1-64

3 Click Insert on the menu bar, point to Picture, and then point to Clip Art.

The Insert menu and Picture submenu display (Figure 1-65).

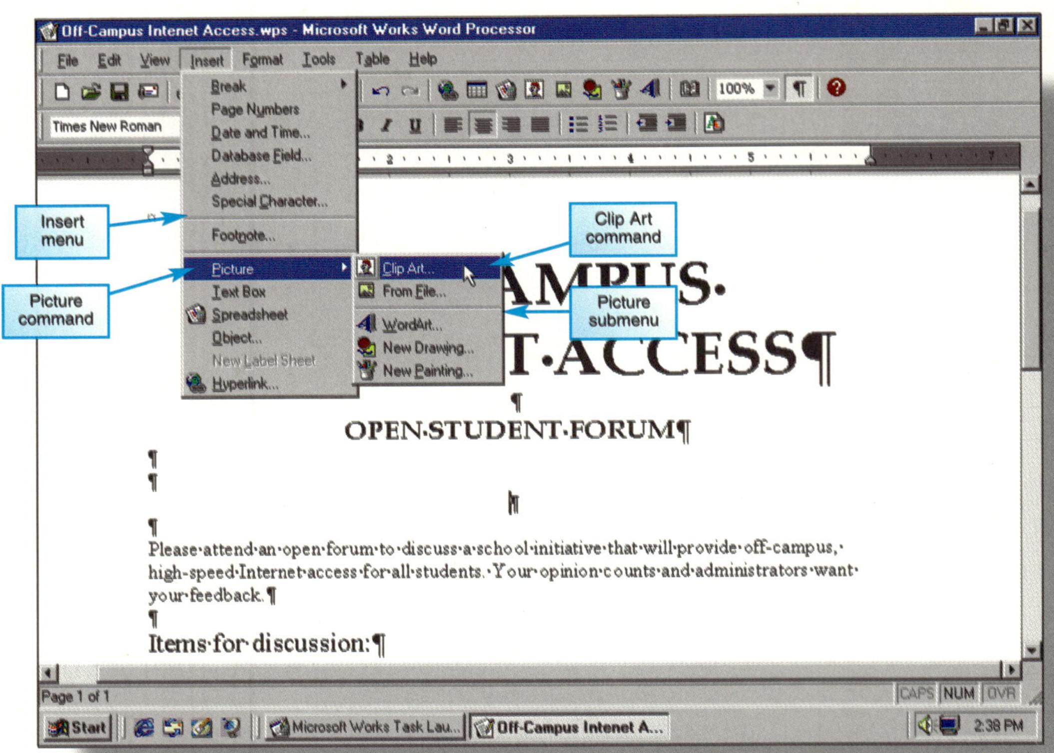

FIGURE 1-65

4 Click Clip Art. When the Insert Clip Art dialog box displays, if necessary click the Find tab, type `globe` **in the Type a keyword text box, click All pictures (clip art and photographs) if necessary in the Select a media type list, and then point to the Search button.**

The Find sheet displays in the Insert Clip Art dialog box (Figure 1-66).

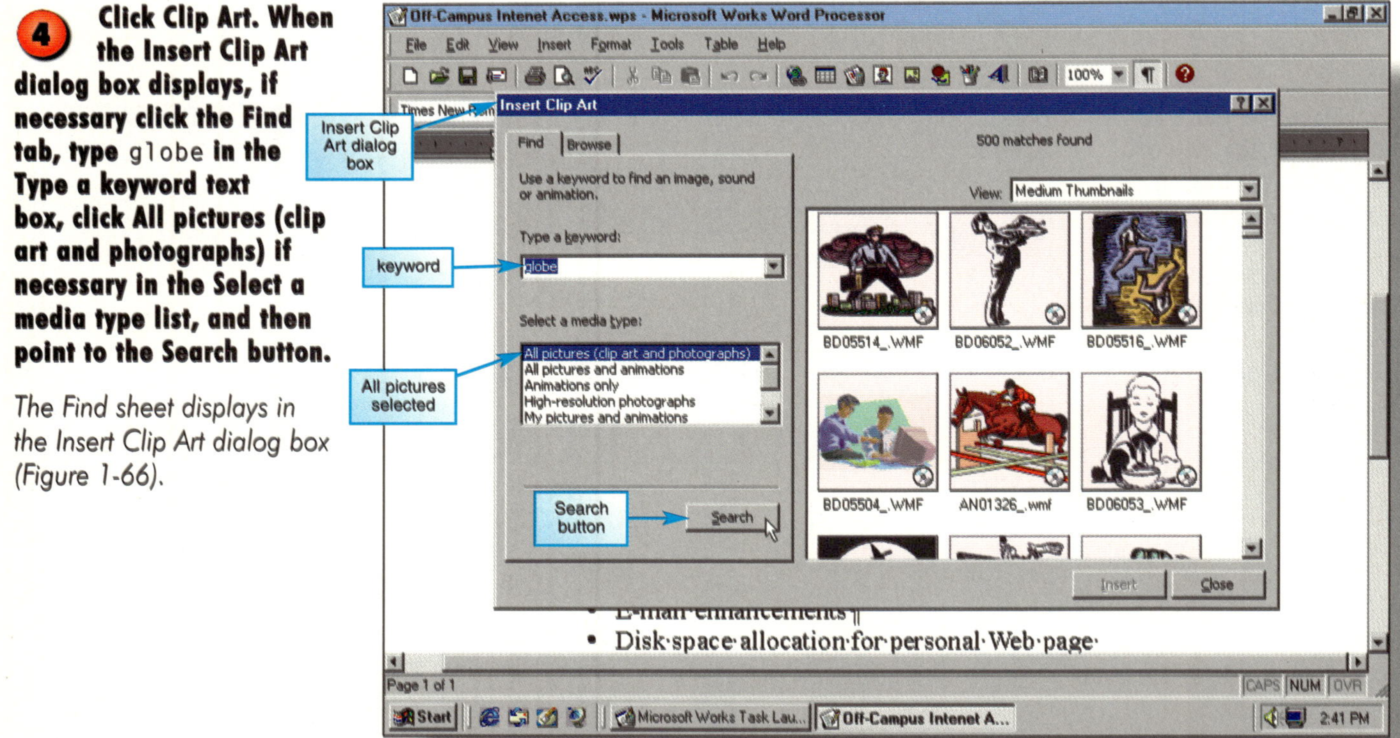

FIGURE 1-66

5 **Click the Search button. When the clip art displays, scroll through the list until the clip art illustrating the world globe with an airplane displays. Click the world globe and then point to the Insert button.**

Works displays the requested clip art images. The clip art illustration of the world globe with an airplane is selected, as indicated by the blue border around the image (Figure 1-67).

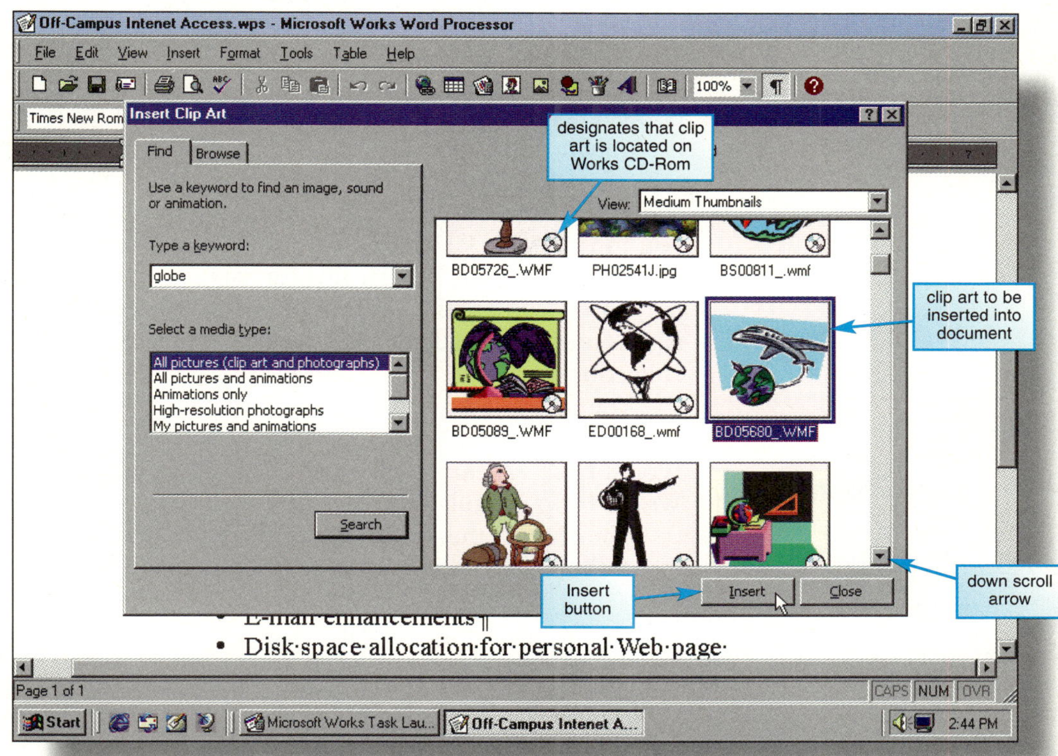

FIGURE 1-67

6 **Click the Insert button.**

Works inserts the clip art in the word processing document at the location of the insertion point (Figure 1-68). A rectangular border that contains small dark squares, called **selection handles**, *displays around the border of the clip art. This border indicates the clip art is selected.*

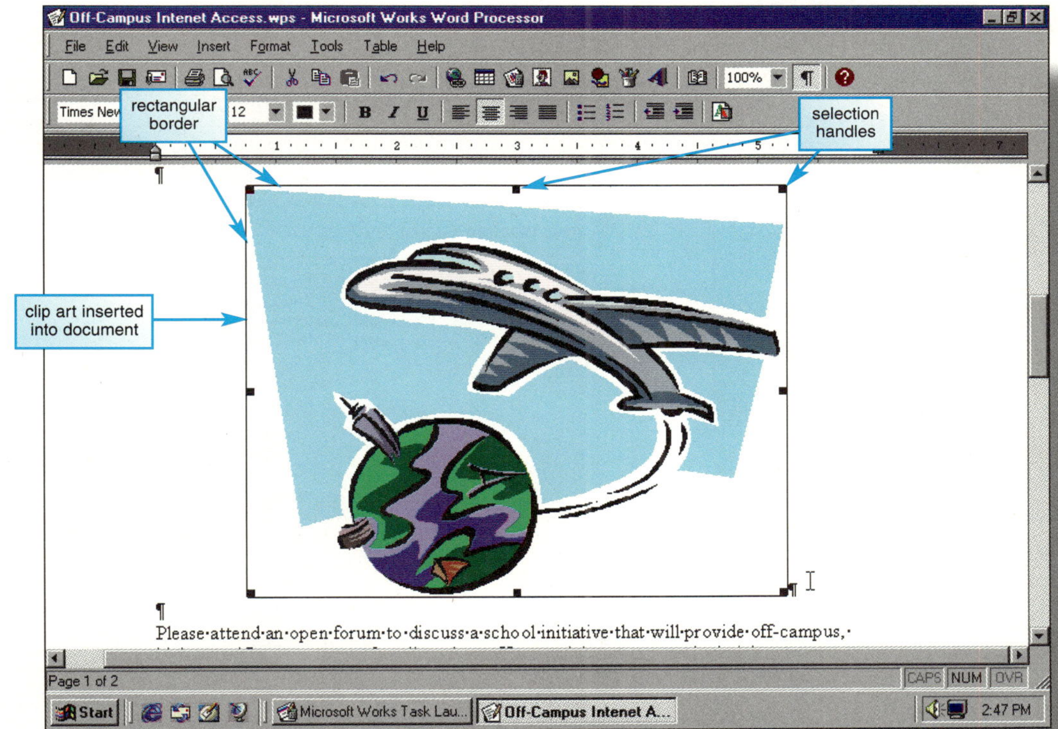

FIGURE 1-68

The Insert Clip Art dialog box contains a collection of approximately 150 clip art images and more than 10,000 **thumbnails**, which are miniature representations of a file, text, or image. The thumbnails that are contained on the Works compact disc (CD-ROM) contain a small picture of a CD-ROM in the lower-right corner of the thumbnail (see Figure 1-67 on the previous page). Clip art images that are stored on the computer's hard drive do not contain the small picture of a CD-ROM. If you choose to install clip art that is available on the Works CD-ROM, Works prompts you to insert the CD-ROM before you can insert the clip art in your document.

Many different clip art images may be purchased and added to Works. You also may insert clip art images that are downloaded from the Internet. One technique is to store downloaded clip art and pictures from the Internet in Works Portfolio collections.

You also can edit clip art using the Microsoft Draw or Microsoft Paint tools that are available with Works. Another option is to wrap text around an object. Use Works Help to learn how to edit clip art or wrap text around an object. Using Works Help is explained later in this project.

The clip art that is placed in the document is called an **object**. Once in the document, the object may be **resized**, that is, made larger or smaller, as required.

More About

Resizing Graphics

When you drag the selection handles to resize a graphic, you might distort its proportions. To maintain the proportions of the graphic, press the SHIFT key while you drag a selection handle.

Changing the Size of Clip Art

After adding the clip art to the document, the size of the clip art must be changed to correspond to Figure 1-1 on page W 1.8. To change the size of the clip art, complete the following steps.

Steps To Resize Clip Art

1 If the clip art is not selected, click the clip art object. Position the mouse pointer on the selection handle in the upper-right corner of the border that surrounds the clip art.

The mouse pointer changes to a two-headed arrow when positioned on a selection handle (Figure 1-69). To resize an object, you drag a selection handle until the object is the desired size.

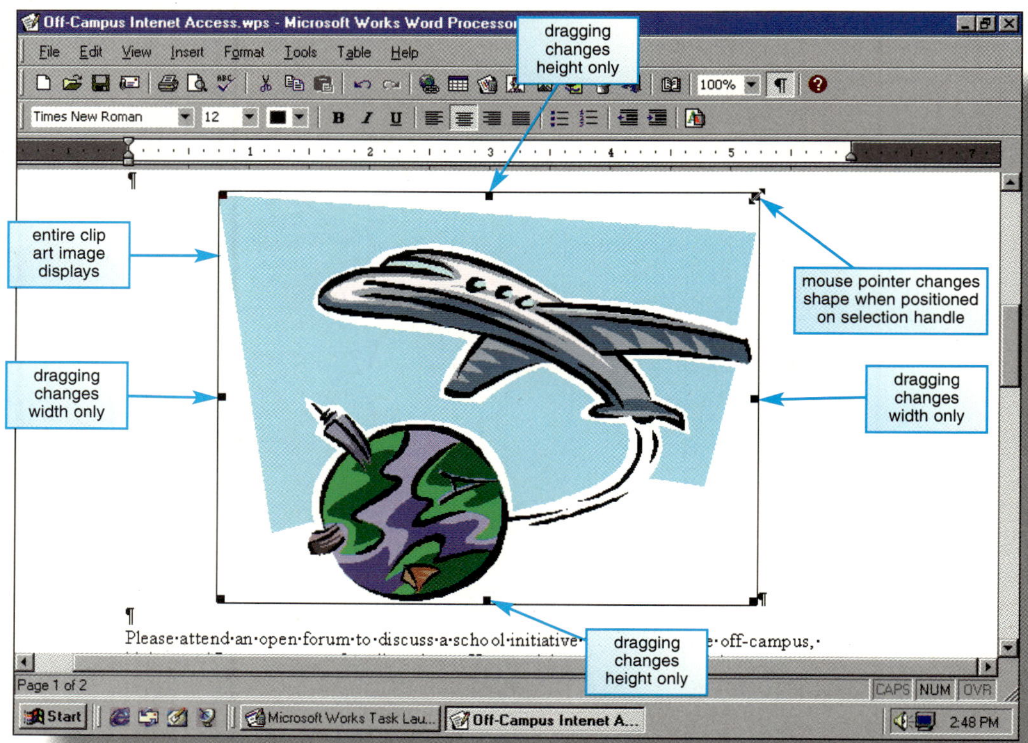

FIGURE 1-69

2 **Drag the selection handle downward and to the left until the selection rectangle is positioned approximately as shown in Figure 1-70.**

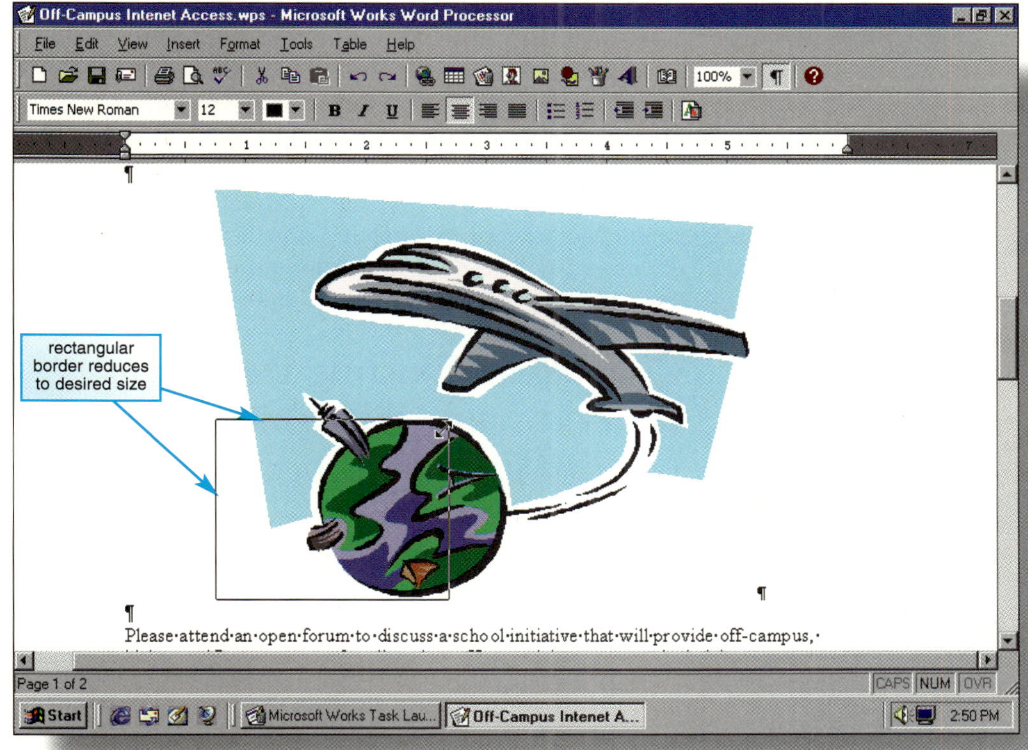

FIGURE 1-70

3 **Release the mouse button. Press CTRL+HOME to display the top of the document.**

Works resizes the object (Figure 1-71). Works also recenters the resized clip art object.

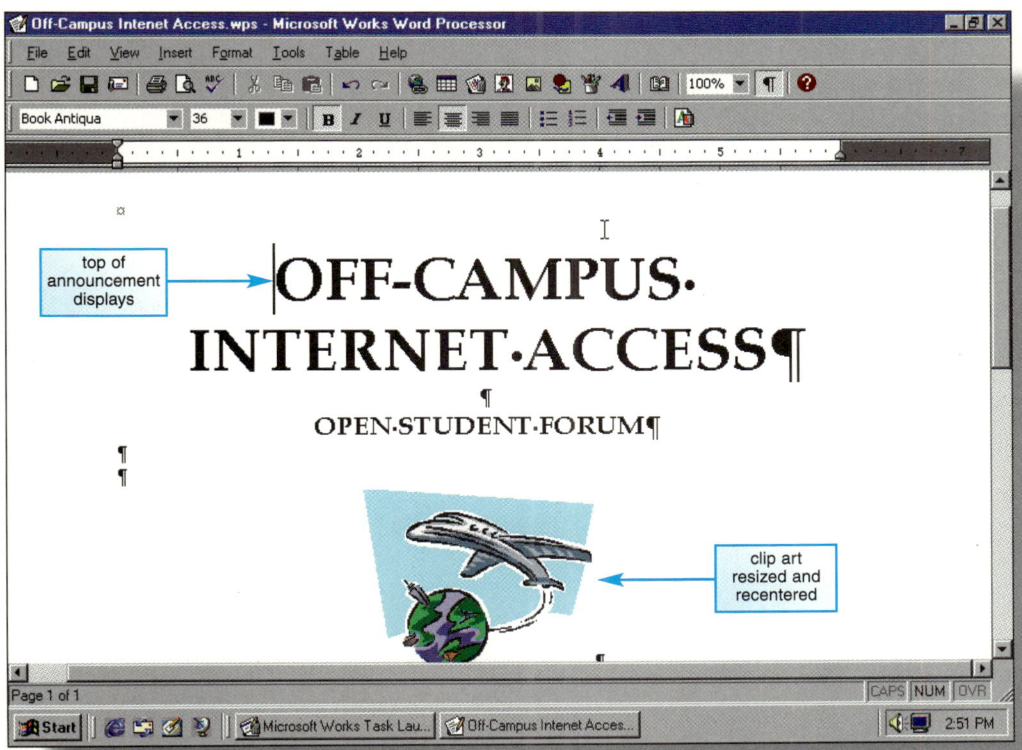

FIGURE 1-71

To resize an object proportionally, you drag one of the corner selection handles. To stretch the object, you drag a top, bottom, or side handle. Dragging one of these selection handles will change the original proportions of the object.

If you ever need to remove a clip art object from a document, select the image and then press the DELETE key. You also can right-click the selected object and then click Clear on the shortcut menu, or use the Clear command on the Edit menu.

If an object has been selected previously, clicking anywhere in the document workspace except the selected object or pressing an arrow key to scroll through a document will remove the rectangular border.

Saving a Document

You have struggled so hard to create the perfect paper on your computer for an English class. Suddenly, a student trips over your power cord and your monitor goes blank. It has been 30 minutes since you last saved your work. Horror stories such as this have happened to most people who have used a computer. There is no such thing as saving too often to protect the work you have completed.

Saving an Existing Document with the Same File Name

The announcement for Project 1 is complete. To save the formatting changes and clip art to your floppy disk in drive A, you must save the document again. When you saved the document the first time, you assigned a file name to it (Off-Campus Internet Access). When you make changes to an already saved document and want to save the modified document without changing the file name, use the **Save button** on the Standard toolbar. Works will save the modified document without displaying the Save As dialog box and asking for a new file name. Perform the following step to save the existing document with the same file name.

Steps To Save an Existing Document with the Same File Name

1 Click the Save button on the Standard toolbar.

Works saves the document on a floppy disk inserted in drive A using the currently assigned file name, Off-Campus Internet Access. When the save is finished, the document remains in memory and displays on the screen (Figure 1-72).

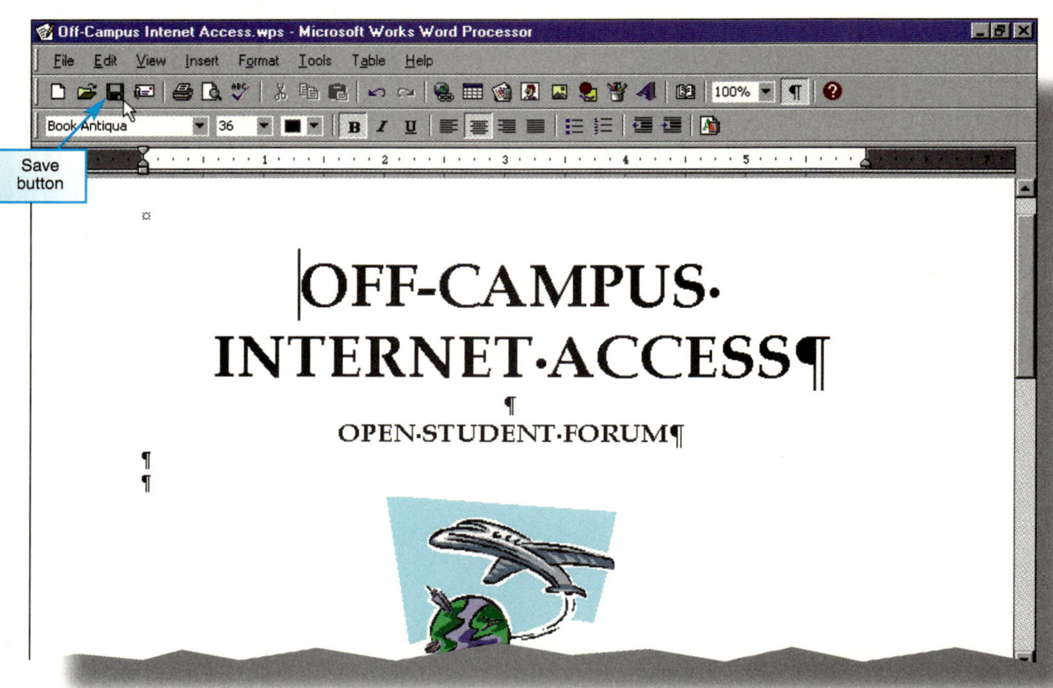

FIGURE 1-72

1. On File menu click Save
2. Press CTRL+S

If you want to save the modified document using a file name different from the name under which the file currently is saved, then you must use the Save As command on the File menu. When you use the **Save As command**, Works will display the Save As dialog box, and then you can enter the new file name, drive, and location. Works will save the document using the new file name in the location you specify. Note, however, that the file saved using the old file name still resides on the disk. The file using the new name does not replace the file with the old name.

Print Preview

After you create and save a Word Processor document, you often will want to print the document. To view the document in reduced size on the screen, use the **print preview** feature. To use print preview, perform the following steps.

To Use Print Preview

1 Point to the Print Preview button on the Standard toolbar (Figure 1-73).

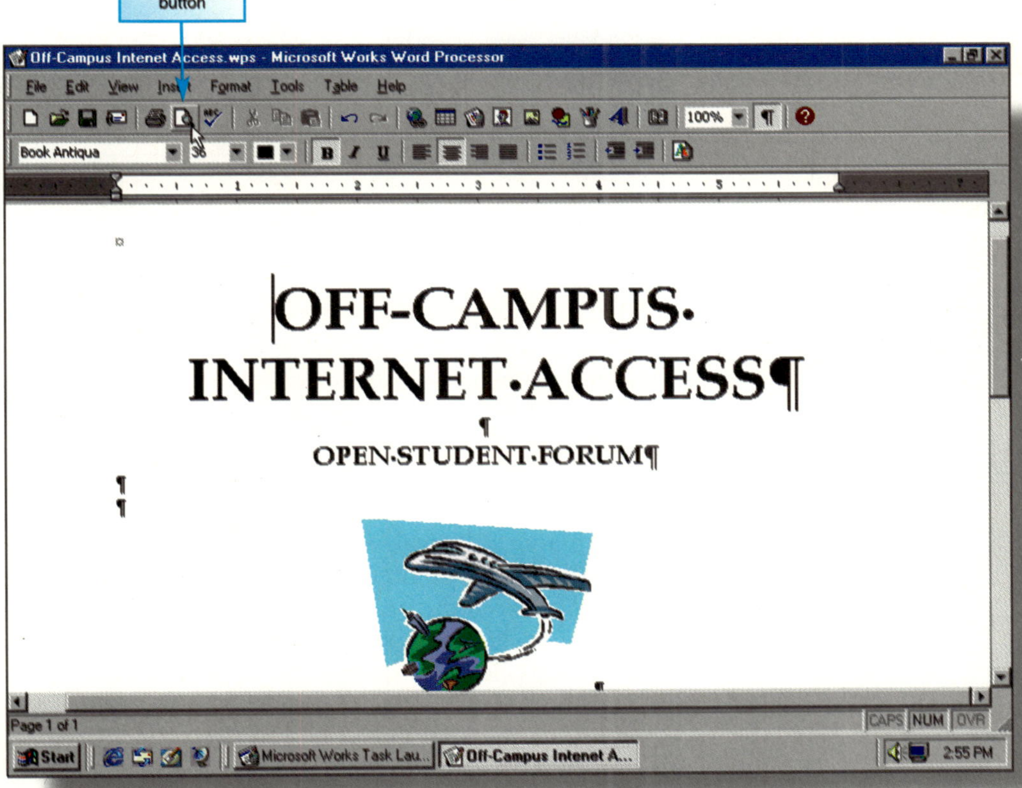

FIGURE 1-73

Click the Print Preview button.

Works displays the document in print preview (Figure 1-74). The Print Preview toolbar displays below the menu bar.

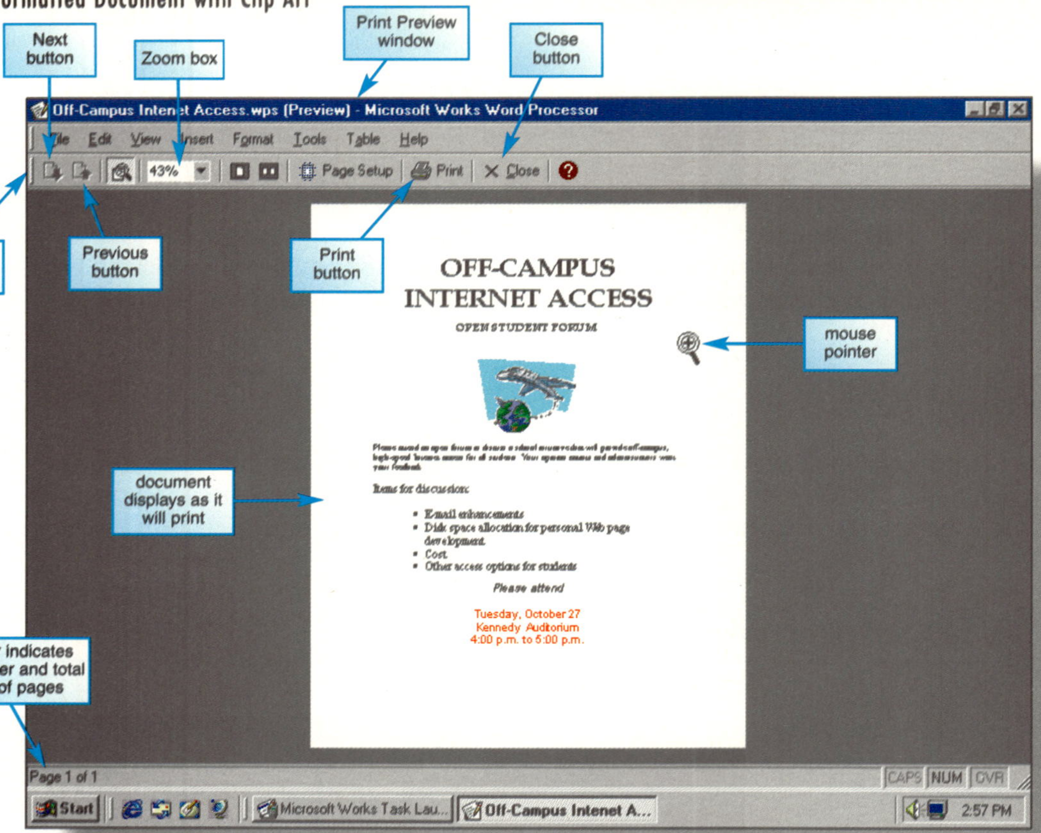

FIGURE 1-74

1. On File menu click Print Preview

If your document contains more than one page, you can click the **Next button** and **Previous button** on the Print Preview toolbar to view different document pages. This document contains only one page and as a result, the Next and Previous buttons are grayed out and unavailable. The number of the pages you are viewing and the total number of pages in a document display on the left side of the status bar.

The document preview that Works displays is reduced in size (43%). It is possible to enlarge the preview. If you position the mouse pointer in the print preview image, the mouse pointer shape changes to a magnifying glass and you can use the mouse to enlarge the print preview image. Clicking the mouse when the mouse pointer is positioned inside the document will enlarge the image to 100%. Clicking the mouse again, reduces the image back to 43%. You also can select other print preview options using the Zoom box on the Print Preview toolbar.

Clicking the **Print button** on the Print Preview toolbar causes Works to print the document. Clicking the **Close Preview button** returns to the Word Processor window where you can enter text.

More About

Printing

If you have a color printer, you can print your document in full color or black and white. If you have only a black and white printer, your document and graphics will print in shades of black, gray, and white.

Printing a Document

The following steps explain how to print a document that displays in the Word Processor window by clicking the **Print command** on the File menu. The first time you print a document on a given computer, you should use the Print command on the File menu to ensure the print options are selected properly.

Steps To Print a Document

1 Click the Close Preview button on the Print Preview toolbar to return to the Word Processor window. Click File on the menu bar and then point to Print.

The File menu displays (Figure 1-75).

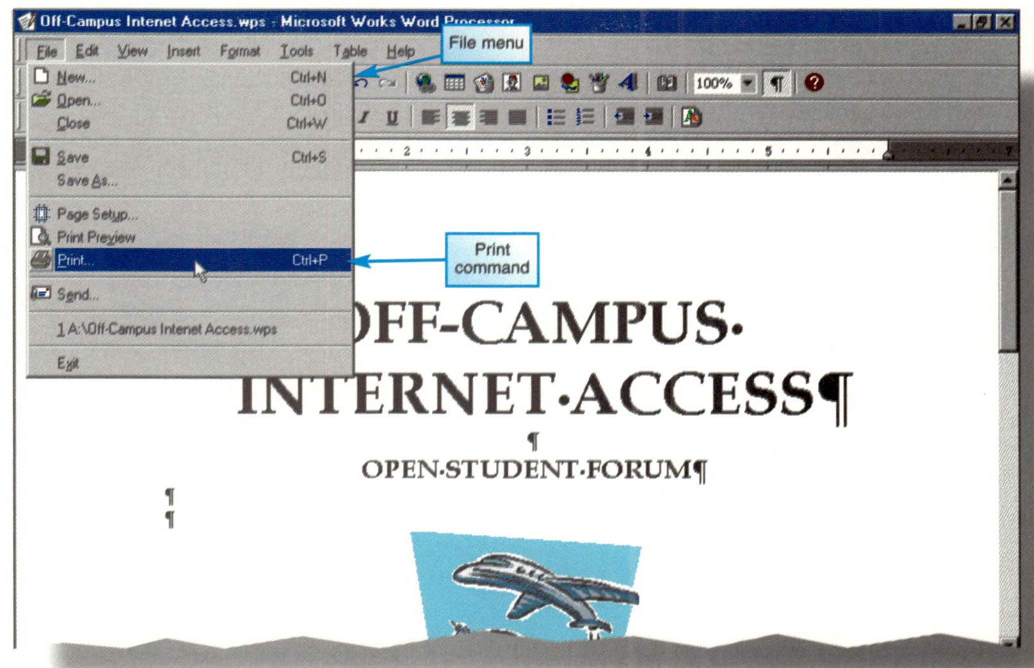

FIGURE 1-75

2 Click Print. When the Print dialog box displays, point to the OK button.

The Print dialog box displays (Figure 1-76). Review the Print dialog box to ensure the Number of copies box contains 1 and All is selected (a small black circle displays in the All option button when it is selected). This indicates all pages will print.

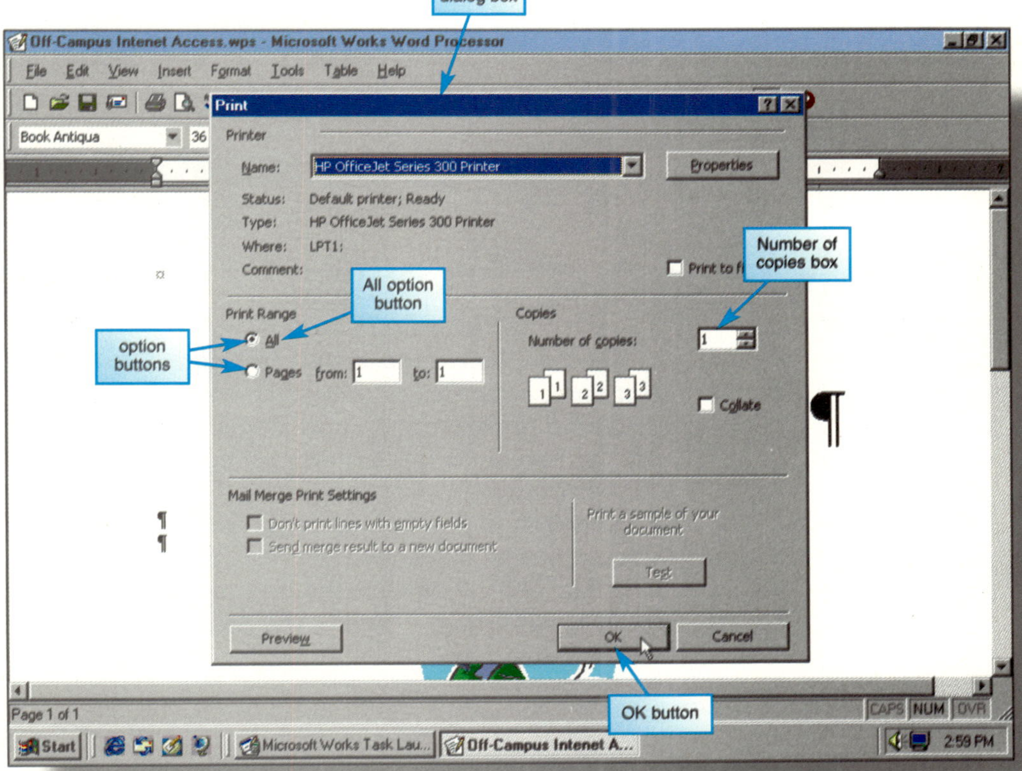

FIGURE 1-76

Click the OK button.

The Printing dialog box displays a brief message describing the status of the printing operation. The document then prints on your printer (Figure 1-77).

OFF-CAMPUS INTERNET ACCESS

OPEN STUDENT FORUM

Please attend an open forum to discuss a school initiative that will provide off-campus, high-speed Internet access for all students. Your opinion counts and administrators want your feedback.

Items for discussion:

- E-mail enhancements
- Disk space allocation for personal Web page development
- Cost
- Other access options for students

Please attend

Tuesday, October 27
Kennedy Auditorium
4:00 p.m. to 5:00 p.m.

FIGURE 1-77

1. Click Print button on Standard toolbar
2. Press CTRL+P

The Print dialog box shown in Figure 1-76 contains two option buttons in the Print range area. **Option buttons** represent options that you can turn on or off. You can select only one option button at a time, however. To select an option button, click the option button. Choosing a new option button automatically turns off the previous option.

After you have made entries in the Print dialog box to assure that printing occurs as you desire, you can use the Print button on the Standard toolbar to print the document. When you click the Print button on the Standard toolbar, the Print dialog box does not display. Printing will result based on previous entries in the Print dialog box.

Closing a Document

When you have completed working on a document, normally you will close the document and begin work on another document or close Works. Closing a document you are working on removes the document from the screen and from random access memory. If you close a document and no other documents are open, Works displays the Works Task Launcher if it is open. This allows you to continue using Works.

You should close a document when you no longer want to work on that document, but want to continue using Works. Complete the following steps to close the document.

To Close a Document

1 Point to the Close button in the upper-right corner of the Word Processor window (Figure 1-78).

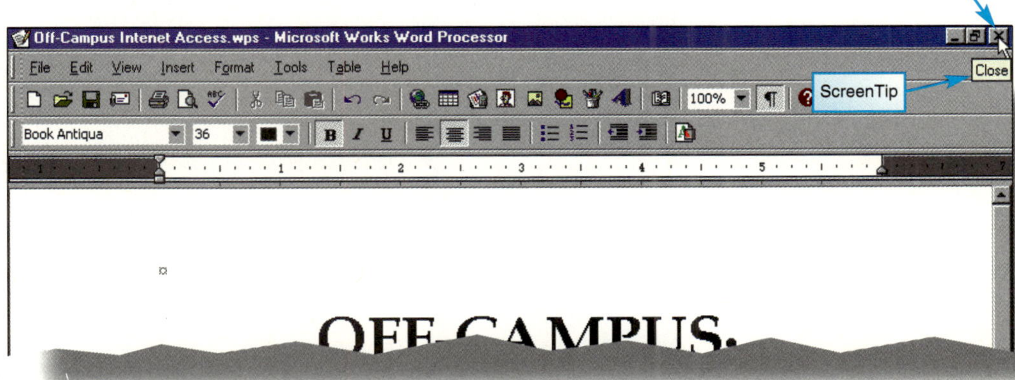

FIGURE 1-78

2 Click the Close button.

The text on the screen disappears and the Works Task Launcher window displays, allowing you to continue to use Works (Figure 1-79).

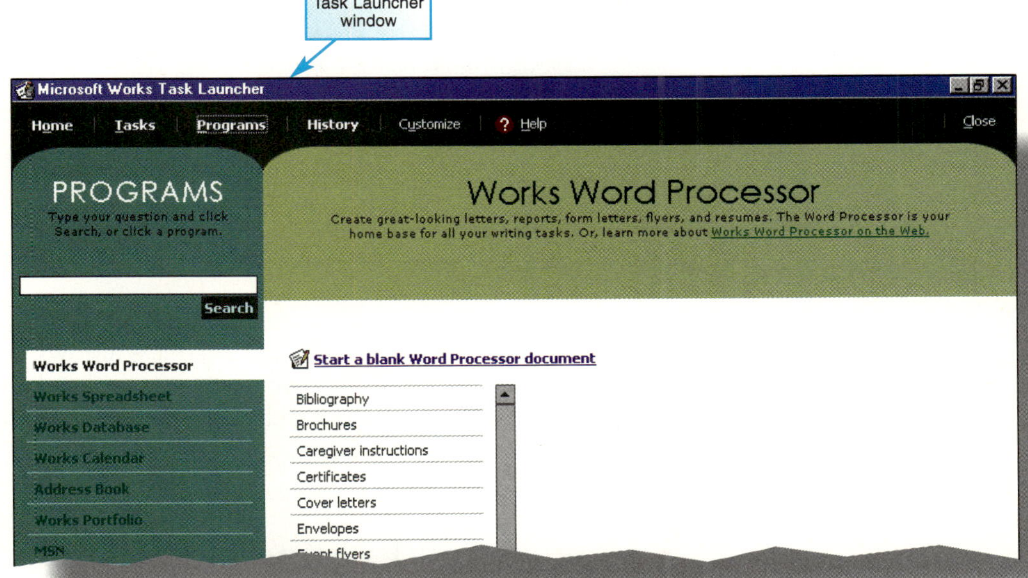

FIGURE 1-79

Other Ways

1. On File menu click Close
2. Press CTRL+W

If you have made any changes to a document after it has been saved, a dialog box displays asking if you want to save the changes before closing the document. Click the Yes button in the dialog box to save changes.

Quitting Works

If you are finished using Works, you should quit Works. The following steps explain how to quit Works.

To Quit Works

1. **Point to the Close button in the upper-right corner of the Works Task Launcher window (Figure 1-80).**

2. **Click the Close button.**

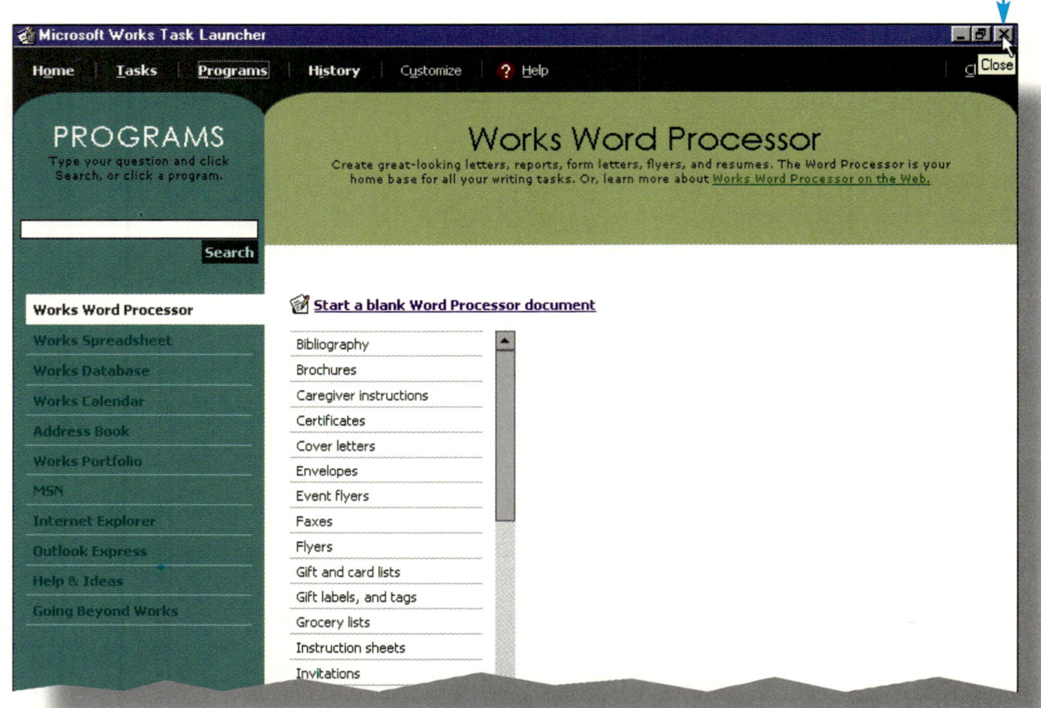

FIGURE 1-80

Other Ways

1. On File menu click Exit
2. On File menu click Exit in Works Task Launcher

Works is terminated and the Microsoft Windows desktop displays. If you have made any changes to an open document after it has been saved, a dialog box displays asking if you want to save the changes before quitting. Click the Yes button in the dialog box to save changes.

Opening an Existing Document

Often after creating, saving, and printing a document and closing Works, you may want to open an existing document to make changes to that document. The easiest way to open an existing document is to use the **My Computer icon** located in the upper-left corner of the desktop. My Computer allows you to access files stored on your hard disk or a floppy disk. To open the file you created in Project 1, Off-Campus Internet Access, double-click the My Computer icon, double-click the 3½ Floppy (A:) icon, where the document is located, and then double-click the file name. Windows will start Microsoft Works and then open Off-Campus Internet Access. Perform the following steps to open an existing document.

To Open an Existing Document

1 Point to the My Computer icon in the upper-left corner of the desktop (Figure 1-81).

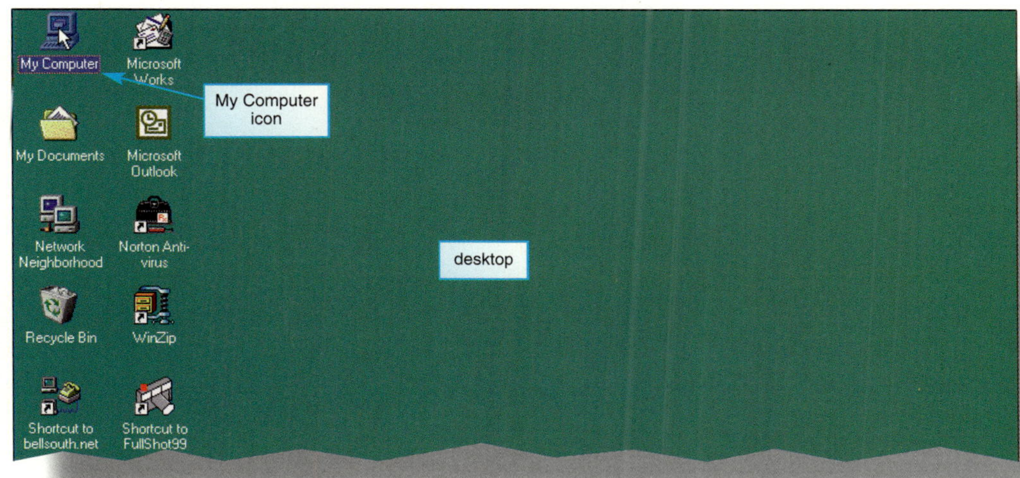

FIGURE 1-81

2 Double-click the My Computer icon. When the My Computer window opens, point to the 3½ Floppy (A:) icon.

When you double-click the My Computer icon, Windows opens the My Computer window (Figure 1-82). The My Computer window contains icons representing the hard disks, floppy disk drive, CD-ROM drive, and command icons. The icons that display on your screen may be different.

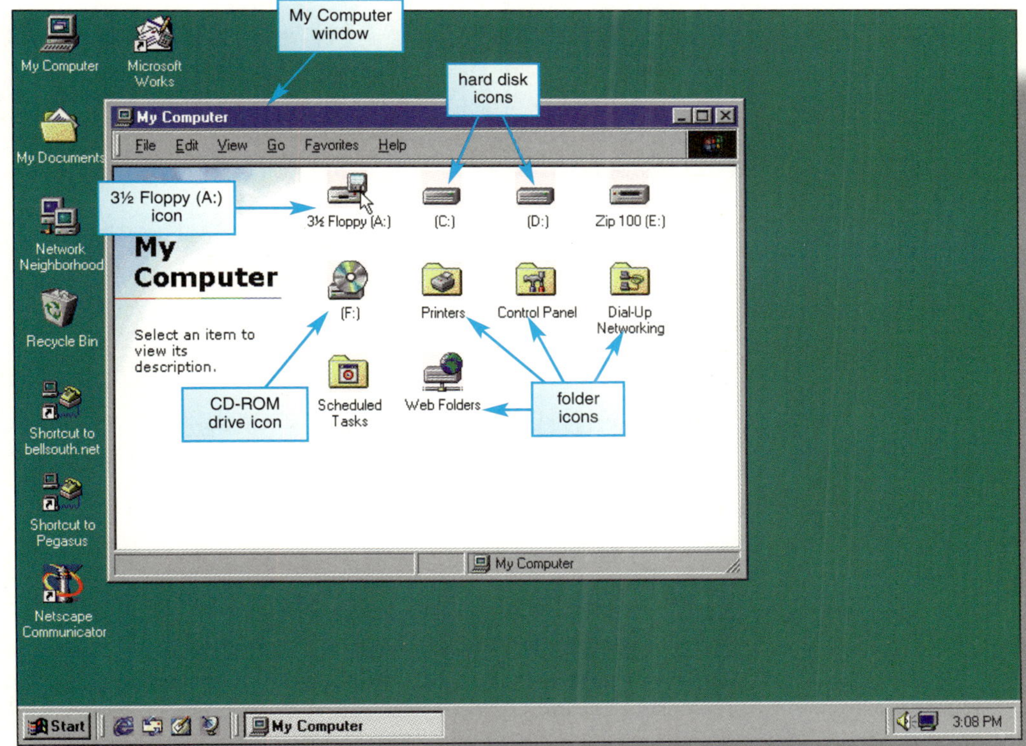

FIGURE 1-82

3 Double-click the 3½ Floppy (A:) icon. When the 3½ Floppy (A:) window displays, point to the Off-Campus Internet Access.wps file icon.

When you double-click the 3½ Floppy (A:) icon, Windows opens the 3½ Floppy (A:) window (Figure 1-83) and displays the file names on drive A.

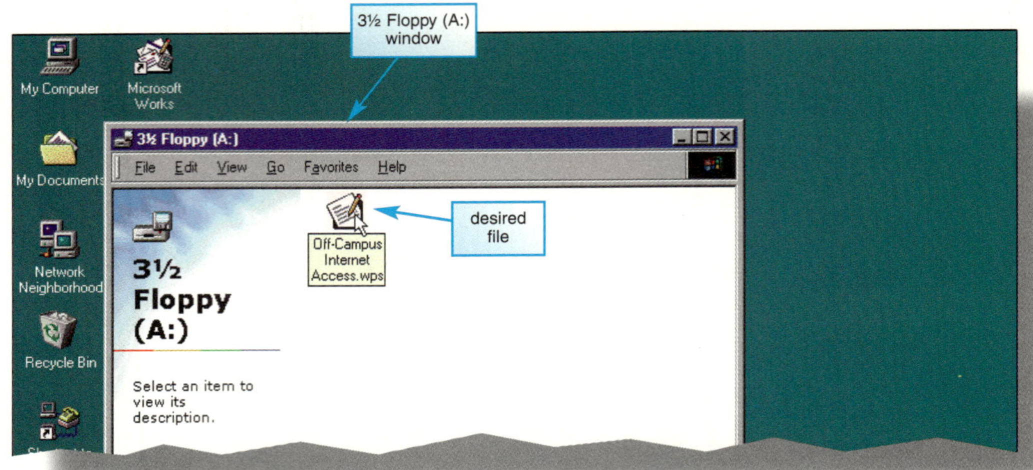

FIGURE 1-83

4 Double-click the Off-Campus Internet Access.wps file icon.

Windows first starts the Works Word Processor and then displays the document, Off-Campus Internet Access (Figure 1-84). You can revise or print the document as required.

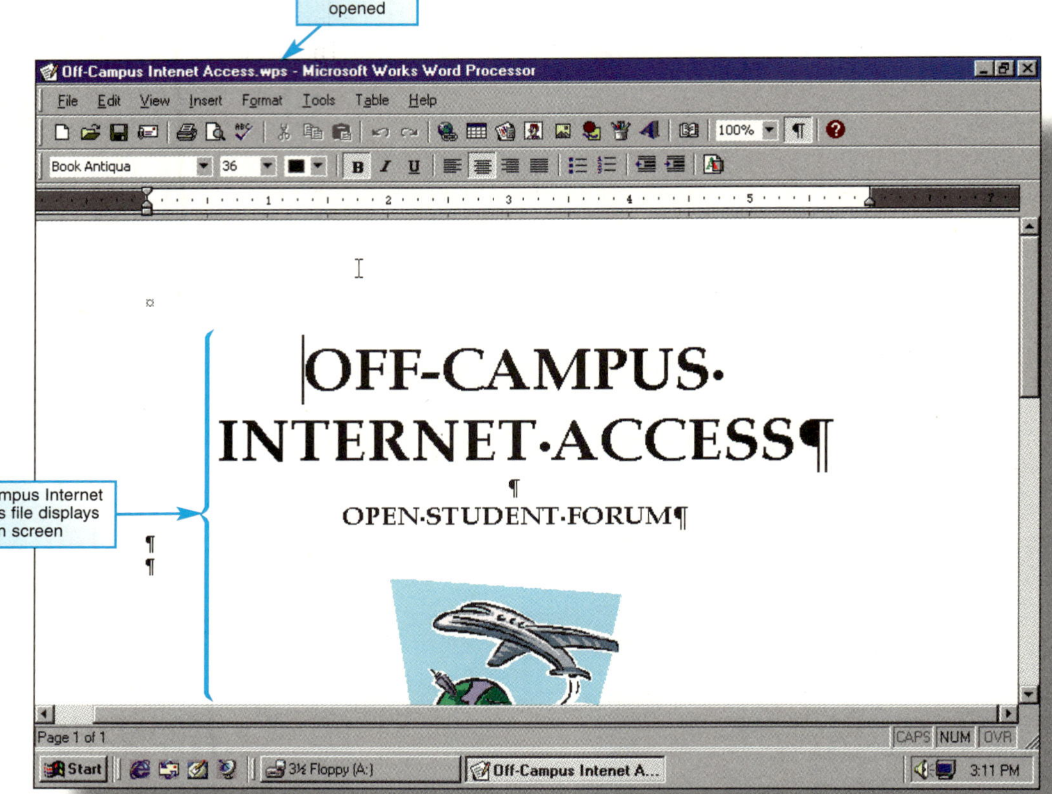

FIGURE 1-84

Other Ways

1. Click History tab in Works Task Launcher, click desired document
2. Click Open button on Standard toolbar
3. On File menu click Open, click desired document, click Open button
4. Press CTRL+O

Another method of opening a file uses file names displayed at the bottom of the File menu (Figure 1-85). Works saves the names of the last four documents on which you have worked and lists their names at the bottom of the File menu. If you want to open one of these documents, click File on the menu bar and then click the file name. The document will open and display in the Word Processor window.

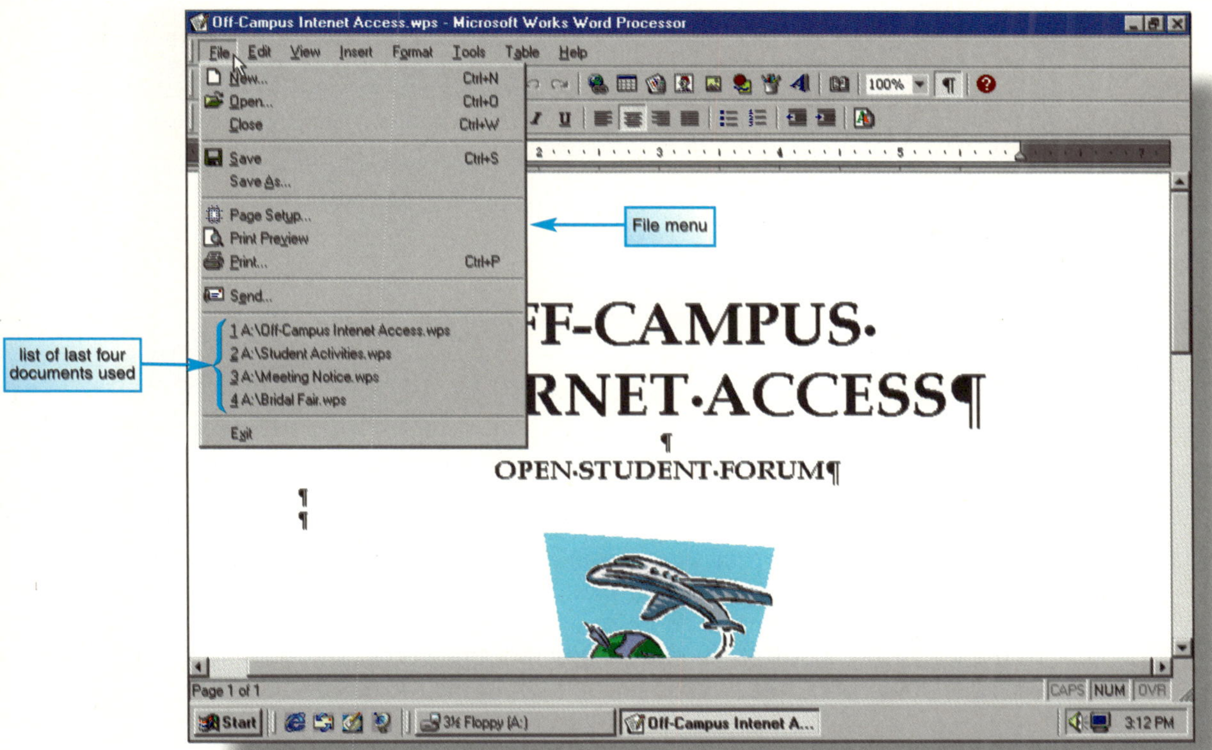

FIGURE 1-85

Moving Around in a Word Processor Document

When you modify a document, you often will have to place the insertion point at different locations within the document. When using the mouse, you can place the insertion point at any location on the screen by pointing to the location and clicking. To place the insertion point at a location in the document that does not display in the document window, use the scroll bars to move the document until the desired location displays, point to the location, and then click the desired location in the document.

In some instances, you may want to use keystrokes to move larger distances in a document. Table 1-2 summarizes useful keystrokes for moving around in a document.

You also can use the UP, DOWN, LEFT, and RIGHT ARROW keys to move the insertion point through a document.

Table 1-2 Keystroke Summary

TASK	KEYSTROKE
Move to the beginning of a document	CTRL+HOME
Move to the end of a document	CTRL+END
Move up one screen	PAGE UP
Move down one screen	PAGE DOWN
Move to the beginning of a line	HOME
Move to the end of a line	END

Deleting and Inserting Text in a Document

When modifying a document, you may find it necessary to delete certain characters, words, sentences, or paragraphs or to insert additional characters, words, or paragraphs. You can use a variety of methods to delete and insert text. Table 1-3 on the next page summarizes methods of deleting text.

Table 1-3 Methods of Deleting Text

METHOD	RESULT
Press the DELETE key	Deletes the character to the right of the insertion point
Press the BACKSPACE key	Deletes the character to the left of the insertion point
Select words, sentences, or paragraphs and then press the DELETE key or click the Clear command on the Edit menu	Deletes selected information

Inserting Text

The Word Processor initially is set to allow you to insert new text between characters, words, lines, and paragraphs without deleting any of the existing text. To insert text in an existing document, place the insertion point where you want the text to display and then type. The text to the right of the text you type will be adjusted to accommodate the insertion. For example, to insert the words, and school, before the word, Web, in the second bulleted paragraph of the announcement in Figure 1-1 on page W 1.8, place the insertion point in the space before the word, Web, by clicking to the left of the word, Web, and then typing the words, and school, followed by a space. Works inserts the words, and school, in the paragraph.

Overtyping Existing Text

Sometimes you may need to **overtype**, or type over, existing text. One method of doing this is to press the INSERT key on the keyboard, which causes the letters OVR to display on the status bar. Then you can type the new text.

When you type, the existing text will be typed over. For example, if a document contains the number 213, and it should contain the number 802, position the insertion point immediately to the left of the 2 in 213, press the INSERT key, and then type 802. The number 802 will replace the number 213. To remove the overtyping status, press the INSERT key again.

Replacing Text with New Text

Another method you can use to replace existing text with new text is to select all the text you want to replace. When you start typing new text, the selected text is deleted and the new text takes its place.

Undo Command

Works provides an **Undo button** on the Standard toolbar that you can use to cancel up to your last 100 command(s) or action(s). For example, if you format text incorrectly, you can undo the format and try it again. If, after you undo an action, you decide you did not want to perform the undo, you can use the **Redo button** to undo the undo. Some actions, such as saving or printing a document, cannot be undone or redone. You also can use the Undo command and Redo command on the Edit menu (Figure 1-86).

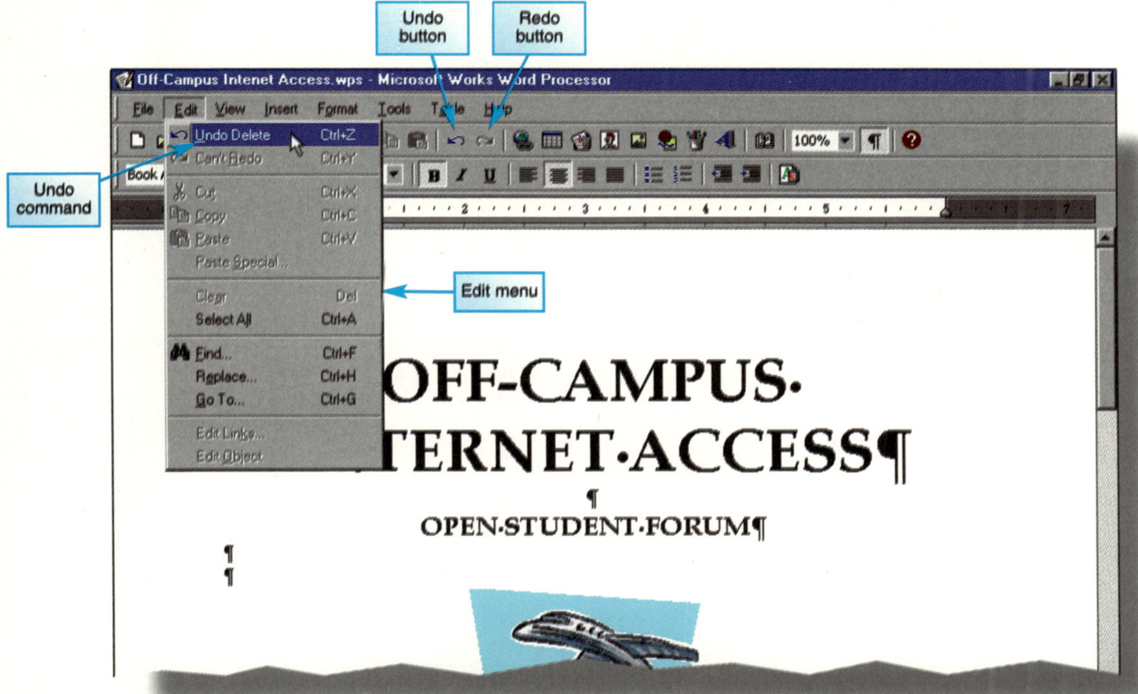

FIGURE 1-86

Undo Paragraph Formatting

To undo all paragraph formatting changes at anytime and revert to the default formatting, select the text you want to undo, hold down the CTRL key, and then press the Q key. For example, if several lines are centered and you no longer want the lines centered, select the lines, hold down the CTRL key, and then press the Q key. You also can change and undo paragraph formatting by clicking the **Paragraph command** on the Format menu and making the appropriate entries in the Format Paragraph dialog box that displays.

Undo Font Styles

To undo font styles and revert to the default font and styles, select the text you want to undo, hold down the CTRL key, and then press the SPACEBAR. For example, if a word displays in bold, italics, and underlined, and you want to remove these font styles from the word, select the word, hold down the CTRL key, and then press the SPACEBAR. You also can click the Bold, Italic, and Underline buttons on the Formatting toolbar to undo their effects when they have been selected. Another method is to click the **Font command** on the Format menu and make the appropriate entries in the Font dialog box that displays.

Microsoft Works Help

To assist you in learning and referencing Works, Works provides an extensive **Help system**. At anytime as you create or edit a document, you can display the Works Help pane on the right side of the window. In Figure 1-87 on the next page, the Start using the Word Processor topic displays in the Works Help pane because a word processing document displays on the screen. In you had a spreadsheet document displayed on the screen, Works Help would display Help information on Start using the spreadsheet. Because you have a word processing document displayed, Works Help provides a list of common tasks on which you may want help when creating or editing a document.

More About

Works Help

If you purchased an application program five years ago, you probably received one or more thick technical manuals explaining the software. With Microsoft Works, you receive a small manual. The Works Help system replaces the reams and reams of printed pages in earlier versions of Works. All the instructions you need are available in Works Help.

More About

Help in a Dialog Box

Do you want the fastest way to get additional help on any Works dialog box option? Just right-click the dialog box option you want help for and Works displays a What's This? command on a shortcut menu. Click What's This? for an explanation. Right-click the explanation and Works displays a shortcut menu with commands that allow you to copy or print the explanation.

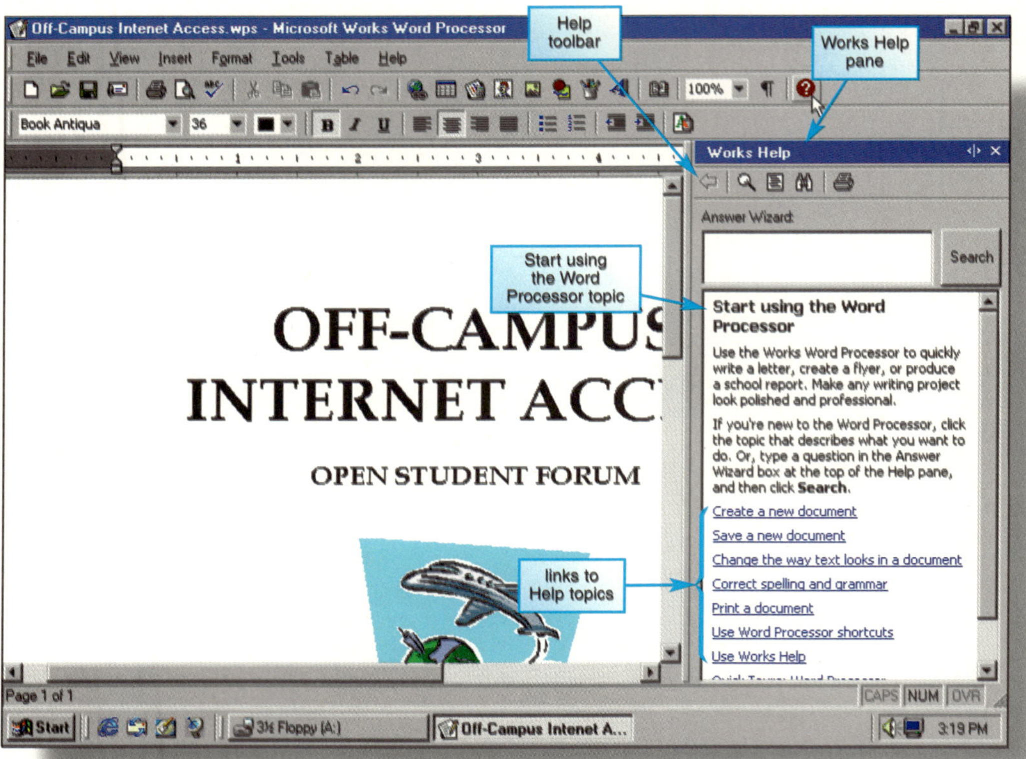

FIGURE 1-87

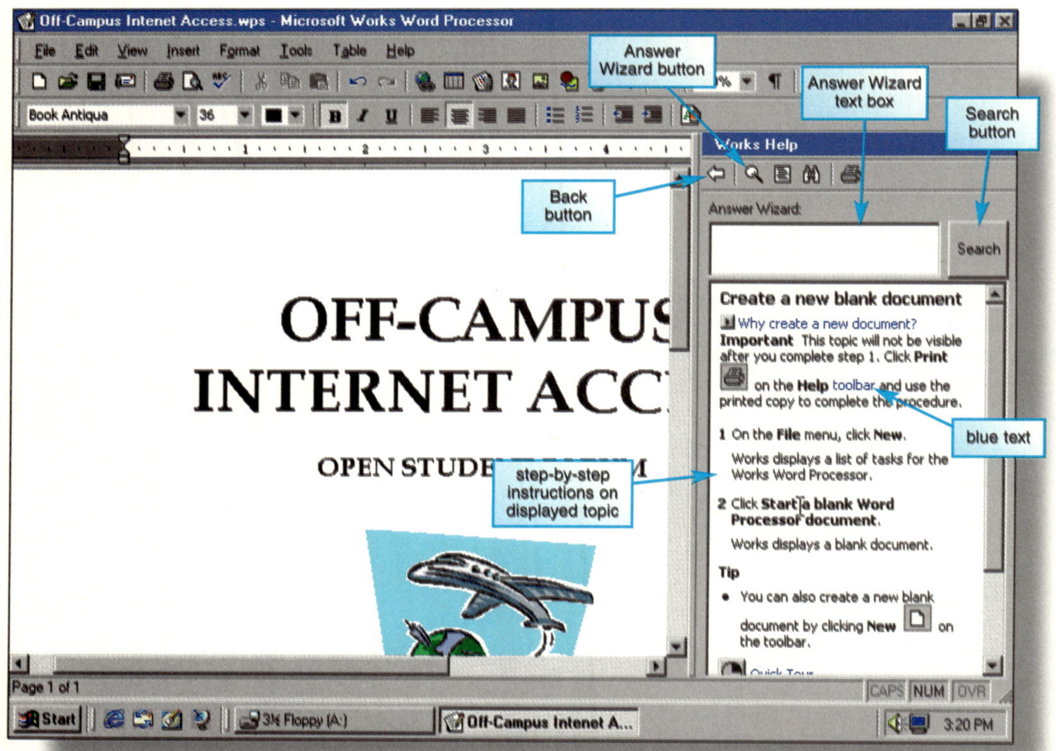

FIGURE 1-88

If you need help with a task, find the topic in the Help pane and then click the topic. Works displays a step-by-step numbered procedure you can follow as you complete the task in the Word Processor window (Figure 1-88). Help also displays tips, related topics, and more. Some step-by-step topics contain blue text that when clicked provides a definition of the term. Click the term again to remove the definition. Use the **Back button** on the Help toolbar to display the previous Help topic.

If the topic you want is not listed in the Help topic, type a question in your own words in the Answer Wizard text box and then click the Search button (see Figure 1-88 on the previous page). The **Answer Wizard** displays a list of topics that relate to your question. If you cannot find a topic that helps you, type the question again with different words. If the Answer Wizard text box is not displayed, click the Answer Wizard button on the Help toolbar.

Click the **Contents button** on the Help toolbar for an overview of Help topics and the Word Processor Table of Contents (Figure 1-89). Click any topic to display additional Help topics and links to Help information on the specific topic.

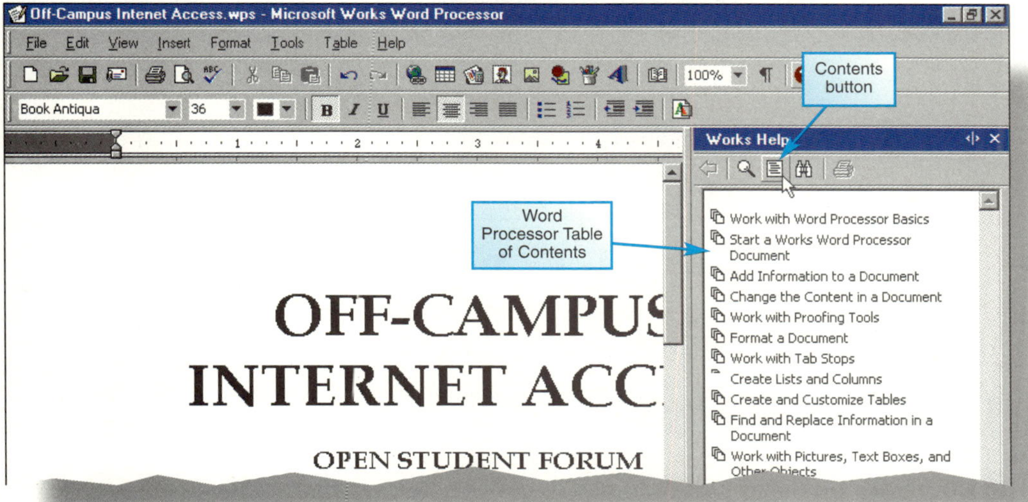

FIGURE 1-89

Clicking the **Index button** on the Help toolbar displays the Works Help Index (Figure 1-90). Type a word or words for the task or item about which you desire information in the top text box or double-click a word or words in the list box. Works displays a list of applicable topics in the Topics found list box. To see a listed topic, click the topic.

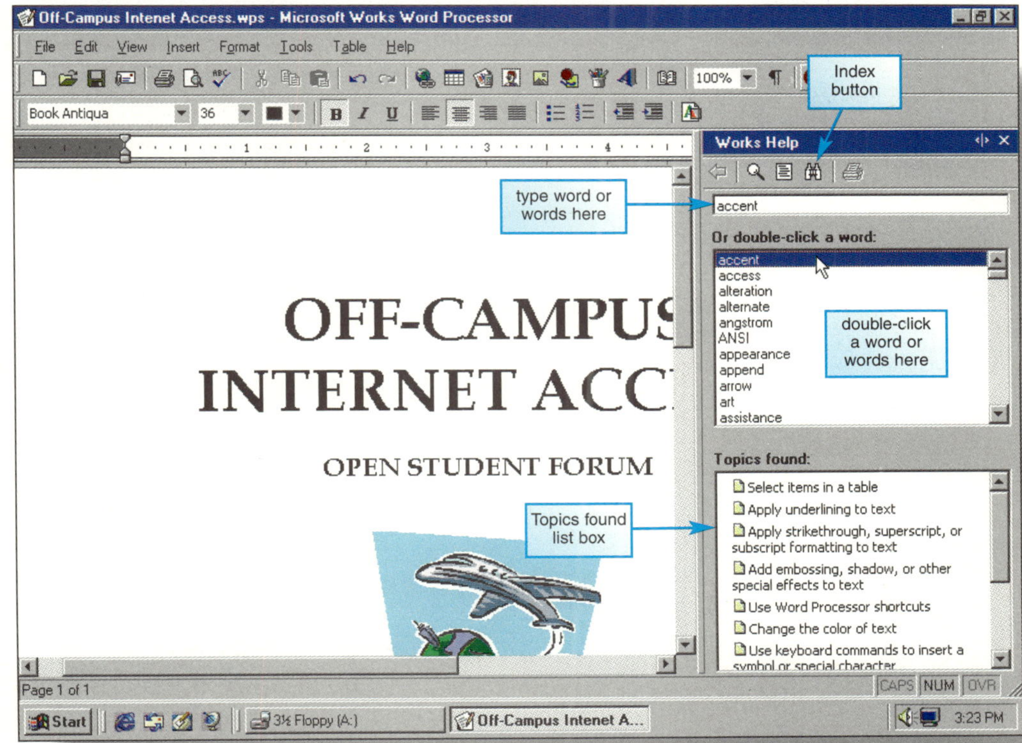

FIGURE 1-90

To learn how to use Works Help, perform the following steps.

To Use Works Help

1 Click Help on the menu bar and then point to Works Help.

Works displays the Help menu (Figure 1-91).

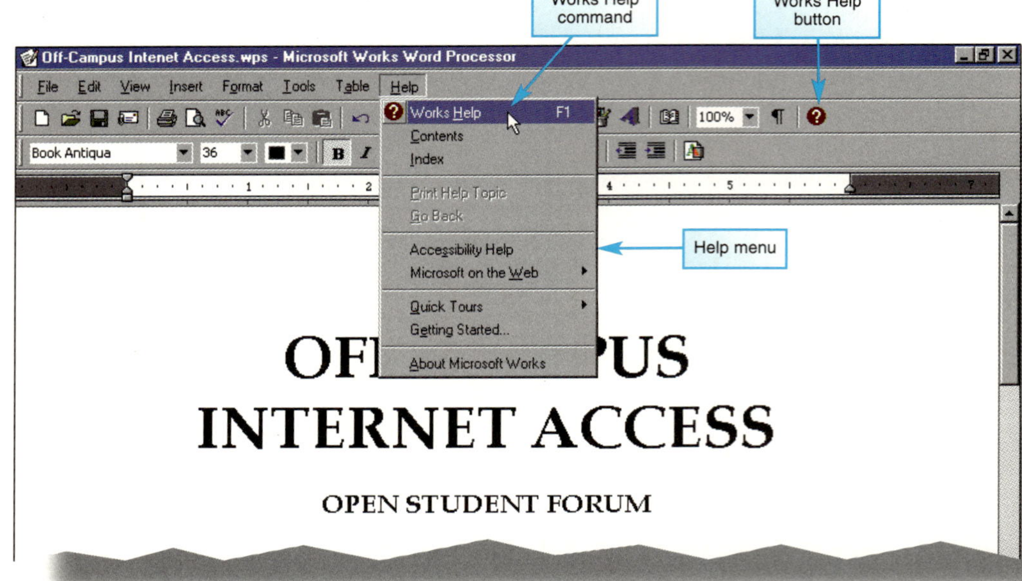

FIGURE 1-91

2 Click Works Help and then point to the Use Works Help topic in the Works Help pane.

Works displays the Works Help pane to the right of the Word Processor window and displays a list of Help topics (Figure 1-92). When you point to a topic, the mouse pointer changes to a hand with a pointing finger, indicating the topics are links.

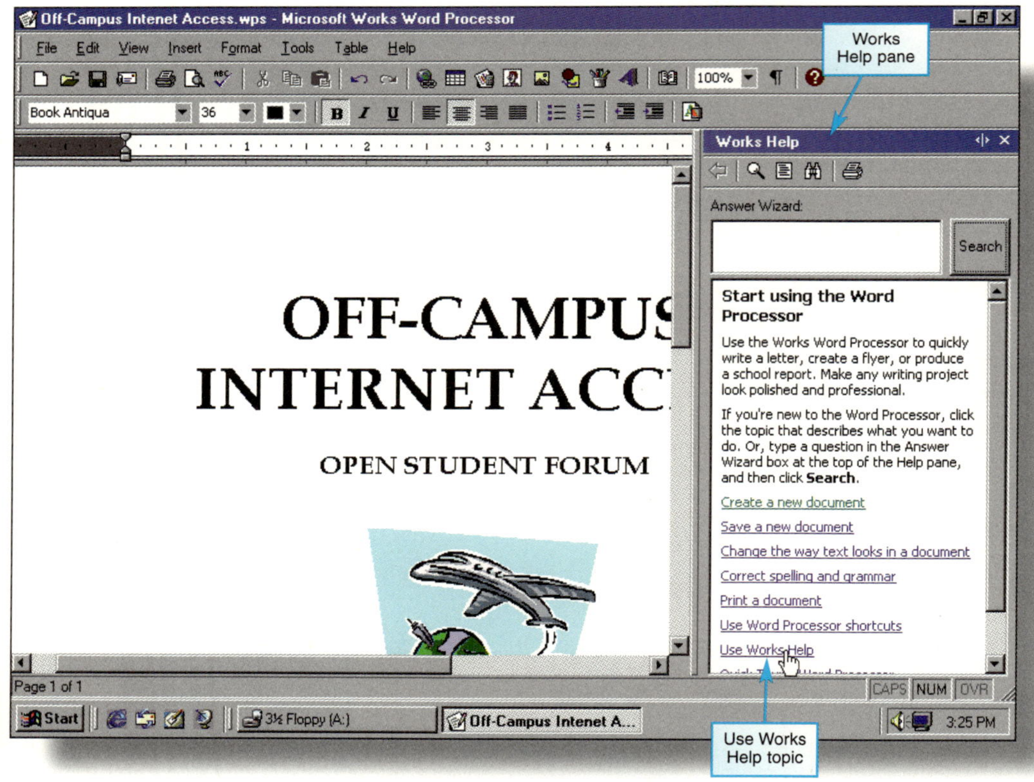

FIGURE 1-92

Other Ways

1. Click Works Help button on Standard toolbar, click Use Works Help topic in Works Help pane
2. Press F1, click Use Works Help topic in Works Help pane

Clicking the Use Works Help link and then reading the topics listed in Use Works Help provides you with the information you need to explore Help further.

The final step in this project is to quit the Works Word Processor.

TO QUIT WORKS WORD PROCESSOR

 Click the Close button in the Works Word Processor window.

Works Word Processor closes.

Project Summary

This project taught you many of the capabilities of the Works Word Processor. Important subject matter included starting Works, entering text, centering text, using fonts, increasing font size, using different font styles, previewing documents, saving a document, closing a document, closing Works, opening an existing document, inserting and deleting data, and using Works Help. With a knowledge of these features of the Word Processor, you now are capable of creating a variety of documents.

What You Should Know

Having completed this project, you now should be able to perform the following tasks:

- Center Paragraphs *(W 1.33)*
- Center Text and Change Font and Font Size *(W 1.43)*
- Change Fonts *(W 1.35)*
- Change Font Size *(W 1.36, W 1.38, W 1.39)*
- Change the Default Font Size *(W 1.19)*
- Check Spelling as You Type *(W 1.26)*
- Close a Document *(W 1.59)*
- Create a Bulleted List *(W 1.41)*
- Display All Characters *(W 1.22)*
- Display Text in Bold *(W 1.47)*
- Display Text in Color *(W 1.45)*
- Enter Text *(W 1.23)*
- Enter Text that Scrolls through the Word Processor Window *(W 1.28)*
- Insert Clip Art into a Document *(W 1.49)*
- Italicize Text *(W 1.44)*
- Open an Existing Document *(W 1.61)*
- Print a Document *(W 1.57)*
- Quit Works *(W 1.60)*
- Quit Works Word Processor *(W 1.69)*
- Resize Clip Art *(W 1.52)*
- Save an Existing Document with the Same File Name *(W 1.54)*
- Save a Document *(W 1.30)*
- Start Microsoft Works *(W 1.9)*
- Start the Word Processor *(W 1.12)*
- Use Print Preview *(W 1.55)*
- Use Wordwrap *(W 1.25)*
- Use Works Help *(W 1.68)*

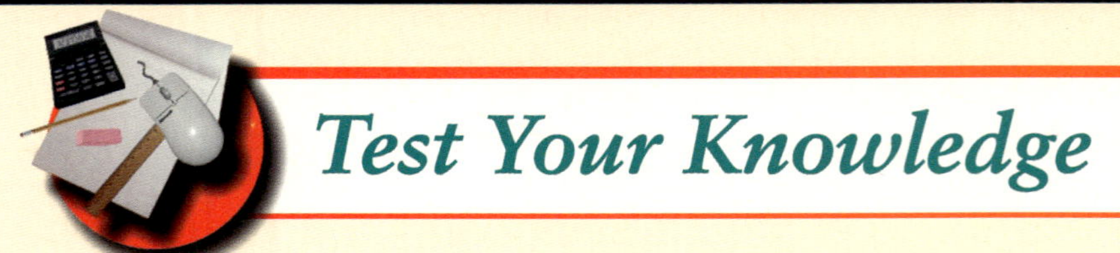

Test Your Knowledge

1 True/False

Instructions: Circle T if the statement is true or F if the statement is false.

T F 1. Microsoft Works has accessories that include Word Art, a Spelling and Grammar feature, Thesaurus, and Microsoft Draw that you can use when creating your Word Processor documents.

T F 2. The menu bar contains buttons that allow you to perform frequently required tasks.

T F 3. Microsoft Works Word Processor Wizards are documents that contain text, settings, and formats that can be reused.

T F 4. With Works, the default font is 12-point Arial.

T F 5. The title bar in the document window contains the name of the document and the application name, Microsoft Works Word Processor.

T F 6. The Microsoft Works Task Launcher contains a Tasks sheet, a Programs sheet, and a History sheet.

T F 7. When you close a document, click the Close button in the upper-right corner of the application window.

T F 8. To highlight a word to be formatted, right-click the word.

T F 9. You must use print preview to make insertions or deletions in a document.

T F 10. The Microsoft Clip Gallery, which contains illustrations you can insert in documents, is an additional accessory to Works and must be purchased separately.

2 Multiple Choice

Instructions: Circle the correct response.

1. Clip art that is placed in a document is called a(n) __________.
   a. picture   b. word art   c. object   d. new drawing
2. To resize an object proportionally, drag one of the __________ selection handles.
   a. side   b. top   c. corner   d. bottom
3. To save an existing document with the same file name, __________.
   a. click the Save button on the Standard toolbar
   b. click Save on the File menu
   c. press CTRL+S
   d. all of the above
4. Before you change the format of a word, you must __________.
   a. select the first character in the word to be formatted
   b. right-click the word to be formatted
   c. select the word to be formatted
   d. underline the word to be formatted
5. By default, Works uses __________-inch left and right margins and __________-inch top and bottom margins.
   a. 1.25, 1   b. 1, 1.25   c. 1.50, 1.25   d. 1.25, 1.25
6. To erase a character to the right of the insertion point, press the __________.
   a. SPACEBAR   b. INSERT key   c. BACKSPACE key   d. DELETE key

Test Your Knowledge

7. When nonprinting characters display in the document window, spaces are indicated by ________.
   a. right-pointing arrows
   b. raised dots
   c. ¶
   d. periods
8. To activate the shortcut menu, point to the selection and ________.
   a. click
   b. right-click
   c. drag
   d. double-click
9. When the mouse pointer is located in the document workspace area of the screen, it appears as a(n) ________.
   a. block arrow
   b. vertical bar
   c. hourglass
   d. I-beam
10. The Undo button on the Standard toolbar will let you undo your last ________ command(s) or action(s).
    a. 100
    b. 200
    c. 5
    d. 50

3 Fill In

Instructions: In Figure 1-93, a series of arrows points to the major components of the Microsoft Works Word Processor window. Identify the parts of the window in the spaces provided.

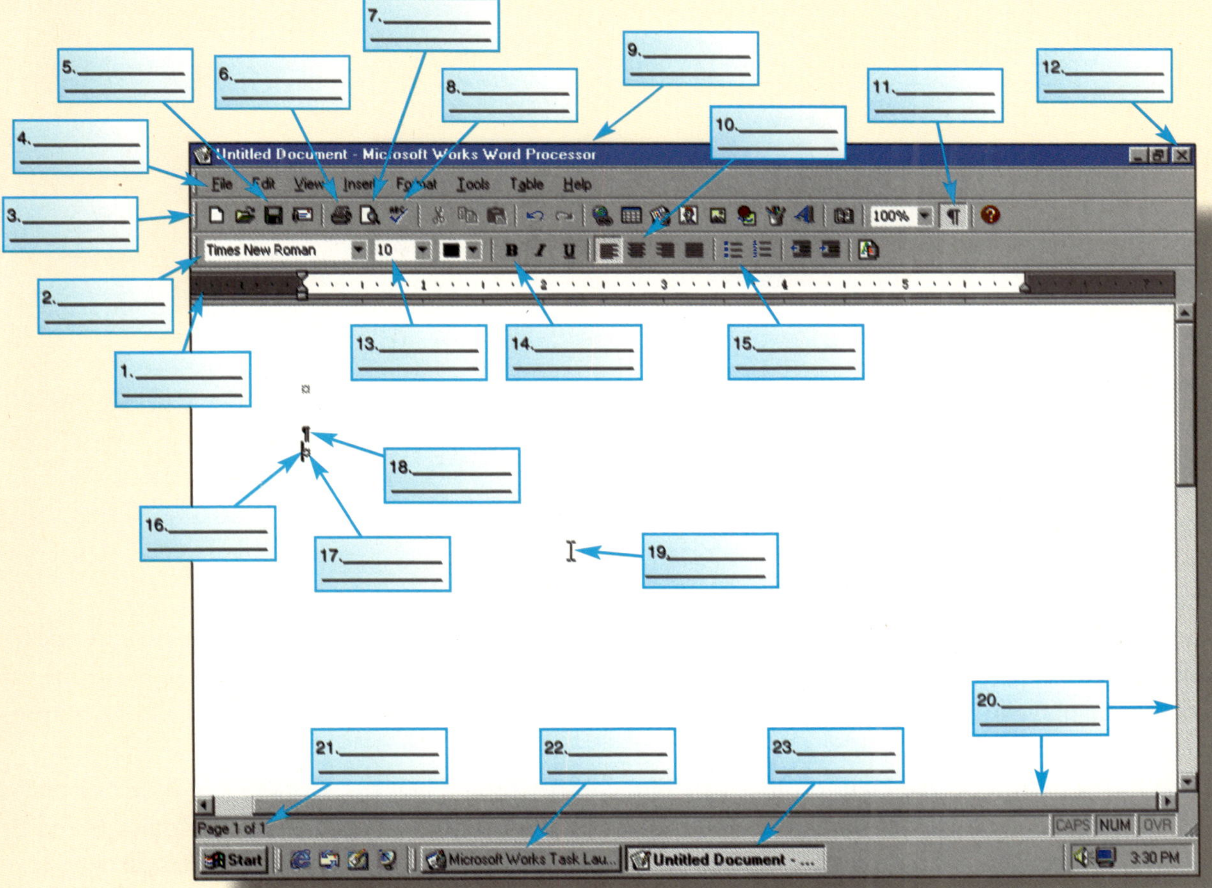

FIGURE 1-93

4 Fill In

Instructions: Write the appropriate command or button name to accomplish each task.

TASK	COMMAND OR BUTTON NAME
Display special characters in the Word Processor window	______________________
Save a new document	______________________
Center a paragraph	______________________
Create a bulleted list	______________________
Remove bullets from a bulleted list	______________________
Change text color	______________________
Bold text	______________________
Insert clip art	______________________
Save an existing document with a different file name	______________________
Print preview a document	______________________
Print a document	______________________

1 Reviewing Project Activities

Instructions: Use your computer to perform the following tasks to obtain experience using Works Help.

1. Start Works Task Launcher and then click Start a blank Word Processor document.
2. Click Help on the menu bar and then click Works Help.
3. The Start using the Word Processor topic displays in the Works Help pane.
4. Click the topic, Use Works Help.
5. Read the list of different ways to obtain information in Works Help.
6. Use the down scroll arrow to read the entire topic. In the Finding and printing help topics section near the bottom of the Help pane, the word, toolbar, displays in blue. Click the blue word, toolbar. Read the information that displays in parentheses after the word, toolbar. Print this topic by clicking the Print button on the Help toolbar.
7. Click the Index button on the Help toolbar (the binoculars icon). When the Works Help Index displays, type `help` in the top text box to display a list of topics related to the word, help. In the Topics found list, click the topic Get help for options in a dialog box. Read the step-by-step instructions that display. Use the down scroll arrow to view the entire topic. Close the Works Help pane.
8. Quit Microsoft Works.

2 Expanding on the Basics

Instructions: Use Works Help to better understand the topics listed below. Print the topic or topics that substantiate your answer.

1. Start a blank Word Processor document, click Help on the menu bar, and then click Works Help. When the Help pane displays, click Quick Tours: What's New in Works. When the Microsoft Works Quick Tours window displays, click the Works Portfolio link and answer the following questions.
   a. What does the Works Portfolio allow you to do?
   b. What sort of information can you save in the Works Portfolio?
   c. How do you copy information into the Works Portfolio?
   d. How do you copy items into other documents?
2. Close the Microsoft Quick Tours window. Using the term, bullet, and the Answer Wizard feature, answer the following questions.
   a. How do you add bullets to a list?
   b. List two ways to remove a bullet from a paragraph.
   c. How can you change a bulleted list to a numbered list?
   d. How can you adjust the spacing between bullets?
3. Close the Microsoft Works Help pane, click Format on the menu bar, and then click Font. When the Font dialog box displays, use the Help (question mark) button located in the upper-right corner of the dialog box to answer the following questions.
   a. What special keyboard characters will not be changed if you click the All caps check box?
   b. What is the difference between the OK button and the Cancel button in the Font dialog box?
   c. What does a check mark specify in the Strikethrough check box in the Font dialog box?
4. Quit Microsoft Works.

1 Checking Spelling of a Document

Instructions: Start Works. Open the document, Meeting Notice, on the Data Disk. If you did not download the Data Disk, see the inside back cover of this book for instructions for downloading or see your instructor.

As shown in Figure 1-94 on the next page, the document is a meeting announcement that contains many spelling and grammar errors. You will right-click each of the spelling errors and then click the appropriate spelling correction on the shortcut menu.

You have learned that Works flags spelling errors with a red wavy underline. Works does not flag grammar errors. To check for grammar errors, click the Spelling and Grammar button on the Standard toolbar, or click Tools on the menu bar, and then click Spelling and Grammar. *Hint*: Use Help to solve any problems.

(continued)

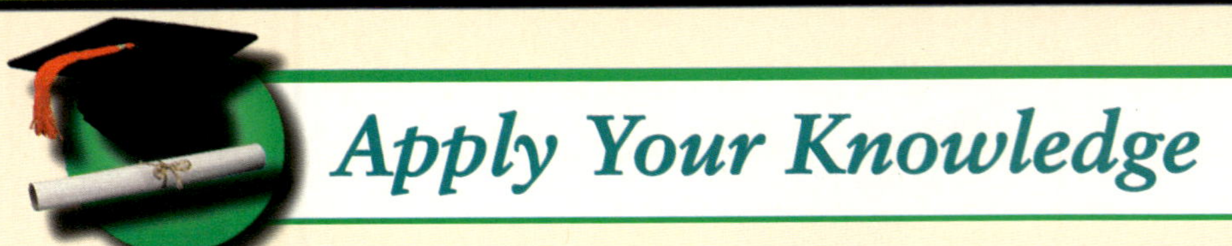

Checking Spelling of a Document *(continued)*

Instructions: Perform the following tasks:

1. Position the insertion point at the beginning of the document. Right-click the flagged word, Employes. Change the incorrect word, Employes, to Employees by clicking Employees on the shortcut menu.
2. Right-click the flagged word, Febuary. Change the incorrect word, Febuary, to February by clicking February on the shortcut menu.
3. Right-click the flagged word, be. Click Delete Repeated Word on the shortcut menu to remove the duplicate word, be.
4. Right-click the flagged word, wellnes. Change the incorrect word, wellnes, to wellness by clicking wellness on the shortcut menu.
5. Right-click the flagged word, nen. Because the shortcut menu does not display the correct word, noon, click outside the shortcut menu to close it. Correct the misspelled word, nen, to the correct word, noon.

MEETING NOTICE

All Employes

NEW WELLNESS PLAN

Effective Febuary 1, Osborne Publishing will be be offering a new wellnes plan for all employees interested in obtaining their optimal level of fitness. Classes will be offered over the nen hour, before 8:00 a.m. and after 5:00 p.m.

Representatives from Funtastic Fitness will be on hand in the Employees' Lounge all day Tuesday, Januery 2, to prepare personal health profiles for interested employees. Profiles take approximately 30 miutes to complete. Sign up at the reception desk.

Your health profiles will be availble Monday, January 8.

FIGURE 1-94

6. Right-click the flagged word, Funtastic. This is the actual name of the company offering the fitness classes. Therefore, you do not want to change the spelling. Click Ignore All on the shortcut menu to remove the red wavy line.
7. Right-click the flagged word, Januery. Change the incorrect word, Januery, to January by clicking January on the shortcut menu.
8. Right-click the flagged word, miutes. Change the incorrect word, miutes, to minutes by clicking minutes on the shortcut menu.
9. Right-click the flagged word, availble. Change the incorrect word, availble, to available by clicking available on the shortcut menu.
10. Click File on the menu bar and then click Save As. Save the document with the file name Corrected Meeting Notice. Print the corrected document.

1 Creating and Formatting the Student Activities Document Using Clip Art

Problem: As the treasurer of the Student Activities Club, you have been asked by the club's advisor to create a flyer recruiting volunteers for upcoming fund-raisers. The flyer is shown in Figure 1-95.

Instructions: Set the default font size to 12. Display the first heading line, STUDENT ACTIVITIES CLUB, in 36-point Curlz MT font. Display the second heading line in 22-point Arial Narrow bold font. The picture is clip art from the Microsoft Clip Gallery, Plant category, and flowers/herbs subcategory. The next three lines display in 14-point Times New Roman font. Display the bulleted list with a one-half-inch margin in 12-point Arial font, bolded. Display the phrases Hot Dog Stand, Bake Sale, and Car Wash in red. The last two lines display in blue 14-point Times New Roman font.

After you have typed and formatted the document, save the document on a floppy disk. Use the file name Student Activities. Print the document, and then follow your instructor's directions for submitting the assignment.

STUDENT ACTIVITIES CLUB

SPRING FLING FUND-RAISER

The Spring Fling is our biggest student body activity. Let's make it the best. Please show your support by volunteering to help at one of the following fund-raisers:

- Hot Dog Stand **Saturday, February 17 from 11:30 a.m. to 3:00 p.m.**
- Bake Sale **Saturday, February 24 from 8:30 a.m. to 2:30 p.m.**
- Car Wash **Saturday, March 10 from 8:00 a.m. to 1:00 p.m.**

Volunteer via e-mail to
Sondra Sunari at ssunari@mail.unl.edu

FIGURE 1-95

2 Creating and Formatting the Southwestern Flyer Document Using Clip Art

Problem: As a college assistant, you have been asked to create a flyer advertising the new Master of Arts in Educational Technology program. The flyer is shown in Figure 1-96 on the next page.

(continued)

Creating and Formatting the Southwestern Flyer Document Using Clip Art *(continued)*

SOUTHWESTERN COLLEGE

Earn A Master's Degree in Educational Technology

The Master of Arts Educational Technology program will prepare you for many technology-related careers including technology coordinator and instructional designer. This cutting-edge program offers the following:

- **Latest educational, presentation, and multimedia software**
- **Flexible class schedules**
- **Online courses**
- **Research**

Fall classes begin August 8

For additional information, call (407) 555-8799

FIGURE 1-96

Instructions: Display the first heading line, SOUTHWESTERN COLLEGE, in 28-point Lucida Sans font. Choose the illustration from the clip art in the Microsoft Clip Gallery, Academic category and graduation subcategory. Display the two lines below the clip art in 22-point Verdana red font. The next four lines display in 16-point Times New Roman font. Display the bulleted list with a one and one-half-inch margin in 14-point Times New Roman font. The line following the bulleted list displays in 18-point Verdana blue font. The last two lines display in 12-point Times New Roman font. Display the entire document in bold.

After you have typed and formatted the document, save the document on a floppy disk with the file name Southwestern Flyer. Print the document, and then follow your instructor's directions for submitting the assignment.

3 Creating and Formatting the Bridal Fair Document Using Clip Art

Problem: The Bridal Fair Committee has asked you to create a flyer announcing the Spring Bridal Fair. The flyer is shown in Figure 1-97.

Instructions: Create the document illustrated in Figure 1-97 using the appropriate fonts, font styles, sizes, colors, and clip art (Special Occasions category and Marriage subcategory). Use Help to determine how to enlarge the clip art object.

After you have typed and formatted the document, save the document on a floppy disk. Use the file name Bridal Fair. Print the document, and then follow your instructor's directions for submitting the assignment.

Spring Bridal Fair

Wedding Planner

The Spring Bridal Fair on April 29, at the Expo Convention Center is your one-stop wedding planner. Fashion shows, merchants, services, and exhibits will help you plan the perfect wedding. Doors open at 10:00 a.m. Drawings and free gifts all day.

- **Attire and accessories**
- **Flowers and decorations**
- **Food, beverages, and catering**
- **Photography and video**
- **Invitations and printing**
- **Music and entertainment**
- **Honeymoon packages**

Admission per person:
$15 at the door - $12 in advance
Call for reservations at (321) 555-EXPO

FIGURE 1-97

The difficulty of these case studies varies:
◗ are the least difficult; ◗◗ are more difficult; and ◗◗◗ are the most difficult.

1 ◗ Many colleges are running out of seats as enrollment is rapidly increasing. You work in the registrar's office at a college where most of the student body commutes. The college has been aggressively developing new online courses. They have asked you to design a poster that will both inform students of the new online course offerings and encourage students to register for these online courses. Design and create the following document:

Line 1: Insert and center an appropriate graphic from the Microsoft Clip Gallery.
Line 2: Save time and money! (36-point Franklin Gothic Heavy centered)
Line 3: Quit fighting traffic! (28-point Franklin Gothic Heavy centered)

(Lines 4 through 9 should be bulleted, 16-point Rockwell with a one-half inch margin)

Line 4: Enroll in one of the NEW online course offerings!
Line 5: Many required courses can now be taken from the convenience of your home.
Line 6: Complete your course work at a time and place convenient for you!
Line 7: Receive individual attention from the instructor.
Line 8: Interact with your classmates virtually!
Line 9: Check out the Online Course section of the catalog for a complete listing of online courses.

Enter blank lines where suitable to properly space the document.

2 ◗ Your nursing sorority is organizing a fund-raising event for a local hospital's healing arts program. This program uses drama and play to help children through difficult illnesses. You are on the advertising committee. Many local businesses have donated items for a silent auction and the door prizes. Your sorority is hosting a Monopoly tournament with the grand prize of a trip to the Cayman Islands that was donated by a local travel agency. You have volunteered to create a flyer to post around campus and the community advertising the event. Create the following document.

Line 1: Help the Children (36-point Century Schoolbook bold centered)
Line 2: Support the Healing Arts Program at Mercy Children's Hospital! (24-point Century Schoolbook centered)
Line 3: Insert and center an appropriate graphic from the Microsoft Clip Gallery.
Line 4: Enter a Monopoly tournament and win! (18-point Arial red centered)
Line 5: Join the fun! Student Union Grand Ballroom (18-point Arial red centered)
Line 6: Saturday, November 11 (18-point Arial red centered)
Line 7: 2:00 p.m. till 8:00 p.m. (18-point Arial red centered)
Line 8: Grand prize is a trip for two to the Cayman Islands! A silent auction will be held and door prizes will be given away. (16-point Century Schoolbook black centered)
Line 9: Help bring a smile to the face of a child! (22-point Lucida Sans black centered)

Enter blank lines where suitable to space the document properly. Use this information to write a press release to promote the fund raising event.

Cases and Places

3 Every year you are faced with writing thank you notes to your relatives for the Christmas gifts they send you. This year you want to expedite the process by using your computer to generate the notes. You create the following form letter:

Dear [Who],
Thank you so much for the nice [what]. I will think of you every time I use it at [where]. It was very kind of you to remember me at Christmas. I will [activity] you soon.

WHO	WHAT	WHERE	ACTIVITY
Francis	brief case	the office	talk to
Barbara	pen and pencil set	my desk	write
Gary	thermos	work	call
Frank	fishing pole	the lake	see

FIGURE 1-98

For each relative, use search and replace to change the words, Who, What, Where, and Activity to those in Figure 1-98. In addition, use the thesaurus to find a synonym for the word, thoughtful, in each letter.

4 Now that you are using a personal computer to complete many of your assignments, you have been suffering from a tingling sensation in your wrists, numbness in your fingers, and difficulty opening and closing your hands. During your next visit to the doctor, you mention these ailments. Your doctor informs you that you are suffering from repetitive stress, or strain, injury (RSI). This term is applied to injuries resulting from repeated movements that irritate nerves and tendons. He describes various actions you can take to alleviate or prevent RSI. They include taking short, frequent breaks of at least ten minutes every hour, stretching the entire body, shrugging your shoulders, and rubbing your hands. You can perform some simple exercises at your desk, such as stretching your fingers, rotating your wrists, and squeezing your thumbs and fingers together. He tells you to adapt your computer workstation to fit your needs, just as you adjust the rearview mirror and seat in your car. For example, you can tilt your monitor so the top line of print on the screen is slightly below eye level and sit 14 to 24 inches away from it. Use ergonomically correct furniture that can be adjusted so the home row of keys is 29 to 31 inches above the floor and your feet are flat on the floor at a 90-degree angle. Have a good desk lamp that illuminates your work, not the screen.

You decide to summarize the doctor's advice by making a reminder list to hang on the side of your monitor. Using this information, create a one-page, bulleted list of the ten major steps you can take to help alleviate or prevent RSI. Title the document, Preventing RSI. Add appropriate clip art from the Microsoft Clip Gallery. Remember to spell check your reminder list.

5 Stress management allows you to use your awareness and mind to control your physical reactions to stress. You can learn to relieve tension and anxiety by relaxing and exercising. In turn, you can decrease your heart rate, blood pressure, and total cholesterol level. Contact a local health club in your area and ask what programs they offer that help reduce stress and improve your cardiovascular fitness. Using the concepts and techniques presented in this project, create a flyer for the health club. Add appropriate clip art from the Microsoft Clip Gallery. Spell check your document.

6 ▶▶▶ Some campus organizations have difficulties with public relations. While the members are dedicated and talented, they simply do not know how to communicate their messages effectively to the student body and community. You have decided to use your computer expertise to help one of these groups. Locate a club on campus that seems to need assistance, whether it be in recruiting new members, promoting an event, or announcing a new program. Talk to the organization's officers and suggest how you can help. Design and create a document advertising one facet of the club. Be creative in your design. Use appropriate clip art from the Microsoft Clip Gallery.

7 ▶▶▶ Many students are unaware of various deadlines that occur during the semester, such as the last day for dropping a class, the first day of advanced registration, the last day of late registration, midterm week, final exam week, and holidays. You see the registrar in the cafeteria and suggest that a one-half page flyer could be distributed at registration. He suggests you provide him with a prototype. Design and create this document, listing important dates during the semester. Be creative in your design. If useful, add appropriate clip art from the Microsoft Clip Gallery.

Microsoft Works 6

Building a Spreadsheet and Charting Data

OBJECTIVES

You will have mastered the material in this project when you can:

- Start the Microsoft Works Spreadsheet tool
- List the steps required to build a spreadsheet
- Describe the parts of a spreadsheet
- Select a cell or range of cells
- Enter text
- Enter numbers
- Use the AutoSum button to sum a range of cells in a row or column
- Copy a cell to a range of adjacent cells
- Format a spreadsheet
- Center text in a range of cells
- Add color to a spreadsheet
- Use the AutoFormat feature
- Change column widths
- Display numbers with the Comma format
- Save a spreadsheet
- Print a spreadsheet
- Create a 3-D Bar chart
- Print a chart
- Close a spreadsheet
- Quit Works
- Open an existing spreadsheet file
- Correct errors in a spreadsheet
- Clear cells and clear an entire spreadsheet

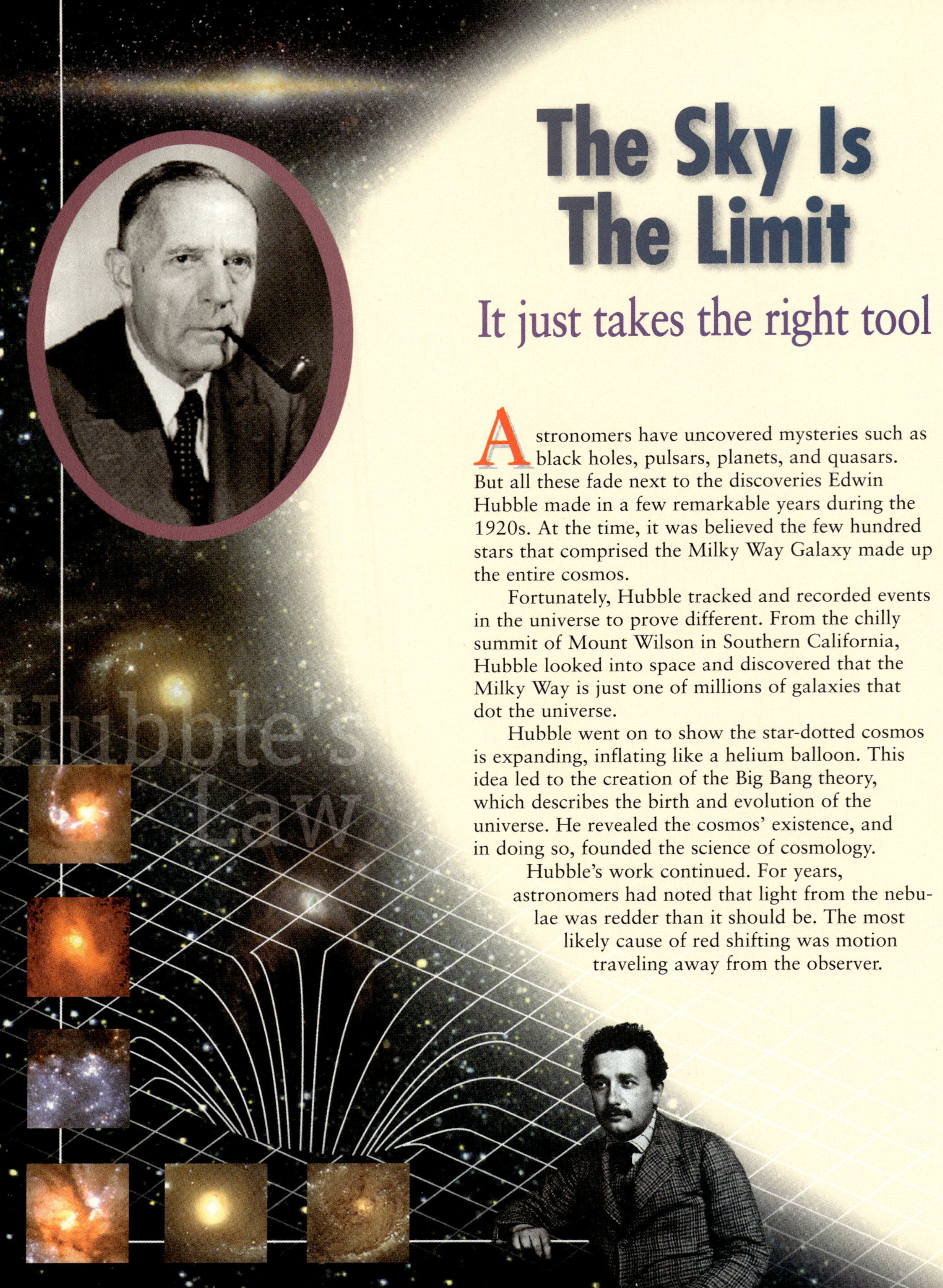

The Sky Is The Limit

It just takes the right tool

Astronomers have uncovered mysteries such as black holes, pulsars, planets, and quasars. But all these fade next to the discoveries Edwin Hubble made in a few remarkable years during the 1920s. At the time, it was believed the few hundred stars that comprised the Milky Way Galaxy made up the entire cosmos.

Fortunately, Hubble tracked and recorded events in the universe to prove different. From the chilly summit of Mount Wilson in Southern California, Hubble looked into space and discovered that the Milky Way is just one of millions of galaxies that dot the universe.

Hubble went on to show the star-dotted cosmos is expanding, inflating like a helium balloon. This idea led to the creation of the Big Bang theory, which describes the birth and evolution of the universe. He revealed the cosmos' existence, and in doing so, founded the science of cosmology.

Hubble's work continued. For years, astronomers had noted that light from the nebulae was redder than it should be. The most likely cause of red shifting was motion traveling away from the observer.

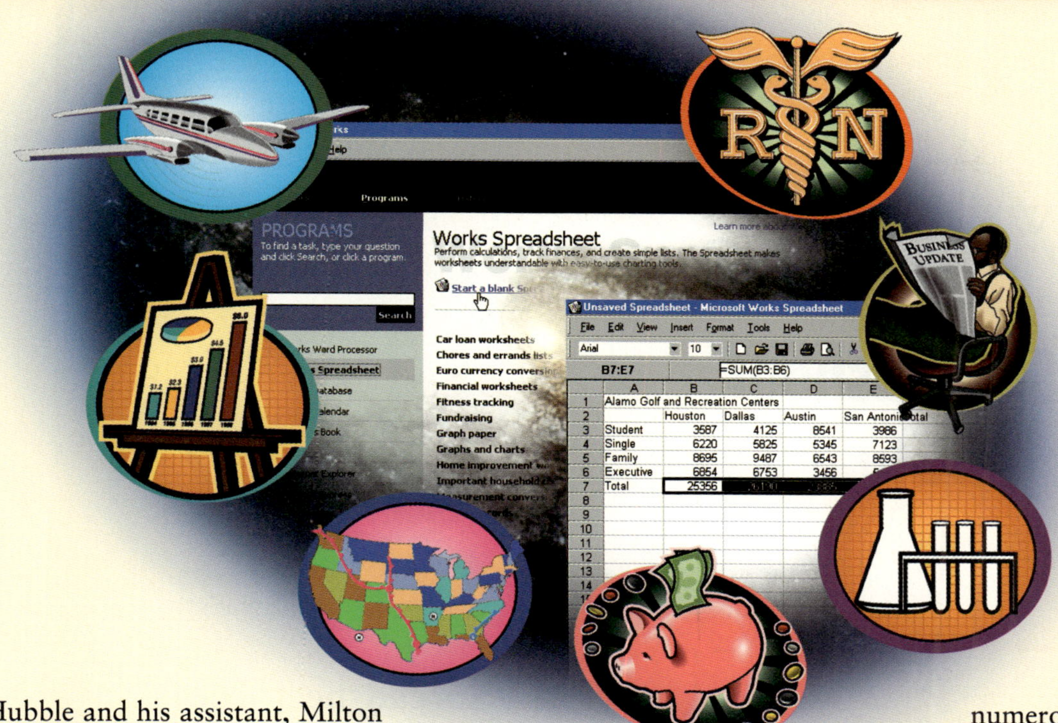

Hubble and his assistant, Milton Humason, began measuring the distance to these receding nebulae and found what is now known as Hubble's Law: the further away a galaxy is from earth, the faster it is racing away.

This key piece of research elated Albert Einstein because he knew the universe must either be expanding or contracting, yet astronomers had told him it was doing neither. With Hubble's finding, Einstein's general theory of relativity, discovered more than a decade earlier, had been confirmed. Einstein also discovered an antigravity force theory, which describes how the universe kept from collapsing in on itself.

Hubble crunched numbers to find exact coordinates, confirming the Milky Way is one among many star clusters in the galaxy. Individuals are seldom faced with documenting discoveries that have such universal impact. The ability to perform calculations in the Microsoft Works Spreadsheet may have helped Hubble discover the Big Bang theory sooner.

For students on a tight budget who need an efficient way to manage personal finances or record schedules, Microsoft Works with record keeping, financial planning and budget capabilities is perfect.

Of course, the potentials of spreadsheets extend beyond college into business, science, and many other fields. Business applications are numerous and familiar, from creating business plans to calculating actuarial tables, from forecasting sales to tracking and comparing airline traffic at airports. Going beyond these traditional uses, geographic data is being merged with statistics to create color-coded maps that track diverse factors such as global warming, health care needs, criminal justice, risk of damage by flood, even maps of what is selling where. For personal use, a number of sophisticated spreadsheet programs help to manage investment portfolios, balance checkbooks, and track household inventories for insurance purposes.

Spreadsheets also have become an important tool for improving productivity in law enforcement, an area that reaches everyone. In one application, the Los Angeles Police Department uses a system based on spreadsheets to save the equivalent of 368 additional police officers by speeding the paperwork. As many as 37 forms per incident is required from those on the force. For certain crimes, such as car theft or home burglaries, spreadsheet data is used to create maps showing crime frequencies. The maps are often distributed to communities in neighborhood watch newsletters.

Whether discovering the expanding universe, the theory of relativity or simply keeping your finances in order, the Microsoft Works Spreadsheet is a tool that is up to the task.

Microsoft Works 6

Building a Spreadsheet and Charting Data

CASE PERSPECTIVE

Alamo Golf and Recreation Centers has experienced explosive growth since its inception four years ago. The facilities provide their customers with two lighted golf ranges with target greens, four chipping/putting greens with sand traps and water hazards, 12 baseball/softball batting cages, a computerized golf-swing analyzer, club rentals, a stocked pro shop, a coffee shop, a special kids' recreational area, professional golf and baseball instruction, and more.

The president of Alamo Golf and Recreation Centers would like a report showing the monthly memberships at each of the four centers. He has asked you to prepare a spreadsheet that specifies the company's current monthly memberships. In particular, he wants to know the total memberships for students, singles, families, and executives in the following four cities: Houston, Dallas, Austin, and San Antonio.

Your task is to develop a spreadsheet to show these memberships. In addition, the director of marketing has asked to see a graphical representation of the memberships. She plans to include the graphical representation in a special fourth anniversary newsletter that will be sent to all employees.

The Works Spreadsheet Tool

A **spreadsheet** is a software tool that is useful when you have a need to enter and calculate data that can be displayed in rows and columns. The Microsoft Works Spreadsheet tool allows you to enter data in a spreadsheet, perform calculations on that data, ask what-if questions regarding the data in the spreadsheet, make decisions based on the results found in the spreadsheet, chart data in the spreadsheet, and share these results with other tools within Works.

As a result of the capabilities of the Works Spreadsheet tool, you can accomplish such tasks as accounting and record keeping, financial planning and budgeting, sales forecasting and reporting, or keeping track of your basketball team's scoring averages. In addition, once you have determined the information you require, you can present it as a spreadsheet or as a chart in printed reports.

Works also allows you to change data and automatically recalculate your spreadsheet. You can place data in a spreadsheet to simulate given conditions, which you then can test and determine the results. For example, you can enter the monthly payment you want to make on a house and then determine the price of the house you can afford based on various interest rates.

Project Two — Spreadsheet with Charted Data

To illustrate the use of the Microsoft Works Spreadsheet tool, this section of the book presents a project similar to the one you created for the Works Word Processor. Project 2 uses the Works Spreadsheet tool to produce the spreadsheet and 3-D Bar chart shown in Figure 2-1(a) and (b).

The spreadsheet contains Alamo Golf and Recreation Centers memberships for Houston, Dallas, Austin, and San Antonio. Memberships fall into four categories: Student, Single, Family, and Executive. Works calculates the total memberships for each city, the total memberships for each category, and the total of all memberships in each city. The spreadsheet in this project also demonstrates the use of the various fonts, font sizes, styles, and colors in the spreadsheet. Proper spreadsheet formatting as shown in this project is an important factor in modern spreadsheet design.

The bar chart, called a 3-D Bar chart, displays the membership categories by city. Works creates the 3-D Bar chart based on the data in the spreadsheet. Each category is represented by the color indicated on the legend below the chart.

More About

Spreadsheets

The first electronic spreadsheet program was VisiCalc written by Bob Frankston and Dan Bricklin in 1979. This product originally was written to run on Apple II computers. Together, VisiCalc and Apple II computers rapidly became successful. Many computer users today consider VisiCalc to be the single most important reason why personal computers gained acceptance in the business world.

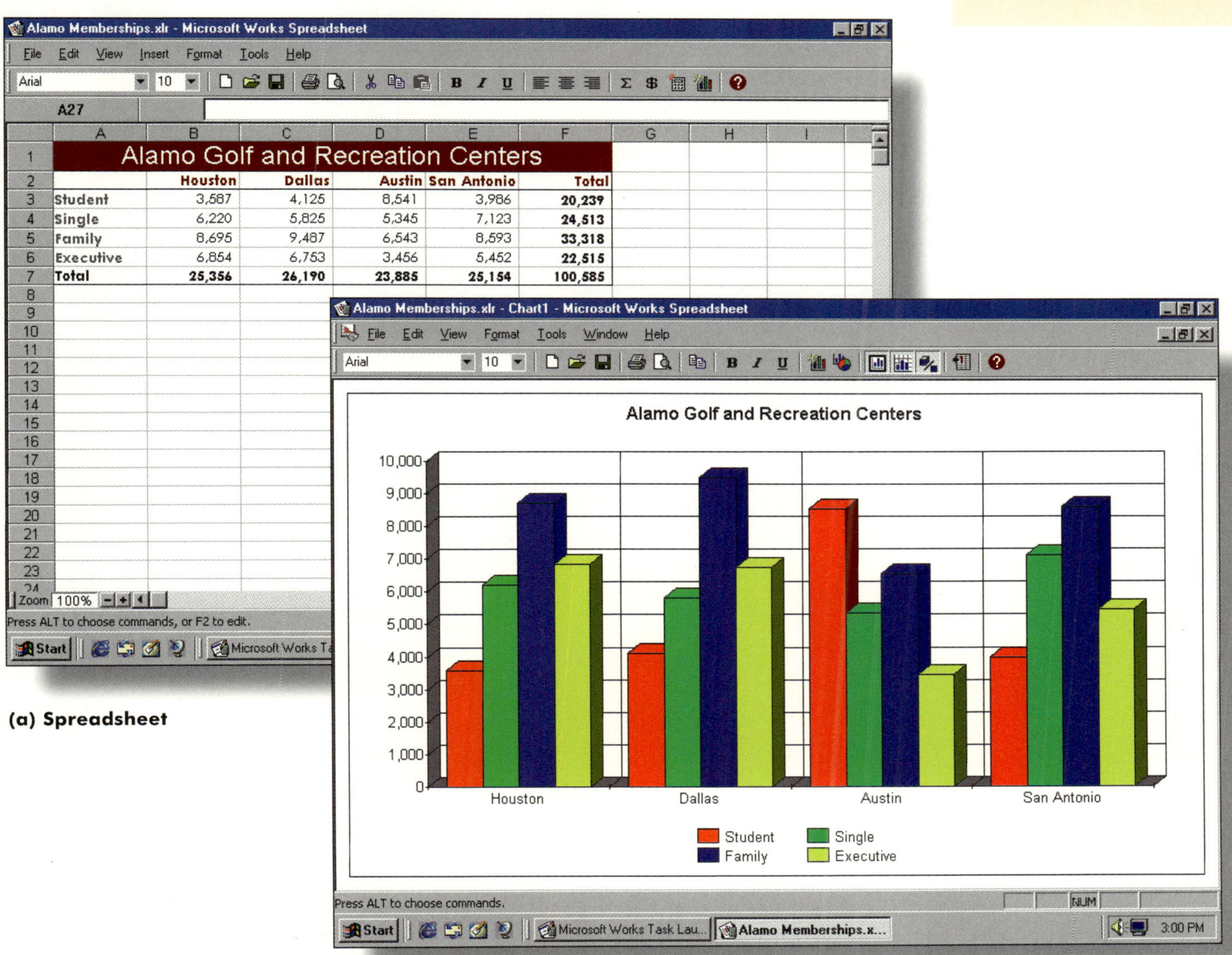

Alamo Golf and Recreation Centers

	Houston	Dallas	Austin	San Antonio	Total
Student	3,587	4,125	8,541	3,986	20,239
Single	6,220	5,825	5,345	7,123	24,513
Family	8,695	9,487	6,543	8,593	33,318
Executive	6,854	6,753	3,456	5,452	22,515
Total	25,356	26,190	23,885	25,154	100,585

(a) Spreadsheet

(b) 3-D Bar Chart

FIGURE 2-1

Starting the Works Spreadsheet

To start the Works Spreadsheet, follow the steps used in the word processing project to open the Microsoft Works Task Launcher (Figure 2-2). Perform the following steps to start the Works Spreadsheet.

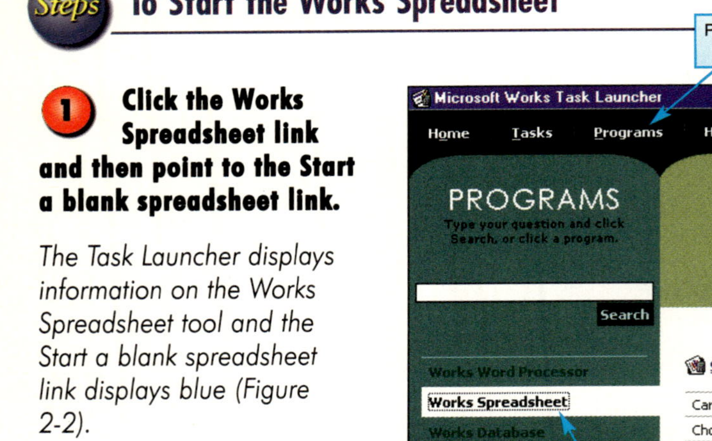

Steps To Start the Works Spreadsheet

1 Click the Works Spreadsheet link and then point to the Start a blank spreadsheet link.

The Task Launcher displays information on the Works Spreadsheet tool and the Start a blank spreadsheet link displays blue (Figure 2-2).

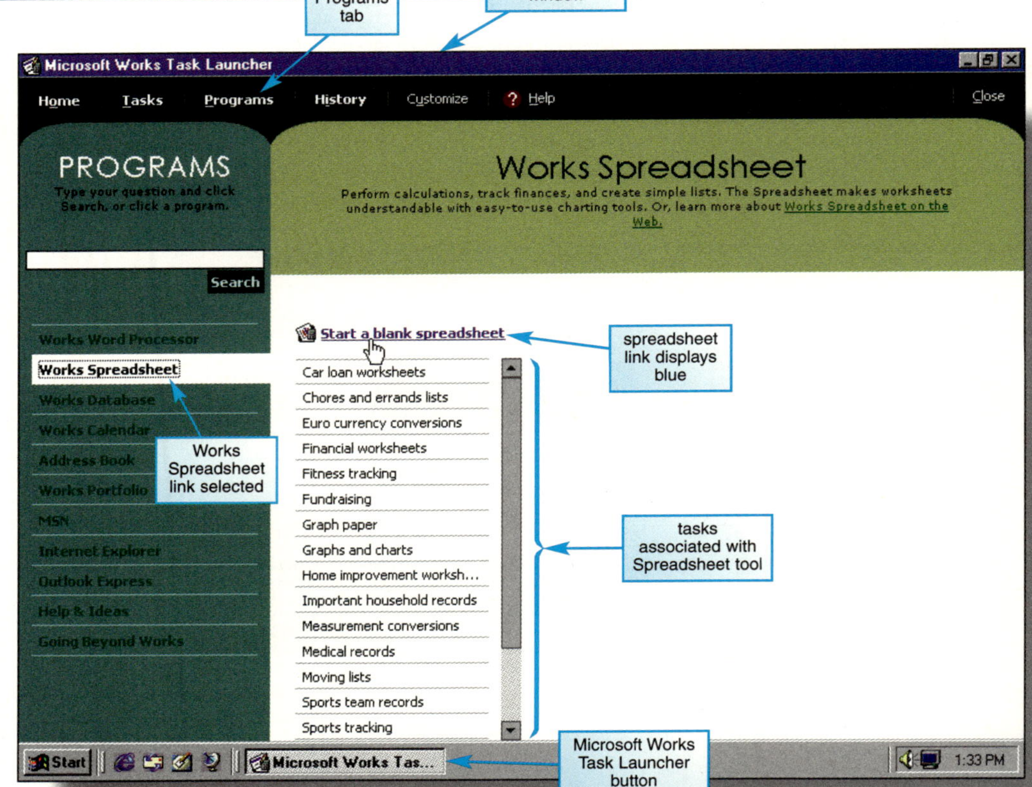

FIGURE 2-2

2 **Click the Start a blank spreadsheet link. If the Help pane displays, close it. If the Portfolio tool displays, close it.**

Works displays the spreadsheet window containing the default name, Unsaved Spreadsheet (Figure 2-3).

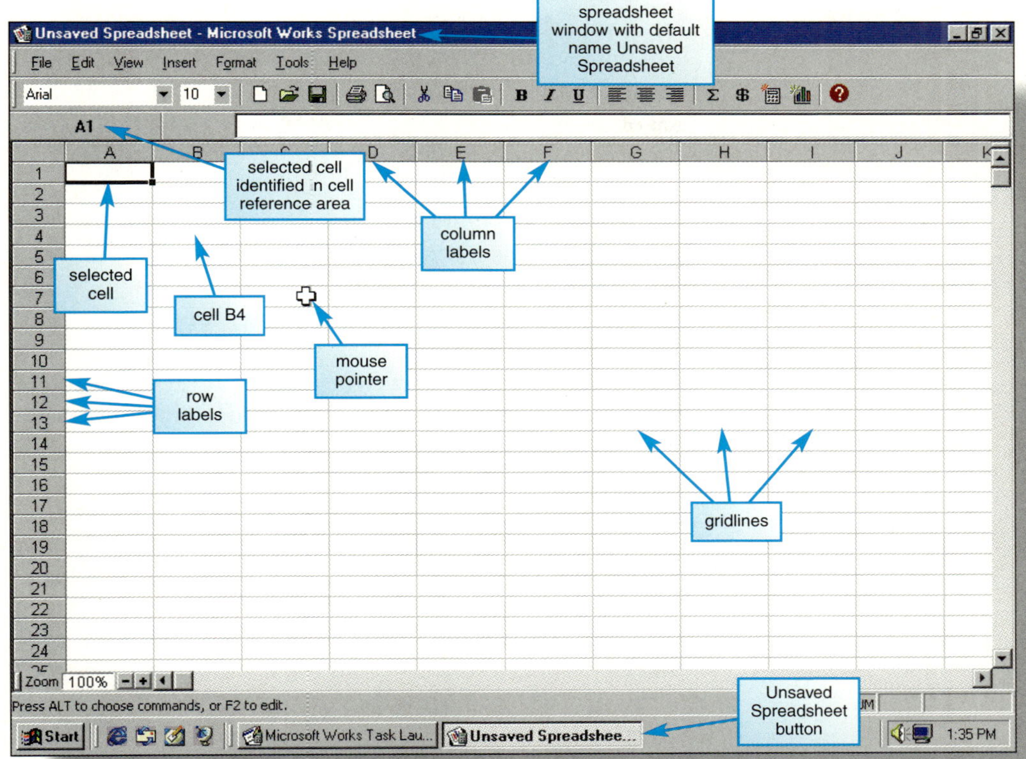

FIGURE 2-3

The following paragraphs describe the elements of the spreadsheet screen identified in Figure 2-3.

The Spreadsheet

The spreadsheet is organized into a rectangular grid containing columns (vertical) and rows (horizontal). A **column label**, which is a letter of the alphabet above the grid, identifies each **column**. A **row label**, which is a number down the left side of the grid, identifies each **row**. In Figure 2-3, eleven columns (letters A through K) and 24 rows (numbers 1 through 24) display on the screen. The number of visible columns and rows may be different depending on the computer.

Cell, Selected Cell, and Mouse Pointer

The intersection of each column and each row is a **cell**. A cell is the basic unit of a spreadsheet into which you enter data. A cell is referred to by its **cell reference**, which is the coordinate of the intersection of a column and a row. To identify a cell, specify the column label (a letter of the alphabet), followed by the row label (a number). For example, cell reference B4 refers to the cell located at the intersection of column B and row 4 (Figure 2-3).

The horizontal and vertical lines on the spreadsheet itself are called **gridlines**. Gridlines are intended to make it easier to see and identify each cell on the spreadsheet. If desired, you can remove the gridlines from the spreadsheet, but gridlines are recommended in most circumstances.

More About

Creating a Spreadsheet

Using the Task sheet listed on the Works Task Launcher, you can create a spreadsheet quickly and easily. For example, car loan worksheets, financial worksheets, fitness tracking, and important household records are wizard-generated spreadsheets that step the user through the creation of predesigned spreadsheets. Spreadsheet wizards and templates are identified in the Works Task Launcher window at the right of the program name.

Scroll Boxes

Dragging the scroll box is the most efficient way to scroll long distances. Drag the scroll boxes in the vertical or horizontal scroll bar to move the spreadsheet view up and down, or left and right, through the document.

One cell in the spreadsheet, designated the **selected cell**, is the one into which you can enter data. The selected cell in Figure 2-3 on the previous page is cell A1. Works identifies the selected cell in two ways. First, Works places a heavy border around it. Second, the cell reference area, which is above the column labels on the left side of the screen, contains the cell reference of the selected cell (see Figure 2-3).

The **mouse pointer** can become a number of shapes when used with the Works Spreadsheet depending on the activity in Works and the location of the mouse pointer on the spreadsheet window. In Figure 2-3, the mouse pointer has the shape of a block plus sign. Normally, the mouse pointer displays as a block plus sign whenever it is located in a cell on the spreadsheet.

Another common mouse pointer shape is the block arrow. The mouse pointer turns into a block arrow whenever you move it outside the spreadsheet window. Other mouse pointer shapes will be described when they display on the screen.

Spreadsheet Window

The Works Spreadsheet contains 256 columns and 16,384 rows for a total of 4,194,304 cells, Figure 2-4(a). The column labels begin with A and end with IV. The row labels begin with 1 and end with 16384. Only a small fraction of the spreadsheet displays on the screen at one time. You view the portion of the spreadsheet displayed on the screen through the spreadsheet window, Figure 2-4(b). Scroll bars, scroll arrows, and scroll boxes you can use to move the window around the spreadsheet are located below and to the right of the spreadsheet window.

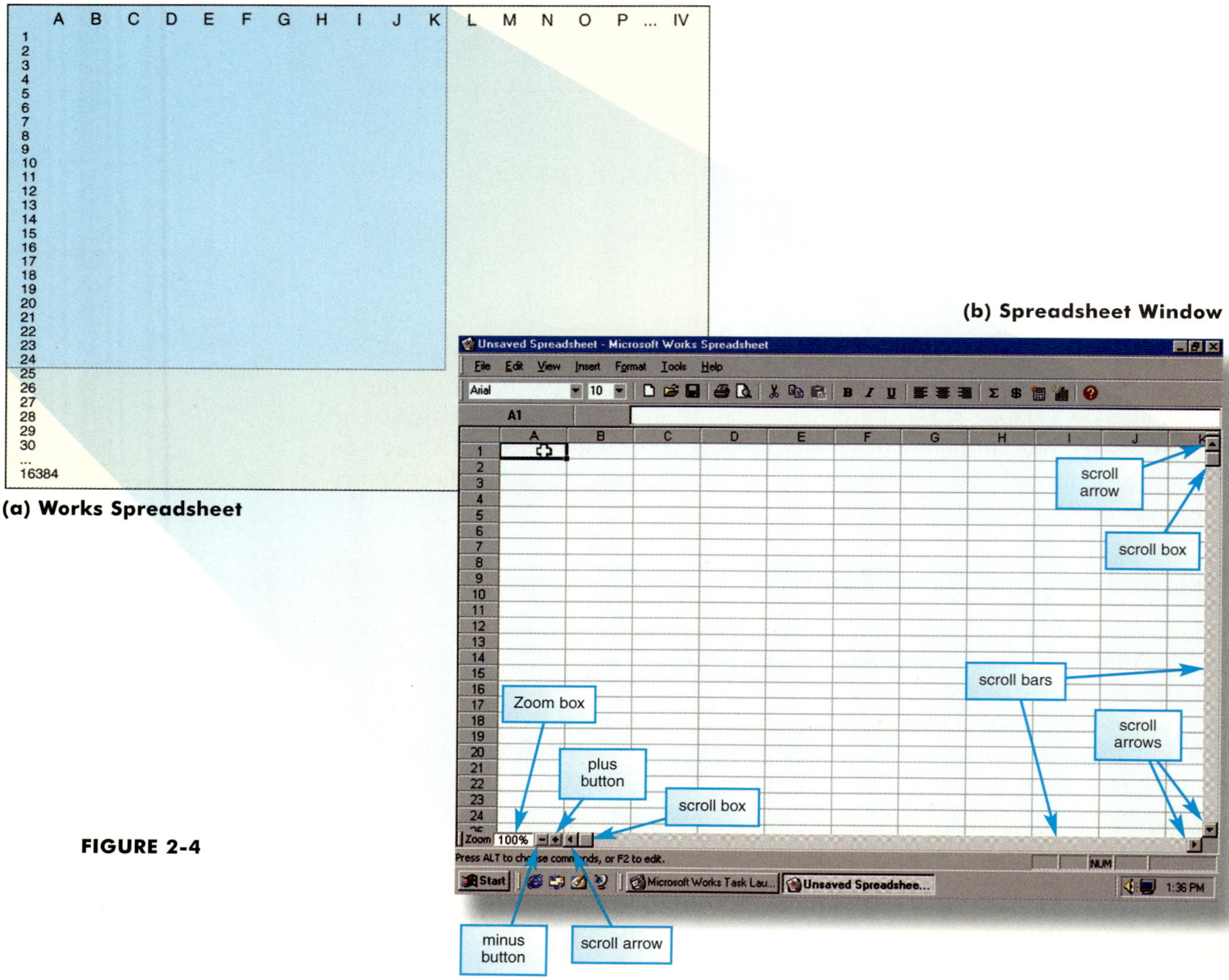

(a) Works Spreadsheet

(b) Spreadsheet Window

FIGURE 2-4

Located in the lower-left corner of the spreadsheet window, the **Zoom box** controls how much of a spreadsheet displays at one time in the spreadsheet window (see Figure 2-4). Clicking the Zoom box displays a list of available zoom percentages to magnify or reduce your spreadsheet on the screen. You also can use the plus or minus buttons next to the Zoom box to control the display. To magnify your spreadsheet, click the plus button; to reduce your spreadsheet, click the minus button. The zoom size of the display has no effect on how the spreadsheet will look when it is printed.

Scroll Bars

Clicking the scroll bar will move the spreadsheet window a full screen up or down.

Menu Bar, Toolbar, Entry Bar, and Status Bar

The menu bar, toolbar, and entry bar display at the top of the screen just below the title bar (Figure 2-5). The status bar displays at the bottom of the screen.

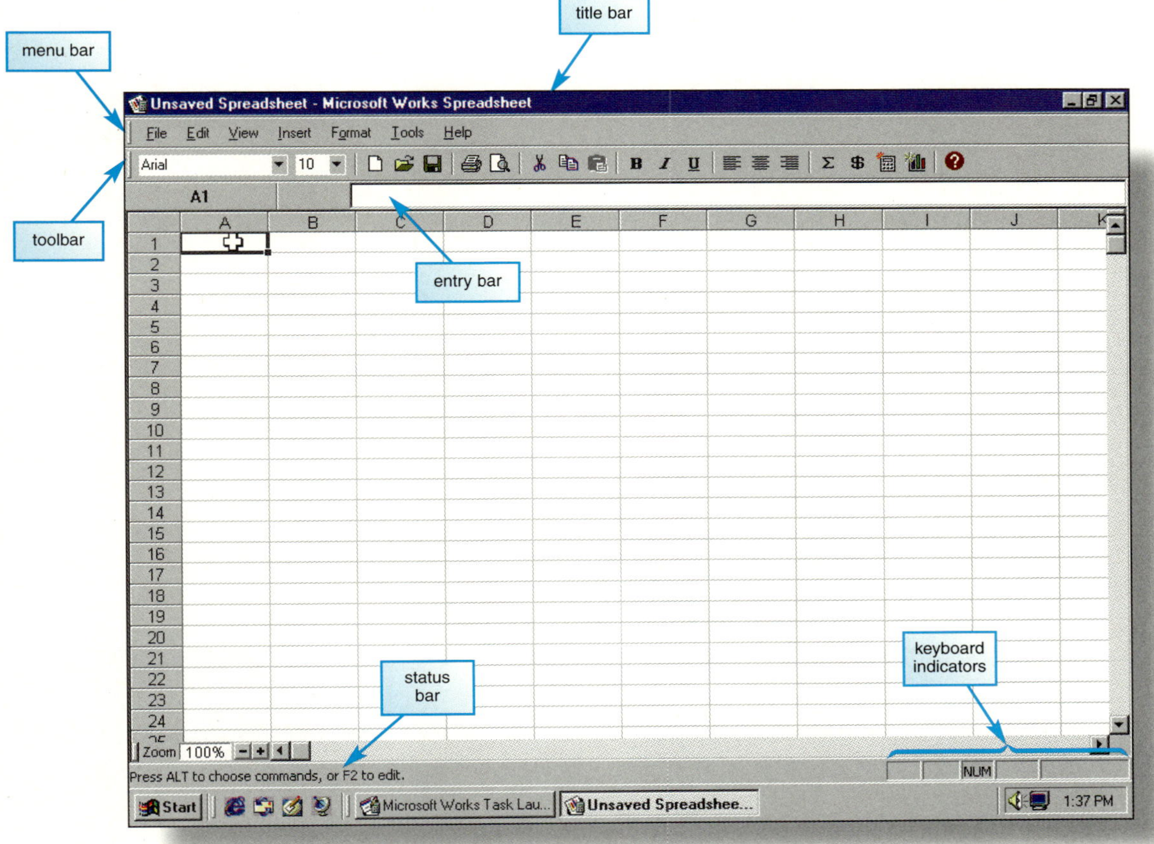

FIGURE 2-5

MENU BAR The **menu bar** displays the Works Spreadsheet menu names (Figure 2-5). Each menu name represents a menu of commands that can retrieve, save, print, and manipulate data in the spreadsheet. To display a menu such as the File menu or the Edit menu, click the menu name.

The menu bar can change to include other menu names and other menu choices depending on the type of work you are doing in the Works Spreadsheet. For example, if you are working with a chart instead of a spreadsheet, the menu bar consists of a list of menu names for use specifically with charts.

Scroll Arrows

To move the spreadsheet up or down one cell at a time, click the scroll arrows at the top or bottom of the vertical scroll bars. Use the scroll arrows on the horizontal scroll bar to move the spreadsheet left or right one cell at a time.

TOOLBAR The **toolbar** (Figure 2-5 on the previous page) contains buttons that allow you to perform tasks more quickly than when using the menu bar. Each button contains a picture that helps you remember its function. If you point to the button, a description of the purpose of the button displays in the status bar and also beneath the button in a yellow rectangle. You click a button to cause a command to execute. Each of the buttons on the toolbar is explained as it is used in the project.

As with the menu bar, Works displays a different toolbar when you work with charts. The buttons on the Charting toolbar are explained when charts are used.

More About

Microsoft Works

You can submit your technical product questions to the Microsoft support technicians online and get a response within 24 hours. For more information on Technicians Online, visit the Works 6 More About Web page (www.scsite.com/works6/more.htm) and then click Technicians Online.

ENTRY BAR Below the toolbar, Works displays the **entry bar** (Figure 2-5). Data that you type displays in the entry bar. Works also displays the selected cell reference in the cell reference area on the left side of the entry bar.

STATUS BAR The left side of the **status bar** at the bottom of the screen displays brief instructions, a brief description of the currently selected command, a brief description of the function of a toolbar button, or one or more words describing the current activity in progress.

Keyboard indicators indicating which keys are engaged, such as NUM (NUM LOCK key active) and CAPS (CAPS LOCK key active), display on the right side of the status bar within the small rectangular boxes.

Selecting a Cell

To enter data into a cell, you must first **select** the cell. The easiest method to select a cell is to position the block plus sign mouse pointer in the desired cell and click.

An alternative method is to use the arrow keys that are located to the right of the keys on the keyboard. After you press an arrow key, the adjacent cell in the direction of the arrow on the key becomes the selected cell. You also can use the TAB key to move from one cell to another in a row.

You know a cell is selected when a heavy border surrounds the cell and the cell reference of the selected cell displays in the cell reference area in the entry bar (Figure 2-6).

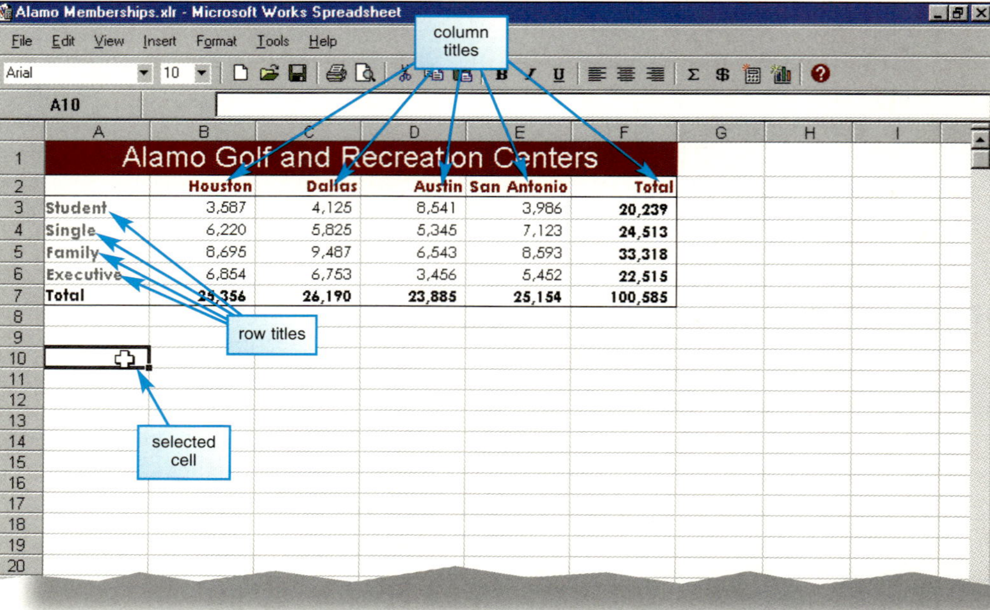

FIGURE 2-6

Entering Text in a Spreadsheet

In the Works Spreadsheet, any set of characters containing a letter is **text**. Text is used for titles, such as spreadsheet titles, column titles, and row titles. In Project 2, the spreadsheet title, Alamo Golf and Recreation Centers, identifies the spreadsheet. The column titles consist of the words Houston, Dallas, Austin, San Antonio, and Total. The row titles (Student, Single, Family, Executive, and Total) identify each row in the spreadsheet (Figure 2-6).

Entering the Spreadsheet Title

The first task to build the spreadsheet is to enter the spreadsheet title into cell A1, as illustrated in the following steps.

To Enter the Spreadsheet Title

1. **If necessary, click cell A1 to select it.**

A heavy border surrounds cell A1, and cell A1 displays in the cell reference area (Figure 2-7).

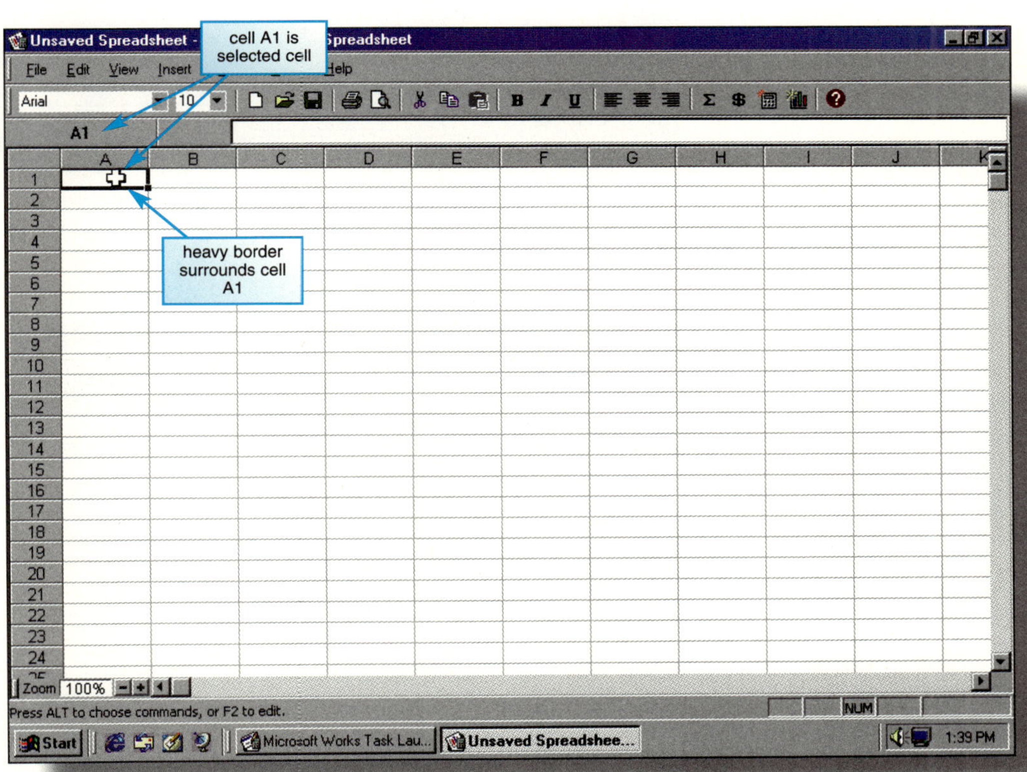

FIGURE 2-7

2 **Type** Alamo Golf and Recreation Centers **in cell A1.**

When you type the first character, the heavy border surrounding the cell changes and a new message displays on the status bar (Figure 2-8). Works displays three boxes; the Cancel box, the Enter box, and the Help box in the entry bar. As you type characters, each character displays in the cell followed immediately by a blinking vertical bar called the insertion point. The ***insertion point*** *indicates where the next character typed will display. Works also displays the data in the entry bar as it is typed. Notice that the mouse pointer changes from a block plus sign to an I-beam. Whenever the mouse pointer is located in the current cell, when you enter data it will change to an I-beam. If you make a typing mistake, press the backspace key until the error is erased, and then retype the text. Clicking the Help box displays the Help pane to the right of the Spreadsheet window.*

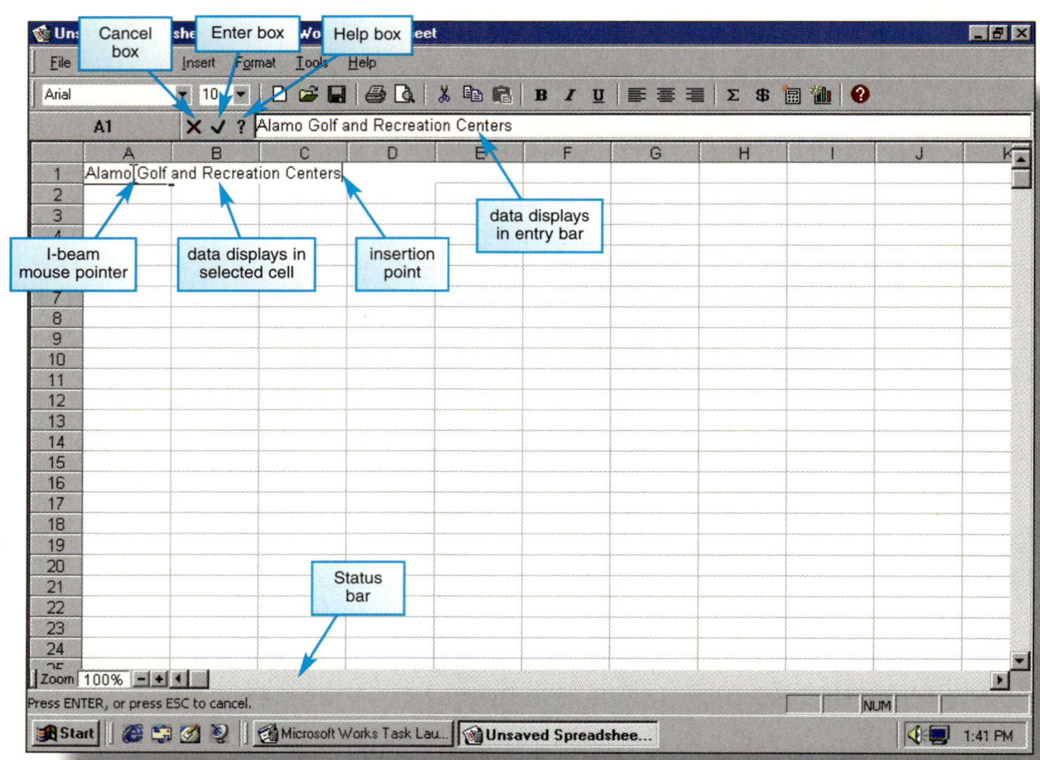

FIGURE 2-8

3 **After you type the text, point to the Enter box (Figure 2-9).**

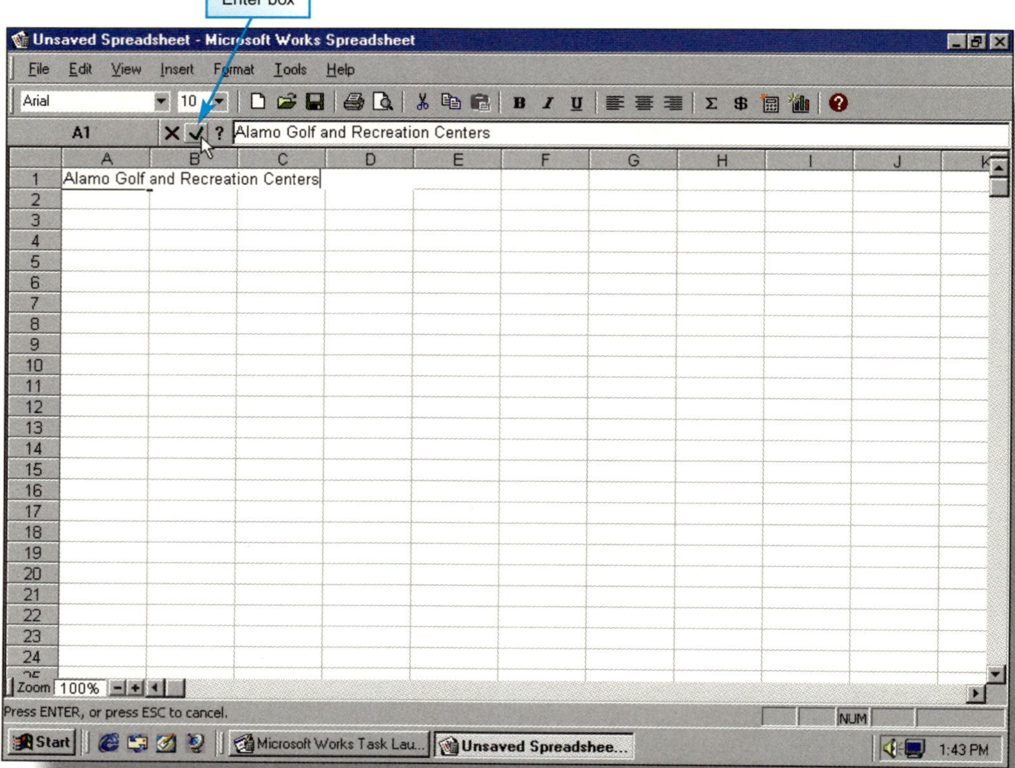

FIGURE 2-9

Click the Enter box to confirm the entry.

When you confirm the entry, Works enters the text in cell A1 (Figure 2-10).

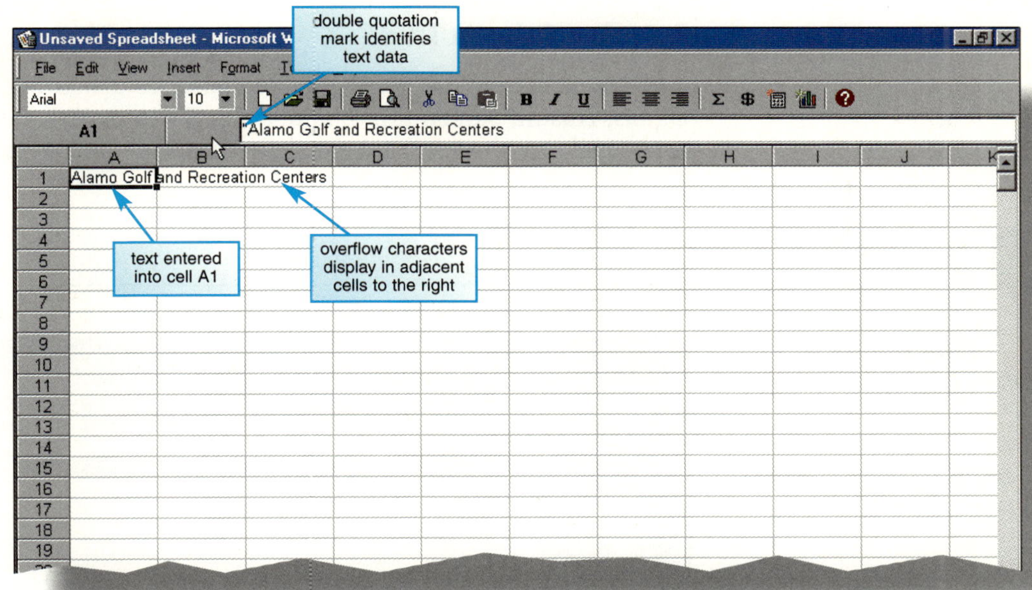

FIGURE 2-10

In the example in Figure 2-10, instead of using the mouse to confirm the entry, you can press the ENTER key after typing the text. Pressing the ENTER key replaces Step 3 and Step 4.

When you confirm a text entry into a cell, a series of events occur. First, when text displays in the entry bar, it displays preceded by a double quotation mark, which indicates the entry is text and not a number or other value.

Second, Works positions the text left-aligned in the selected cell. Therefore, the A in Alamo begins in the leftmost position of cell A1.

Third, when the text you enter contains more characters than can be displayed in the width of the cell, Works displays the overflow characters in adjacent cells to the right as long as these cells do not contain data. In Figure 2-10, cell A1 is not wide enough to contain 29 characters plus four blank spaces. Thus, Works displays the overflow characters in cells B1 and C1 because the cells are empty.

Fourth, when you confirm an entry into a cell by clicking the Enter box, the cell into which the text is entered remains the selected cell. If you confirm an entry into a cell by pressing the ENTER key, the selection will move to the cell directly below the cell that contains the entered text.

Correcting a Mistake while Typing

If you type the wrong letter and notice the error before clicking the Enter box or pressing the ENTER key, use the BACKSPACE key to erase all the characters back to and including the ones that are wrong. The insertion point will indicate where in the text the next character you type will display. Then retype the remainder of the text entry.

To cancel the entire entry before confirming the entry, click the Cancel box or press the ESC key.

If you see an error in data you already have entered into a cell, select the cell and retype the entire entry. Later in this project, additional error-correction techniques are explained.

Entering Column Titles

The next step is to enter the column titles consisting of the words, Houston, Dallas, Austin, San Antonio, and Total. To enter the column titles, select the appropriate cell and then enter the text, as illustrated in the following steps.

To Enter Column Titles

Click cell B2 to select it.

A heavy border surrounds cell B2, and B2 displays in the cell reference area (Figure 2-11).

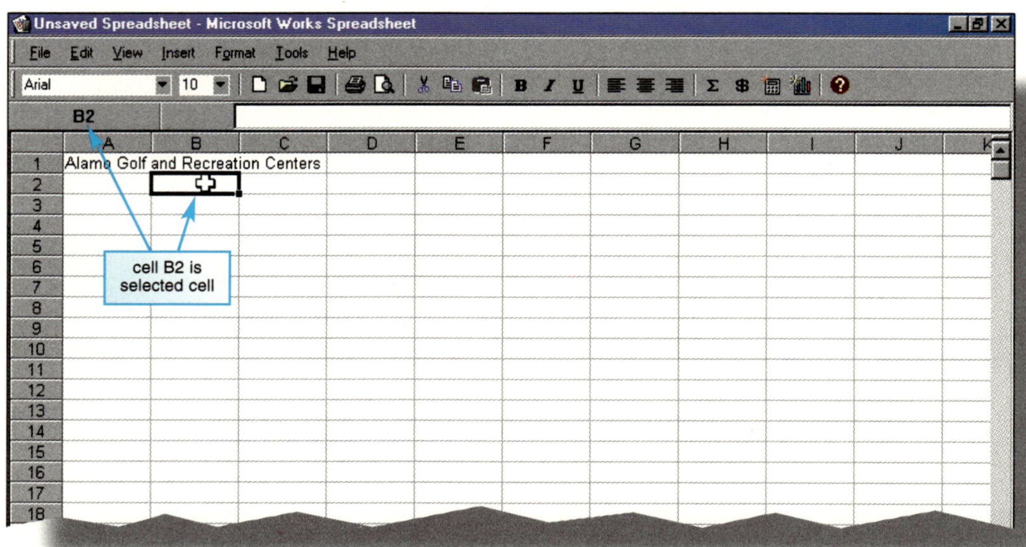

FIGURE 2-11

Type `Houston` **as the column title.**

Works displays Houston in the entry bar and in cell B2, which is the selected cell (Figure 2-12). Because the mouse pointer is located in the selected cell while data is entered, it changes to an I-beam.

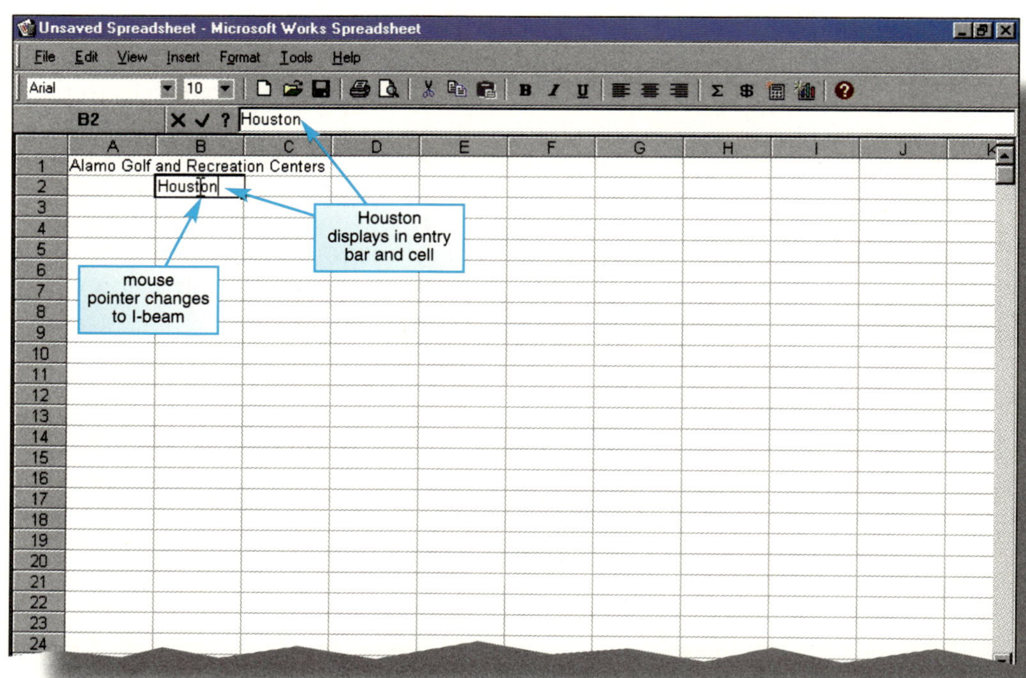

FIGURE 2-12

3 Press the RIGHT ARROW key.

Works selects cell C2 (Figure 2-13). When you press an arrow key to confirm an entry, Works enters the data and then makes the adjacent cell in the direction of the arrow (up, down, left, or right) the selected cell.

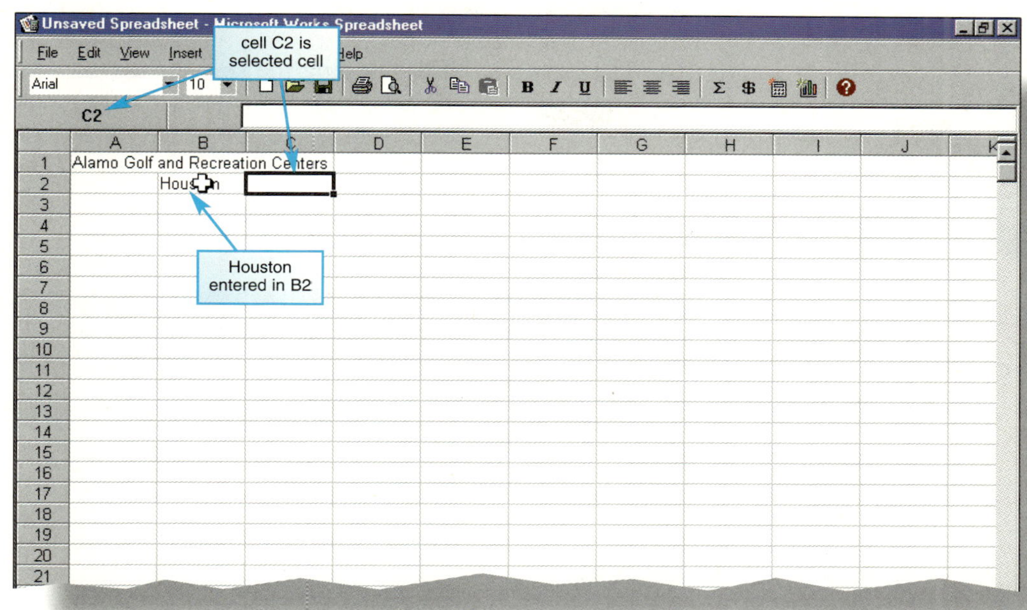

FIGURE 2-13

4 Repeat Steps 2 and 3 for the remaining column titles. That is, enter `Dallas` **in cell C2,** `Austin` **in cell D2,** `San Antonio` **in cell E2, and** `Total` **in cell F2. Confirm the last column title entry in cell F2 by pressing the ENTER key.**

The column titles display as shown in Figure 2-14.

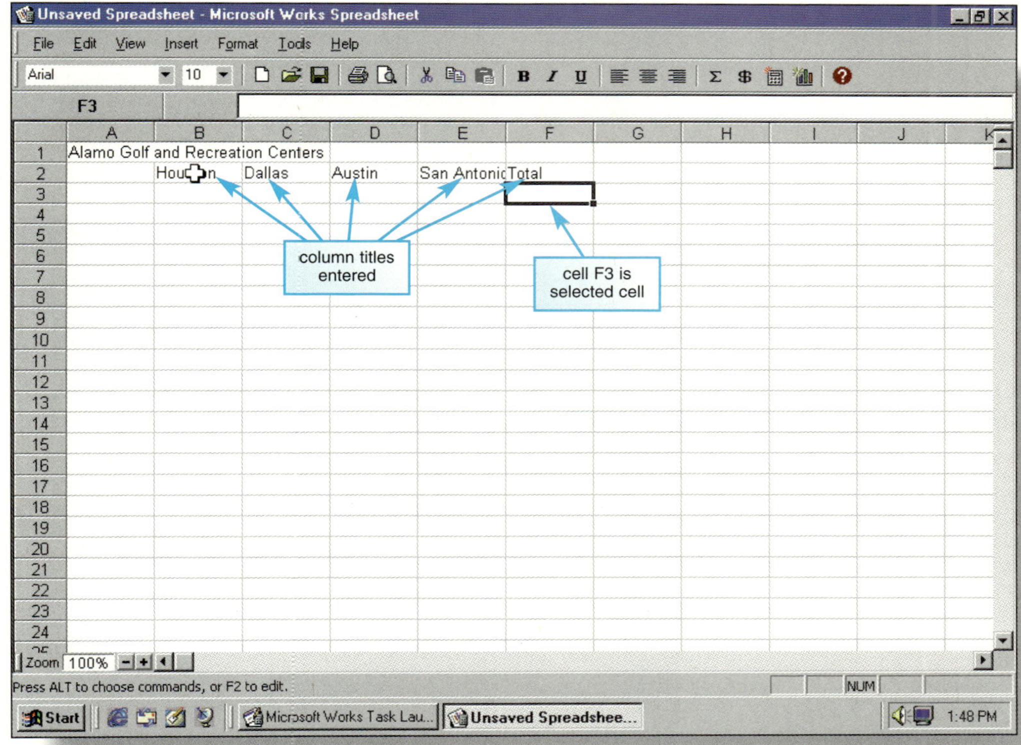

FIGURE 2-14

When confirming an entry in a cell, use the arrow keys if the next entry is in an adjacent cell. If the next entry is not in an adjacent cell, click the Enter box in the entry bar or press the ENTER key, and then use the mouse to select the appropriate cell for the next entry.

Entering Row Titles

The next step in developing the spreadsheet is to enter the row titles in column A. Complete the following steps to enter the row titles.

To Enter Row Titles

1 Click cell A3 to select it (Figure 2-15).

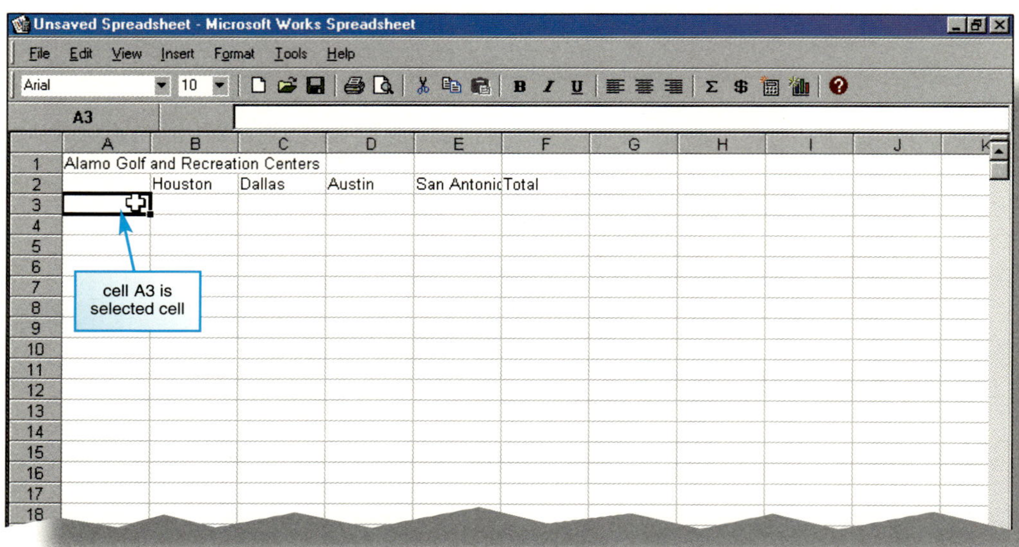

FIGURE 2-15

2 Type the row title `Student` **and then press the DOWN ARROW key.**

When you press the DOWN ARROW key, Works enters the row title, Student, in cell A3 and makes cell A4 the selected cell (Figure 2-16).

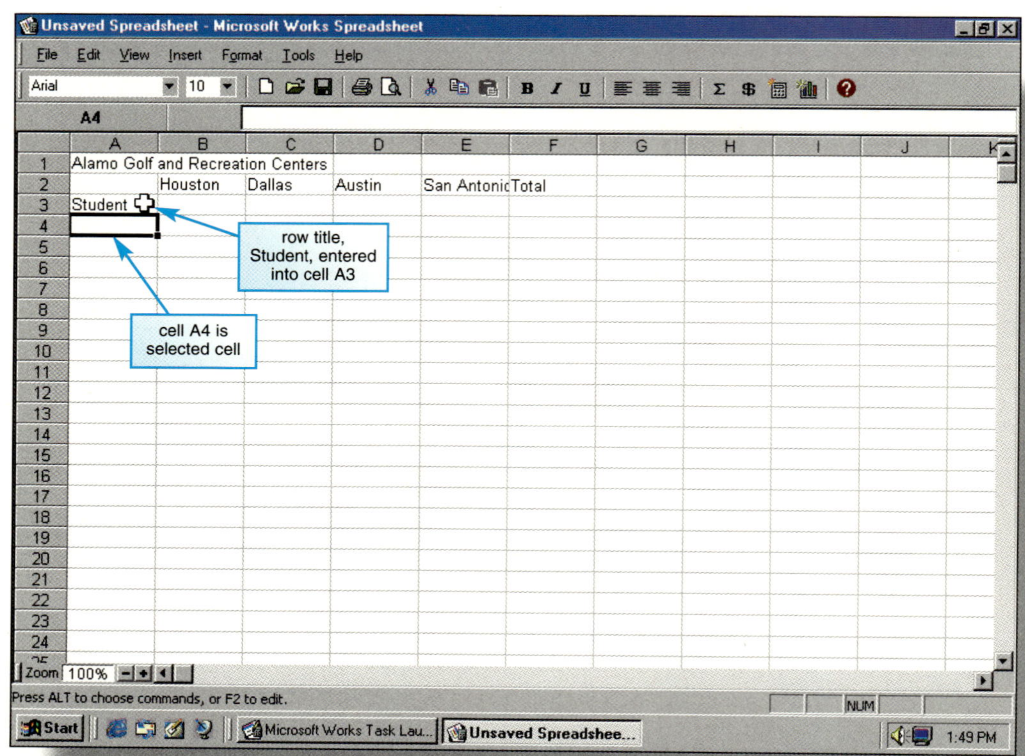

FIGURE 2-16

3 **Type** `Single` **in cell A4 and then press the DOWN ARROW key. Type** `Family` **in cell A5 and then press the DOWN ARROW key. Type** `Executive` **in cell A6 and then press the DOWN ARROW key. Type** `Total` **in cell A7 and then confirm the entry by pressing the ENTER key.**

The row titles display as shown in Figure 2-17. The row titles are left-aligned in each cell. Cell A8 is the selected cell.

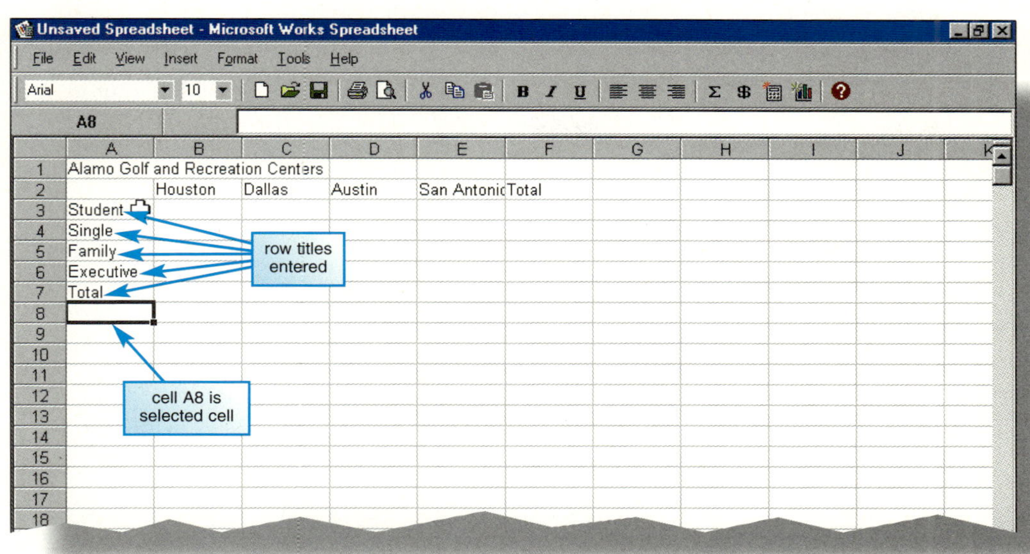

FIGURE 2-17

Entering Numbers

You can enter numbers that represent amounts and other numeric values into cells. Numbers can include the digits zero through nine and any one of the following characters:

( ) , . / $ % E e

The use of these characters is explained when they are required in a project. If a cell entry contains any other character from the keyboard, Works interprets the entry as text or a date and treats it accordingly.

In this project, you must enter the memberships for Houston, Dallas, Austin, and San Antonio for each of the categories, Student, Single, Family, and Executive in rows 3, 4, 5, and 6. The steps below and on the next two pages illustrate how to enter these values one row at a time.

Numbers

To enter numbers in a cell, you can use the number keys at the top of the keyboard, or when the NUM LOCK key is on, you can use the numeric keypad at the right of the keyboard. Using the keypad at the right of the keyboard generally is the fastest way to enter numbers.

To Enter Numeric Data

1 **Click cell B3 to select it (Figure 2-18).**

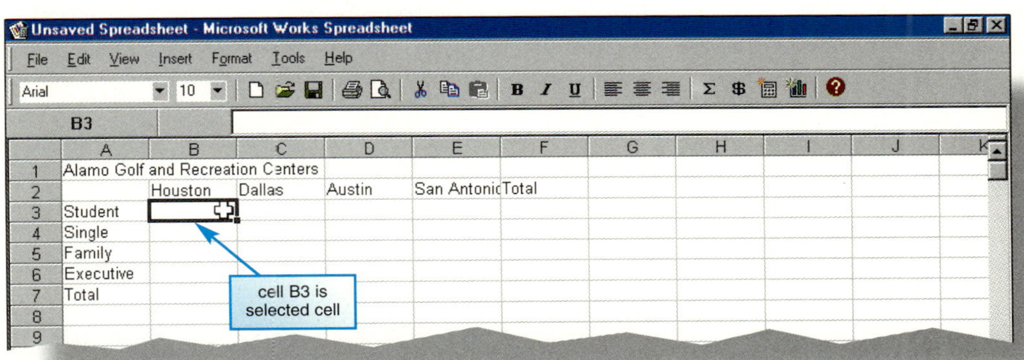

FIGURE 2-18

Type 3587 **in cell B3.**

The number 3587 displays in the entry bar and in the selected cell (Figure 2-19). Enter the number without a comma. You will format the numbers in the spreadsheet with commas in a later step. The mouse pointer changes from a block plus sign to an I-beam.

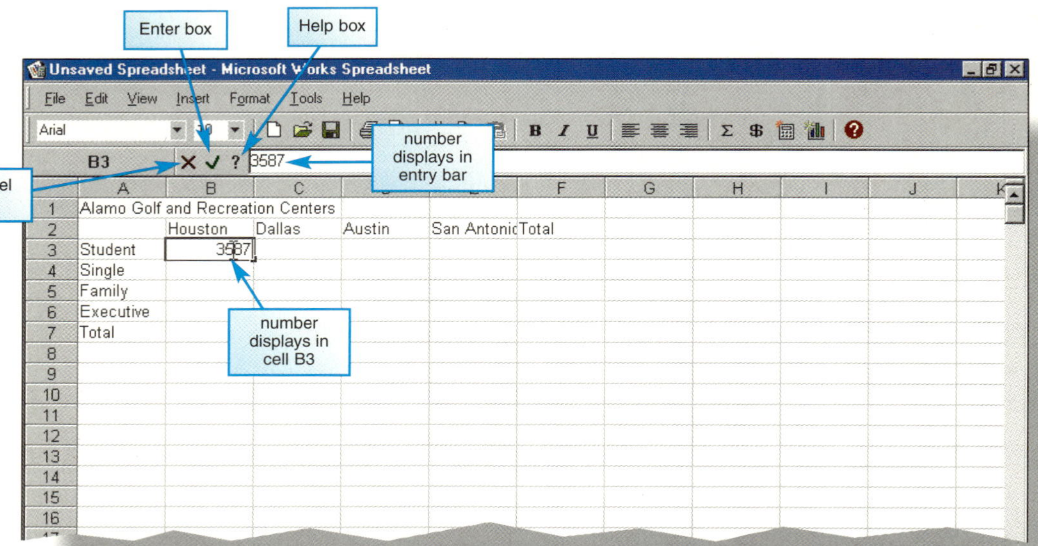

FIGURE 2-19

Press the RIGHT ARROW key.

Works enters the number 3587 into cell B3 and selects cell C3 (Figure 2-20).

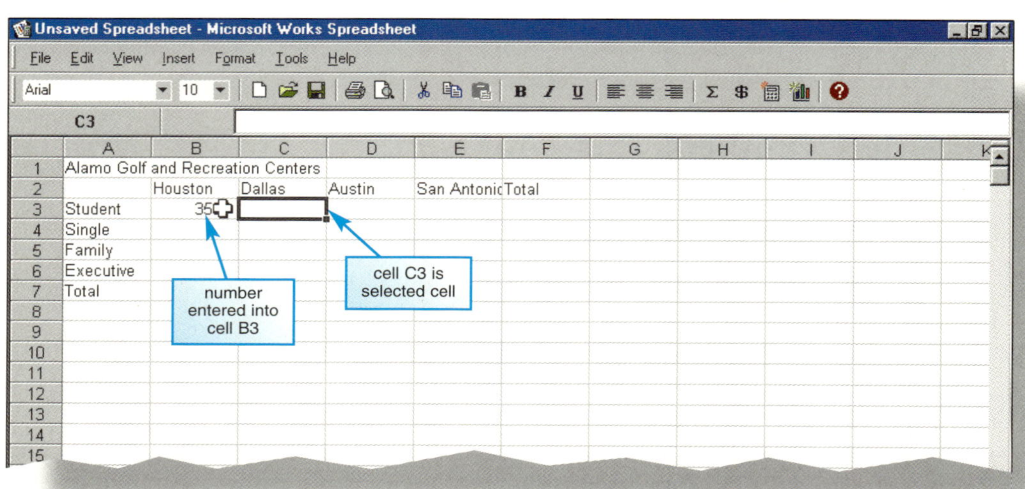

FIGURE 2-20

4 **Type** 4125 **in cell C3 and then press the RIGHT ARROW key. Type** 8541 **in cell D3 and then press the RIGHT ARROW key. Type** 3986 **in cell E3 and then press the ENTER key.**

Row 3 contains the student memberships and cell E4 is selected (Figure 2-21).

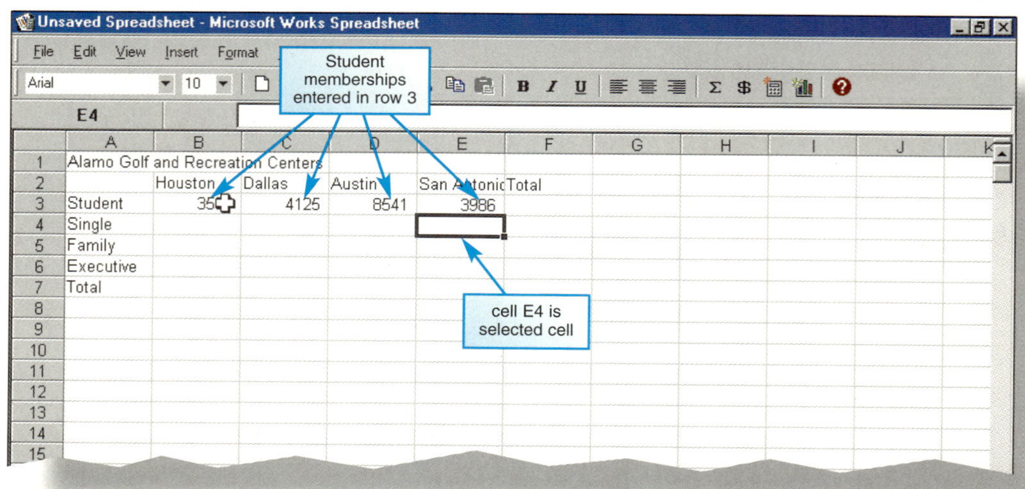

FIGURE 2-21

5 **Click cell B4 to select it (Figure 2-22).**

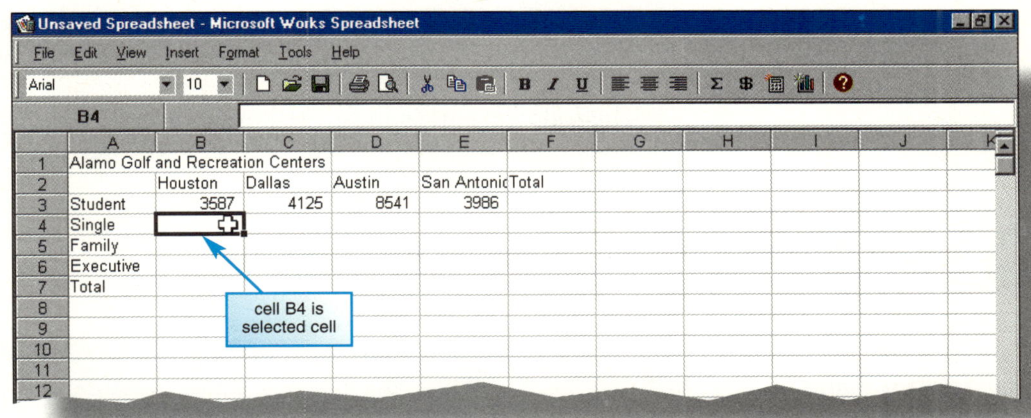

FIGURE 2-22

6 **Refer to Figure 2-23 and repeat the procedures used in Steps 2 through 4 to enter the single memberships, family memberships, and executive memberships.**

The single, family, and executive memberships are entered in rows 4, 5, and 6, respectively (Figure 2-23).

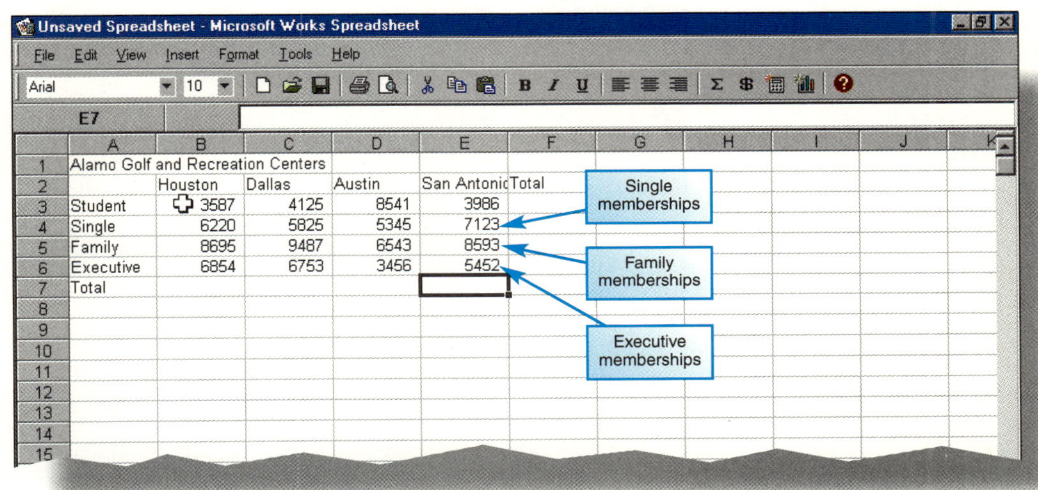

FIGURE 2-23

You now have entered all the numbers required for this spreadsheet. Notice several important points. First, commas, which are used to separate every third digit, are not required when you enter numbers. You will add them in a later step. Second, Works enters numbers right-aligned in the cells, which means they occupy the rightmost position in the cells. Third, Works will calculate the totals in row 7 and column F. The capability of the Works Spreadsheet tool to perform calculations is one of its major features.

Calculating a Sum

The next step in creating the Alamo Golf and Recreation Centers spreadsheet is to calculate the total memberships for Houston. To calculate this value and enter it into cell B7, Works must add the numbers in cells B3, B4, B5, and B6. The SUM function available in the Works Spreadsheet tool provides a convenient means to accomplish this task.

To use the SUM function, you first must identify the cell into which the sum will be entered after it is calculated. Then, you can use the **AutoSum button** on the toolbar to actually sum the numbers.

The following steps illustrate how to use the AutoSum button to sum the sales for Houston in cells B3, B4, B5, and B6 and enter the answer in cell B7.

Steps To Sum a Column of Numbers Using the AutoSum Button

Click cell B7 to select it. Point to the AutoSum button on the toolbar.

Cell B7 is selected (Figure 2-24).

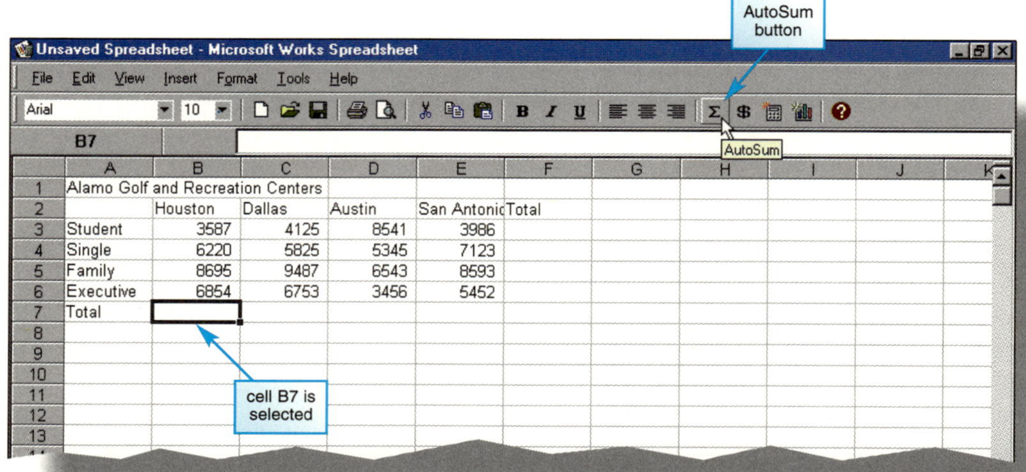

FIGURE 2-24

Click the AutoSum button.

Works responds by displaying =SUM(B3:B6) in the entry bar and in the selected cell (Figure 2-25). The =SUM entry identifies the SUM function. The B3:B6 entry within parentheses following the function name SUM is the way Works identifies cells B3, B4, B5, and B6 as the cells containing the values to be summed. Works also places a dark background behind the proposed cells to sum. The word POINT displays on the status bar indicating the SUM function is pointing to a range to be summed.

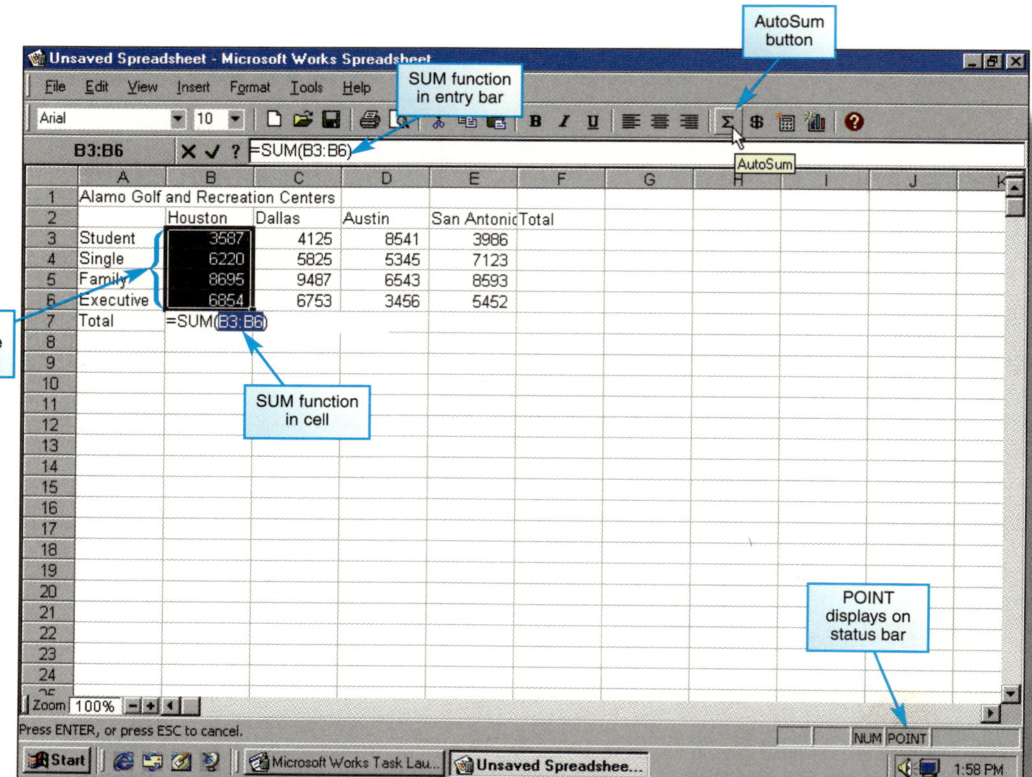

FIGURE 2-25

3 Click the AutoSum button a second time.

Works displays the sum of the memberships for Houston (3587 + 6220 + 8695 + 6854 = 25356) in cell B7 (Figure 2-26). Although the SUM function assigned to cell B7 is not displayed in the cell, it remains in the cell and displays in the entry bar when the cell is selected.

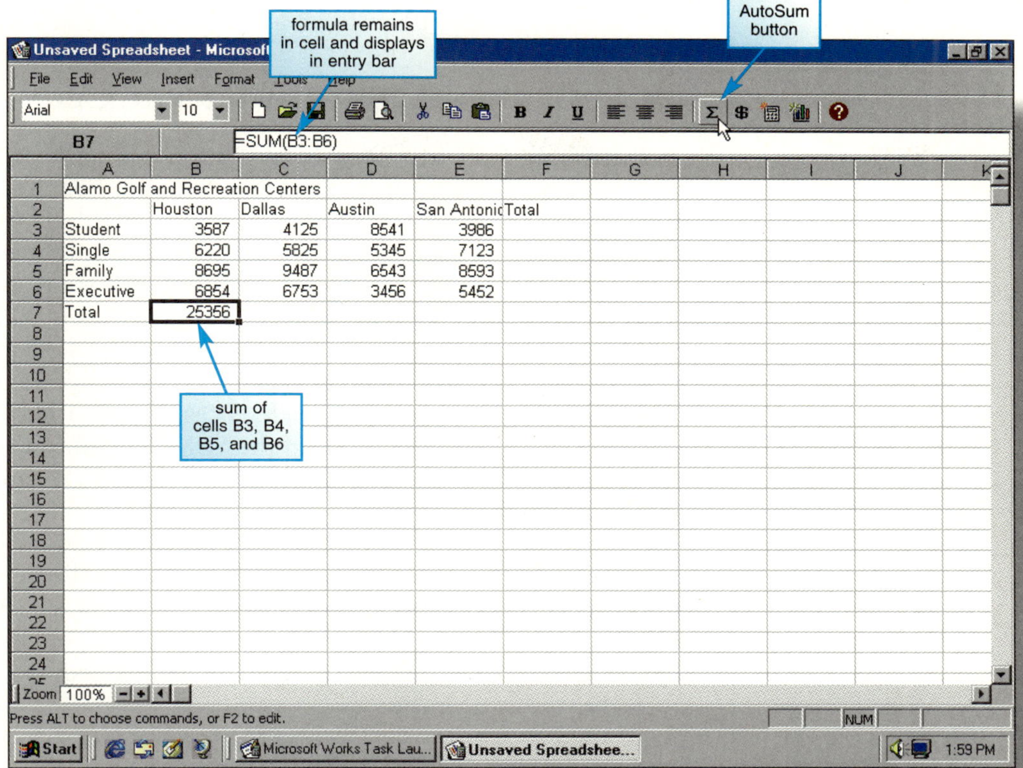

FIGURE 2-26

1. Press CTRL+M

To display the SUM function in a cell instead of the sum, click the cell and then click in the entry bar area.

When you enter the SUM function using the AutoSum button, Works automatically selects what it considers to be your choice of cells to sum. The group of cells, B3, B4, B5, and B6, is called a range. A **range** is a block of adjacent cells in a spreadsheet. Ranges can be as small as a single cell and as large as an entire spreadsheet. Once you define a range, you can work with all the cells in the range instead of one cell at a time. In Figure 2-26, clicking the AutoSum button defines the range, which consists of cells B3 through B6 (designated B3:B6 by Works).

When selecting the range of cells to sum using the AutoSum button, Works first looks for a range above the selected cell, and then to the left. If Works selects the wrong range, drag through the correct range any time before clicking the AutoSum button a second time. You also can enter the correct range in the selected cell to receive the sum by typing the beginning cell reference, a colon (:), and the ending cell reference, followed by clicking the AutoSum button a second time. A third method to fix an incorrect range specified by Works is to enter the correct range in the entry bar by dragging through the range specified in the entry bar and then by typing the beginning cell reference, a colon (:), and the ending cell reference, followed by clicking the AutoSum button a second time.

When using the AutoSum button, you can click it once and then click the Enter box or press the ENTER key to complete the entry. Clicking the AutoSum button a second time, however, is the quickest way to enter the SUM function.

AutoSum

Consider how fast Works completes the following sophisticated operations after clicking the AutoSum button twice: (1) enters the equal sign and function name; (2) scans the spreadsheet and selects cells to be summed; (3) calculates the total; and (4) displays the result of the calculation.

Copying a Cell to Adjacent Cells

In the Alamo Golf and Recreation Centers spreadsheet, Works also must calculate the totals for Dallas, Austin, and San Antonio. For the Dallas memberships, the total is the sum of the values in the range C3:C6. Similarly, for the Austin memberships, the range to sum is D3:D6 and for the San Antonio memberships, the range is E3:E6.

To calculate these sums, you can follow the steps shown in Figures 2-24 through 2-26 on pages W 2.20 and W 2.21. A more efficient method, however, is to copy the SUM function from cell B7 to the range C7:E7. The copy cannot be an exact duplicate, though, because different columns must be referenced for each respective total. Therefore, when you copy cell references, Works adjusts the cell references for each column. As a result, the range in the SUM function in cell C7 will be C3:C6, the range in the SUM function in cell D7 will be D3:D6, and the range in SUM function in cell E7 will be E3:E6.

The easiest way to copy the SUM function from cell B7 to cells C7, D7, and E7 is to use the fill handle. The **fill handle** is the small rectangular dot located in the lower-right corner of the heavy border around the selected cell. To copy using the fill handle, first select the cell that includes the data you want to copy, then drag the fill handle to select the range to which you want to copy. Complete the following steps to perform this operation.

To Copy One Cell to Adjacent Cells in a Row

1 If necessary, click the cell to copy – cell B7 – and position the mouse pointer on the fill handle located in the lower-right corner of cell B7.

Cell B7 is selected (Figure 2-27). When you position the mouse pointer on the fill handle, the mouse pointer changes to the word FILL with a cross indicating the fill handle is selected.

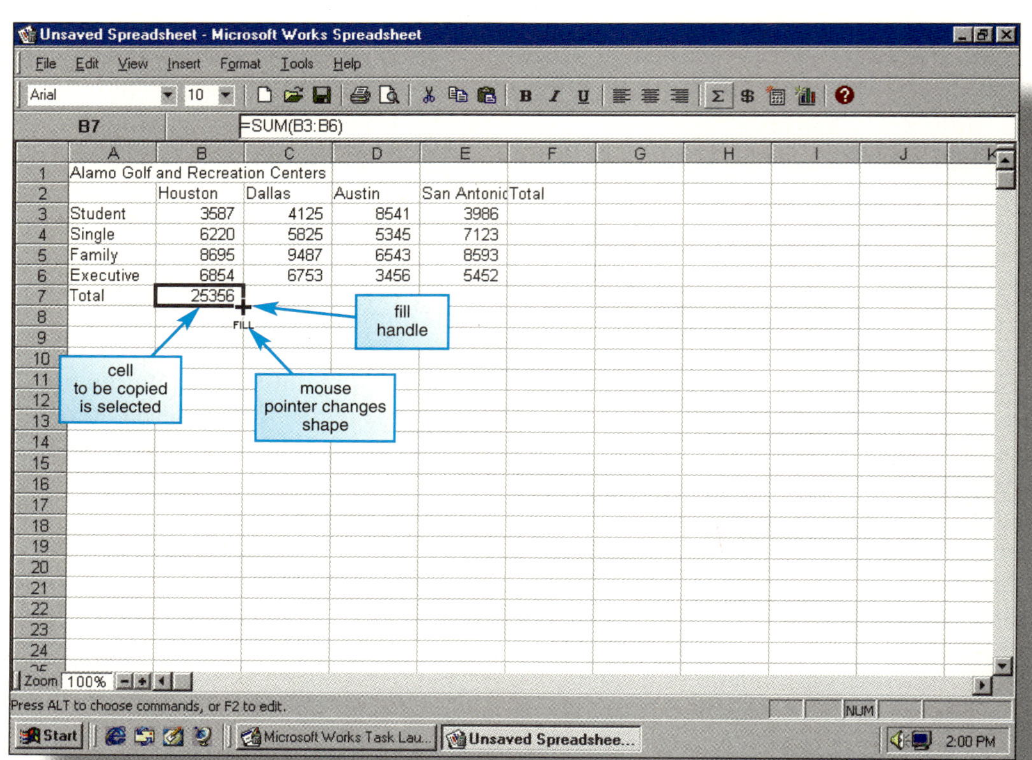

FIGURE 2-27

2 Drag through the range into which you want to copy (cells C7, D7, and E7).

When you drag the fill handle through the cells, Works places a border around the cell you want to copy (B7) and an outline around the range into which you want to copy (C7:E7) (Figure 2-28). The contents of cell B7 display in the entry bar.

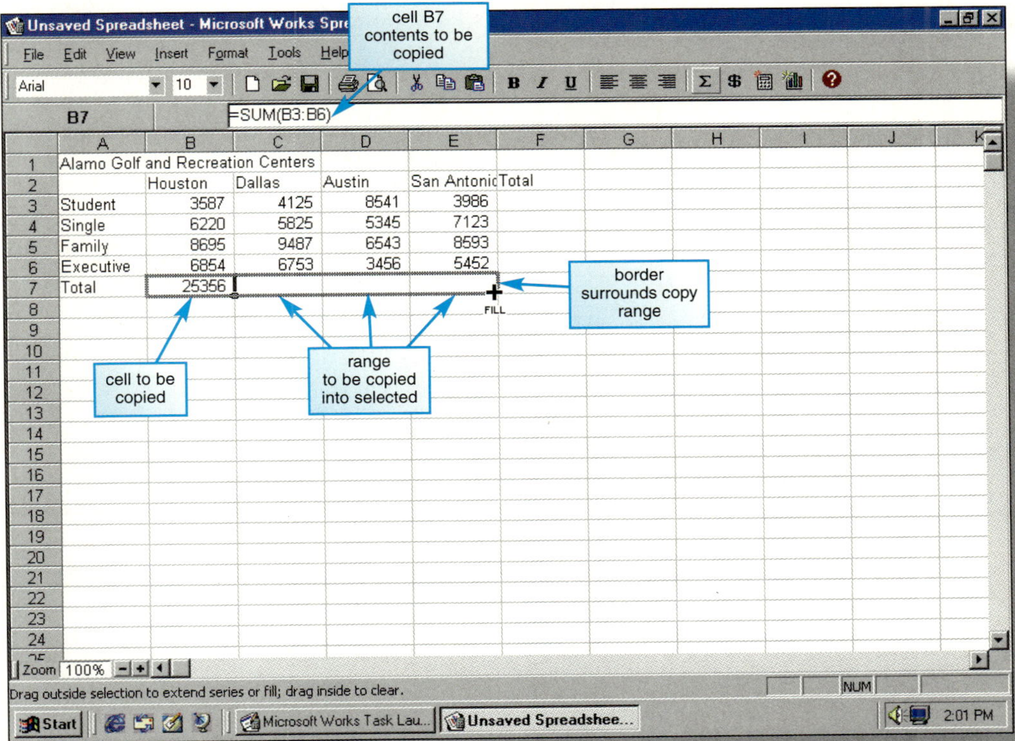

FIGURE 2-28

3 Release the mouse button.

When you release the mouse button, Works copies the SUM function from cell B7 into the range C7:E7 (Figure 2-29). In addition, Works performs calculations based on the formula in each of the cells and displays sums in cells C7, D7, and E7. The mouse pointer changes back to a block plus sign.

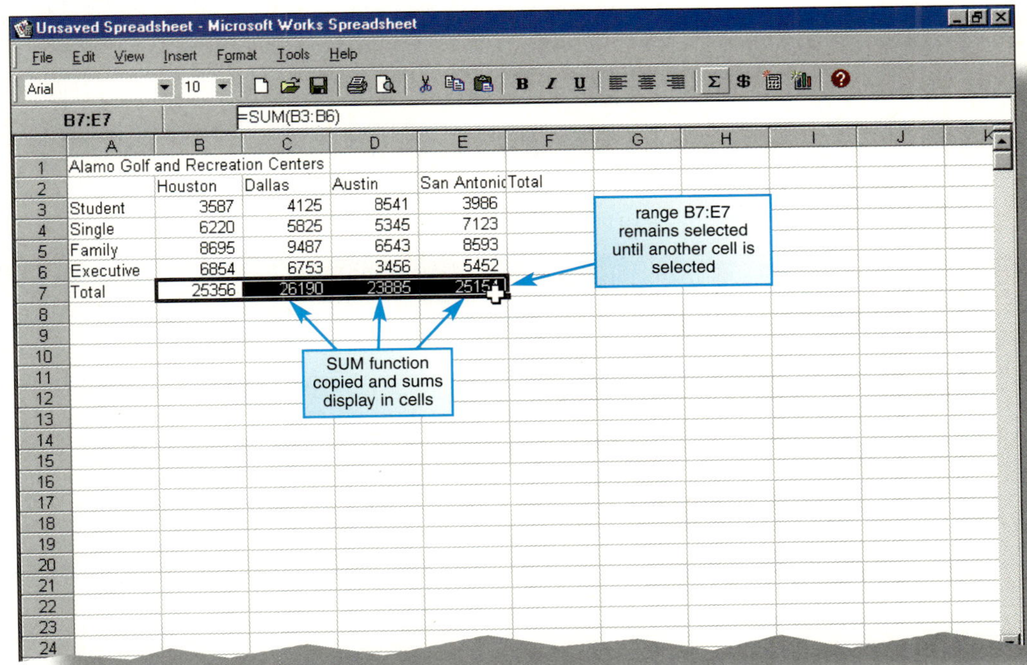

FIGURE 2-29

Other Ways

1. On Edit menu click Fill Right
2. Press CTRL+R

After Works has copied the contents of a cell into a range, the range remains selected. To remove the selection, click any cell in the spreadsheet.

Summing a Row Total

The next step in building the Alamo Golf and Recreation Centers spreadsheet is to total the student memberships, single memberships, family memberships, and executive memberships, and then to calculate the total memberships for the centers. These totals will be entered in column F. The SUM function is used in the same manner as totaling the memberships in row 7. Perform the following steps to sum the row numbers.

Steps To Sum a Row of Numbers Using the AutoSum Button

1 Click cell F3, which will contain the total for Student. Point to the AutoSum button on the toolbar.

Cell F3 is selected (Figure 2-30).

AutoSum button

cell F3 is selected

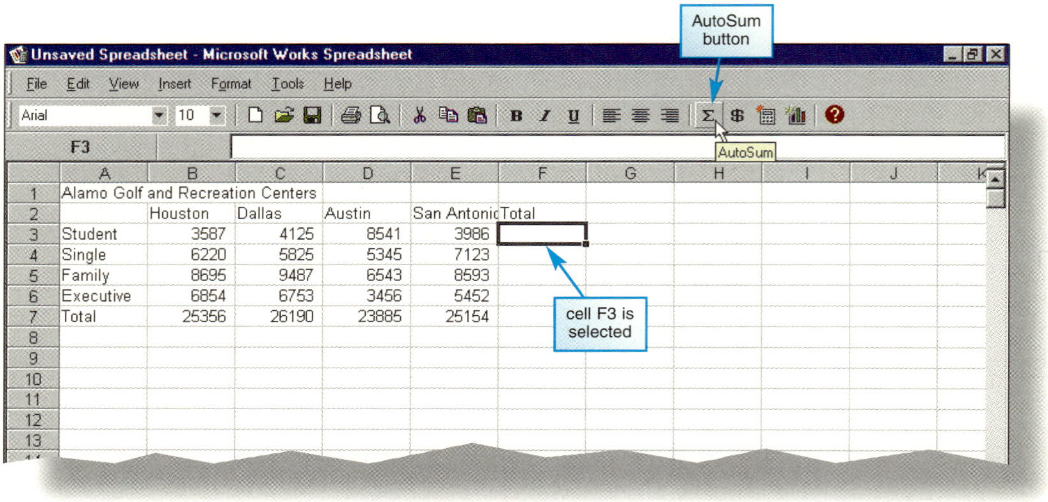

FIGURE 2-30

2 Click the AutoSum button.

Works responds by displaying =SUM(B3:E3) in the entry bar and in the selected cell (Figure 2-31). Works also places a dark background behind the proposed cells to sum. The =SUM entry identifies the SUM function. The B3:E3 entry within parentheses following the function name SUM is the way Works identifies cells B3, C3, D3, and E3 as the cells containing the values to be added.

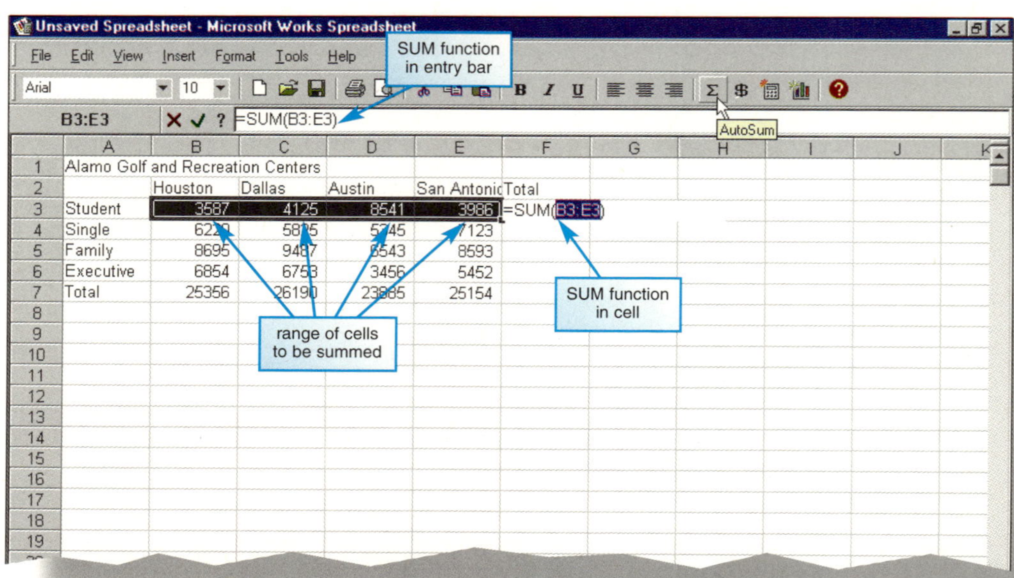

FIGURE 2-31

3 Click the AutoSum button a second time.

Works enters the formula in cell F3, displays the sum in the cell, and displays the SUM function from cell F3 in the entry bar (Figure 2-32).

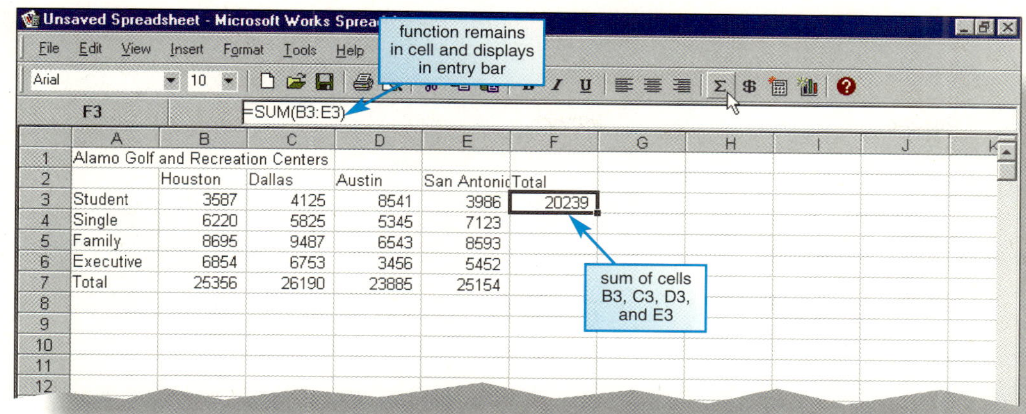

FIGURE 2-32

1. Press CTRL+M

As shown previously, you can accomplish Step 3 by clicking the Enter box or pressing the ENTER key.

Copying Adjacent Cells in a Column

The next task is to copy the SUM function from cell F3 to the range F4:F7 to obtain the total memberships for single, family, executive, and to obtain the total memberships for the Alamo Golf and Recreation Centers. The steps to accomplish this task follow.

To Copy One Cell to Adjacent Cells in a Column

1 If necessary, select cell F3. Position the mouse pointer on the fill handle located in the lower-right corner of cell F3. When the mouse pointer changes to the word FILL with a cross, drag through the range to cell F7.

When you drag the fill handle through the cells, Works places a border around the cell you want to copy (F3) and an outline around the range into which you want to copy (F4:F7) (Figure 2-33). The contents of cell F3 display in the entry bar.

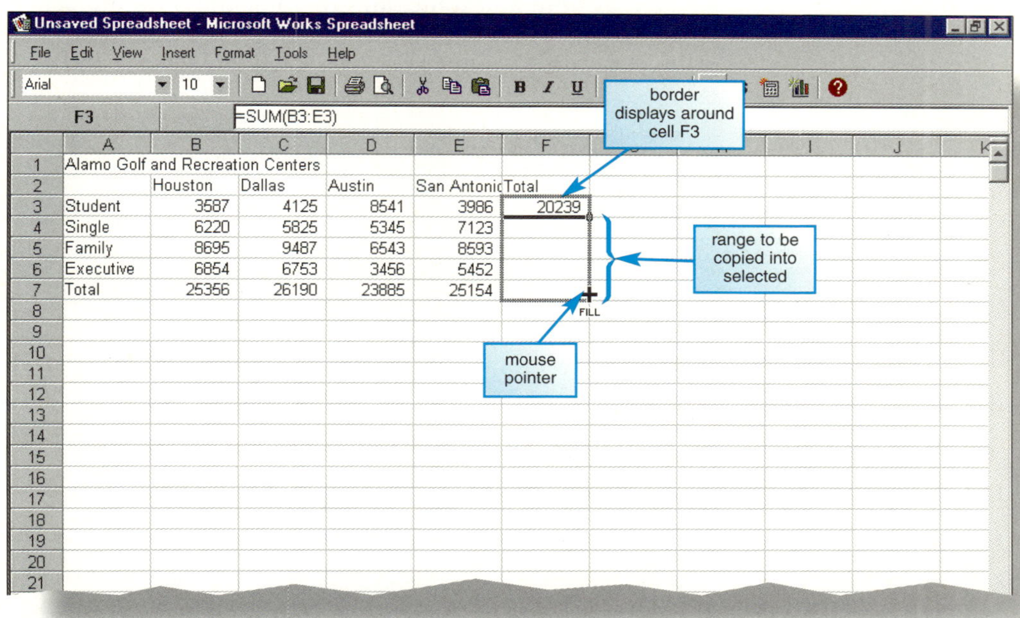

FIGURE 2-33

Release the mouse button.

When you release the mouse button, Works fills the selected range with the SUM function and displays the calculated sums in each of the cells (Figure 2-34). When Works copies the function, each range reference in the function is adjusted to reflect the proper rows of numbers to sum. The mouse pointer changes back to a block plus sign.

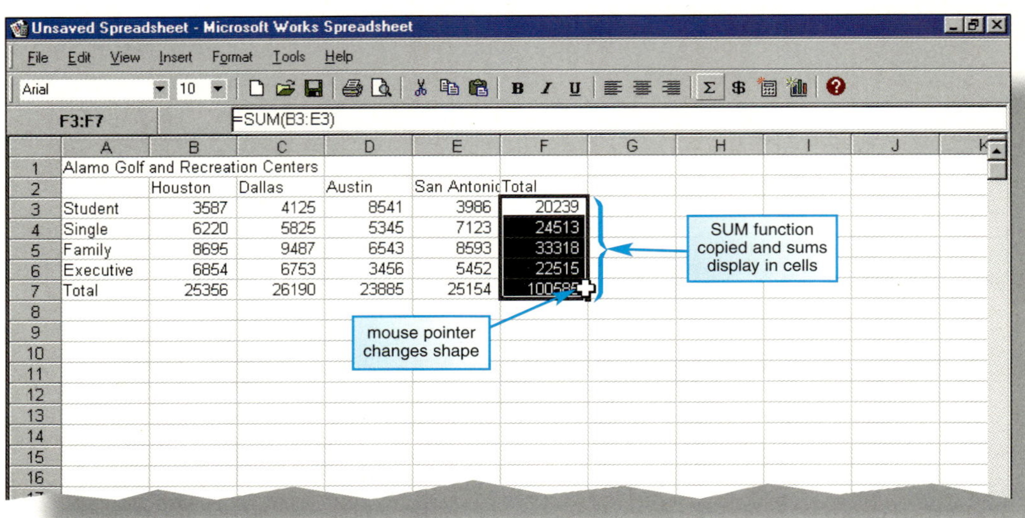

FIGURE 2-34

1. On Edit menu click Fill Down
2. Press CTRL+D

After Works copies the cell contents, the range F3:F7 remains selected. You can remove this selection by clicking any cell in the spreadsheet.

Formatting the Spreadsheet

You now have entered all the text, numeric entries, and functions for the spreadsheet. The next step is to format the spreadsheet. You **format** a spreadsheet to emphasize certain entries and make the spreadsheet attractive to view and easy to read and understand.

With Works, you have the ability to change fonts, font sizes, and font styles such as bold and italic, and to color the font and cells containing the data in the spreadsheet. On the following pages, you will learn how to format the spreadsheet as shown in Figure 2-35.

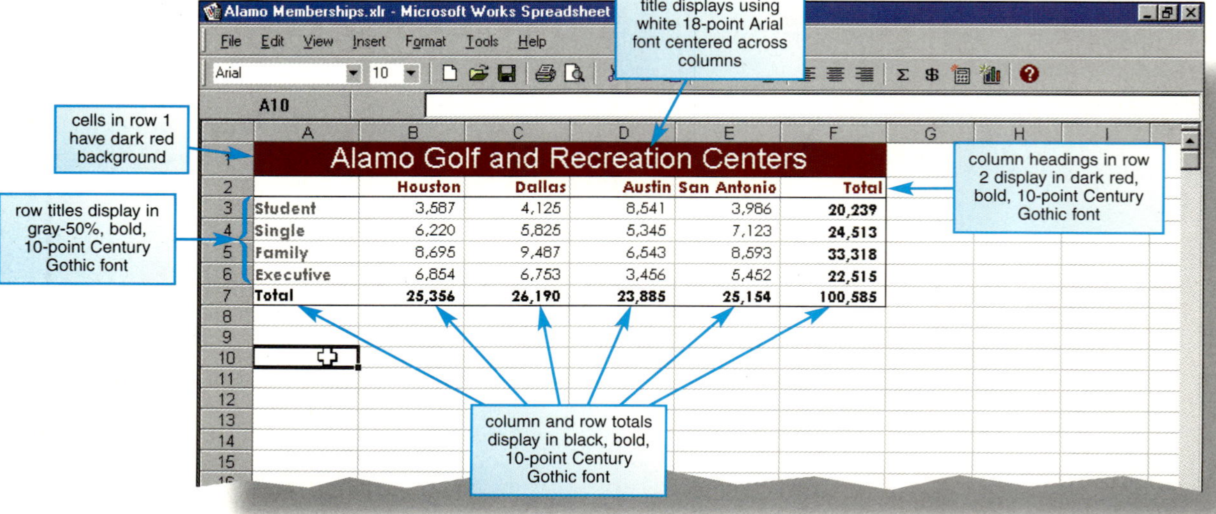

FIGURE 2-35

In Figure 2-35, the spreadsheet title displays in white 18-point Arial font. The cell background is dark red, and the title is centered over the columns in the spreadsheet. The color of the column titles (dark red), row titles (gray), and the remainder of the spreadsheet display as illustrated. The fonts, font sizes, styles, and colors are determined by the AutoFormat feature of Works. The membership numbers, column totals, and row totals display with commas. The following sections describe how to accomplish this formatting.

Right-Clicking

Right-clicking selected cells was not even available in earlier versions of Works, so you may find people familiar with Works not even considering right-clicking. Because it always produces a shortcut menu containing frequently used commands, right-clicking can be the fastest way to access commands.

Formatting Text and Changing the Color of Cells

The first step in formatting the spreadsheet is to format the title of the spreadsheet in cell A1. The spreadsheet title displays in white 18-point Arial font and is centered over columns A through F. The cell background is dark red. Formatting can be accomplished using the Format command on the shortcut menu. Complete the following steps to format the title.

To Format Cells

1 Select the range of cells A1:F1. Right-click the selected range. Point to Format on the shortcut menu.

Cells A1 through F1 are selected and the shortcut menu displays (Figure 2-36).

FIGURE 2-36

2 Click Format. When the Format Cells dialog box displays, point to the Alignment tab.

Works displays the Format Cells dialog box (Figure 2-37). The Format Cells dialog box contains five tabbed sheets: Number, Alignment, Font, Border, and Shading. The Number sheet displays in front of the other tabbed sheets.

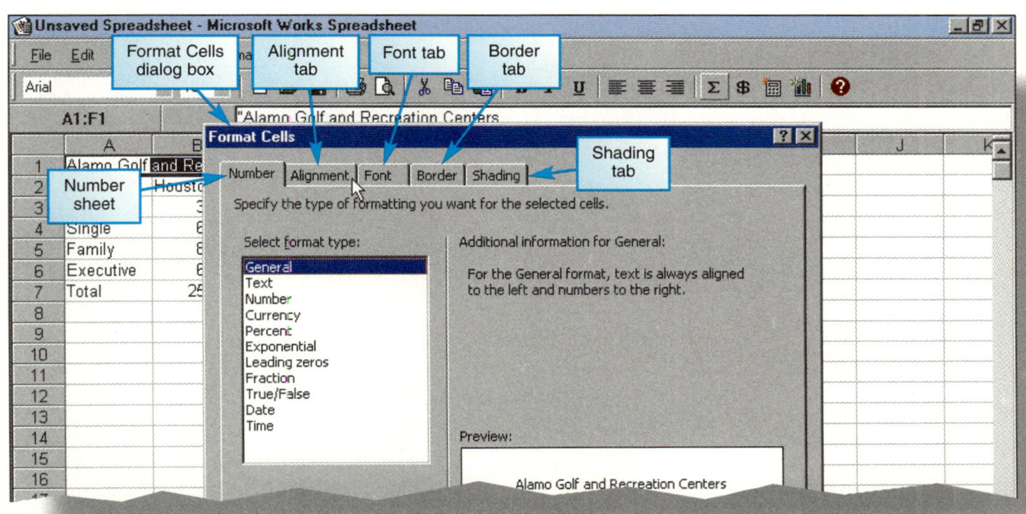

FIGURE 2-37

3 **Click the Alignment tab. When the Alignment sheet displays, click Center across selection in the Select horizontal position area. Click Center in the Select vertical position area. Point to the Font tab.**

When you click the Alignment tab, the Alignment sheet moves to the front (Figure 2-38). Selecting the Center across selection option button in the Select horizontal position area indicates the title should be centered horizontally across the selected columns. The selection of the Center option button in the Select vertical position area indicates that the title is to be centered vertically in the cells.

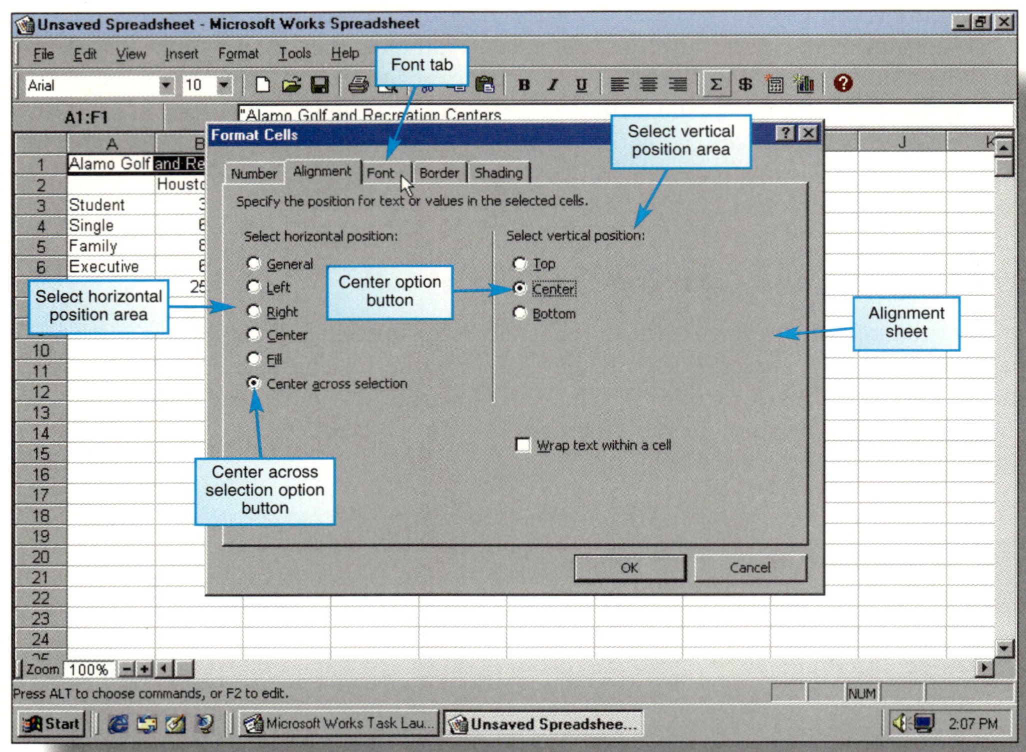

FIGURE 2-38

4 **Click the Font tab. When the Font sheet displays, scroll to and then point to the number 18 in the Size list.**

Works displays the Font sheet (Figure 2-39). The default values are Arial font, 10-point size, Automatic color, and Regular selections in the Font style area. The Preview area displays an example of the text with these options in effect. Automatic color displays text in black.

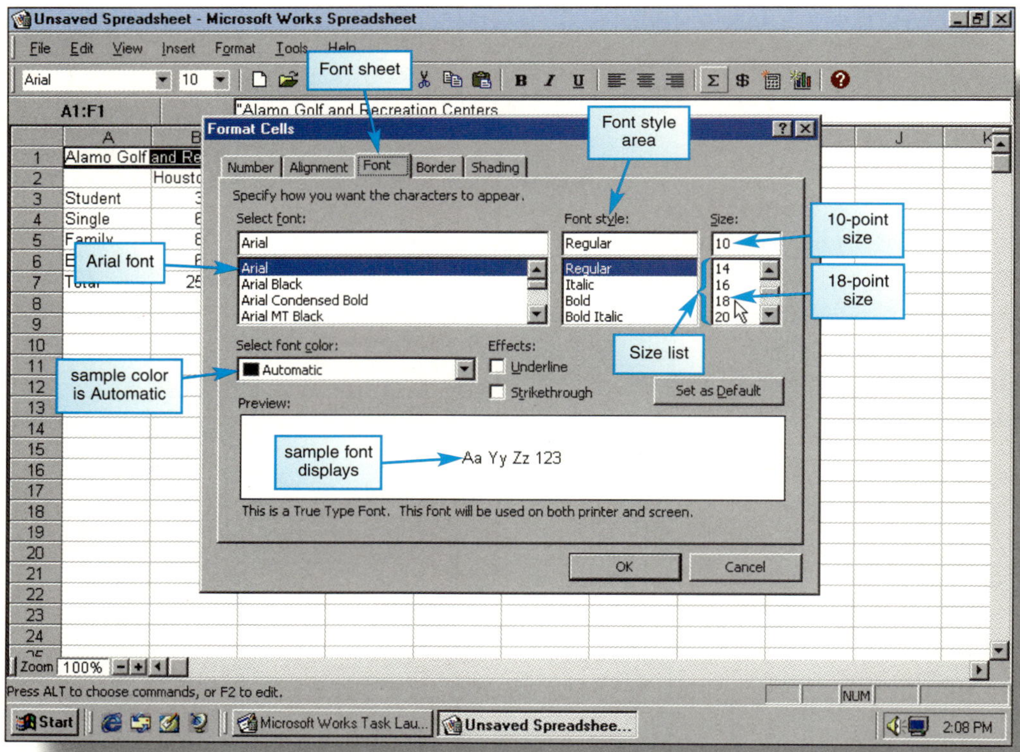

FIGURE 2-39

5 Click 18. Point to the Select font color box arrow.

Works displays a preview of 18-point Arial text in the Preview area (Figure 2-40).

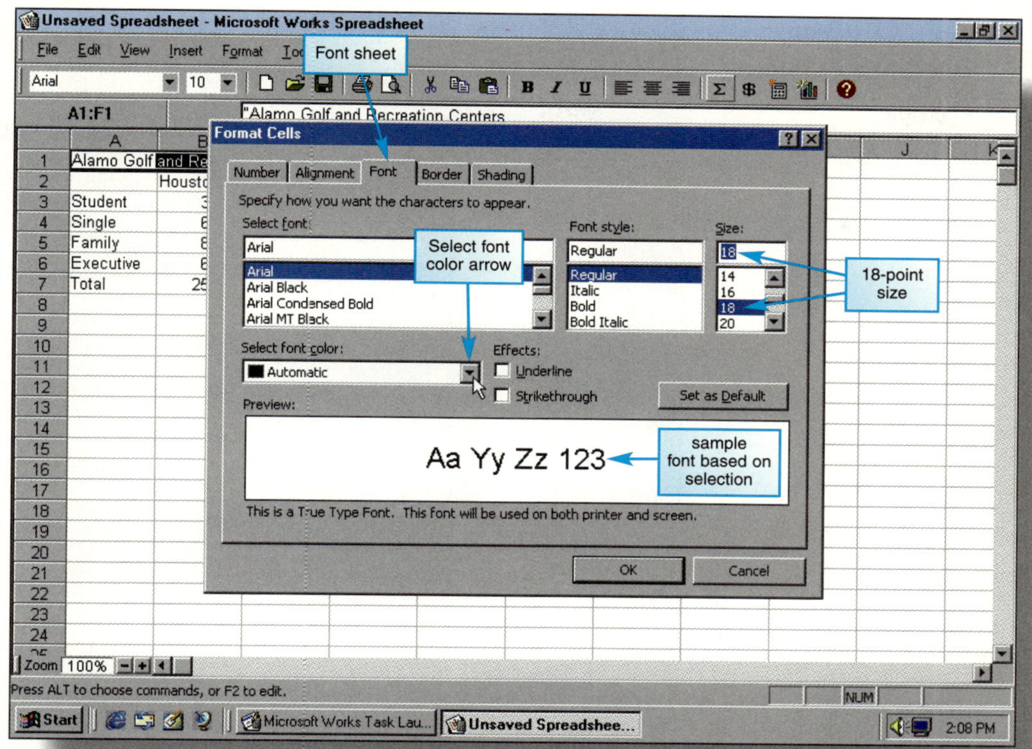

FIGURE 2-40

6 Click the Select font color box arrow. Scroll down and then point to the color White.

The Select font color list displays (Figure 2-41).

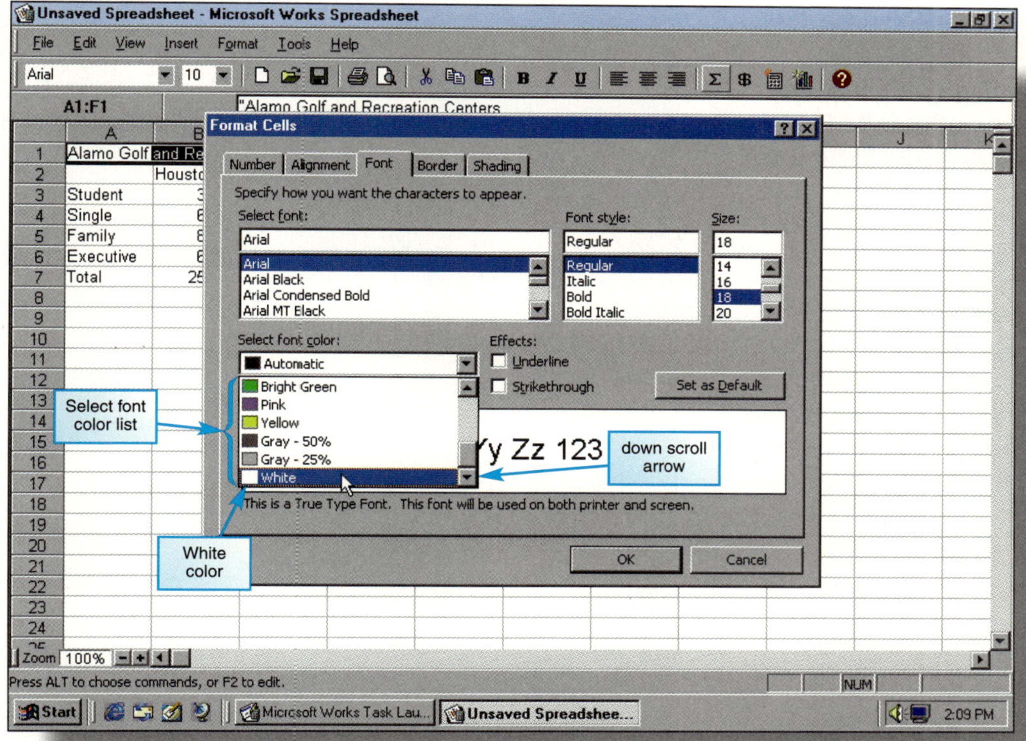

FIGURE 2-41

7 Click White and then point to the Shading tab.

The color white and the word, White, display in the Select font color list (Figure 2-42).

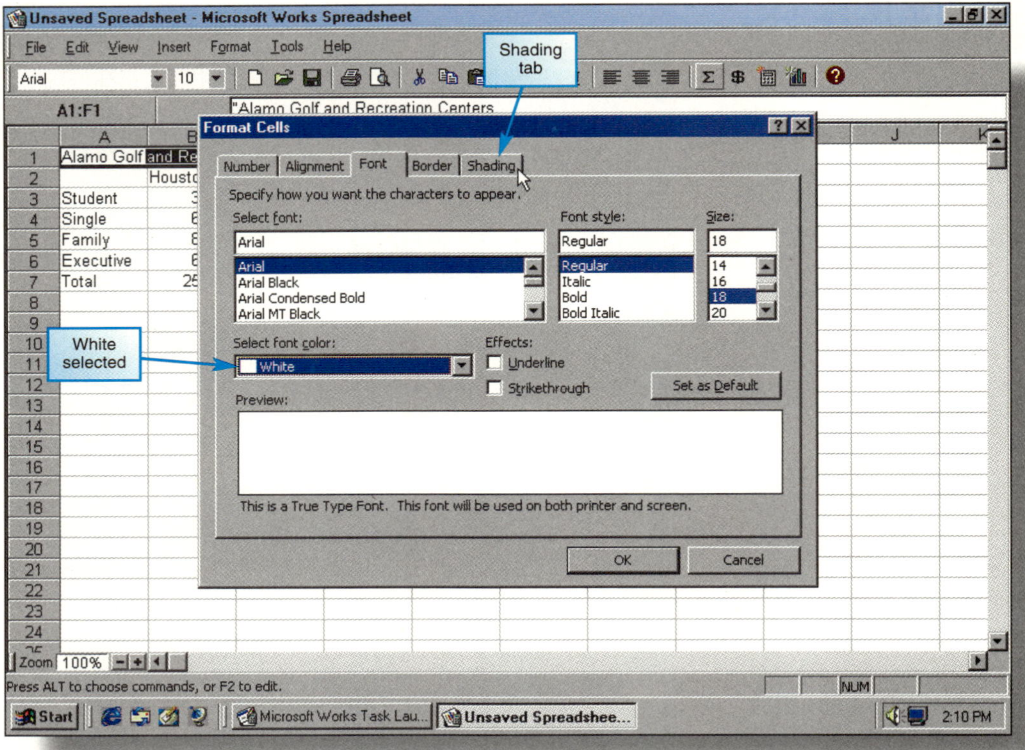

FIGURE 2-42

8 Click the Shading tab. When the Shading sheet displays, point to the Solid (100%) pattern in the Pattern list.

Works displays the Shading sheet (Figure 2-43). A series of options display in the Pattern list. The first option is selected and contains the word, None. This option is followed by a series of boxes with various patterns you can select. The first pattern below None is the Solid (100%) pattern.

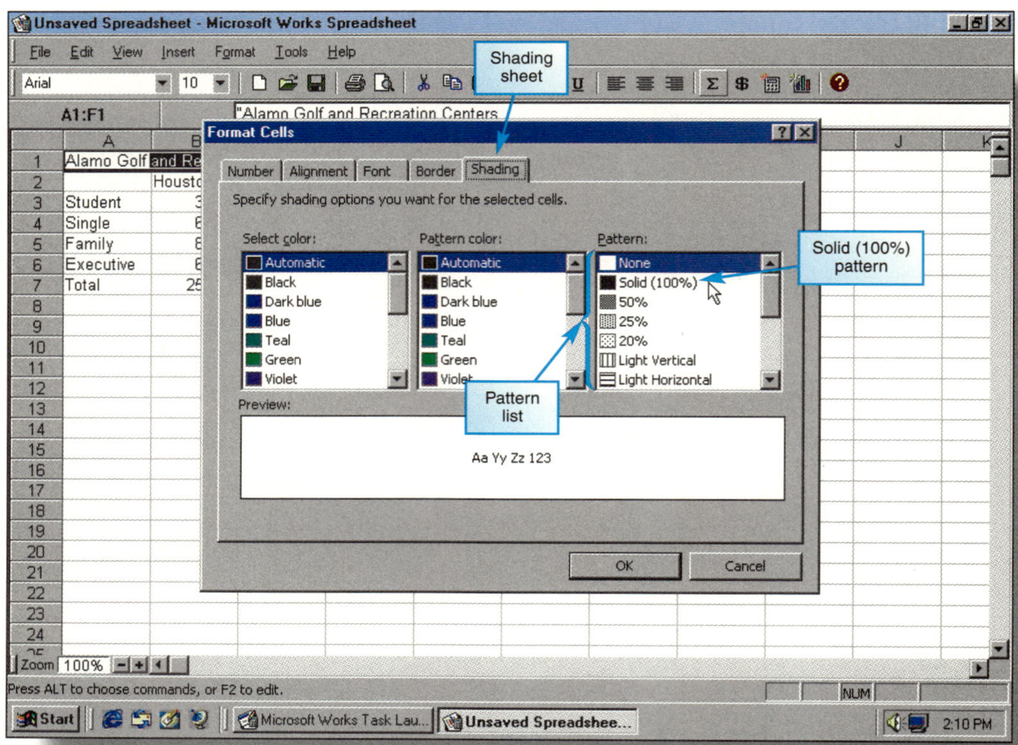

FIGURE 2-43

9 Click Solid (100%). In the Pattern color list, scroll through and then point to the color Dark Red.

The Solid (100%) pattern in the Pattern list is selected (Figure 2-44).

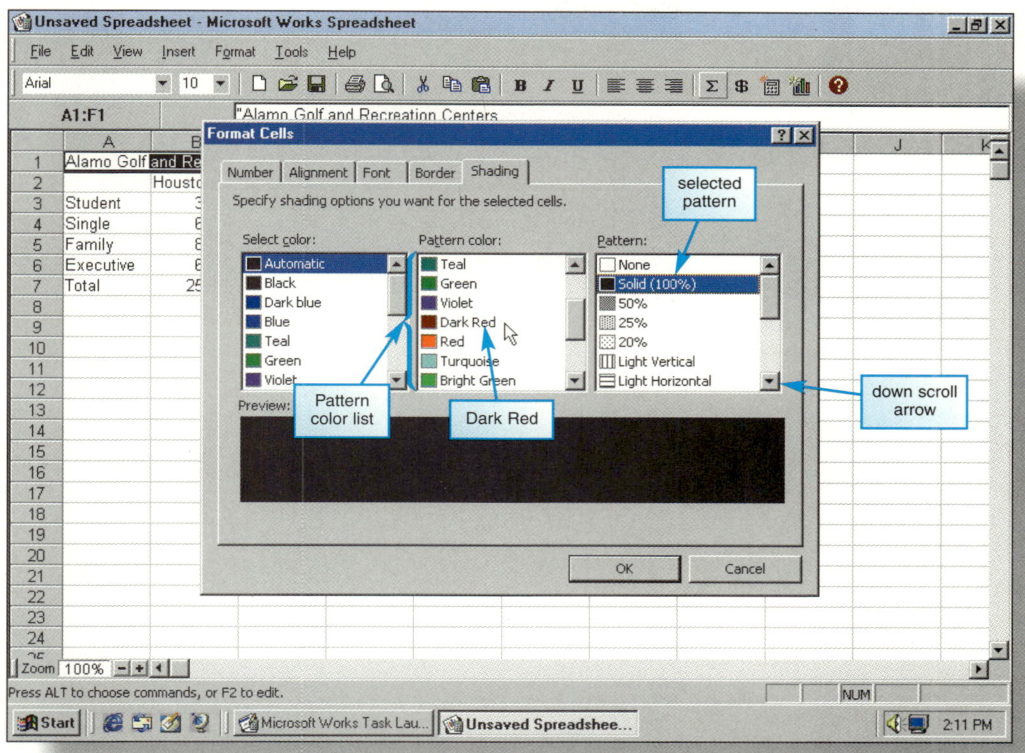

FIGURE 2-44

10 Click Dark Red. Point to the OK button.

Dark Red is selected in the Pattern color list. The Solid (100%) pattern changes to dark red. A preview of the Solid (100%) dark red pattern displays in the Preview area (Figure 2-45).

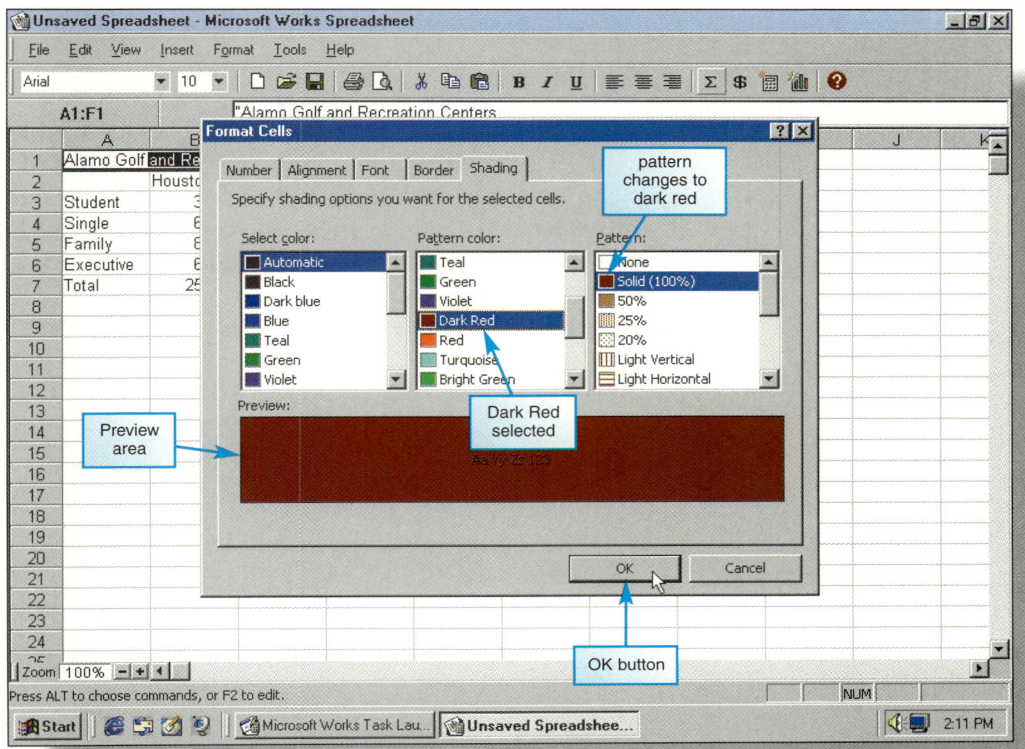

FIGURE 2-45

11 Click the OK button. Click any cell to remove the selection.

Works displays a dark red color in cells A1 through F1 (Figure 2-46). The title displays in white 18-point Arial font and is centered across columns A through F. Notice that when the font size is increased to 18 points, Works automatically increases the height of row 1 so the enlarged text displays properly.

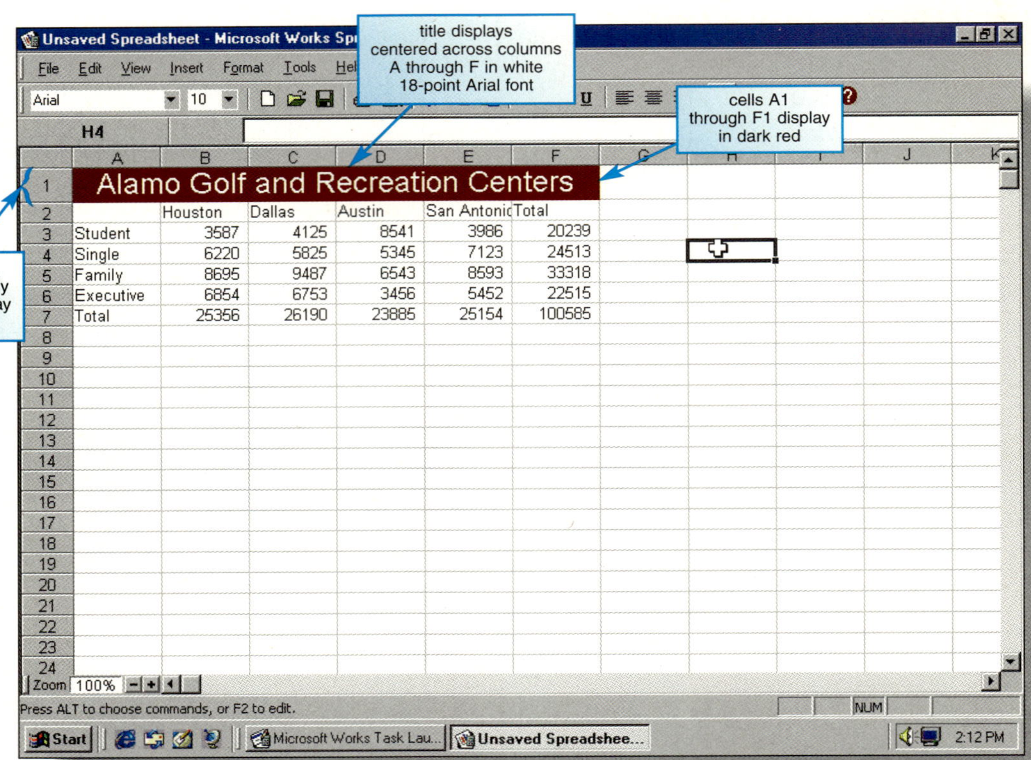

	A	B	C	D	E	F
1	Alamo Golf and Recreation Centers					
2		Houston	Dallas	Austin	San Antonic	Total
3	Student	3587	4125	8541	3986	20239
4	Single	6220	5825	5345	7123	24513
5	Family	8695	9487	6543	8593	33318
6	Executive	6854	6753	3456	5452	22515
7	Total	25356	26190	23885	25154	100585

FIGURE 2-46

Other Ways

1. On Format menu click Alignment, Font, Border, or Shading, click OK button

More About

AutoFormat

After you apply a format to a selected range with the AutoFormat command, you can apply additional formatting. For example, you can increase the thickness of a border or change the shading color of the cells.

Using the AutoFormat Command

Works provides an AutoFormat feature that enables you to format a spreadsheet in a variety of styles without going through a series of individual steps to select color, font and font styles, borders, and so forth. AutoFormat allows you to select one of 19 different, predefined formats to apply to a spreadsheet. AutoFormat sets the alignment, fonts, patterns, column width, cell height, and borders automatically to match the style option you select.

The following steps explain how to use the Works AutoFormat feature.

Steps To Use AutoFormat

1 **Select cells A2:F7 by dragging the mouse pointer from cell A2 through cell F7. Click Format on the menu bar and then point to the AutoFormat command.**

Cells A2 through F7 are selected (Figure 2-47). The Format menu displays.

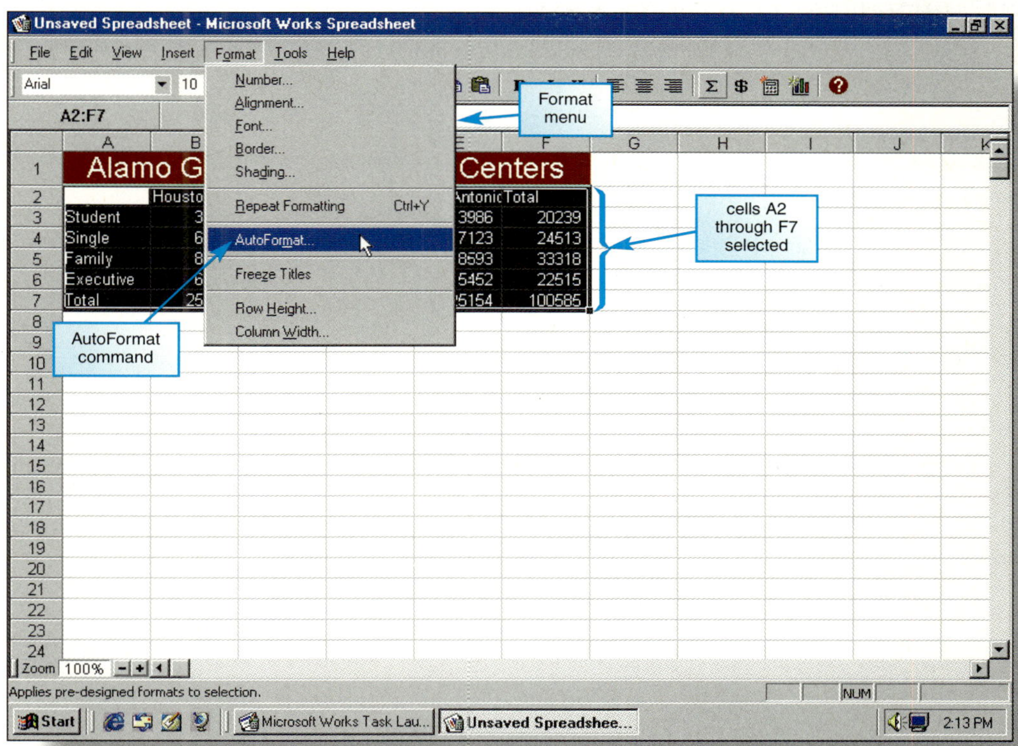

FIGURE 2-47

2 **Click AutoFormat.**

Works displays the AutoFormat dialog box (Figure 2-48). The Select a format list displays a list of preformatted styles. You can click the down scroll arrow to display additional styles. None is the default format. A sample of this style displays in the Preview area. The Preview area shows how the selected cells in the spreadsheet will display based on the selection in the Select a format list.

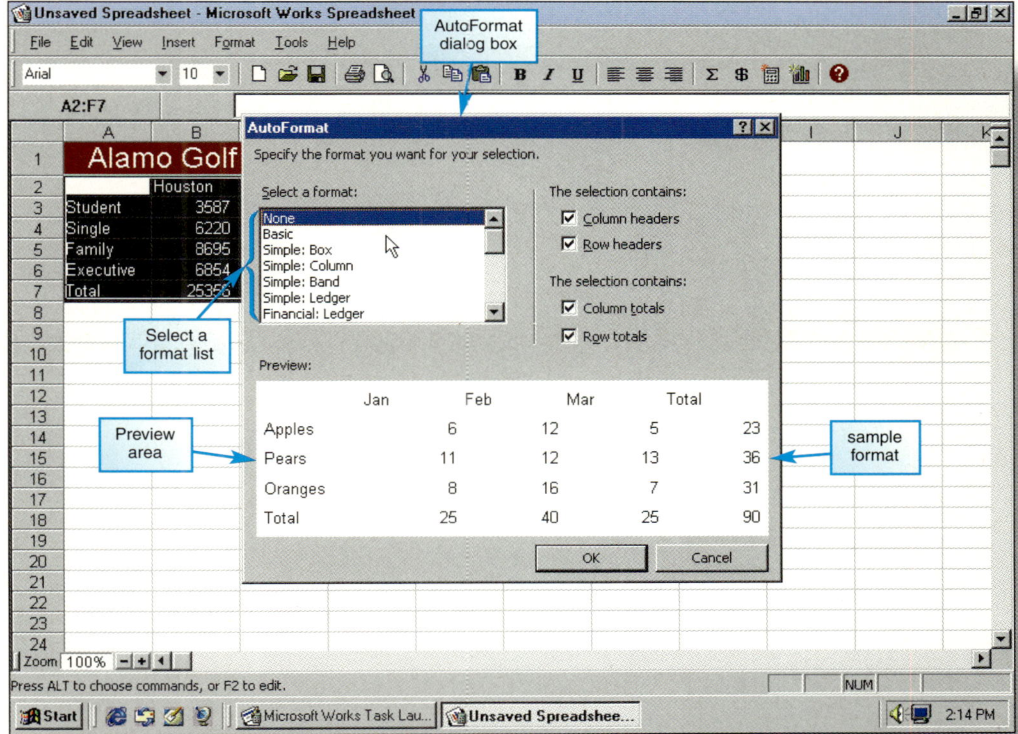

FIGURE 2-48

3 **In the Select a format list, click Simple: Box. Make certain that the Column headers, Row headers, Column totals, and Row totals check boxes are selected and then point to the OK button.**

Works displays a sample of the Simple: Box style in the Preview area (Figure 2-49). A check mark in the four check boxes specifies that you want Works to format the column titles, row titles, column totals, and row totals for easy identification as shown in the Preview area.

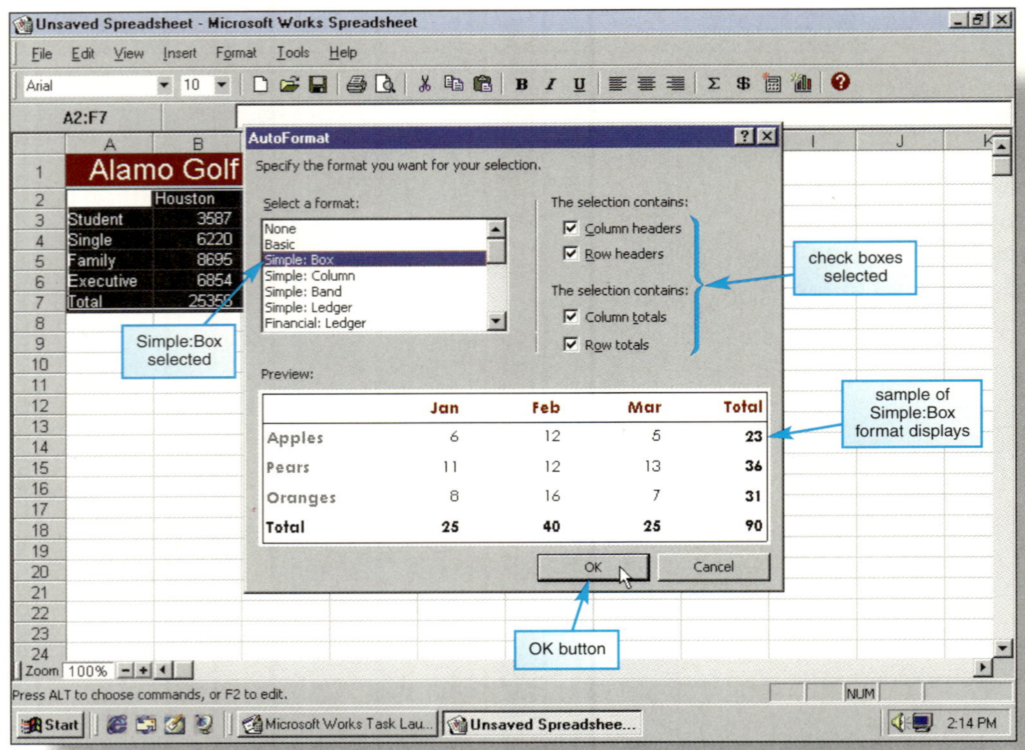

FIGURE 2-49

4 **Click the OK button. Click any cell to remove the selection.**

Works applies the predefined format style Simple:Box to the spreadsheet (Figure 2-50). The spreadsheet displays with the fonts, font styles, colors, and borders as illustrated.

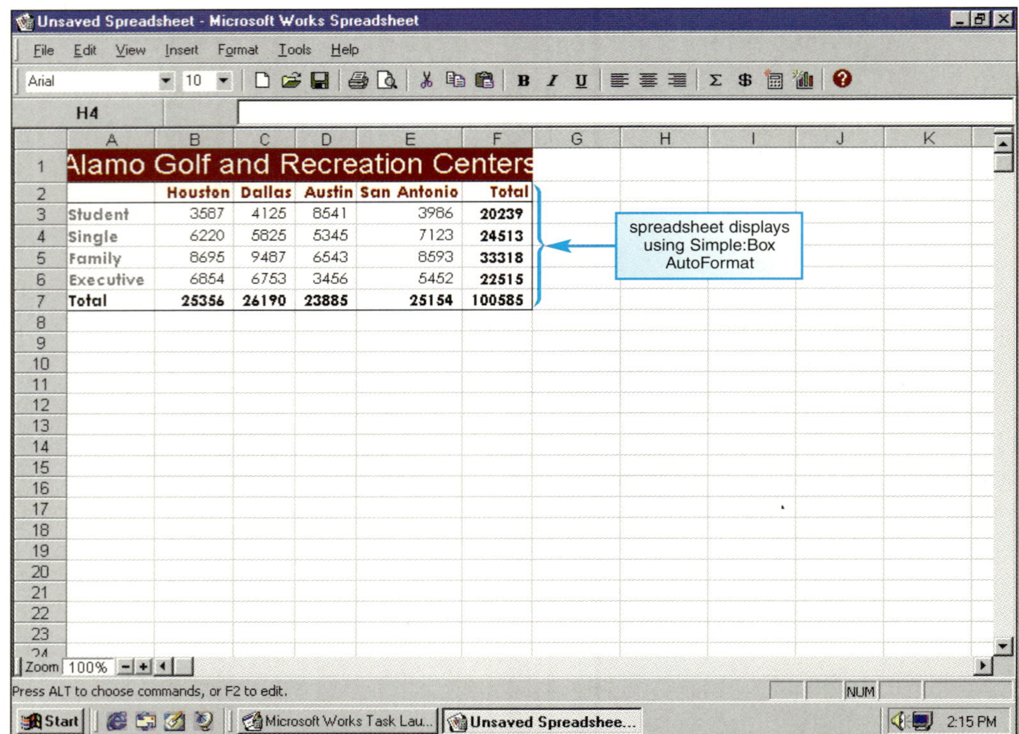

FIGURE 2-50

The AutoFormat feature changes column width to accommodate the numbers in each of the columns. As a result, the first letter and the last letter of the previously formatted title are partially cutoff due to the column widths created by the Simple:Box AutoFormat. Therefore, the column width of columns A through F should be changed to 12 to improve the readability of the spreadsheet and to allow the entire title to display.

The Undo Feature

Remember the Undo feature from the Word Processor tool? It is available with the Spreadsheet tool as well. Click Undo on the Edit menu immediately after performing the operation you want to undo.

Changing Column Widths

Works provides the capability to change each column individually or you can change the width of a group of columns. In the following example, the columns will be changed as a group, which requires selecting all columns to be changed and then clicking the Column Width command on the shortcut menu. To complete this task, perform the following steps.

To Change Column Widths

1 Position the mouse pointer on column heading A and drag through column headings B, C, D, E, and F to select columns A through F. Click Format on the menu bar and then point to Column Width.

Columns A through F are selected (Figure 2-51). The Format menu displays.

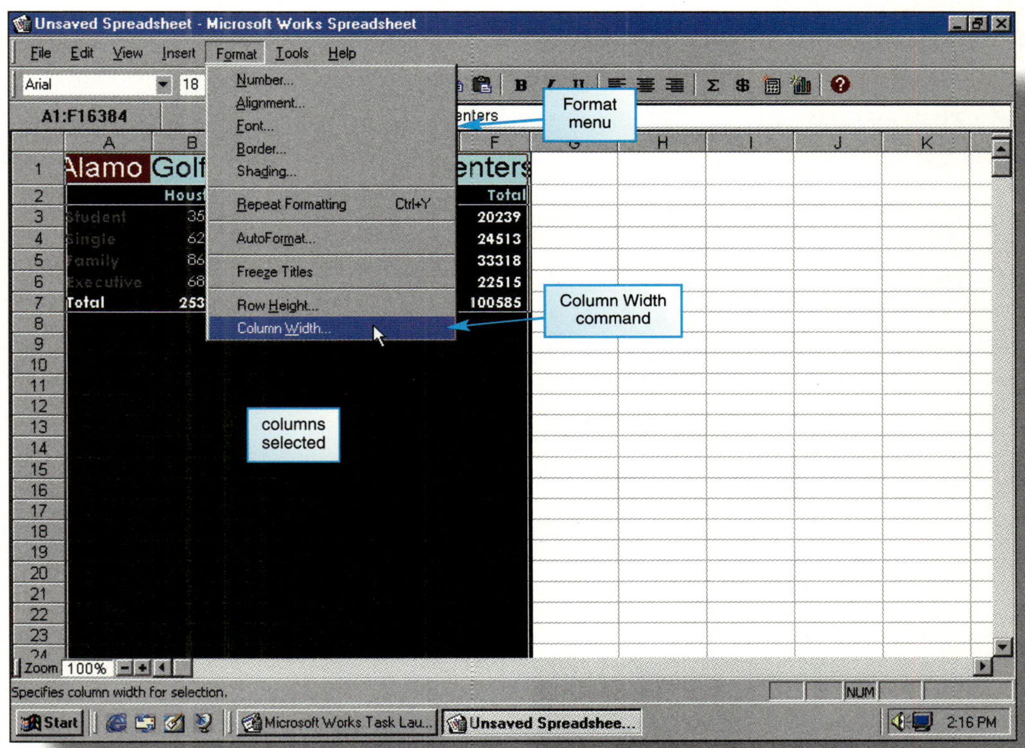

FIGURE 2-51

2 Click Column Width. When the Column Width dialog box displays, make sure the Set column width (in characters) to option button is selected, click the up arrow twice in the Set column width (in characters) to text box to display the number 12. Point to the OK button.

Works displays the Column Width dialog box (Figure 2-52). The Set column width (in characters) to option button is selected, and 12 displays in the text box.

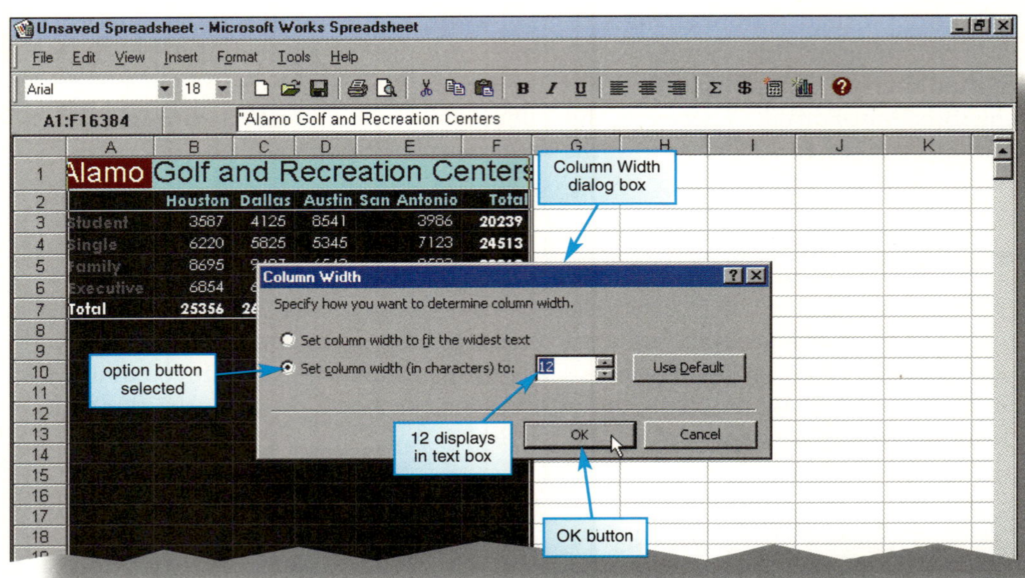

FIGURE 2-52

3 Click the OK button. Click any cell to remove the selection.

Works makes columns A through F twelve characters wide (Figure 2-53). Notice most of column J and all of column K have moved off the screen.

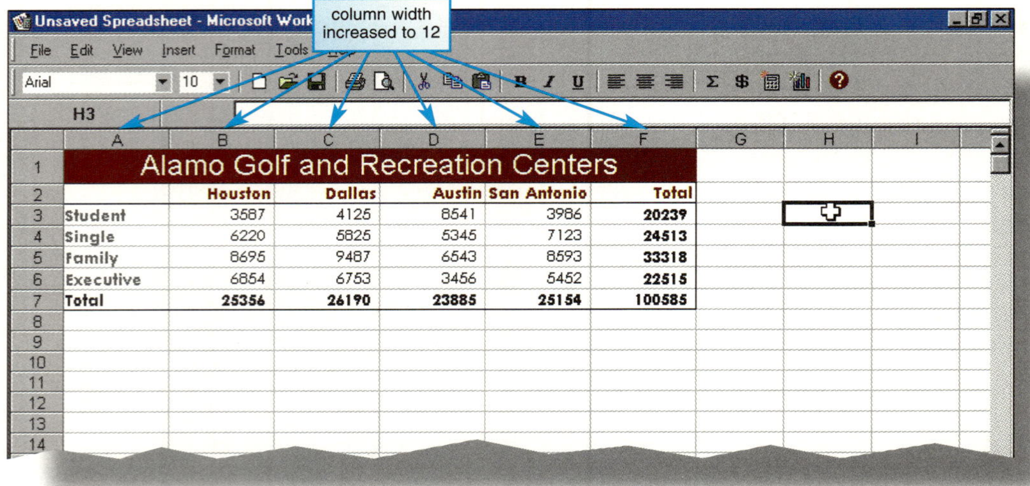

FIGURE 2-53

The default column width is 10 characters. You change column widths for several reasons. First, changing the column width increases the space between each column and often makes the spreadsheet easier to read. Also, in some instances, the values you enter into a cell or the values Works calculates in a cell will not fit in a 10-character wide cell. When this occurs, you must change the width of the column to a size that can accommodate the entry in the cell. In addition, adding formatting such as the Comma format may require increasing the column width.

Works provides a number of methods that can be used to change the column width. To quickly change the width of a single column, place the mouse pointer over the column border (the right or left vertical line in the column label area) and drag. When the column is as large or small as you want, release the mouse button.

To quickly adjust the column width for best fit, double-click the column letter. This will adjust the column width to fit the longest entry in the column. To obtain best fit, you also can click the Set column width to fit the widest text option button in the Column Width dialog box. If more than one column is selected, Works applies an appropriate width to each column.

If, at a later time, you want to change these columns back to the default value, select the desired columns, right-click the selected columns, click the Column Width command on the shortcut menu, and then click the Standard button in the Column Width dialog box.

Microsoft Works 6

Now you can view Webcast seminars and training online. You will find sessions on the Basics of Works troubleshooting, and other relevant topics and products. For more information on Webcast Training and Seminars, visit the Works 6 More About Web page (www.scsite.com/works6/more.htm) and then click Seminars.

Number Format

The numeric values in rows 3, 4, 5, 6, and 7 are to be formatted with commas. In Works, this requires the use of the Number format. When you use the **Separators or Number format**, by default, Works places two digits to the right of the decimal point (including zeroes), and a comma separates every three digits to the left of the decimal point. Because the numeric values in rows 3 through 7 are whole numbers, you will apply the Number format and specify zero digits to the right of the decimal point and a comma separating every three digits to the left of the decimal point. To format numeric values in the Number format, complete the following steps.

To Display Numbers with the Number Format

1 Select the range of cells B3:F7 by dragging through cells B3 through F7. Right-click the selected range and point to the Format command on the shortcut menu.

Cells B3 through F7 are selected (Figure 2-54). The shortcut menu displays.

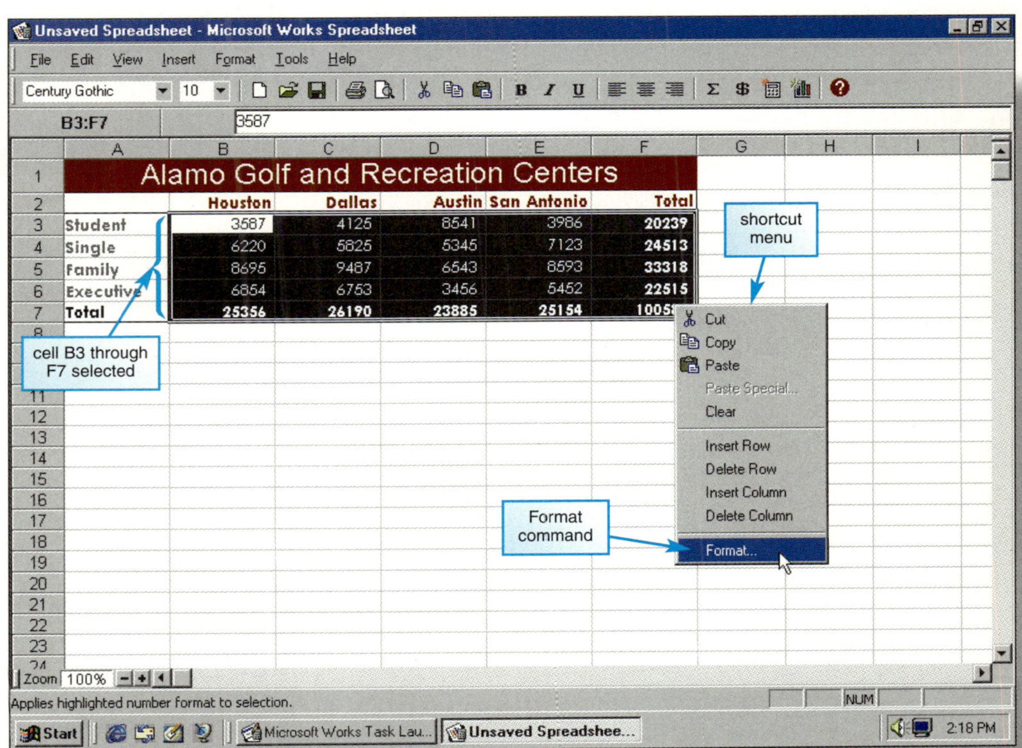

FIGURE 2-54

2 **Click Format. If necessary, when the Format Cells dialog box displays, click the Number tab. Click Number in the Select format type list. Click the down arrow in the Set decimal places text box twice to display the number 0. Make sure that the Use separators in numbers over 999 check box is selected and then point to the OK button.**

The Format Cells dialog box displays (Figure 2-55). Number is selected in the Select format type box and zero displays in the Set decimal places text box. The Use separators in numbers over 999 check box is selected, and a sample of the designated format displays in the Preview area.

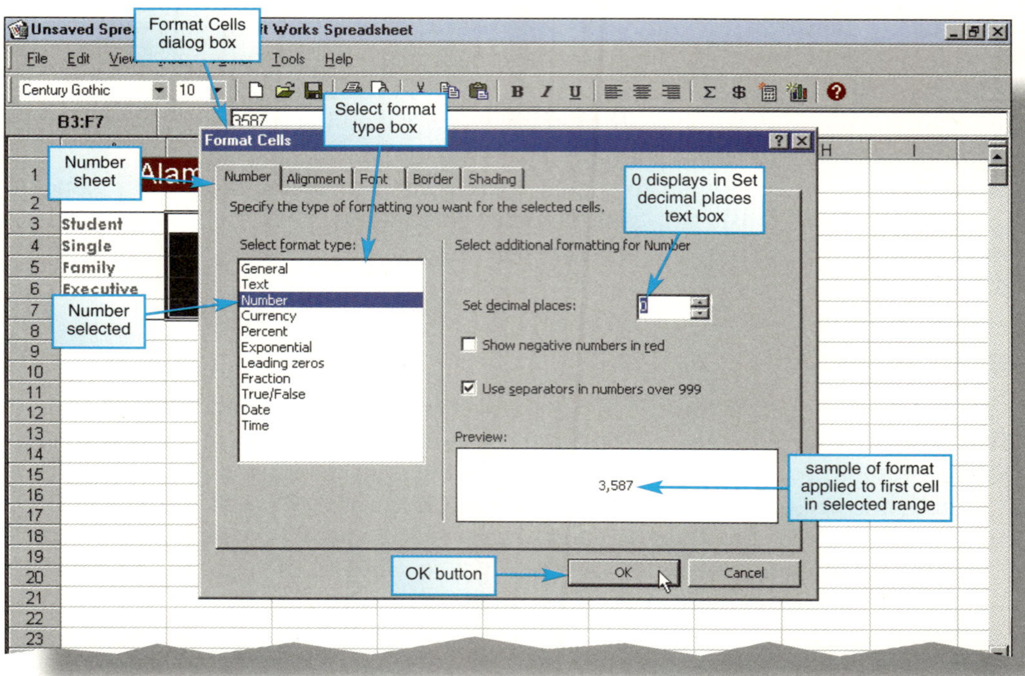

FIGURE 2-55

3 **Click the OK button. Click any cell to remove the selection.**

Works formats the range of cells B3:F7 using the Number format with commas every three digits to the left (Figure 2-56).

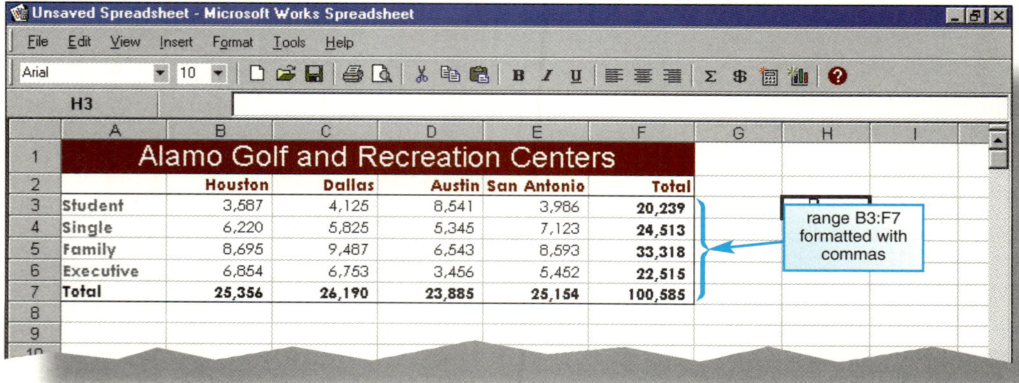

FIGURE 2-56

Other Ways

1. On Format menu click Number, click Number, click OK button
2. Press CTRL+, (comma)

Checking the Spelling on the Spreadsheet

The spreadsheet now is complete. All the text and data have been entered and formatted. You now should check the spelling on the spreadsheet using the Spelling command on the Tools menu. To check the spelling, complete the following steps.

TO CHECK SPELLING

1. Click Tools on the menu bar.
2. Click Spelling.
3. If any errors are found, perform the steps to correct the errors.

Saving a Spreadsheet

If you accidentally turn off your computer or if electrical power fails, you will lose all your work on the spreadsheet unless you have saved it on disk. Therefore, after you have worked on a spreadsheet for a period of time, or when you complete the spreadsheet, you should save it. When saving the spreadsheet for the first time, use the Save button on the toolbar.

You can save a spreadsheet on hard disk or on a floppy disk. In this project, you are to save the spreadsheet on a floppy disk located in drive A. You can use the following procedure, however, for either hard disk or floppy disk. Perform the following steps to save the spreadsheet on a floppy disk.

Saving a Works Spreadsheet

When saving a Works spreadsheet for the first time, check to make sure that Works 6.0 (*.xlr) displays in the Save as type box. If it is not displayed, click the Save as type box arrow and then click Works 6.0 (*.xlr).

To Save a Spreadsheet

1 **Point to the Save button on the toolbar (Figure 2-57).**

Unsaved Spreadsheet - Microsoft Works Spreadsheet

Save button

	A	B	C	D	E	F
1	Alamo Golf and Recreation Centers					
2		Houston	Dallas	Austin	San Antonio	Total
3	Student	3,587	4,125	8,541	3,986	20,239
4	Single	6,220	5,825	5,345	7,123	24,513
5	Family	8,695	9,487	6,543	8,593	33,318
6	Executive	6,854	6,753	3,456	5,452	22,515
7	Total	25,356	26,190	23,885	25,154	100,585

FIGURE 2-57

2 **Click the Save button. When the Save As dialog box displays, type** `Alamo Memberships` **in the File name text box. Click the Save in box arrow. Click 3½ Floppy (A:) in the Save in list and then point to the Save button.**

Works displays the Save As dialog box (Figure 2-58). The file name you type displays in the File name text box. This is the name Works will use to store the file. Drive A is selected in the Save in box.

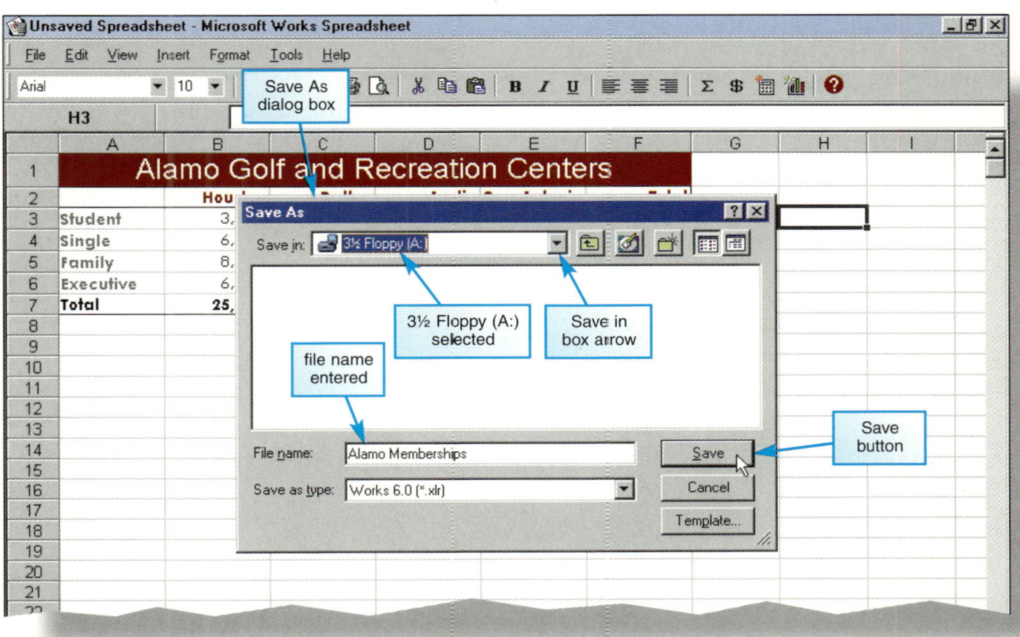

FIGURE 2-58

Click the Save button.

Works saves the file on drive A and displays the file name, Alamo Memberships.xlr, on the title bar (Figure 2-59). The Works spreadsheet extension, .xlr, may not display depending on how your computer is configured.

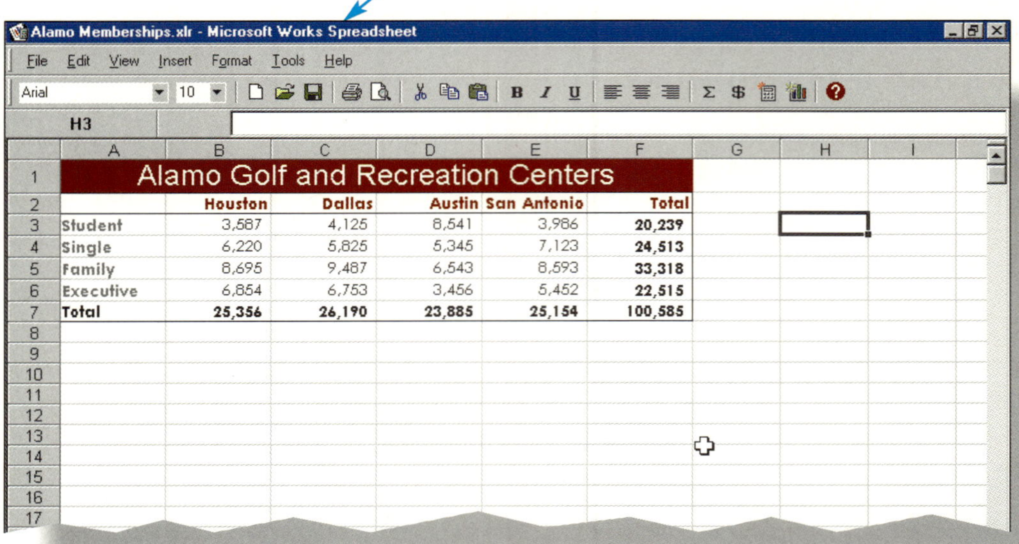

FIGURE 2-59

Other Ways

1. On File menu click Save As, enter file name, click OK button
2. Press CTRL+S

Printing a Spreadsheet

After you save the spreadsheet, the next step is to print it. To print a spreadsheet, click Print on the File menu, as explained in the following steps.

To Print a Spreadsheet

1 Click File on the menu bar and then point to Print.

The File menu displays (Figure 2-60).

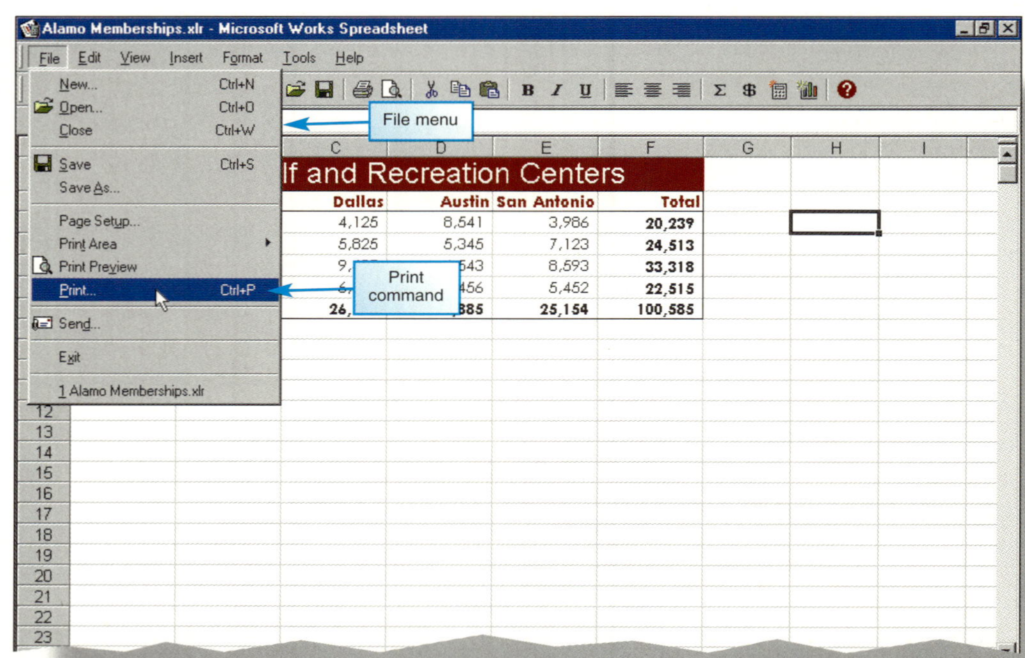

FIGURE 2-60

2 **Click Print. When the Print dialog box displays, point to the OK button.**

The Print dialog box displays (Figure 2-61). The default settings in the dialog box are that one copy of the spreadsheet is to print and all pages in the document are to print.

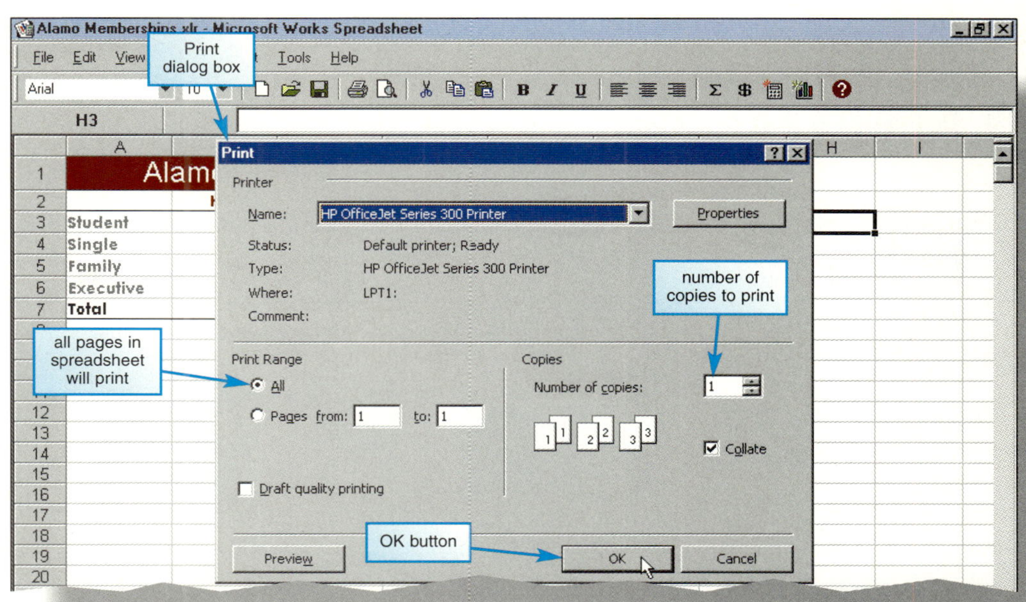

FIGURE 2-61

3 **Click the OK button.**

Works momentarily displays a Printing dialog box, then prints the document on the printer (Figure 2-62).

Alamo Golf and Recreation Centers

	Houston	Dallas	Austin	San Antonio	Total
Student	3,587	4,125	8,541	3,986	**20,239**
Single	6,220	5,825	5,345	7,123	**24,513**
Family	8,695	9,487	6,543	8,593	**33,318**
Executive	6,854	6,753	3,456	5,452	**22,515**
Total	**25,356**	**26,190**	**23,885**	**25,154**	**100,585**

FIGURE 2-62

Other Ways

1. Click Print button on toolbar
2. Press CTRL+P

If a color printer is used, the output will appear as shown in Figure 2-62. If a black and white printer is used, the spreadsheet will print in shades of black, gray, and white.

If you have used the Print command previously and know that the entries you want are contained in the Print dialog box, you can click the Print button on the toolbar to print the spreadsheet.

Charting a Spreadsheet

In addition to creating and printing the spreadsheet, Project 2 requires a portion of the data in the spreadsheet to be charted. A **chart** is a graphical representation of the data in the spreadsheet. A spreadsheet file can contain a total of eight charts. You are to create a 3-D Bar chart of the memberships for Houston, Dallas, Austin, and San Antonio for each of the four categories (Student, Single, Family, and Executive). With a 3-D Bar chart, memberships are represented by a series of vertical bars that are shaded to give a three-dimensional effect.

To create the 3-D Bar chart, perform the steps below.

To Create a 3-D Bar Chart

1 Select the cells to be charted (A2:E6) and then point to the New Chart button on the toolbar.

The selected cells include the column titles, row titles, and memberships for Houston, Dallas, Austin, and San Antonio (Figure 2-63). The totals are not included because they do not present meaningful comparisons on a Bar chart.

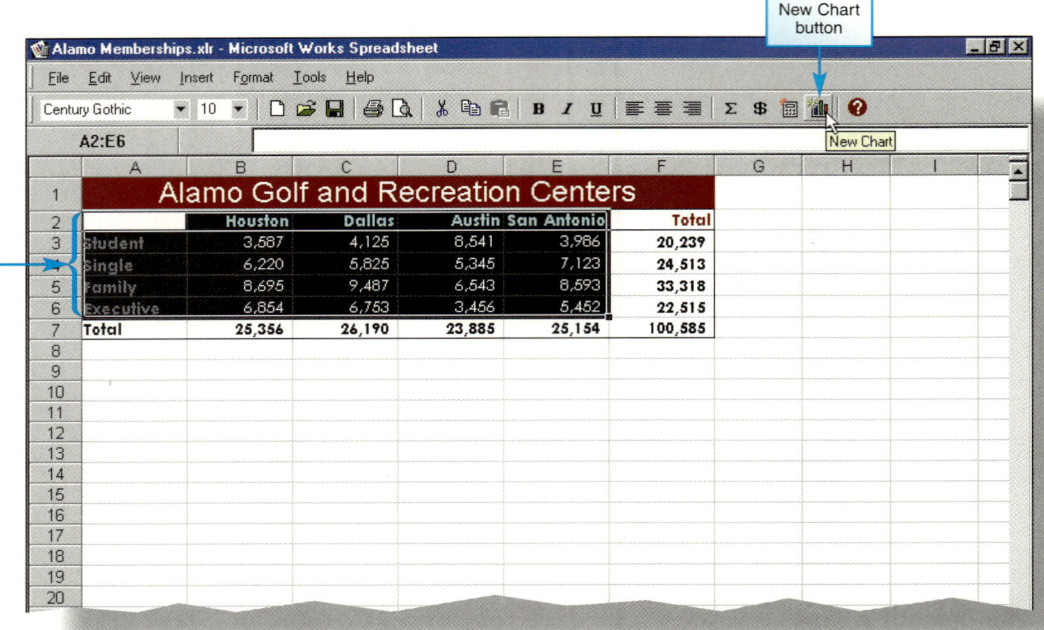

FIGURE 2-63

2 Click the New Chart button. When the New Chart dialog box displays, point to the 3-D Bar chart in the Chart type area located on the Basic Options sheet.

Works displays the New Chart dialog box (Figure 2-64). Twelve types of charts display in the Chart type area on the Basic Options sheet. The Works default chart (Bar chart) is selected. The chart name that is selected (Bar) displays above the chart types. A sample of the chart that will display is shown in the Preview area.

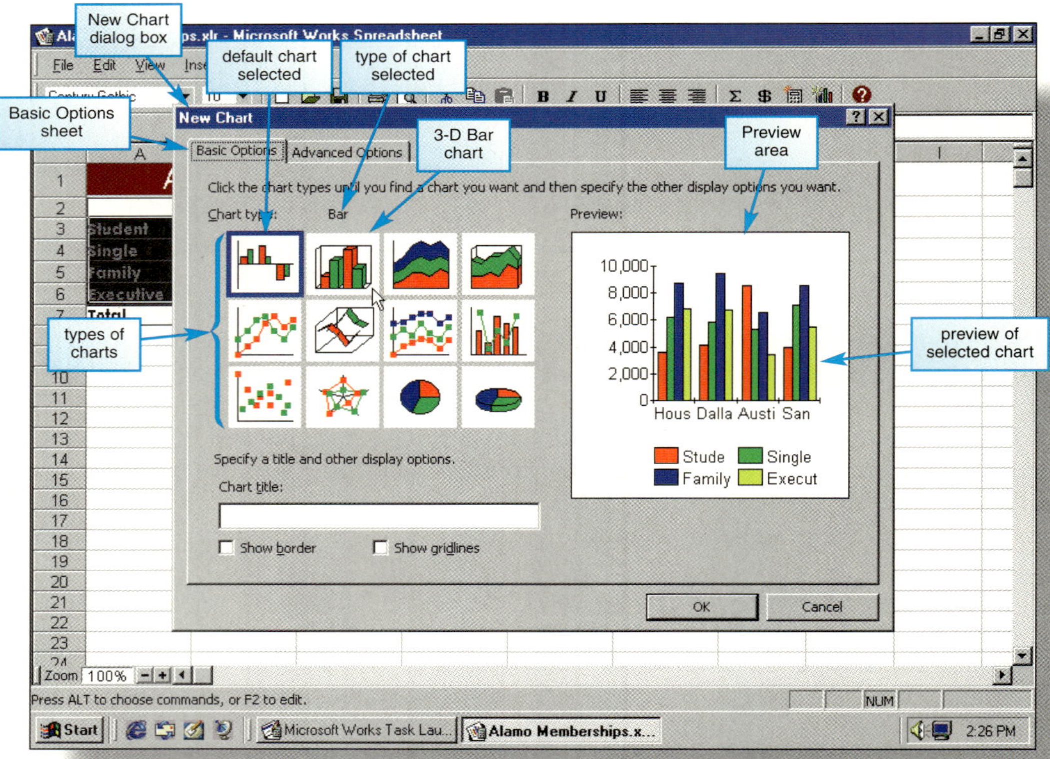

FIGURE 2-64

3 **Click the 3-D Bar chart icon in the Chart type area. Press the TAB key and type** `Alamo Golf and Recreation Centers` **in the Chart title text box. Click Show border and then click Show Gridlines below the chart title. Point to the OK button.**

The 3-D Bar chart is selected in the Chart type area (Figure 2-65). The title for the chart displays in the Chart title text box. The check mark in the Show border check box instructs Works to place a border around the chart. The check mark in the Show gridlines check box informs Works to include gridlines on the chart. The Preview area contains a sample of the chart that will display. You can enter a maximum of 39 characters including spaces in the Chart title text box.

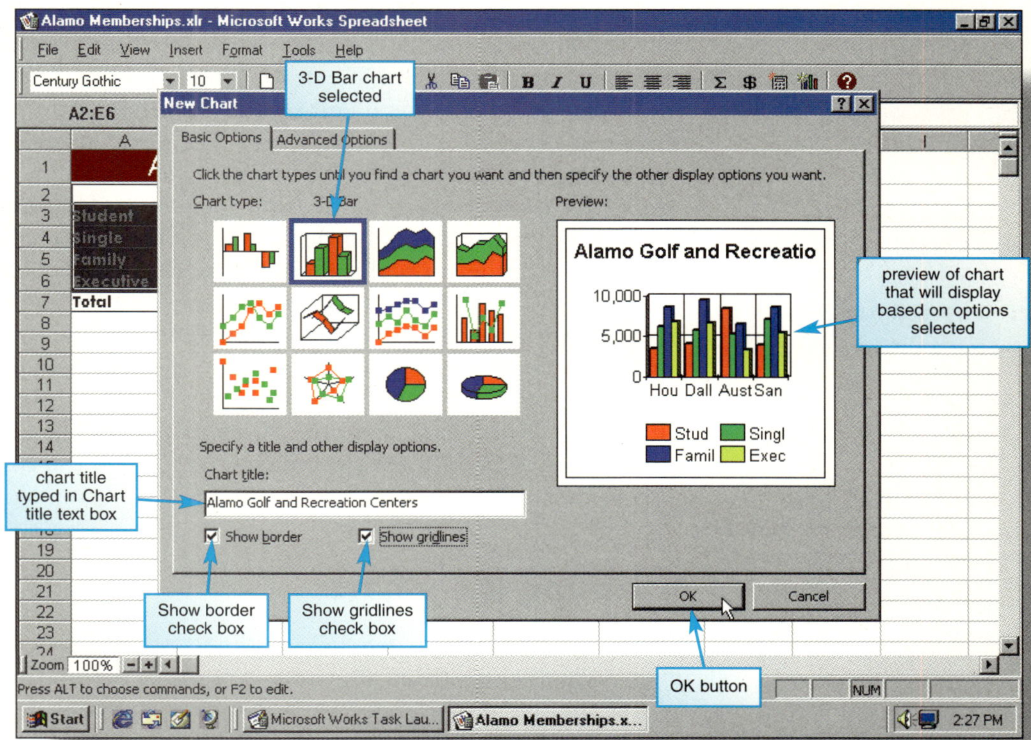

FIGURE 2-65

Click the OK button.

Works displays the chart with the title, Alamo Memberships.xlr - Chart1, in the title bar (Figure 2-66). The chart title displays centered above the chart. The extension, .xlr, may not display depending on how your computer is configured.

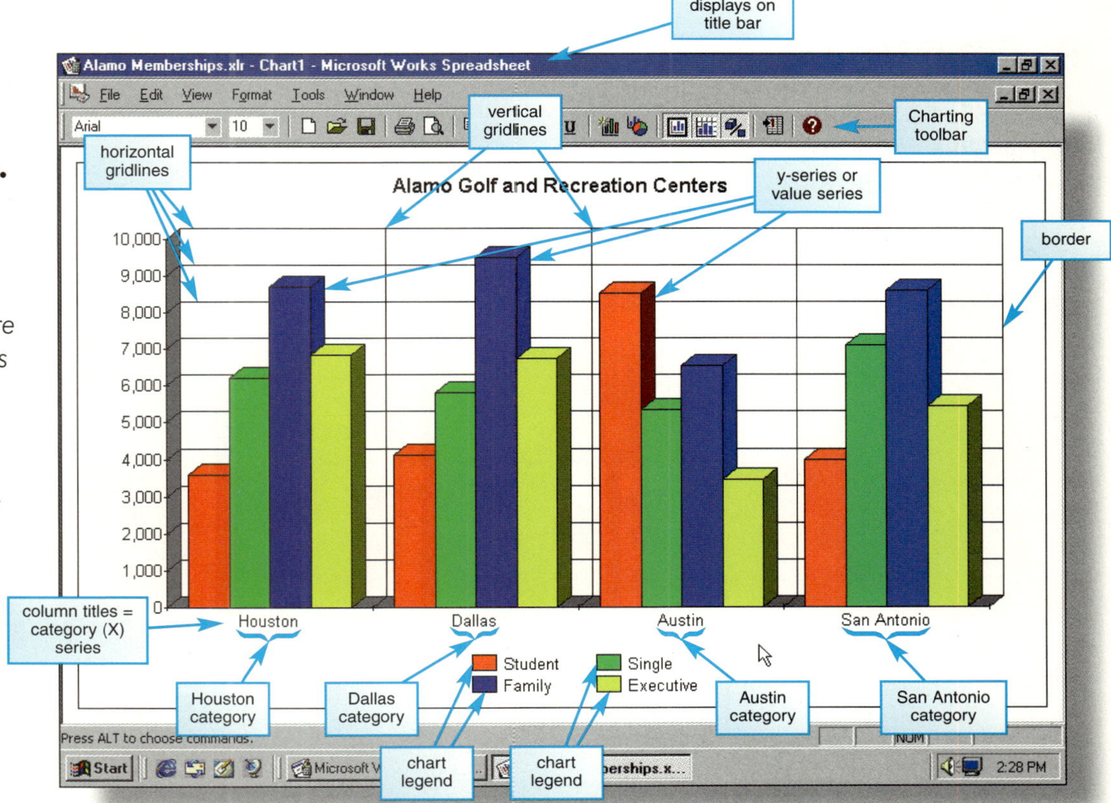

FIGURE 2-66

The cluster of bars for each city (Houston, Dallas, Austin, and San Antonio) is called a **category**. All the category labels together are called the **category (X) series**. Each bar (red for Student, green for Single, blue for Family, and yellow for Executive) represents the memberships for each item in the spreadsheet and is called the **Y-series**, or the **value series**. The chart legend indicates the item each color represents. The Charting toolbar displays below the menu bar. The horizontal gridlines originate from each number on the y-axis. The vertical gridlines separate each category on the x-axis. A border displays around the chart.

To remove the vertical gridlines from the chart, click the Vertical (Y) axis command on the Format menu in the chart window. In the Format Vertical Axis dialog box, remove the check mark from the Show gridlines check box. To remove the horizontal gridlines from the chart, click the Horizontal (X) axis command on the Format menu in the chart window. In the Format Horizontal Axis dialog box, remove the check mark from the Show gridlines check box.

To remove the border around the chart, click the Border command on the Format menu.

> **More About**
>
> **Printing a Chart**
>
> If you work with a color monitor but print in black and white, the colors you see on screen are replaced with patterns in black and white. To view the chart, as it will appear when printed, click Display as Printed on the View menu. Works displays the chart as it will appear when printed in black and white. If you would like to print in color, however, and you have a color printer, this option will display how the chart will print in color.

Printing the Chart

You can print the chart by clicking the Print button on the Charting toolbar. By default, Works will print the chart in portrait orientation. Most users find it better to print bar charts in landscape orientation to better duplicate display proportions. Other charts may look better when printed in portrait orientation. Perform the following steps to print the chart in landscape orientation.

To Print a Chart

1 Click File on the menu bar and then point to the Page Setup command.

The File menu displays (Figure 2-67).

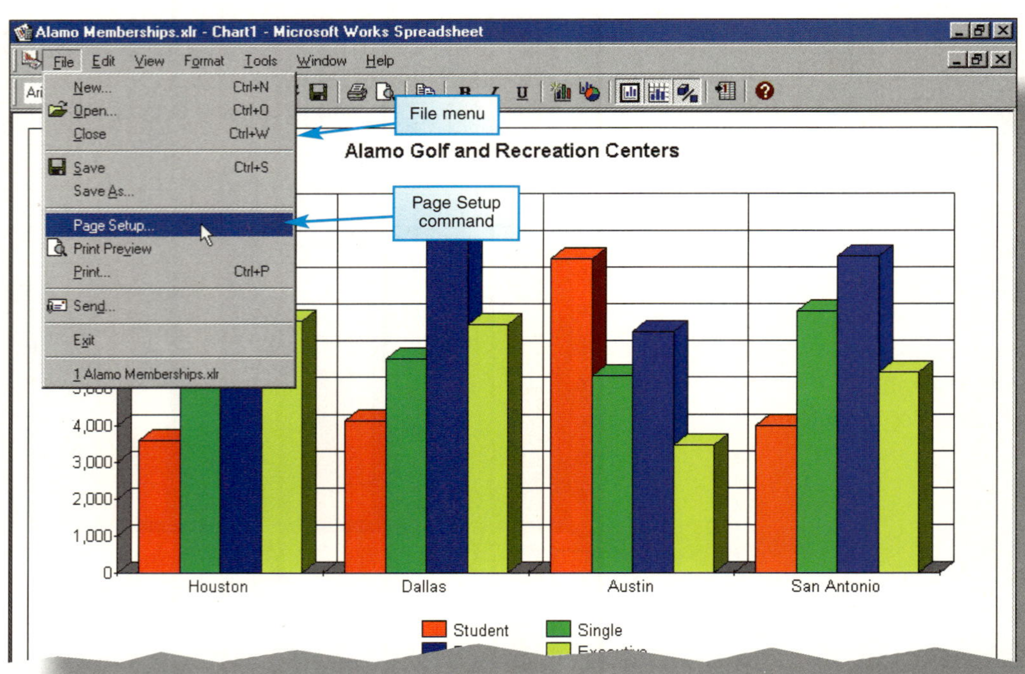

FIGURE 2-67

2 Click Page Setup. When the Page Setup dialog box displays, point to the Source, Size & Orientation tab.

The Page Setup dialog box displays (Figure 2-68).

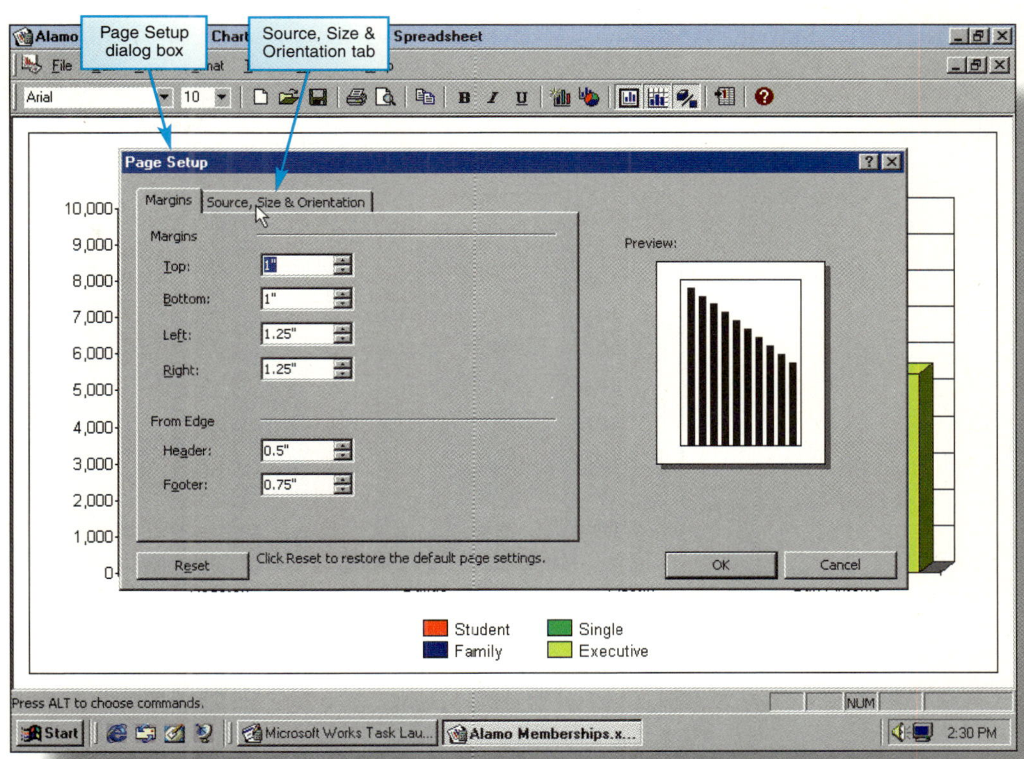

FIGURE 2-68

3 Click the Source, Size & Orientation tab. Click Landscape in the Orientation area. Point to the OK button.

Works displays the Source, Size & Orientation sheet (Figure 2-69). The Landscape option instructs Works to print the chart in landscape orientation.

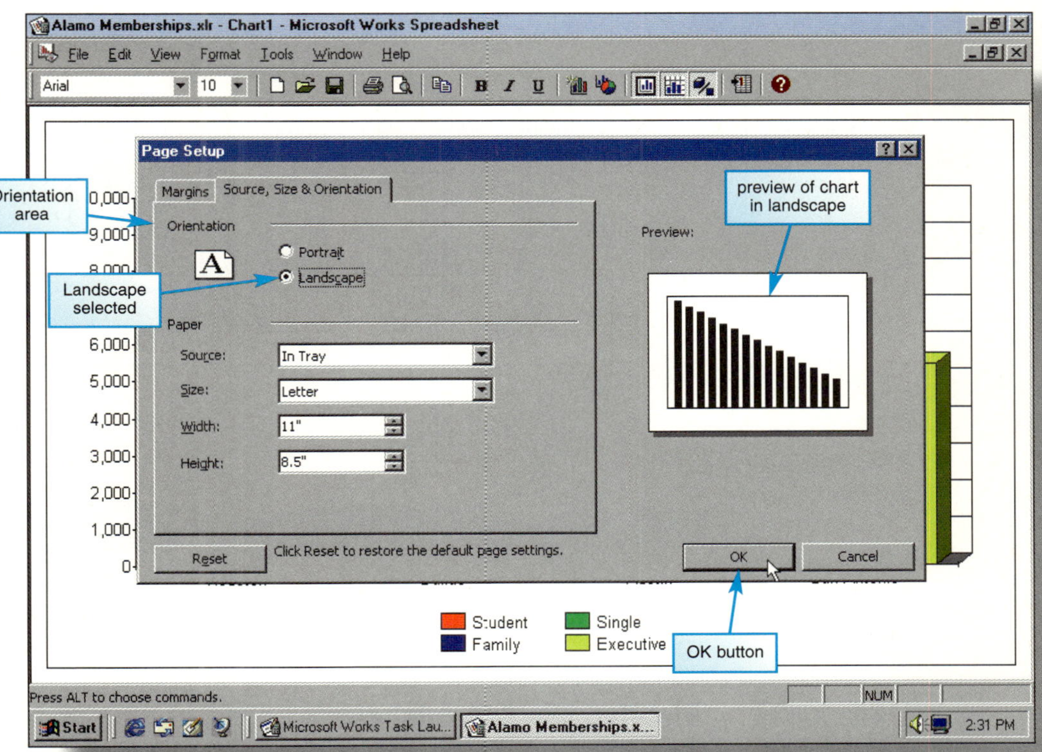

FIGURE 2-69

4 Click the OK button. Point to the Print button on the Charting toolbar.

The Page Setup dialog box closes (Figure 2-70).

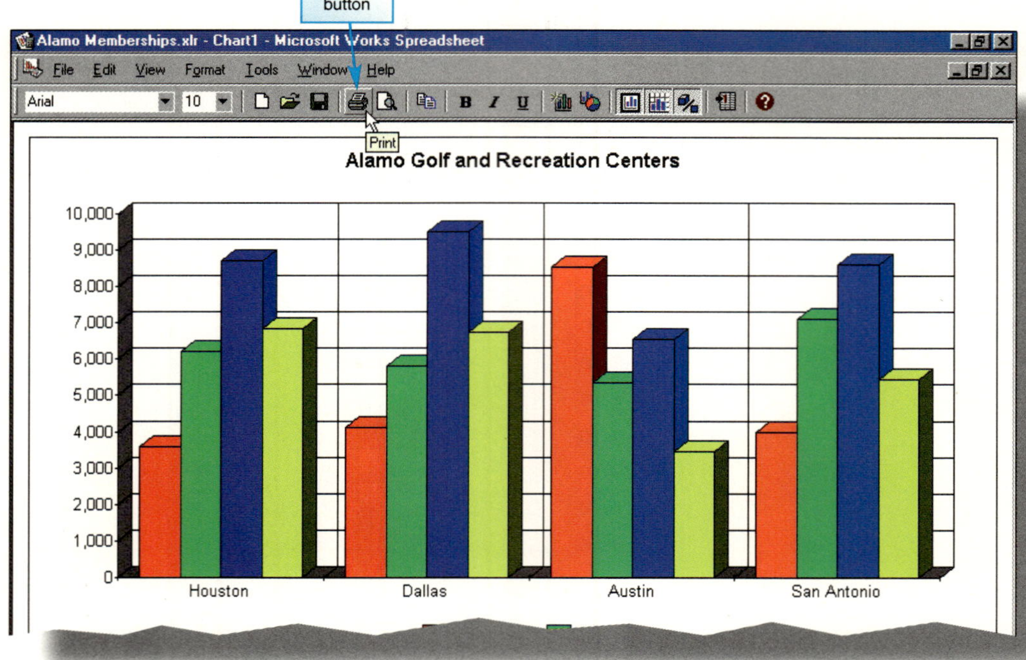

FIGURE 2-70

5 Click the Print button.

Works prints the chart on the top one-quarter of the page (Figure 2-71).

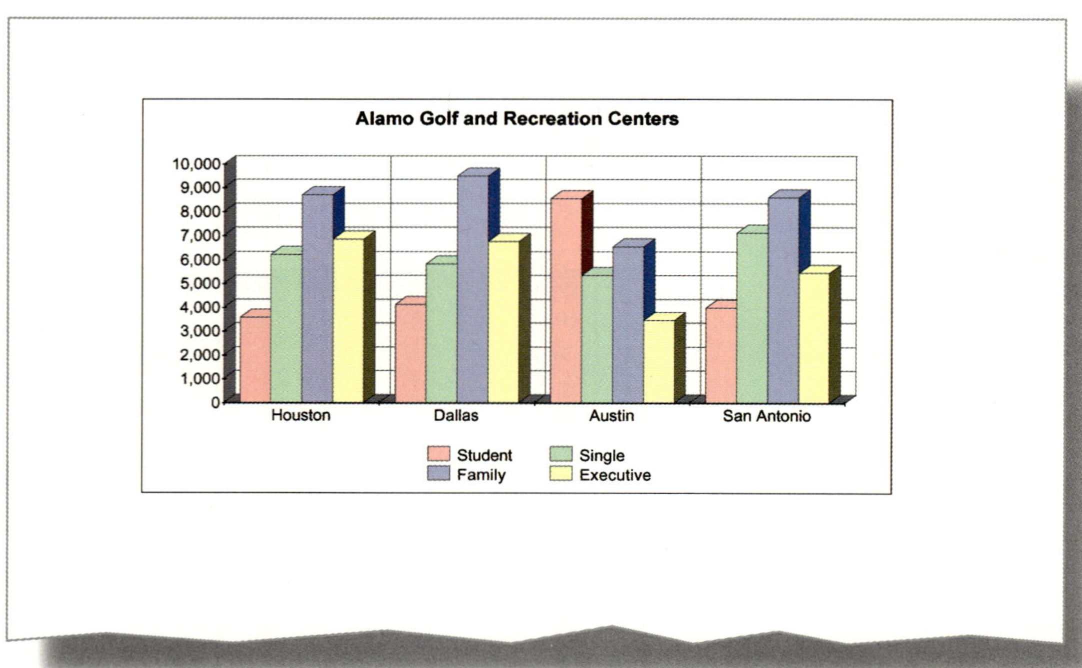

FIGURE 2-71

Other Ways

1. On File menu in the chart window click Print
2. Press CTRL+P

Viewing the Spreadsheet

When you create a chart, Works displays the chart window on top of the spreadsheet. To view the spreadsheet, click the file name of the spreadsheet on the Window menu in the chart window as illustrated in the following steps.

To View the Spreadsheet

1 Click Window on the menu bar in the chart window and point to Alamo Memberships.xlr, the file name of the spreadsheet.

The Window menu displays and lists the open windows in the application (Figure 2-72). The chart is the active window, and Works indicates this by the check mark next to the chart name Alamo Memberships.xlr - Chart1.

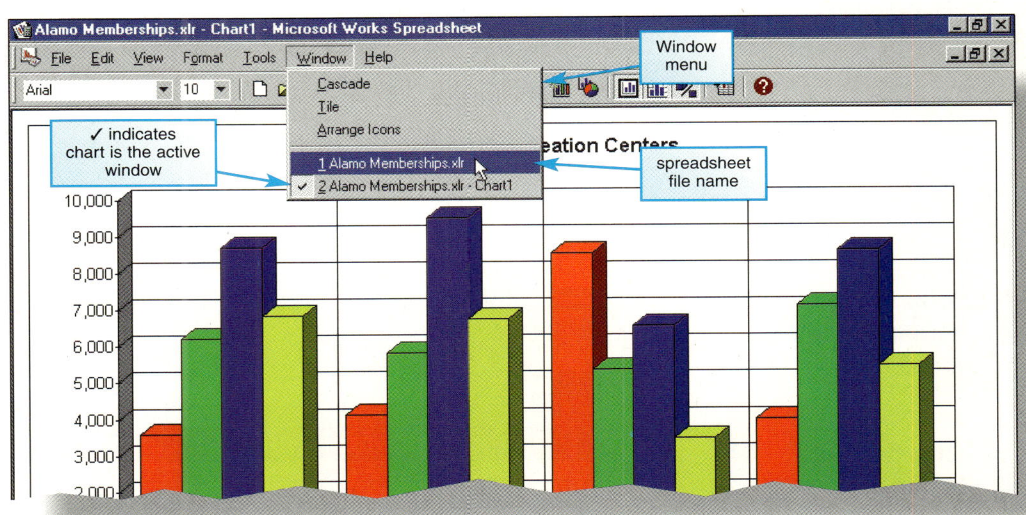

FIGURE 2-72

2 Click Alamo Memberships.xlr. Click any cell to remove the selection from the cells.

Works displays the spreadsheet and makes the Spreadsheet window the active window (Figure 2-73).

	A	B	C	D	E	F
1	Alamo Golf and Recreation Centers					
2		Houston	Dallas	Austin	San Antonio	Total
3	Student	3,587	4,125	8,541	3,986	20,239
4	Single	6,220	5,825	5,345	7,123	24,513
5	Family	8,695	9,487	6,543	8,593	33,318
6	Executive	6,854	6,753	3,456	5,452	22,515
7	Total	25,356	26,190	23,885	25,154	100,585

FIGURE 2-73

Other Ways

1. On View menu click Spreadsheet

To redisplay the chart window, click the chart name on the Window menu.

Saving the Spreadsheet and Chart

After creating a chart, you should save the spreadsheet again to save the chart with the spreadsheet. To save the chart with the spreadsheet, perform the following step.

TO SAVE THE SPREADSHEET AND CHART

Click the Save button on the toolbar.

The spreadsheet is saved as specified in the last save process; that is, on drive A with the file name, Alamo Memberships. The chart is saved with the spreadsheet.

Closing a Spreadsheet

Once you complete the spreadsheet and chart, you can close the spreadsheet and work on another spreadsheet or another Works project. To close the spreadsheet, perform the following steps.

To Close a Spreadsheet

1 Point to the Close button on the title bar (Figure 2-74).

2 Click the Close button.

The spreadsheet closes and the Works Task Launcher displays, allowing you to continue using Works.

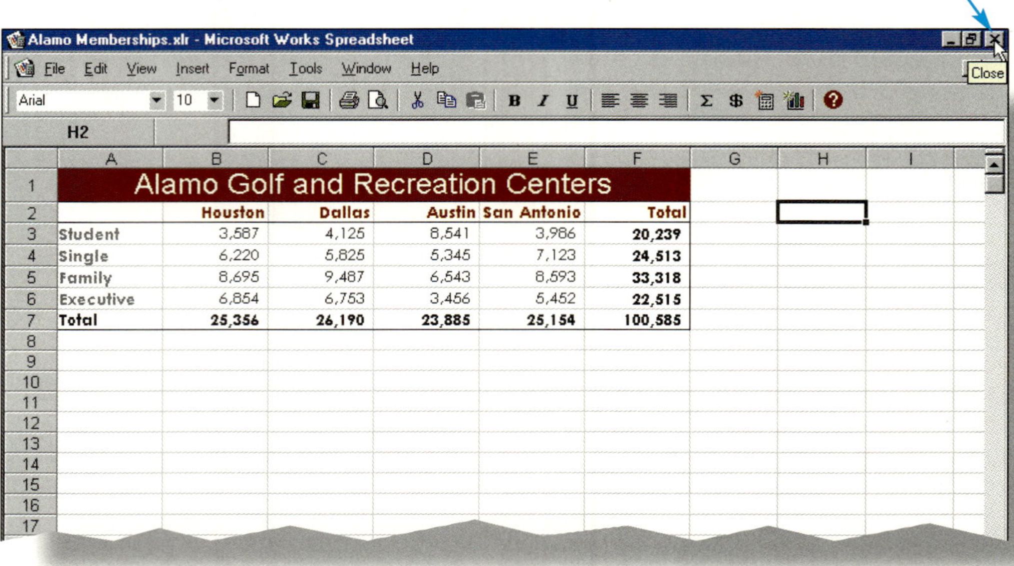

	Houston	Dallas	Austin	San Antonio	Total
Student	3,587	4,125	8,541	3,986	20,239
Single	6,220	5,825	5,345	7,123	24,513
Family	8,695	9,487	6,543	8,593	33,318
Executive	6,854	6,753	3,456	5,452	22,515
Total	25,356	26,190	23,885	25,154	100,585

FIGURE 2-74

Other Ways

1. On File menu click Close
2. Press CTRL+W

You can close a chart without closing the entire spreadsheet file by clicking the Close command on the File menu in the chart window.

If you have made any changes to a spreadsheet after it has been saved, a dialog box displays asking if you want to save the changes before closing the spreadsheet. Click the Yes button in the dialog box to save changes.

Quitting Works

After you have completed all your tasks, normally you will want to quit Works and return to the Windows desktop. To quit Works, perform the following steps.

TO QUIT WORKS

1. Point to the Close button in the Works Task Launcher Window's title bar (Figure 2-75).
2. Click the Close button.

Works is terminated, and the Microsoft Windows desktop will redisplay.

Other Ways

1. On File menu click Exit
2. Press ALT+F4

FIGURE 2-75

More About

Microsoft Works Task Launcher Connectivity

The improved Task Launcher has direct connectivity in the program area to Internet Explorer, and under each program, you will find a connection to the Microsoft Works Web site. To learn more about how you can get the most out of Work, click the links on the Task Launcher.

Opening an Existing Spreadsheet File

Once you have saved a spreadsheet on disk, you may need to retrieve, or open, the spreadsheet to make changes to it or otherwise process it. Opening a spreadsheet means the spreadsheet is retrieved from the disk into main memory. The easiest way to open an existing document is to use the My Computer icon located on the desktop. Perform the following steps to open an existing spreadsheet.

Steps To Open an Existing Spreadsheet File

1 Point to the My Computer icon on the desktop (Figure 2-76).

FIGURE 2-76

2 Double-click the My Computer icon. When the My Computer window opens, point to 3½ Floppy (A:).

When you double-click the My Computer icon, Windows opens the My Computer window (Figure 2-77). The My Computer window contains icons representing the hard disk, floppy disk drive, CD-ROM drive, and folder icons. Drive A in Figure 2-77 is a 3½ floppy disk drive. The icons that display on your screen may be different.

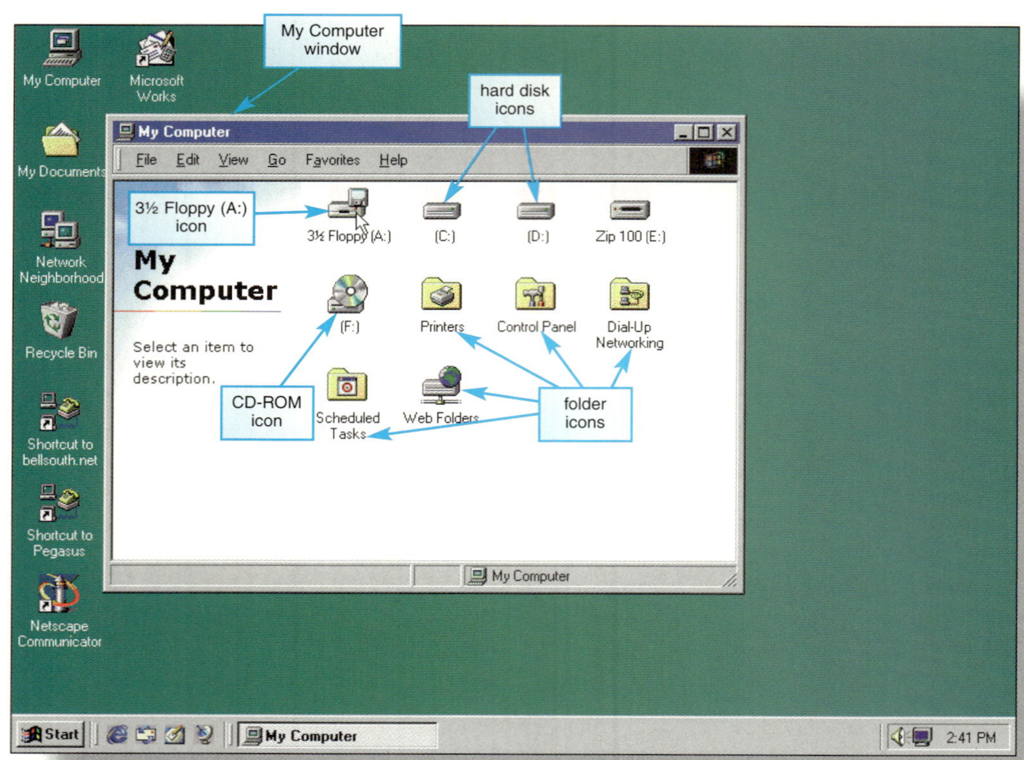

FIGURE 2-77

3 Double-click 3½ Floppy (A:). When the 3½ Floppy (A:) window opens, point to the Alamo Memberships.xlr icon.

When you double-click the 3½ Floppy (A:) icon, Windows opens the 3½ Floppy (A:) window (Figure 2-78) and displays the file names on drive A. The charting icon identified with the file indicates the file is a spreadsheet.

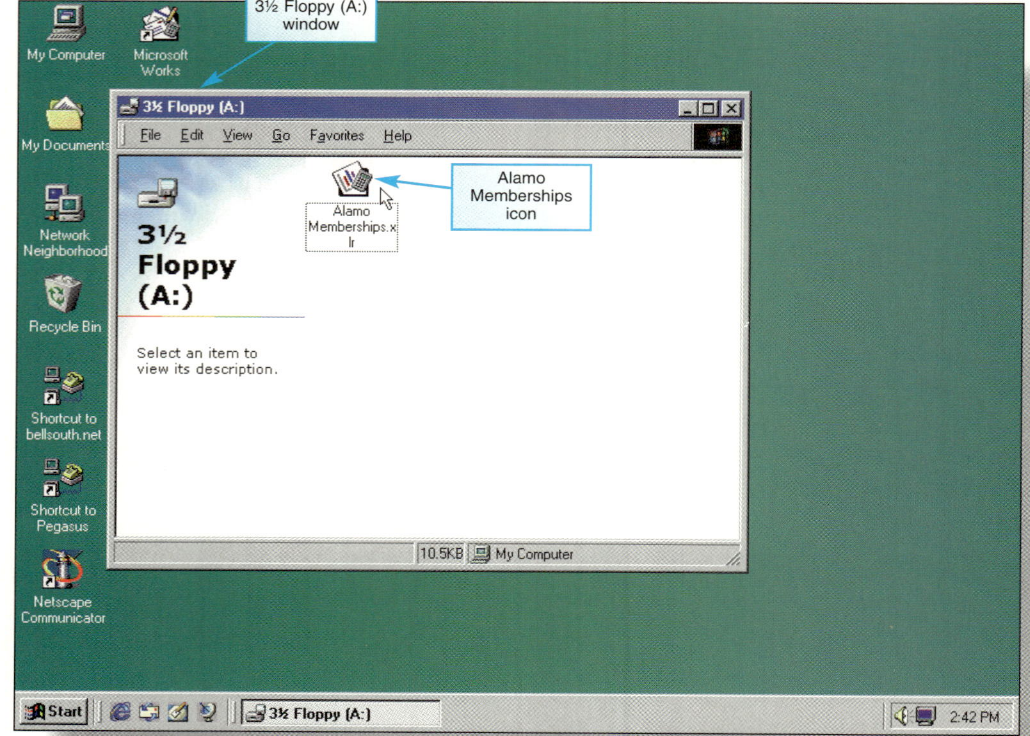

FIGURE 2-78

4 **Double-click the Alamo Memberships.xlr icon.**

Windows first starts Works and then opens the spreadsheet, Alamo Memberships.xlr, and displays it on the screen (Figure 2-79). You can revise or print the spreadsheet as required.

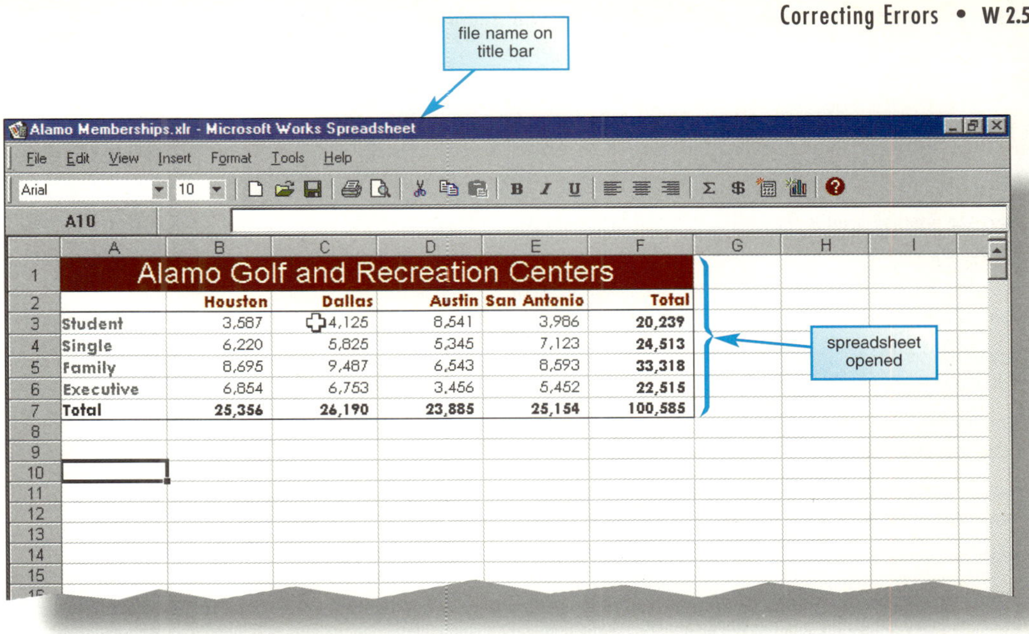

file name on title bar

Alamo Memberships.xlr - Microsoft Works Spreadsheet

	A	B	C	D	E	F
1	Alamo Golf and Recreation Centers					
2		Houston	Dallas	Austin	San Antonio	Total
3	Student	3,587	4,125	8,541	3,986	20,239
4	Single	6,220	5,825	5,345	7,123	24,513
5	Family	8,695	9,487	6,543	8,593	33,318
6	Executive	6,854	6,753	3,456	5,452	22,515
7	Total	25,356	26,190	23,885	25,154	100,585

spreadsheet opened

FIGURE 2-79

5 **Click File on the menu bar and then click the Close command to close the spreadsheet.**

You also can open files by clicking the desired file name listed at the bottom of the File menu. As mentioned earlier, the Works extension, .xlr, may not display depending on the configuration of your computer.

Other Ways

1. Click Task Launcher button, click History tab, click desired document
2. On File menu click Open, click desired document, click Open button
3. Press CTRL+O
4. Click Open button on toolbar, click desired document, click Open button

Correcting Errors

When you create a spreadsheet, the possibility exists that you may make an error by entering the wrong text or data in a cell. In addition, it is possible that you must change a value in a cell even though it was correct when you entered it.

Works provides several methods for changing data in a spreadsheet and correcting errors. These methods are explained in the next section.

Correcting Errors Prior to Entering Data into a Cell

If you notice an error in the entry bar prior to confirming the entry, you can use the BACKSPACE key to erase the error and then type the correct characters. If the error is too severe, click the Cancel box in the entry bar or press the ESC key to erase the entire entry in the entry bar and reenter the data from the beginning.

Editing Data in a Cell

If you notice an error in the spreadsheet after confirming the entry, you can correct it using one of two methods. If the entry is short, retype it and click the Enter box or press the ENTER key. The new entry will replace the old entry. Remember that you must select the cell containing the error before you begin typing. If the entry in the cell is long and the errors are minor, you may want to edit the entry rather than retype it. To edit an entry in a cell, first select the cell containing the error. In the entry bar, click the first character in error. Works places the insertion point at the location you clicked in the entry bar. After the insertion point is positioned properly, make your changes. When you type characters in the entry bar, Works inserts the characters to the left of the insertion point and moves all following characters one position to the right.

Table 2-1 Methods of Moving the Insertion Point in the Entry Bar

TASK	MOUSE	KEYBOARD
Move the insertion point to the beginning of text	Click to left of first character	Press HOME
Move the insertion point to the end of text	Click to right of last character	Press END
Move the insertion point one character to the left	Click one character to left	Press LEFT ARROW
Move the insertion point one character to the right	Click one character to right	Press RIGHT ARROW
Move the insertion point anywhere in the entry bar	Click entry bar at appropriate position	Press LEFT ARROW or RIGHT ARROW
Select one or more characters	Drag mouse pointer through the characters	Press SHIFT+LEFT ARROW or SHIFT+RIGHT ARROW
Delete selected characters	None	Press DELETE

To delete a character in the entry bar, place the insertion point to the left of the character you want to delete and then press the DELETE key, or place the insertion point to the right of the character you want to delete and then press the BACKSPACE key.

While the insertion point is located in the entry bar, you may have occasion to move it to various points in the bar. Table 2-1 illustrates the means for moving the insertion point in the entry bar.

When you have finished editing an entry, click the Enter box or press the ENTER key. Understanding how to correct errors or change entries in a spreadsheet is an important skill.

Clearing a Cell or Range of Cells

It is not unusual to enter data into the wrong cell or range of cells. In such a case, to correct the error you may want to delete, or clear, the data. Never select a cell and press the SPACEBAR to enter a blank character and assume you have cleared the cell. A blank character is text and is different from an empty cell, even though the cell may appear empty.

Works provides a variety of methods to clear the contents of a cell or a range of cells. The various methods are explained in the following steps.

TO CLEAR CELL CONTENTS – DELETE KEY

1. Select the cell or range of cells.
2. Press the DELETE key.

TO CLEAR CELL CONTENTS – EDIT MENU AND CLEAR COMMAND

1. Select the cell or range of cells.
2. Click Edit on the menu bar and then click Clear.

TO CLEAR CELL CONTENTS – EDIT MENU AND CUT COMMAND OR CUT BUTTON

1. Select the cell or range of cells.
2. Click Edit on the menu bar and click Cut; or click the Cut button on the toolbar.

Each of these methods has differences you should understand. In the first method, when you press the DELETE key, the data in the cell or cells is cleared but the formatting remains. Thus, even after you clear the cells using the DELETE key, formatting such as dollar formats, bold, italic, underlining, and so on remain. To clear the formatting, you must individually turn off each of the formatting features or use the Cut command for clearing the cells.

When you use the Edit menu and Clear command, the data in the cell or range of cells is cleared, but the formatting remains. This method has the same effect as using the DELETE key.

When you use the Cut command from the Edit menu or click the Cut button on the toolbar, Works clears both the data and the formatting from the cell or range of cells. Actually, the data and the associated formatting are placed on the Windows Clipboard for potential pasting elsewhere, but if you never paste the data into the same or another Works document, in effect, the data and formatting have been entirely cleared from the spreadsheet.

Clearing the Entire Spreadsheet

Sometimes so many major errors are made with a spreadsheet that it is easier to start over. To clear an entire spreadsheet, follow these steps.

TO CLEAR THE ENTIRE SPREADSHEET

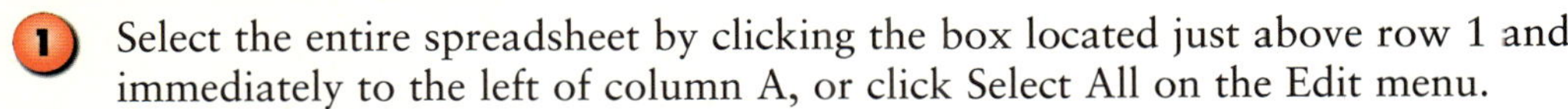

1. Select the entire spreadsheet by clicking the box located just above row 1 and immediately to the left of column A, or click Select All on the Edit menu.

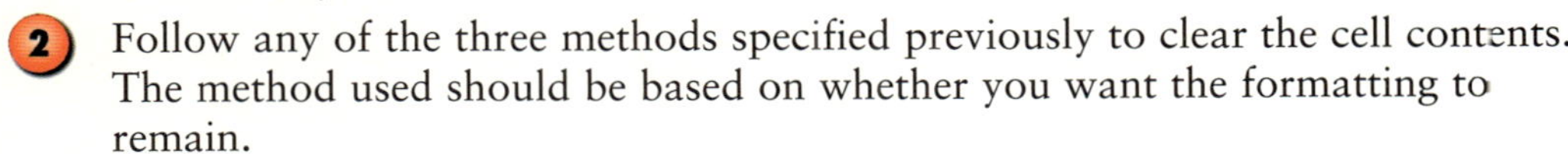

2. Follow any of the three methods specified previously to clear the cell contents. The method used should be based on whether you want the formatting to remain.

An alternative to the previous steps is to click Close on the File menu and not save the spreadsheet. Works closes the spreadsheet. You then can click the Open a blank Spreadsheet link in the Works Task Launcher window to begin working on your new spreadsheet.

Project Summary

In this project, you learned to start the Microsoft Works Spreadsheet tool, enter both text and numeric data into the spreadsheet, calculate the sum of numeric values in both rows and columns, and copy formulas to adjacent cells in both rows and columns. In addition, you displayed the title centered across columns, added color to the title, and used the AutoFormat feature to format a spreadsheet. Using the steps and techniques presented, you changed column widths and formatted numeric data in the Comma format. You learned to save a spreadsheet, print a spreadsheet, create a chart from spreadsheet data, print the chart, and open a spreadsheet. After completing the project, you learned various error correction techniques.

What You Should Know

Having completed this project, you should now be able to perform the following tasks:

- Change Column Widths *(W 2.35)*
- Check Spelling *(W 2.38)*
- Clear Cell Contents *(W 2.52)*
- Clear the Entire Spreadsheet *(W 2.53)*
- Close a Spreadsheet *(W 2.48)*
- Copy One Cell to Adjacent Cells in a Column *(W 2.25)*
- Copy One Cell to Adjacent Cells in a Row *(W 2.22)*
- Create a 3-D Bar Chart *(W 2.42)*
- Display Numbers with the Comma Format *(W 2.37)*
- Enter Column Titles *(W 2.14)*
- Enter Numeric Data *(W 2.17)*
- Enter Row Titles *(W 2.16)*
- Enter the Spreadsheet Title *(W 2.11)*
- Format Cells *(W 2.27)*
- Open an Existing Spreadsheet File *(W 2.49)*
- Print a Chart *(W 2.45)*
- Print a Spreadsheet *(W 2.40)*
- Quit Works *(W 2.48)*
- Save a Spreadsheet *(W 2.39)*
- Save the Spreadsheet and Chart *(W 2.47)*
- Start the Works Spreadsheet *(W 2.6)*
- Sum a Column of Numbers Using the AutoSum Button *(W 2.20)*
- Sum a Row of Numbers Using the AutoSum button *(W 2.24)*
- Use AutoFormat *(W 2.33)*
- View the Spreadsheet *(W 2.47)*

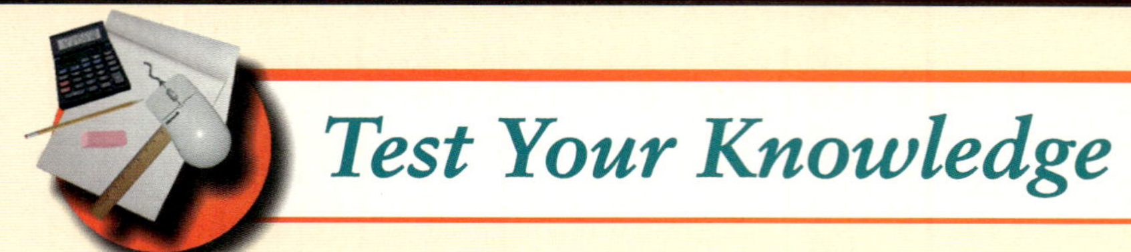

Test Your Knowledge

1 True/False

Instructions: Circle T if the statement is true or F if the statement is false.

T F 1. When using the Works Spreadsheet tool, the shape of the mouse pointer changes depending on the location of the mouse pointer in the Spreadsheet window.

T F 2. Any set of characters that contains a letter is considered text in the Works Spreadsheet tool.

T F 3. Works displays the same toolbar when you work with spreadsheets or charts.

T F 4. The intersection of each column and each row is a cell.

T F 5. To print a spreadsheet, click the Print button on the Charting toolbar.

T F 6. You can use the fill handle to copy the contents of one cell to adjacent cells in a column or row.

T F 7. To quickly adjust the column width for best fit, double-click the cell displaying the largest entry in the column.

T F 8. When using the AutoSum button to sum a column or row of values, Works always selects the correct range to sum.

T F 9. Works enters numbers right-aligned in cells.

T F 10. If text you enter in a cell contains more characters than can be displayed in the width of the cell, the overflow characters always will display in adjacent cells to the right.

2 Multiple Choice

Instructions: Circle the correct response.

1. To confirm a cell entry, click or press the __________.
   a. TAB key b. Enter box c. ENTER key d. all of the above
2. To enter data into a cell, the cell must be __________.
   a. empty b. selected c. defined as a number d. formatted
3. To cancel an entry before confirming the entry, click the __________.
   a. BACKSPACE key b. DELETE key c. Cut button d. Cancel box
4. To clear both the data and the formatting from a cell, __________.
   a. press the BACKSPACE key
   b. click the Cut button on the toolbar
   c. press the DELETE key
   d. click the Clear command on the Edit menu
5. To delete a character in the entry bar, __________.
   a. place the insertion point to the left of the character to delete and then press the SPACEBAR
   b. place the insertion point to the right of the character to delete and then press the BACKSPACE key
   c. place the insertion point to the right of the character to delete and then click the Cancel button
   d. place the insertion point to the left of the character to delete and then press the BACKSPACE key
6. To print a chart, __________.
   a. click the Print command on the File menu in the Charting window
   b. click the Print command on the File menu in the Spreadsheet window
   c. press CTRL+P in the Spreadsheet window
   d. click the Print button in the Spreadsheet window

7. A chart title may contain up to __________ characters including spaces.
   a. 40 b. 9 c. 30 d. 39
8. You can save up to __________ charts for each spreadsheet.
   a. two b. six c. eight d. ten
9. After selecting a range to chart, clicking the New Chart button on the toolbar will display __________.
   a. the New Chart dialog box
   b. a 3-D Bar chart
   c. a blank chart window with a Charting toolbar
   d. a 2-D Bar chart
10. Works enters numbers __________-aligned in a cell.
   a. center b. right c. left d. decimal

3 Fill In

Instructions: In Figure 2-80, a series of arrows point to the major components of the Microsoft Works Spreadsheet window. Identify the parts of the window in the space provided.

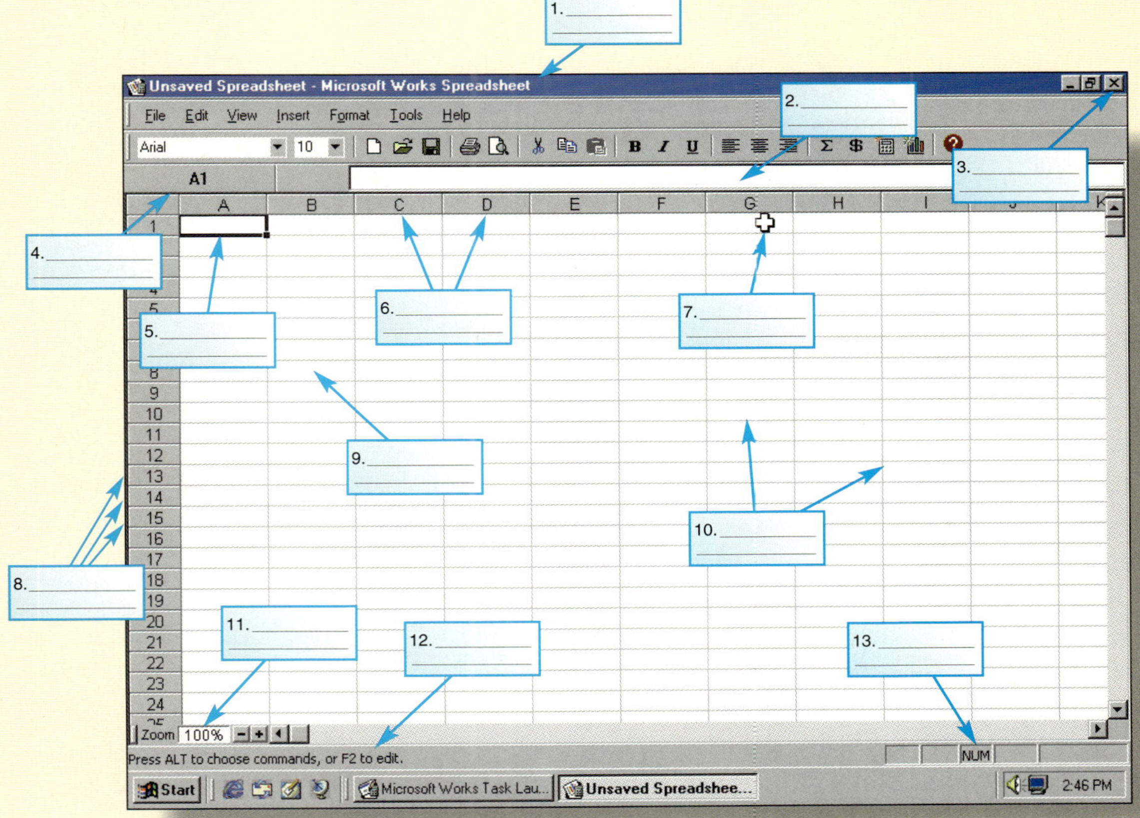

FIGURE 2-80

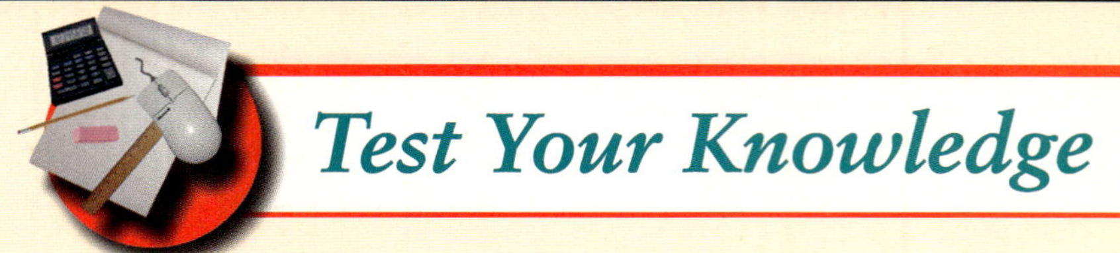

4 Fill In

Instructions: In Figure 2-81, arrows point to buttons on the Spreadsheet toolbar. Identify the various buttons in the spaces provided.

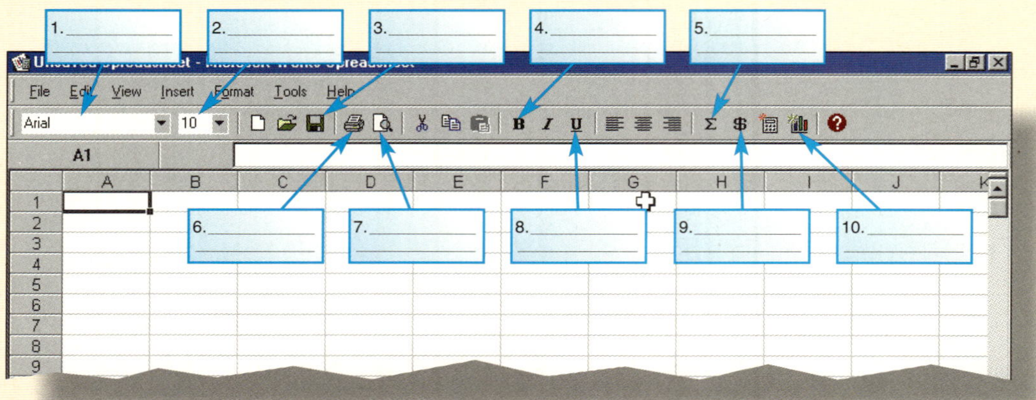

FIGURE 2-81

1 Reviewing Project Activities

Instructions: Use your computer to perform the following tasks to obtain experience using Works Help.

1. Start Works Task Launcher and then click Start a blank Spreadsheet.
2. Click Help on the menu bar and then click Works Help.
3. Click QuickTours: Spreadsheet and then click the Creating a Chart link. View the quick tour on Creating a Chart. Click the Close button.
4. Click the topic Create a chart on the Start using the Spreadsheet menu. When the Create a chart topic displays in the Help pane, read and print the numbered information on the topic.
5. Click the Contents button on the Help toolbar to display the Spreadsheet Table of Contents. Click Final Checklist Before Printing, click the Preview a Spreadsheet Before Printing, and then click Preview a spreadsheet before printing.
6. When the Preview a spreadsheet before printing topic displays in the Help pane, read the step-by-step instructions. Locate the Related topics list. Click Print a document to view the topic. Read and print the Print a document topic.
7. Close the Works Help pane.
8. Quit Microsoft Works.

2 Expanding on the Basics

Instructions: Use Works Help to better understand the topics listed below. Print the topic or topics that substantiate your answer.

1. Use the key term, formula, and the Index sheet to display various topics on formulas. Access the various topics and view the QuickTours to answer the following questions.
   a. How do you type your own formula?
   b. How do you insert a range in a formula?
   c. How do you delete a formula?
2. Using the key term, format, and using the Index sheet, display the topic, Change the number format. Read the step-by-step instructions and Related topics links and then answer the following questions.
   a. What is a number format?
   b. What are the different ways the Works Spreadsheet tool will format a number?
   c. What are the definitions of range and data entries?
3. Close Works Help and then quit Microsoft Works.

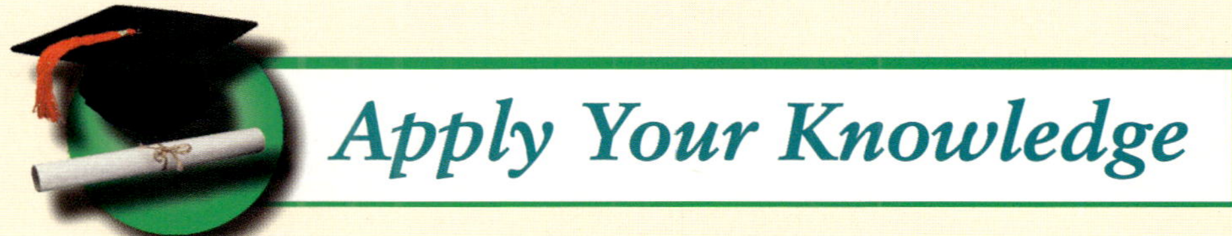

1 Charting Spreadsheet Data

Instructions: Start the Microsoft Works Spreadsheet Tool. Open the spreadsheet, Sports Equipment Sales (Figure 2-82), on the Data Disk. If you did not download the Data Disk, see the inside back cover of this book for instructions for downloading or see your instructor. Chart the range A2:E8 as a 3-D Bar chart. Add the title, Sports Equipment Sales Projections. Add a border and gridlines to the 3-D Bar chart. Print the chart. Save the spreadsheet with the file name, Modified Equipment Sales.

Sports Equipment Sales.xlr - Microsoft Works Spreadsheet

File Edit View Insert Format Tools Help

Arial 10

A17

	A	B	C	D	E	F
1	SPORTS EQUIPMENT SALES PROJECTIONS					
2		2001	2002	2003	2004	TOTAL
3	Footballs	$14,325	$15,138	$16,295	$17,344	$63,102
4	Soccer Balls	$19,553	$23,441	$27,678	$30,514	$101,186
5	Tennis Rackets	$17,663	$19,234	$20,998	$23,312	$81,207
6	Roller Blades	$25,867	$28,698	$32,214	$36,597	$123,376
7	Hockey Skates	$18,776	$22,534	$26,798	$31,879	$99,987
8	Ice Skates	$13,596	$16,852	$18,002	$19,870	$68,320
9	Total	$109,780	$125,897	$141,985	$159,516	$537,178
10						

FIGURE 2-82

1 Building an International Athletic Shoes Sold Spreadsheet

Problem: As the international sales manager for Swift Feet Athletic Shoes Company, you have been asked to analyze the yearly shoe sales for the international market and compare it to the North American market. The shoe sales are shown in Table 2-2. The spreadsheet and chart are shown in Figure 2-83(a) and (b).

Table 2-2 Shoe Sales Data

	NORTH AMERICA	SOUTH AMERICA	EUROPE	ASIA
Pro Sport	151256	80968	101234	98254
Pro Air	175678	85769	123417	101628
Pro Walker	132867	100233	113845	105864
Pro Runner	196967	104267	154693	102475

	A	B	C	D	E	F
1		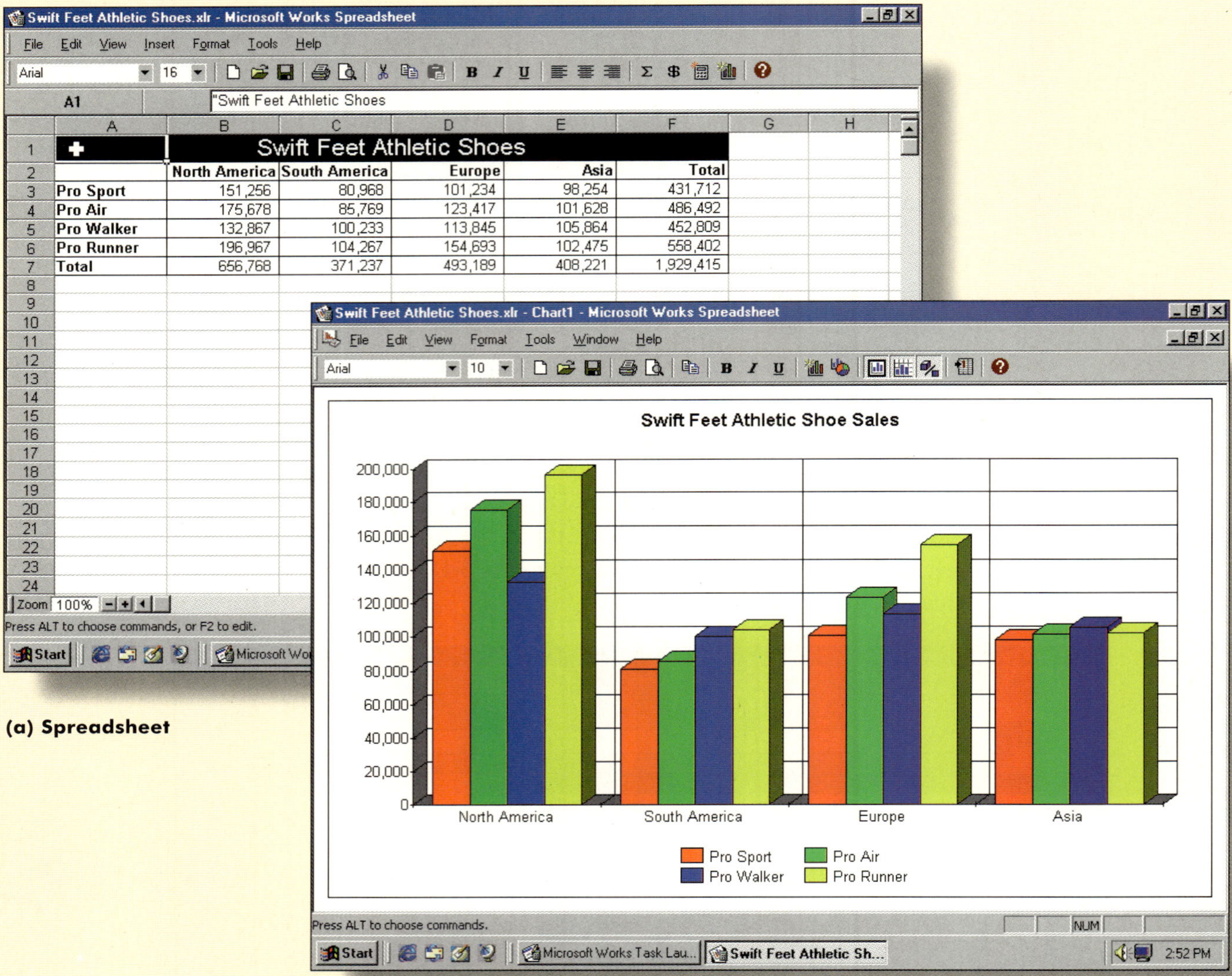 Swift Feet Athletic Shoes				
2		North America	South America	Europe	Asia	Total
3	Pro Sport	151,256	80,968	101,234	98,254	431,712
4	Pro Air	175,678	85,769	123,417	101,628	486,492
5	Pro Walker	132,867	100,233	113,845	105,864	452,809
6	Pro Runner	196,967	104,267	154,693	102,475	558,402
7	Total	656,768	371,237	493,189	408,221	1,929,415

(a) Spreadsheet

Swift Feet Athletic Shoe Sales

(b) 3-D Bar Chart

FIGURE 2-83

In the Lab

Instructions: Perform the following tasks:

1. Create the spreadsheet shown in Figure 2-83(a) using the numbers in Table 2-2.
2. Calculate the totals for the four areas, the shoe categories, and the entire company.
3. Format the spreadsheet title, Swift Feet Athletic Shoes, as white 16-point Arial font and centered over columns A through F. Add a black solid pattern to the foreground of cells A1:F1.
4. Use AutoFormat and the Basic table format for the remaining portion of the spreadsheet. The numbers display using the Number format.
5. The column width should be 14 for columns A through F.
6. Select cells A2:F7. Format the font to 10-point Arial.
7. Print the spreadsheet.
8. Create the 3-D Bar chart from the spreadsheet data. Add the title, Swift Feet Athletic Shoe Sales, to the chart. Also include a border and gridlines for the chart.
9. Print the 3-D Bar chart.
10. Save the spreadsheet with the chart using the filename, Swift Feet Athletic Shoes.
11. Follow directions from your instructor for turning in this assignment.

2 Building a Student Enrollment Spreadsheet

Problem: As the director of human resources for the College of St. Sebastian, you have been asked to prepare a report of the undergraduate student enrollment by department and class. The current student enrollment is shown in Table 2-3. The spreadsheet and chart are shown in Figure 2-84 on the next page.

Table 2-3 College Enrollment

	FRESHMAN	*SOPHOMORE*	*JUNIOR*	*SENIOR*
Education	1638	1533	1857	1723
Technology	525	475	589	625
Nursing	989	876	1025	1143
Engineering	376	402	475	466
Fine Arts	1235	1637	1867	1951

(continued)

Building a Student Enrollment Spreadsheet *(continued)*

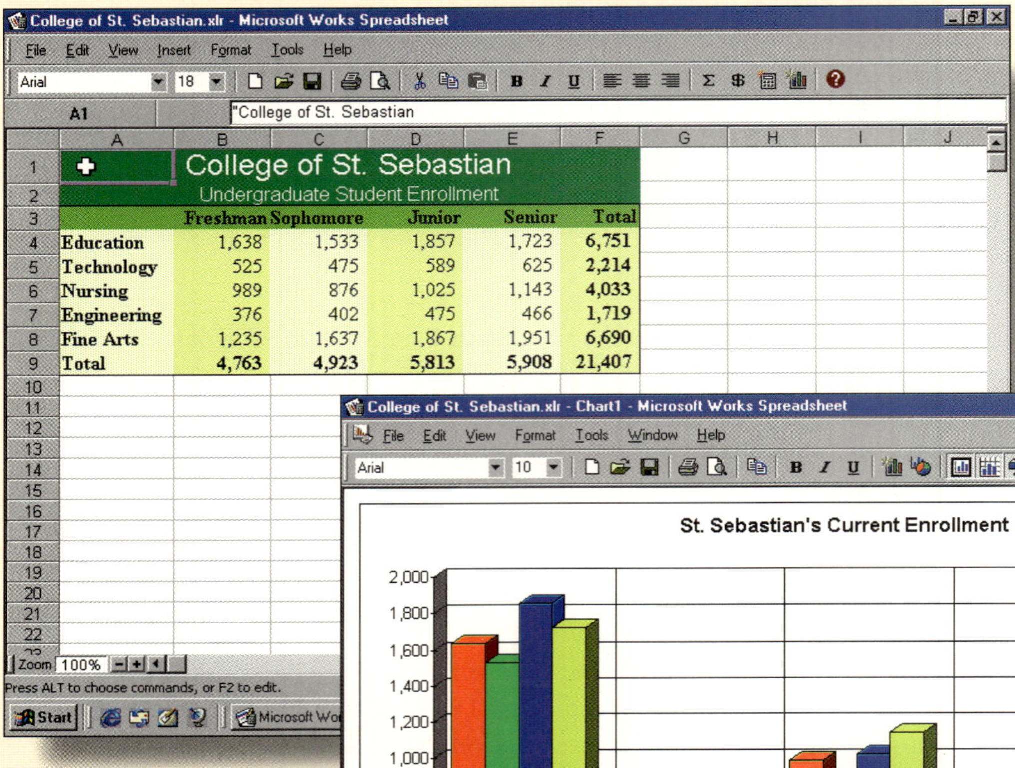

College of St. Sebastian.xlr - Microsoft Works Spreadsheet

	A	B	C	D	E	F
1		College of St. Sebastian				
2		Undergraduate Student Enrollment				
3		Freshman	Sophomore	Junior	Senior	Total
4	Education	1,638	1,533	1,857	1,723	6,751
5	Technology	525	475	589	625	2,214
6	Nursing	989	876	1,025	1,143	4,033
7	Engineering	376	402	475	466	1,719
8	Fine Arts	1,235	1,637	1,867	1,951	6,690
9	Total	4,763	4,923	5,813	5,908	21,407

(a) Spreadsheet

College of St. Sebastian.xlr - Chart1 - Microsoft Works Spreadsheet

St. Sebastian's Current Enrollment

Education, Technology, Nursing, Engineering, Fine Arts

Freshman, Sophomore, Junior, Senior

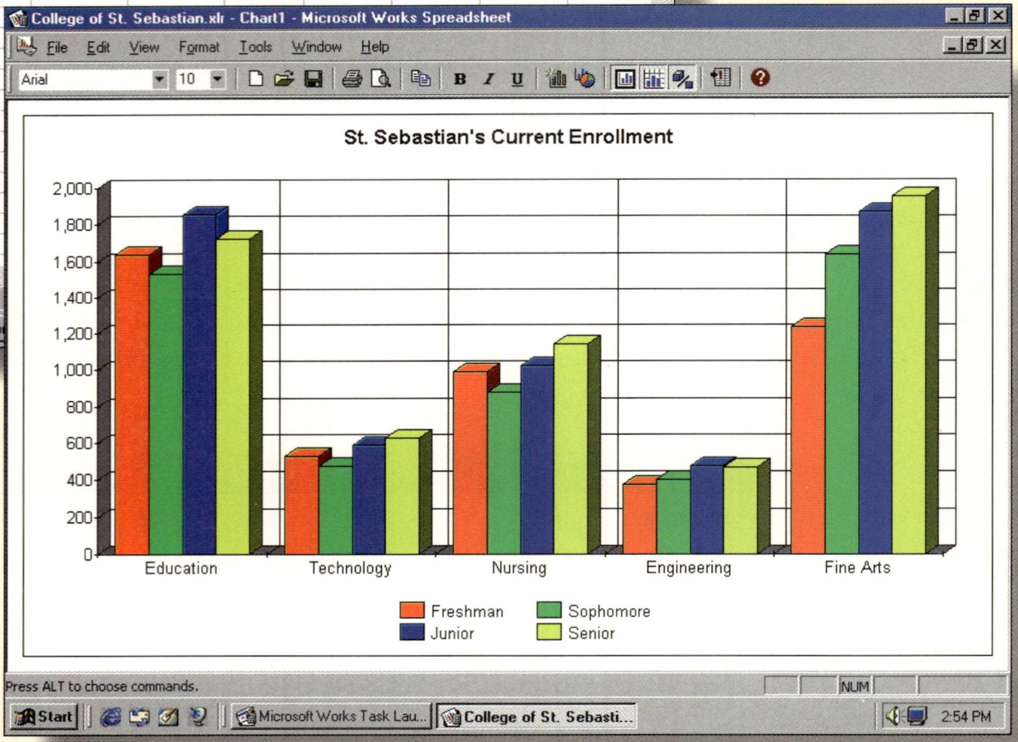

(b) 3-D Bar Chart

FIGURE 2-84

Instructions: Perform the following tasks:

1. Create the spreadsheet shown in Figure 2-84(a) using the numbers in Table 2-3 on the previous page.
2. Calculate the totals for the four classes, the college categories, and the entire college.
3. Format the spreadsheet title, College of St. Sebastian, as white 18-point Arial font and centered over columns A through F. Add a green solid pattern to the foreground of cells A1:F2.
4. Format the subtitle, Undergraduate Student Enrollment, as white 12-point Arial font and centered over columns A through F.

In the Lab

5. Use AutoFormat and the Creative: Column table format for the remaining portion of the spreadsheet. The numbers display using the Number format.
6. The font should be 12-point Times New Roman for A3:F9.
7. The column width should be 13 for column A, 11 for columns B through E, and 9 for column F.
8. Print the spreadsheet.
9. Create the 3-D Bar chart from the spreadsheet data. Add the title, St. Sebastian's Current Enrollment, to the chart. Also include a border and gridlines for the chart.
10. Print the 3-D Bar chart.
11. Save the spreadsheet with the chart using the filename, College of St. Sebastian.
12. Follow directions from your instructor for turning in this assignment.

3 Building a Movie Sales Spreadsheet

Problem: As market researcher for Videos, Inc., you have been asked to prepare a report of movies purchased by age group during the past year. The sales are shown in Table 2-4. The spreadsheet and chart are shown in Figure 2-85(a) and (b) on the next page.

Table 2-4 Videos, Inc. Customer Data

	16-20	*21-35*	*36-49*	*50+*
Musical	5622	7321	11986	13663
Comedy	33527	34897	42582	22460
Action	22520	38539	31855	6289
Romantic	12798	31022	41957	21739
Sci-fi	18602	28527	8253	321

Instructions: Perform the following tasks:

1. Create the spreadsheet shown in Figure 2-85(a) using the numbers in Table 2-4.
2. Calculate the totals for the four age categories, the movie categories, and the entire company.
3. Format the spreadsheet title, Videos, Inc. Sales, as white 18-point Arial font and centered over columns A through F. Add a dark blue solid pattern to the foreground of cells A1:F1.
4. Use AutoFormat and the Professional: Band table format for the remaining portion of the spreadsheet.
5. The font size should be 12-point for A2:F8
6. The column width should be 10 for columns A through F.
7. Print the spreadsheet.
8. Create the 3-D Bar chart from the spreadsheet data. Add the title, Video Sales by Age Group, to the chart. Also include gridlines for the chart.
9. Print the 3-D Bar chart.
10. Save the spreadsheet with the chart using the filename, Videos, Inc.
11. Follow directions from your instructor for turning in this assignment.

(continued)

Building a Movie Sales Spreadsheet (continued)

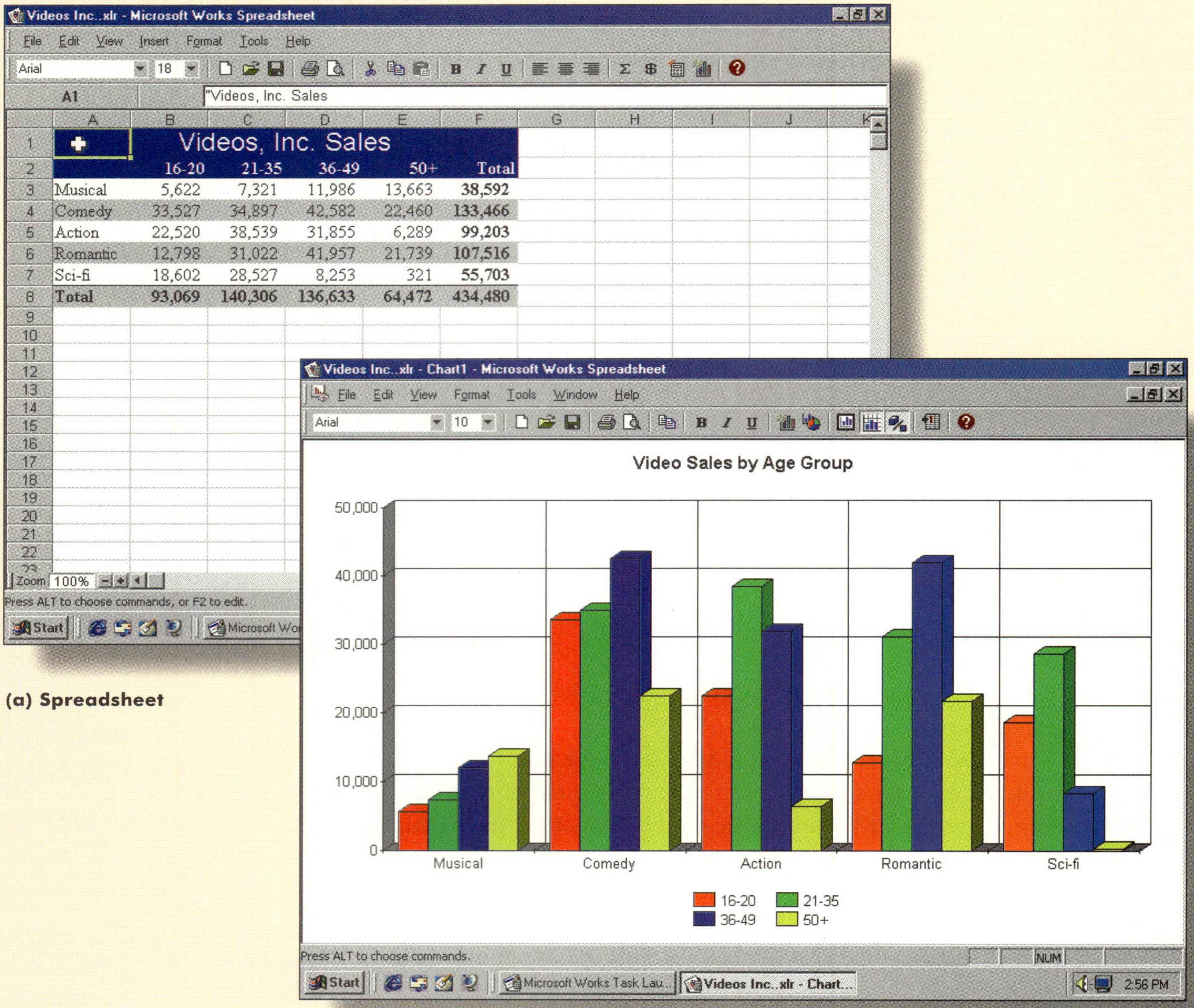

Videos Inc..xlr - Microsoft Works Spreadsheet

	A	B	C	D	E	F
1		Videos, Inc. Sales				
2		16-20	21-35	36-49	50+	Total
3	Musical	5,622	7,321	11,986	13,663	**38,592**
4	Comedy	33,527	34,897	42,582	22,460	**133,466**
5	Action	22,520	38,539	31,855	6,289	**99,203**
6	Romantic	12,798	31,022	41,957	21,739	**107,516**
7	Sci-fi	18,602	28,527	8,253	321	**55,703**
8	**Total**	**93,069**	**140,306**	**136,633**	**64,472**	**434,480**

(a) Spreadsheet

Videos Inc..xlr - Chart1 - Microsoft Works Spreadsheet

Video Sales by Age Group

50,000
40,000
30,000
20,000
10,000
0

Musical Comedy Action Romantic Sci-fi

16-20 21-35
36-49 50+

(b) 3-D Bar Chart

FIGURE 2-85

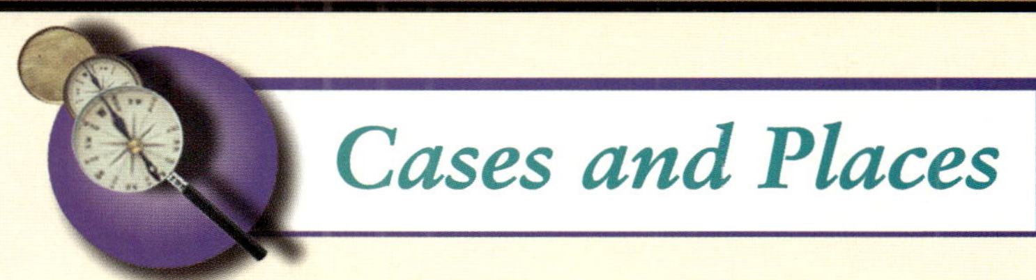

Cases and Places

The difficulty of these case studies varies:
◗ are the least difficult; ◗◗ are more difficult; and ◗◗◗ are the most difficult.

1 ◗ You just started working as an assistant in an optometrist's office. Your employer, Dr. Phillips, has asked you to prepare a worksheet to help him determine what age groups of patients are more likely to wear contacts than glasses. He has compiled some of the data, as shown in Figure 2-86.

AGES	21-30	31-40	41-50	51-60	61+
Glasses	56	62	66	70	78
Contacts	76	66	55	42	15

FIGURE 2-86

With this data, design a spreadsheet and a 3-D chart to present to Dr. Phillips. Use the concepts and techniques presented in this project to create the spreadsheet and chart.

2 ◗ You regularly contribute to a variety of charities. In an attempt to make your tax preparation easier, you keep a record of the money given to four different charities during each quarter of the year (Figure 2-87). Use the concepts and techniques presented in this project to prepare a spreadsheet to summarize your donations to each charity during each quarter.

CHARITY	QTR1	QTR2	QTR3	QTR4
Church	400	350	400	350
Shelter for the Homeless	150	140	125	175
Cancer Foundation	100	0	150	75
Cystic Fibrosis	0	125	75	75
Aid to Children	150	200	150	125

FIGURE 2-87

3 ◗◗ The Main Street Rib House restaurant is trying to decide whether it is feasible to open another restaurant in a neighboring community. The owner has asked you to develop a spreadsheet totaling all of the revenues received for a four-week period (Figure 2-88). The restaurant is closed on Sundays and Mondays. Create a spreadsheet and a 3-D chart to illustrate revenues by day and totals by day and for the four- week period.

	TUESDAY	WEDNESDAY	THURSDAY	FRIDAY	SATURDAY
Week 1	$8,850	$9,220	$11,760	$19,870	$17,450
Week 2	$9,200	$8,930	$12,890	$20,980	$18,450
Week 3	$8,900	$9,120	$12,340	$19,250	$18,890
Week 4	$9,100	$9,050	$11,900	$20,240	$18,200

FIGURE 2-88

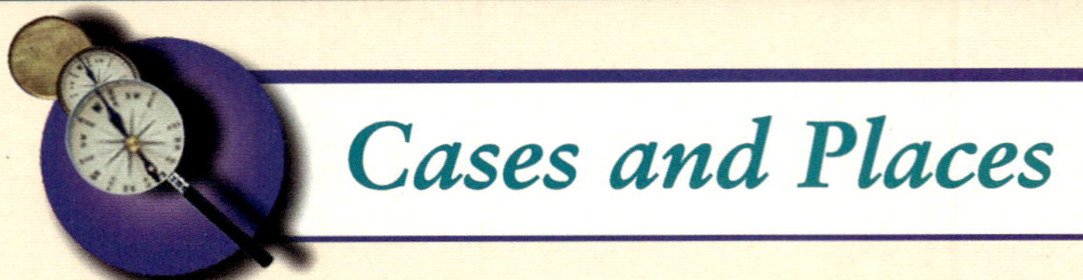

Cases and Places

4 ▶▶ The director of your school's fitness center has asked you to help her arrange more efficient scheduling of the facilities. She has asked you to determine which activities appeal to various age groups during the day. You administer a survey to all students and staff using the fitness center during the week and collect data on their ages and preferred activities. You discover that among students aged 17–21, 2,050 participate in aerobics, 1,795 in toning, 963 in running or walking, and 540 in tennis. Among students aged 22–29, 3,467 participate in aerobics, 3,984 in toning, 1,952 in running or walking, and 541 in tennis. Among students aged 30–39, 769 participate in aerobics, 970 in toning, 1,019 in running or walking, and 357 in tennis. Among students aged 40–49, 467 participate in aerobics, 647 in toning, 572 in running or walking, and 409 in tennis. Using this information, create a spreadsheet showing the age groups that participate in each of these activities. Include a bar chart to illustrate your data.

5 ▶▶ Medical and fitness experts recommend aerobic exercise for at least 30 minutes three times weekly. You have decided to visit your campus' fitness center between classes and on weekend mornings in an attempt to improve your health. You speak with a fitness trainer who develops an aerobic training schedule for you. In addition, she recommends 30 minutes of spot toning on alternate days. You decide to exercise by using the treadmill for 24 minutes on Monday, Wednesday, and Friday, the stepper for 18 minutes on Tuesday, Thursday, and Saturday, and the rower for 18 minutes on Sunday, Wednesday, and Saturday. Also, you plan to use free weights for 30 minutes every other day beginning on Monday. Use the concepts and techniques presented in this project to prepare a spreadsheet to record the total minutes spent exercising weekly on each piece of equipment and with the free weights. Chart the amount of time spent on each activity for four weeks. Then create a bar chart illustrating your exercise efforts.

6 ▶▶▶ Health experts recommend individuals obtain 10-20 percent of their total daily calories from fat, which for most people would be approximately 20-40 grams per day. Keep track of the total fat grams you consume daily during breakfast, lunch, dinner, and snacks for one week. You can determine the number of fat grams by examining the labels on the products, tables in nutrition books, or pamphlets at local fast food restaurants. Use the concepts and techniques presented in this project to prepare a spreadsheet. Include totals for each day of the week and each meal of the week to determine which days and meals are the healthiest for you. Include a bar graph to illustrate your data.

7 ▶▶▶ Drugstores often advertise that they have the lowest prices. Make a list of seven items that can be purchased from any drugstore. Visit at least three drugstores and obtain a price for each of the items listed. Make sure your prices are for similar items. Using this data, together with the techniques presented in this project, create a spreadsheet showing the price of each individual item in the drugstore and the total price for all seven items in a particular drugstore. Include a 3-D chart to illustrate your data.

Microsoft Works 6

Using Form Design to Create a Database

OBJECTIVES

You will have mastered the material in this project when you can:

- Define the elements of a database
- Start the Works Database tool
- Identify all elements on the Works Database window
- Change margins and field sizes in form design view
- Correct errors when entering field names
- Save a database file
- Position fields in form design view
- Insert and format clip art
- Enter a title in form design view using WordArt
- Format a title in form design view using WordArt
- Insert a rectangular bar into a form
- Add color to an object
- Format the field names in form design view
- Enter and format a text label in form design view
- Enter text and numeric data into a database in form view
- Display the next record, previous record, first record, and last record in form view
- Format the database in list view
- Set field widths in list view
- Print the database in form view and list view

Storing, Sorting, and Retrieving Mountains of Data

The faces of large electronic-commerce Web sites are deceptively simple. Friendly booksellers such as Amazon.com and Borders.com hide huge, humming servers that store mass quantities of data with sophisticated systems. These large servers quickly direct your Web clicks through a maze of database accesses and network routers.

Amazon.com created a database to store and list more than 18 million unique items in various categories ranging from books, CDs, toys, electronics, videos, and DVDs to home improvement products, software and video games. The company has used this database to serve more than 17 million customer accounts in 150 countries since opening its virtual doors on the Internet in July 1995. Today, Amazon.com also offers online auctions and free electronic greeting cards.

E-commerce Web sites are just one example of the many business, scientific, and personal databases that help people organize and process mountains of information systems. A computer database such as one developed using Microsoft Works Database tool, is a catalog of information about a particular subject: books, movies, planets, people, and sales. Using the computer's speed, data on a subject can be rapidly sorted according to specific criteria to find common denominators. For example, all the movies Sandra Bullock appeared in during the last five years. The more information about a given subject, the more useful a database becomes.

From keeping track of names, addresses, and phone numbers to creating a personal inventory of books, CDs, and videos, managing information is as important for students as it is for businesses. To make it easier to get started, Microsoft Works Database provides wizards and templates. All you must do is add data.

In addition to the many home and personal applications, databases are used for a multitude of business and scientific functions. Some databases keep track of genetic factors that aid in developing new disease-fighting drugs. Others organize satellite data for use in oil exploration or receive information from point-of-sale transactions that help refine retail merchandising. Still others track demographics and buying patterns to enhance consumer marketing.

The world expanded into the era of convergence with the help of the Internet and private networks, and sharing data became more flexible than ever before. The storage medium where the data is kept can physically reside with one individual or a group, yet anyone, anywhere who has access clearance can use, even update the information. Numerous data storage locations, often separated by thousands of miles, also can be linked electronically to form a single virtual database.

Databases have become a vital component in e-business strategies. Behind the scenes, computer databases assume greater importance everyday in the management of business, government, science, and personal activities. For those who use them, databases can offer a wonderful tool to store, sort, and retrieve information.

Microsoft Works 6

Using Form Design to Create a Database

CASE PERSPECTIVE

Alamo Golf and Recreation Centers has grown rapidly as an entertainment facility for the entire family. The management of Alamo Golf and Recreation Centers has asked you to design and create a database of current customers.

The information for the database can be found in the Alamo Golf and Recreation Centers marketing department. Jennifer Reeves, Director of Marketing, maintains current information on all customers. As the new assistant director of marketing, your first task is to design and then create a database that contains demographic and other information on each customer. Jennifer Reeves has requested an attractively designed database form that can be used to enter customer information.

You are to analyze the data available on each customer and create a database of all current customers of Alamo Golf and Recreation Centers. Once the database form is designed, you are to enter the information for each customer in the database. This database will allow you to keep customer information current and accurate while Jennifer Reeves and other management personnel can analyze the data for trends and produce a variety of useful reports.

Introduction

In earlier projects, you used the Microsoft Works Word Processor and Spreadsheet tools. In this project, you will be learning about and using the Database tool.

The **Works Database tool** allows you to create, store, sort, and retrieve data. Many people record data such as the names, addresses, and telephone numbers of friends and business associates, records of investments, and records of expenses for income tax purposes. These records must be arranged so the data can be accessed easily when required.

The term **database** describes a collection of data organized in a manner that allows access, retrieval, and use of that data. The Works Database tool allows you to create a database; add, delete, and change data in the database; sort the data in the database; retrieve the data in the database; and create reports using the data in the database.

Project Three — Creating a Database

Project 3 shows you how to create a database using Microsoft Works. The database created in this project is shown in Figure 3-1. This database contains information about customers belonging to the Alamo Golf and Recreation Centers. The information for each customer is stored in a record. A **record** contains all the information for a given person, product, or event. For example, the first record in the database contains information about Mr. Joseph A. Semora.

DATE JOINED	TITLE	FIRST NAME	MI	LAST NAME	ADDRESS	CITY	STATE	ZIP	OCCUPATION	TYPE	DUES	CHARGE	REC CENTER
06/12/01	Mr.	Joseph	A.	Semora	79 Fuller	Dallas	TX	75391	Retired	Executive	$110.00	Y	$16.50
06/12/01	Dr.	Hector	G.	Gonzales	14 Alamo	Garland	TX	75040	Doctor	Family	$80.00	Y	$16.50
06/15/01	Ms.	Kim	W.	Sanchez	1539 Centre	Dallas	TX	75201	Attorney	Single	$50.00	N	
06/16/01	Dr.	Doug	R.	Guen	26 Concord	Dallas	TX	75222	Doctor	Family	$80.00	N	$16.50
06/17/01	Mr.	Rubin	E.	Gordin	4 Hyde Park	Irving	TX	75063	Teacher	Family	$80.00	Y	
06/19/01	Mr.	Ivan	L.	Fenton	502 Beacon	Dallas	TX	75222	Accountant	Single	$50.00	Y	
06/25/01	Mr.	Jacob	L.	Reeves	205 Kent	Mesquite	TX	75149	Retail	Student	$35.00	Y	
06/26/01	Mr.	Michael	W.	Bovie	14 St. Lukes	Garland	TX	75040	Teacher	Family	$80.00	Y	$16.50
06/29/01	Mr.	Gabriel	G.	Vidal	234 Fendal	Dallas	TX	75222	Retail	Student	$35.00	Y	
07/01/01	Mrs.	Susan	D.	Johnson	26 Bexar	Irving	TX	75063	Retired	Family	$80.00	Y	
07/03/01	Mr.	Edward	A.	Fowler	12 Michigan	Irving	TX	75063	Retail	Family	$80.00	Y	$16.50
07/07/01	Mr.	Ron	G.	Gurtler	766 Dover	Dallas	TX	75391	Teacher	Single	$50.00	N	
07/11/01	Mr.	Bei	V.	Wo	2550 Park	Mesquite	TX	75149	Retail	Executive	$110.00	Y	$16.50
07/15/01	Ms.	Jenny	U.	Smith	342 Lindon	Irving	TX	75063	Teacher	Student	$35.00	Y	
07/16/01	Ms.	Kristen	E.	Wade	12 Kent	Dallas	TX	75391	Technician	Single	$50.00	Y	
07/18/01	Dr.	David	J.	Setaro	3454 Lake	Dallas	TX	75222	Retired	Executive	$110.00	Y	$16.50

FIGURE 3-1

A record consists of a series of fields. A **field** contains a specific piece of information within a record. For example, in the database shown in Figure 3-1, the first field is the Date Joined field, which contains the date on which the person joined. The Title field identifies the person as Mr., Mrs., Ms., or Dr. The First Name, MI, and Last Name fields contain the first name, middle initial, and last name of each of the customers.

The remaining fields in each of the records are:

1. Address: Street address of the customer.
2. City: City in which the customer lives.
3. State: State in which the customer lives.
4. Zip: Zip code of the customer's city.
5. Occupation: The occupation of the customer.
6. Type: The type of membership held by the customer. Four memberships are available – Student, Single, Family, and Executive.
7. Dues: The monthly amount paid by each customer for the use of the golf and baseball facilities.
8. Charge: Specifies whether the customer and family members have been approved to charge food and merchandise in the center to their account. If a customer has charge privileges, this field will contain a Y; otherwise the field contains an N.
9. Rec Center: The additional monthly amount paid by each customer for unlimited use of the Rec Center, including free use of all video games.

Microsoft Works 6

To find new ideas and information about how to use all that Microsoft Works has to offer, visit the Works 6 More About Web page (www.scsite.com/works6/more.htm) and then click Ideas and Projects.

Each of these fields contains information for each customer record. Thus, for record one, the customer's first name is Joseph, the middle initial is A., the last name is Semora, and he lives at 79 Fuller, Dallas, TX. In record two, the First Name field contains Hector, the middle initial contains G., and the Last Name field contains Gonzales. Dr. Gonzales lives in Garland, TX, has a family membership on which he has charge privileges. He pays $80 a month for use of the facility and $16.50 a month for unlimited use of the Rec Center.

It is important to understand that a record consists of one or more fields. When you define the database, you will define each field within a record. After you define the fields, you can enter data for as many records as are required in your database.

Creating a Database

Using the Task sheet listed on the Works 6 Task Launcher, you can create a database quickly and easily. For example, the home inventory databases and recipe book are wizard-generated databases that step the user through the creation of predesigned forms based on the Database tool. Database wizards are identified in the Works 6 Task Launcher window at the right of the program name.

Starting Microsoft Works

To start Microsoft Works, follow the steps you have used in previous projects to open the Microsoft Works Task Launcher (Figure 3-2). The following step summarizes the procedure.

TO START MICROSOFT WORKS

1. Click the Start button on the taskbar, point to Programs on the Start menu, and then click Microsoft Works. When the Microsoft Works Task Launcher window displays, if necessary click the Programs tab, click the Works Database link on the Programs sheet, and then point to the Start a blank database link.

The Microsoft Works Task Launcher displays information on the Works Database tool and the Start a blank database link displays blue (Figure 3-2).

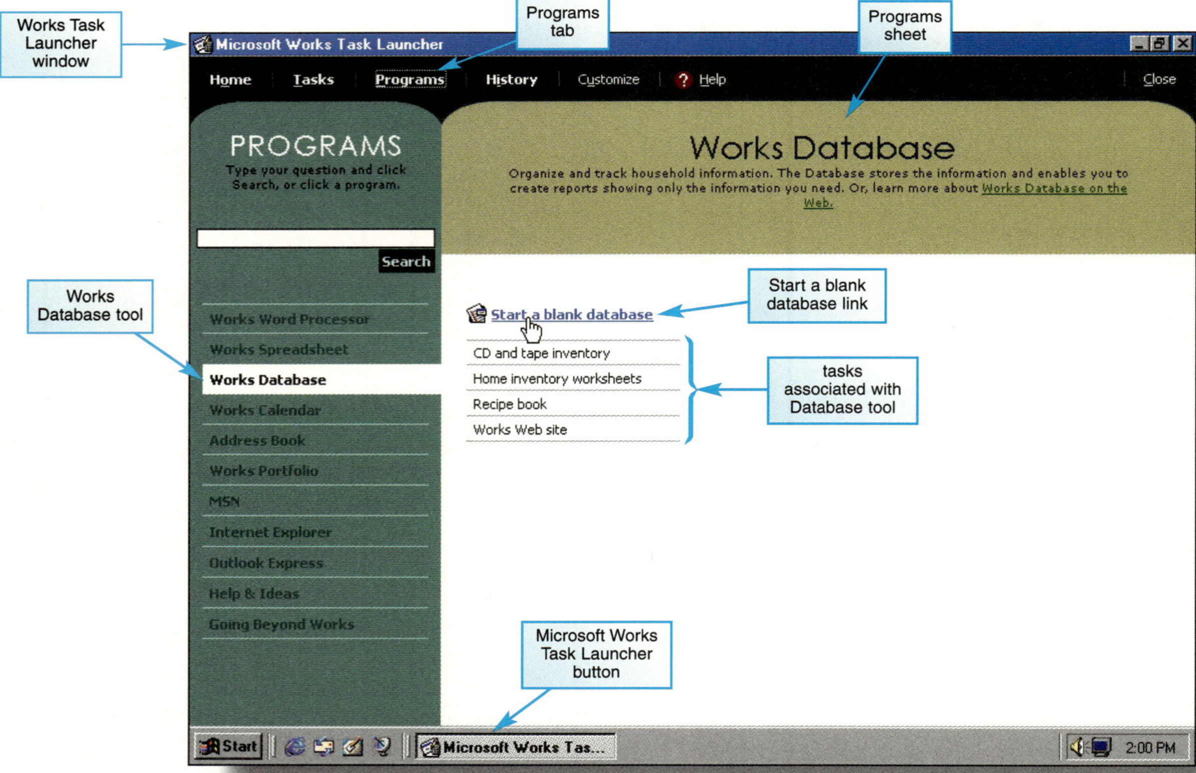

FIGURE 3-2

You now have started Works and are ready to use the Database tool.

Creating a Database

The next step is to start the Microsoft Works Database tool. When you start the Microsoft Works Database tool, Works displays the Create Database dialog box where you add fields to create your database. Each field has a format that indicates the type of data that can be stored in the field. The formats you will use in this project are:

1. **Text** – The field can contain any characters.
2. **Number** – The field can contain only numbers. Fields are assigned this type so they can be used in arithmetic operations. Fields that contain numbers but will not be used for arithmetic operations usually are assigned a format of Text. The Dues field and Rec Center field contain numbers and are assigned the Number format. The values in these fields display with dollar signs and decimal points.
3. **Date** – The field can contain text or numbers in a recognizable date format, such as 06/12/01 or June 12, 2001. The Date Joined field is assigned the Date format.

The field names and field formats are shown in Table 3-1. To create the database, perform the following steps.

Table 3-1 Field Names and Field Formats

FIELD NAME	FIELD FORMAT	FIELD NAME	FIELD FORMAT
Date Joined	Date	State	Text
Title	Text	Zip	Text
First Name	Text	Occupation	Text
MI	Text	Type	Text
Last Name	Text	Dues	Number
Address	Text	Charge	Text
City	Text	Rec Center	Number

Steps To Create a Database

1 Click the Start a blank database link on the Programs sheet. If the First-time Help pane displays, click the OK button.

Works displays the Database window containing the document name, Unsaved Database (Figure 3-3). Works also displays the Create Database dialog box. The default name for the first field in the database, Field 1, displays selected in the Field name text box.

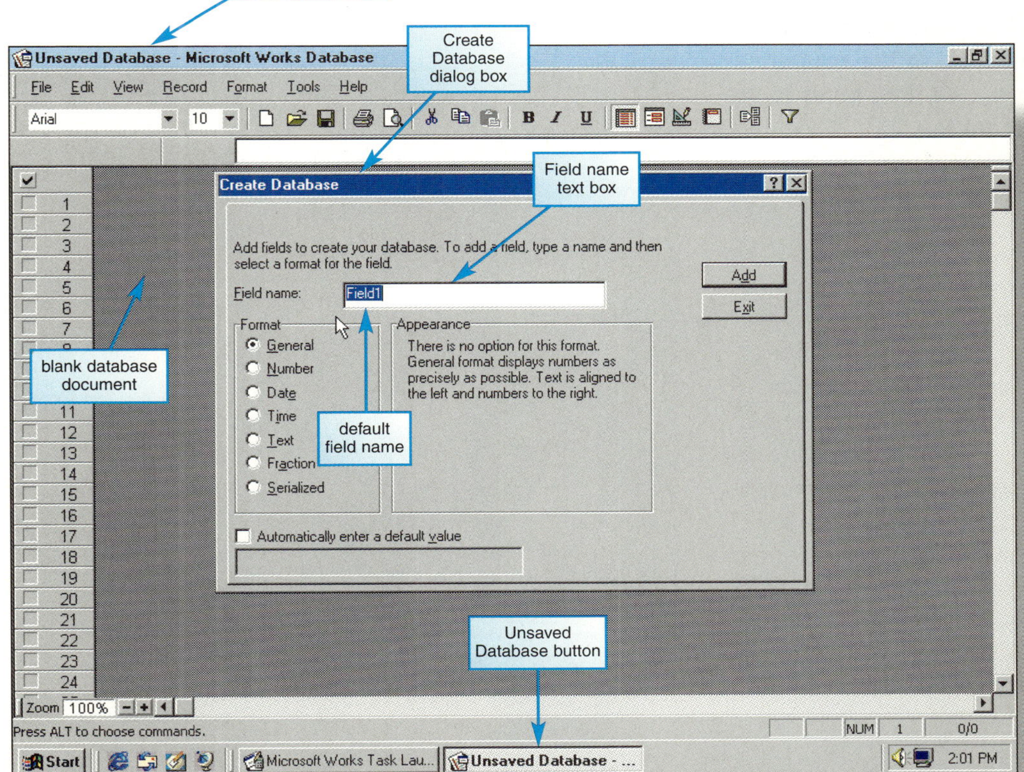

FIGURE 3-3

2 **Type** `Date Joined` **in the Field name text box. Click Date in the Format area. Verify that the first date format is selected in the Appearance list and then point to the Add button.**

Works displays the field name you typed in the Field name text box (Figure 3-4). When you click Date in the Format area, Works displays the Appearance list with a list of available formats for a date. The current date in the MM/DD/YY format is selected in the Appearance list.

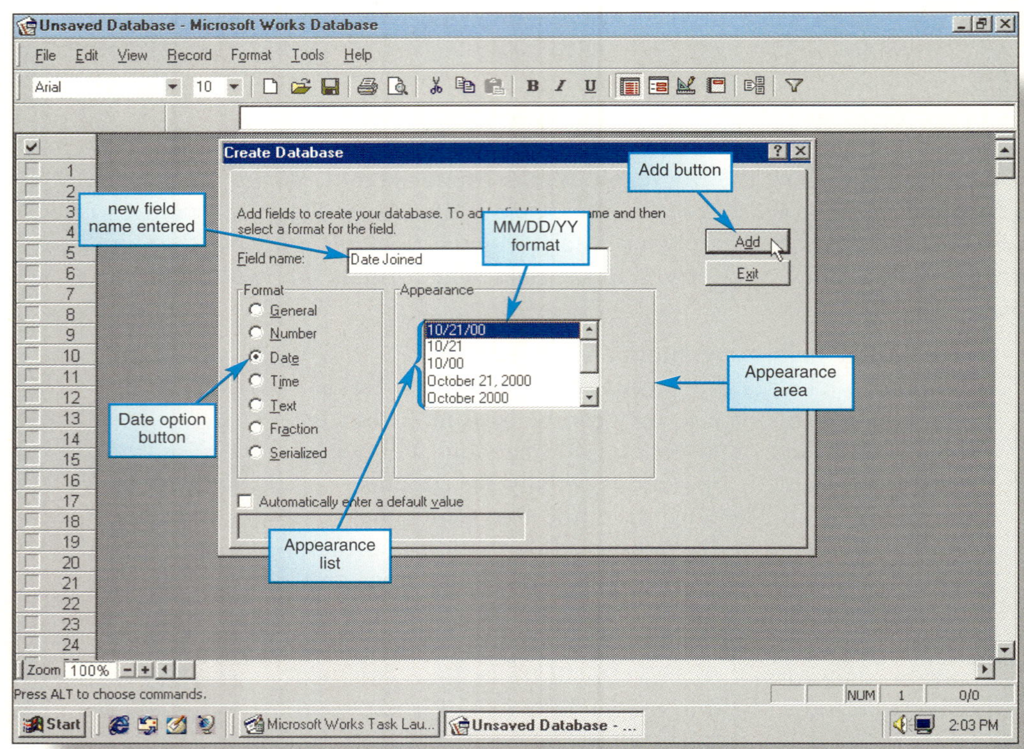

FIGURE 3-4

3 **Click the Add button. Type** `Title` **in the Field name text box, click Text in the Format area, and then point to the Add button.**

Works adds the Date Joined field to the database document (Figure 3-5). The dialog box remains open, ready to accept another field definition. The field name, Title, displays in the Field name text box. The Text option button is selected, indicating any characters, symbols, or numbers can be entered in the field. Works displays information on the Text format in the Appearance area.

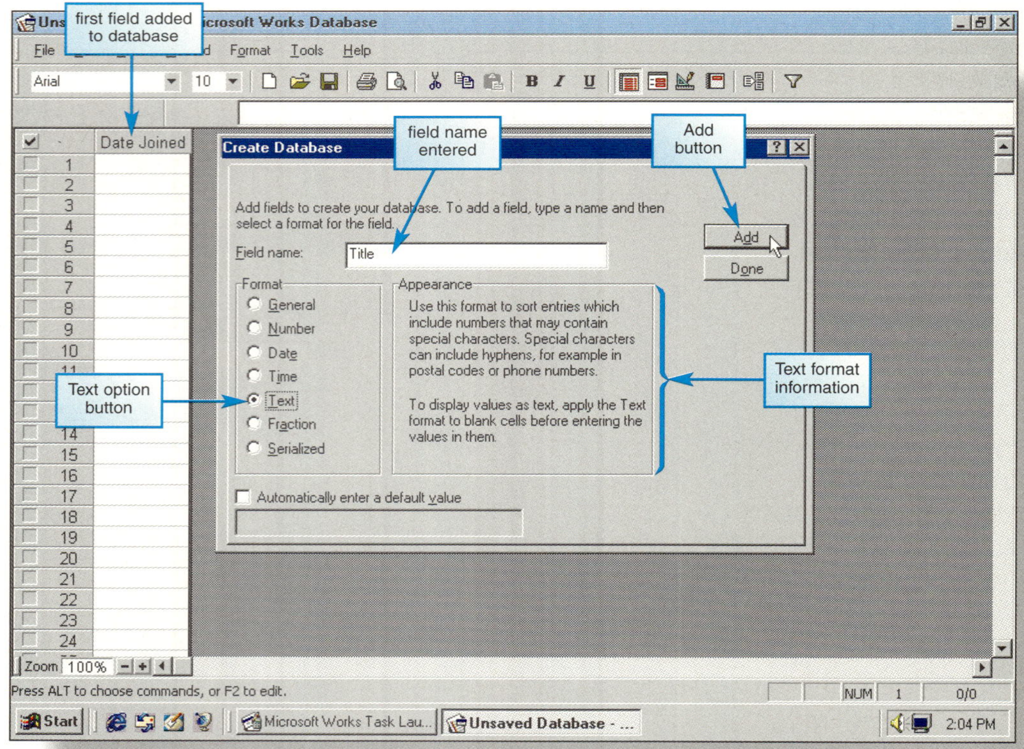

FIGURE 3-5

4 Click the Add button to enter the Title field. Repeat Step 3 to enter the field names for First Name, MI, Last Name, Address, City, State, Zip, Occupation, and Type using the format specified in Table 3-1 on page W 3.7.

Works adds the fields for Title, First Name, MI, Last Name, Address, City, State, Zip, Occupation, and Type to the database document (Figure 3-6). Only the first ten fields display on the screen, therefore the Type field does not show on the screen.

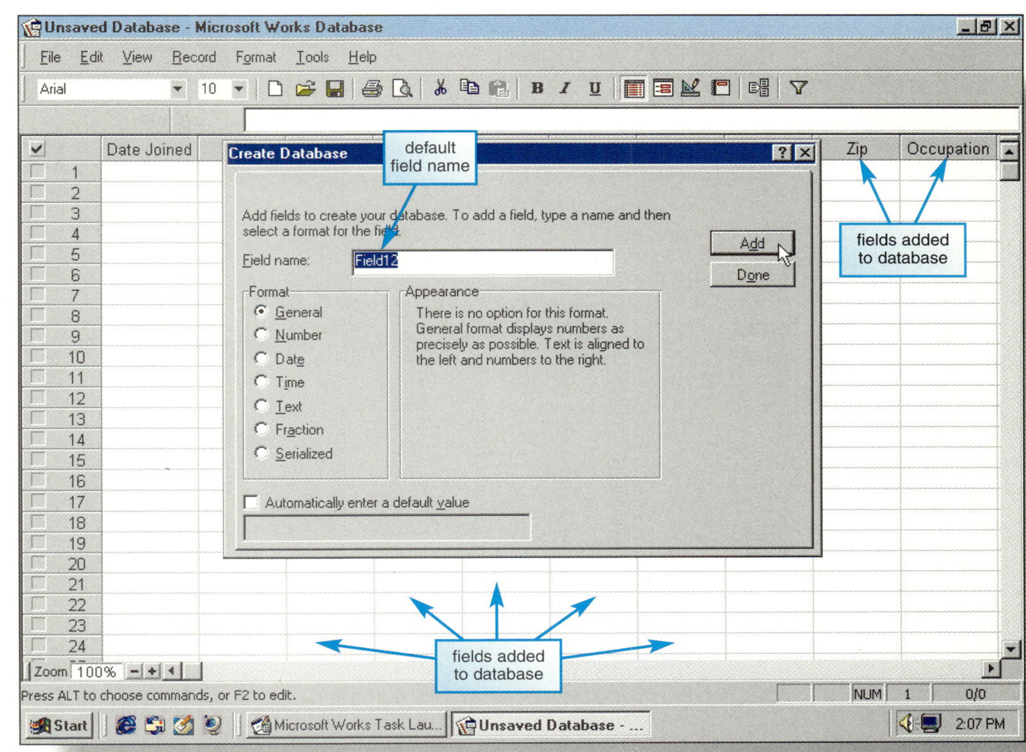

FIGURE 3-6

5 Type Dues **in the Field name text box. Click Number in the Format area. Click $1,234.56 in the Appearance list. Verify that the number 2 displays in the Decimal places list and then point to the Add button.**

The field name, Dues, displays in the Field name text box (Figure 3-7). When you click the Number option button, Works displays a list of available formats for a number. The $1,234.56 format is selected and the value 2 displays in the Decimal places list box. These selections instruct Works to add a dollar sign, a comma every three digits to the left of the decimal point, and two decimal places to a number.

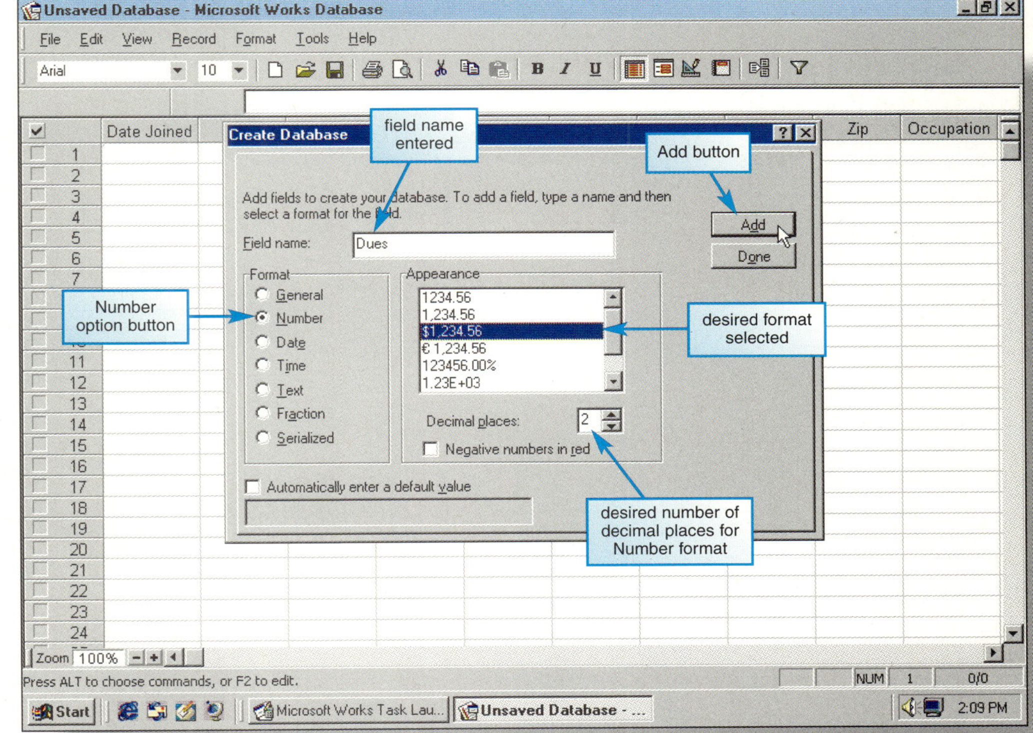

FIGURE 3-7

6 **Click the Add button. Type** Charge **in the Field name text box, click Text in the Format area, and then click the Add button. Type** Rec Center **in the Field name text box and then click Number in the Format area. Verify that $1,234.56 in the Appearance list is selected. Verify that the number 2 displays in the Decimal places list and then point to the Add button.**

Works adds the Charge field to the database. The field name, Rec Center, displays in the Field name text box (Figure 3-8). The $1,234.56 format is selected.

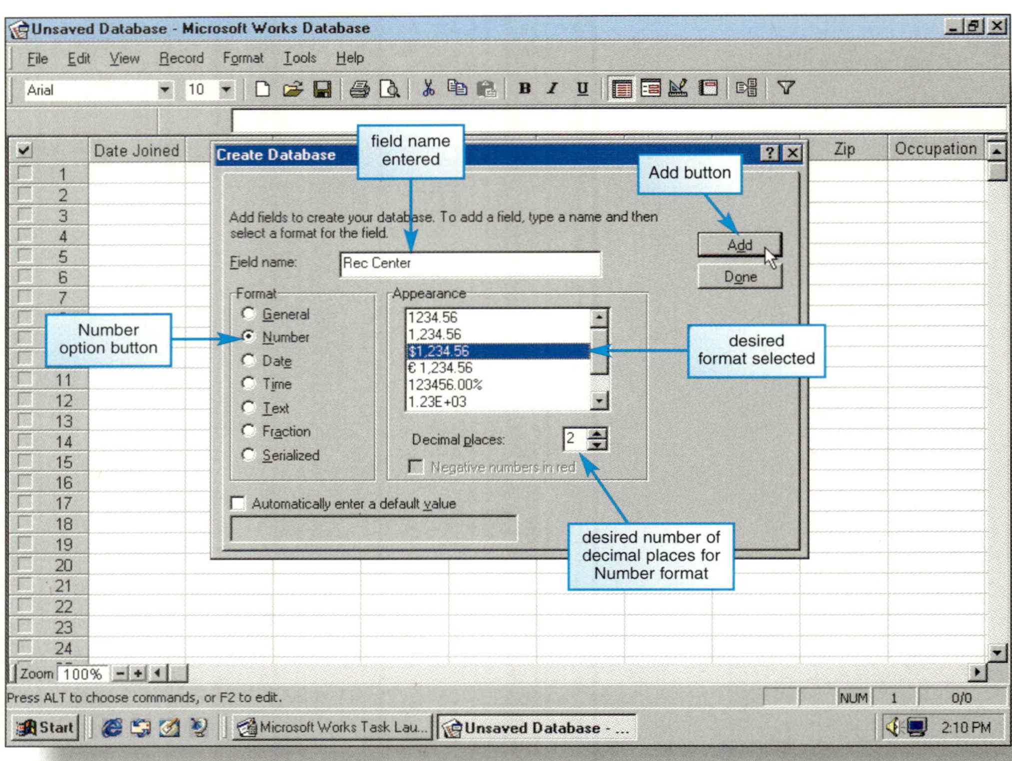

FIGURE 3-8

7 **Click the Add button. When Works displays Field 15 in the Field name text box, point to the Done button.**

Works adds the Rec Center field to the database. The default field name, Field 15, displays in the Field name text box (Figure 3-9).

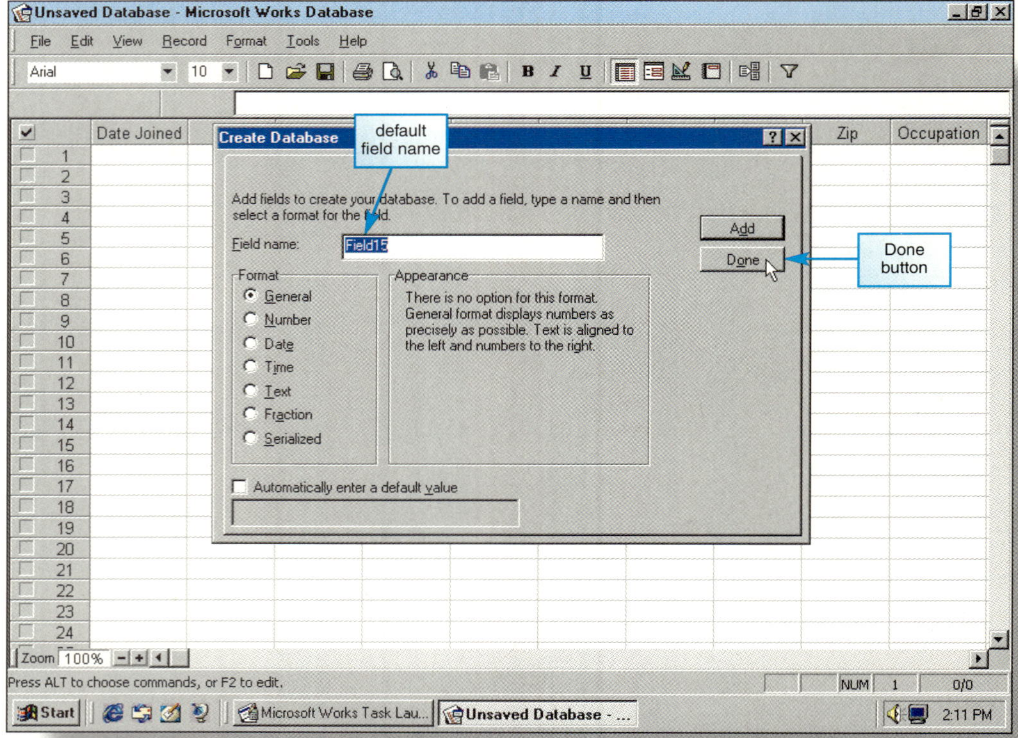

FIGURE 3-9

8 Click the Done button in the Create Database dialog box. If the Help pane displays to the right of the Database window, close the Help pane. If the Portfolio tool displays, close it.

Works displays the records in the database in a grid that resembles a spreadsheet (Figure 3-10). The screen in Figure 3-10 is presented in **list view**, *which allows you to view multiple records at the same time. The field names identify each column and the record numbers identify each row. The Date Joined field for record 1 is selected, designated by a dark border around the field. Only the first ten fields display. Use the scroll arrows, scroll boxes, or scroll bars to view the additional fields. The right side of the toolbar contains six new buttons. These buttons are explained as they are used. The List View button is light gray and is recessed, indicating the screen is showing the database in list view.*

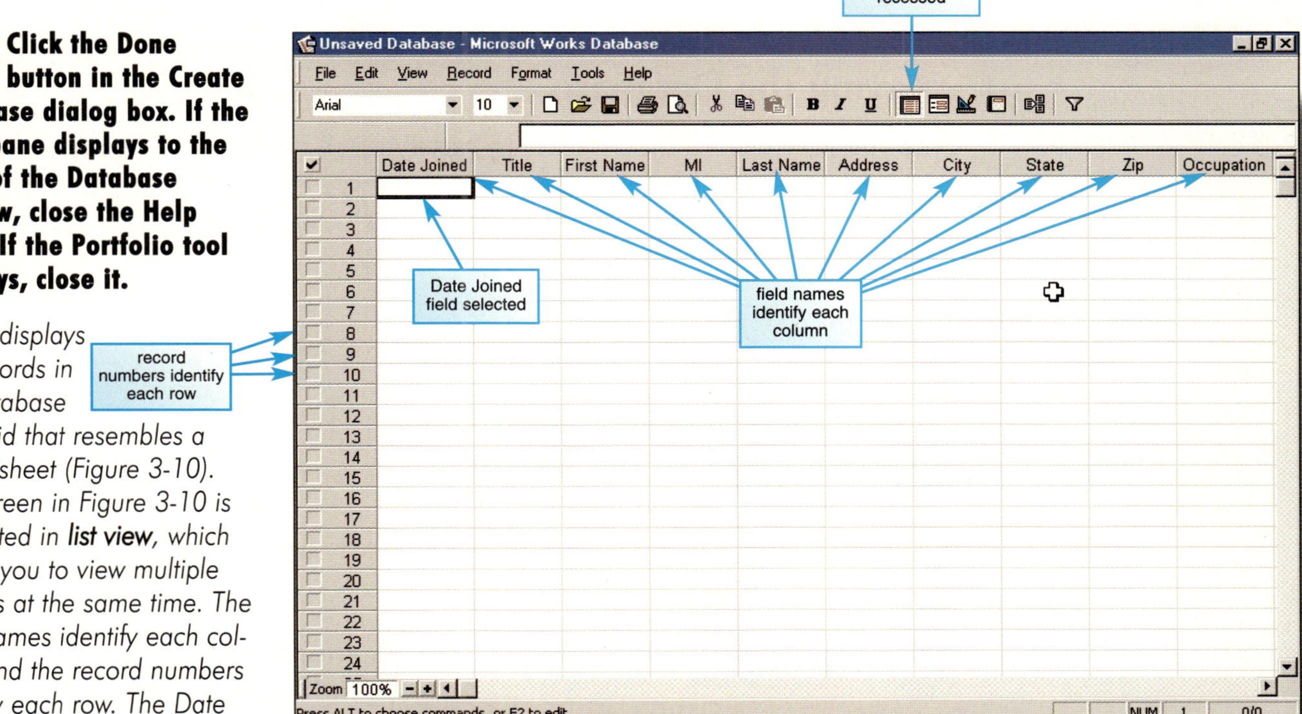

FIGURE 3-10

You should note several points when entering data into the fields for a database. First, choose the field names with care so that they accurately reflect the contents of the field. In all subsequent uses of the database, you will refer to the data in the fields by these names, so it is important to be able to easily identify the contents of the fields. The maximum number of characters in a field name is 15 characters, including spaces and punctuation. A field name can contain any character except a single quotation mark. You can enter up to 256 fields into a database.

Second, if you make an error while typing a field name in the Create Database dialog box, you can correct the error by backspacing to remove the error and then typing the correct characters. If you notice an error in a field name in list view, click any cell in the column that contains the incorrect field name. Then click Field on the Format menu and enter the correct field name in the Format dialog box. Click the OK button in the Format dialog box and Works will change the field name.

More About

Database Formats

When assigning formats to fields that contain numbers but will not be used for arithmetic operations, use the Text format. For example, a Zip code field should be assigned the Text format because Zip codes will not be involved in any arithmetic. In addition, Zip codes and telephone numbers that include hyphens cannot use the Number format.

Saving the Database

Once you have defined the database by specifying all the field names, normally you should save your work so an accidental loss of power does not destroy it. To save your work on a floppy disk in drive A using the file name Alamo Customers, complete the following steps.

TO SAVE THE DATABASE

1. Insert a floppy disk into drive A.
2. Click the Save button on the toolbar.
3. When the Save As dialog box displays, type the file name, `Alamo Customers`, in the File name text box.
4. If necessary, click 3½ Floppy (A) in the Save in list.
5. Click the Save button.

Works will save the file on the floppy disk in drive A and will place the name, Alamo Customers.wdb, on the title bar of the Works Database window. The Works Database extension, .wdb, may not display depending on how your computer is configured.

Databases in Works 6

In some Database Management System software, every table, filter, form, or report is stored in separate files. This is not the case in Works, in which a database is stored in a single file. A Works database file contains the filters and reports you create for the database.

Form Design View

After you have entered the field names into the database, the next step is to position the fields on a form so they are easy to read and use. You use form design view to arrange fields on a form. **Form design view** is a database view in which you position fields on a form, insert objects, or customize the form by adding color, labels, and borders. The final form design view of the database in this project is shown in Figure 3-11. Notice that each of the fields in the database is arranged on the page for ease of reading.

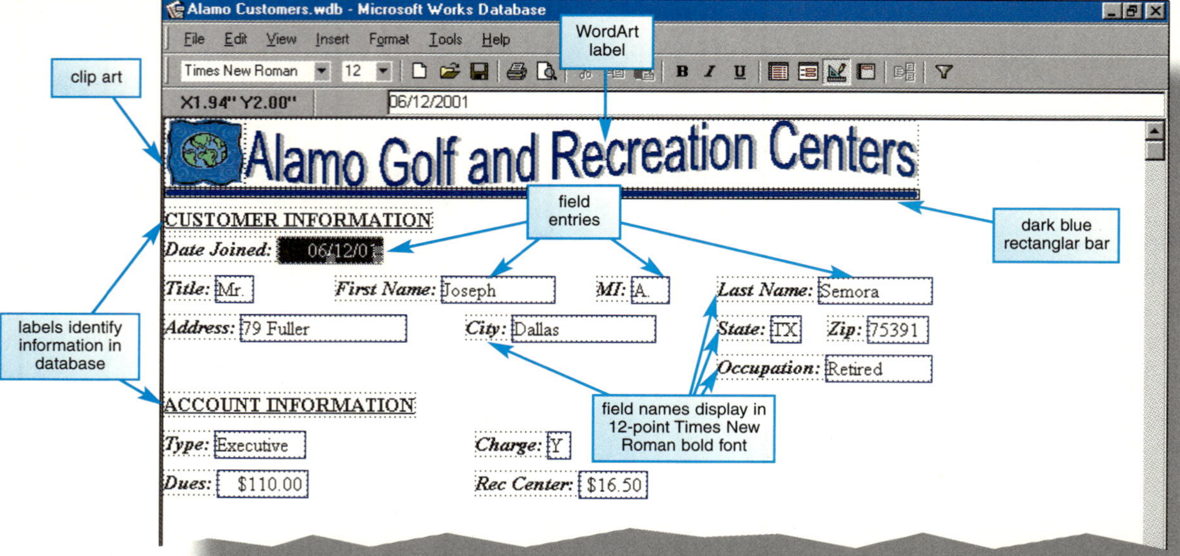

FIGURE 3-11

Four different elements are displayed in the form shown in Figure 3-11. The first is a clip art display in the upper-left corner of the form. The second element contains the words, Alamo Golf and Recreation Centers, which is the name of the company. The words, Alamo Golf and Recreation Centers, were created using a Works accessory called WordArt. **WordArt** allows you to display words on a database form in a variety of shapes and styles. You also may display a title on a database form using the standard fonts available as part of Works. In database terminology, when using standard font styles, the title would be called a **text label**. CUSTOMER INFORMATION and ACCOUNT INFORMATION shown in Figure 3-11 are text labels. A dark blue rectanglar bar displays below the clip art and WordArt.

The third element on the form is the field name. A **field name** distinguishes a field from all other fields in the database. For example, in Figure 3-11, you can see that the field containing the date joined is called Date Joined, the field name for title is Title, the field for the first name is First Name, and so on. A field name always ends with a colon (:). In form design view, you can format each of the field names in a style that makes the form easy to read. In the database for Project 3, each of the field names displays in bold and italics.

The fourth element on the form is the field entry. A **field entry** is the actual data in the field. In Figure 3-11, the field entry for the Date Joined field is 06/12/01. The field entry for the Title field is Mr., the field entry for the First Name field is Joseph, and so on. Field entries can contain any characters you wish and can be a maximum of 256 characters. By default, Works assigns a field width of 20 to each field. The default font is Times New Roman, and the default point size is 10.

Notice that dotted lines display around all elements in form design view. This indicates you can select the elements for editing or change their locations on the form. In Figure 3-11, the field entry for Date Joined is highlighted, indicating it is selected. Three square selection handles display in the selected area that you can use to resize the field. You can select the field name and the field entry area separately in form design view.

An important design decision is to determine the width of the field. You want a field to be large enough to contain the largest field entry, but no larger. In most cases, you will be able to determine the proper width based on the maximum number of characters in the field entry, but the field width you specify when defining the field will not always correspond to the number of characters actually in the field because many fonts, such as Times New Roman, use variable-width characters. For example, when using 12-point Times New Roman font, to place twenty letter i's in a field requires a width of 10, while placing twenty letter m's in a field requires a width of 37. If you use a font with a fixed width for each character, such as Courier New font, then the width you choose will correspond exactly to the number of characters in the field. When you choose the width, estimate as closely as you can while remembering you can easily change the width of a field at a later time.

The field widths for the form design view of the database in Project 3 are shown in Table 3-2.

Table 3-2 Field Widths

FIELD NAME	FIELD WIDTH	FIELD NAME	FIELD WIDTH
Date Joined	14	State	4
Title	5	Zip	8
First Name	15	Occupation	14
MI	5	Type	12
Last Name	15	Dues	12
Address	22	Charge	3
City	19	Rec Center	9

More About

Field Widths and Heights

In form view, the field height can be between 1 and 325 lines. When a field's height is more than one line, Works wraps the text to the next line when the text is longer than the field's width.

Form Design View

When you set up a database in form design view, you need to be careful how you set up fields in the database. Where you place the fields now affect what you can do with your database later, whether it is sorting, searching, adding, or deleting. The more logically you set up your fields, the easier it will be to sort, search, add, or delete records and fields.

Formatting the Database Form in Form Design View

After you have entered the field names, the next step is to format the form so it is easy to read and use. You use the form design view of the database to format the form. Because someone may have to enter thousands of records into the database, the form should be easy to read and use.

Formatting the form consists of a number of separate tasks. The first is to change the margins of the form in form design view. The next task is to change the size of the fields. Then the fields are positioned on the form. Next you are to insert clip art in the title area; type, position, and format the title, Alamo Golf and Recreation Centers, on the database form; place a border below the title; and add color in the title area. You then must change the style of the field names. The final step is to add a border around the field entries. Figure 3-11 on page W 3.12 illustrates the form for Project 3 after formatting. The technique for formatting is explained on the following pages.

Displaying the Database in Form Design View

The first step in formatting the form is to display the database in form design view. Perform the following steps to display the database in form design view.

Steps To Display the Database in Form Design View

1 Point to the Form Design button on the toolbar (Figure 3-12).

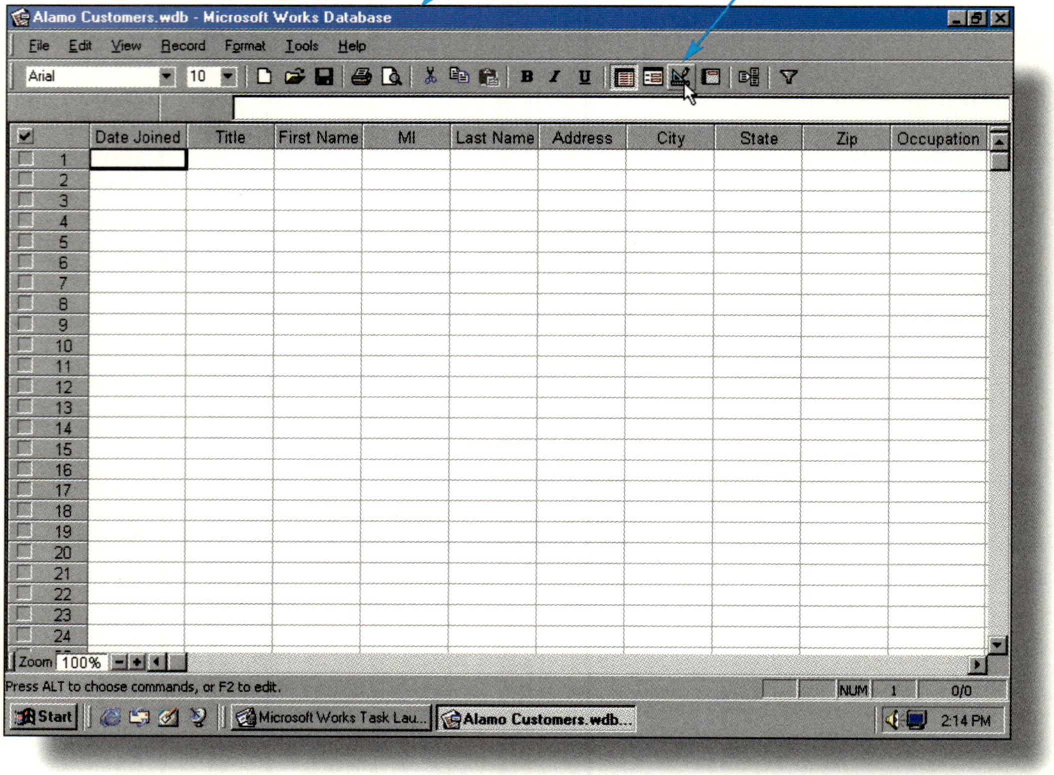

file name displays on title bar

Form Design button

FIGURE 3-12

2 **Click the Form Design button.**

Works displays the database in form design view (Figure 3-13). The field names you entered display on the form.

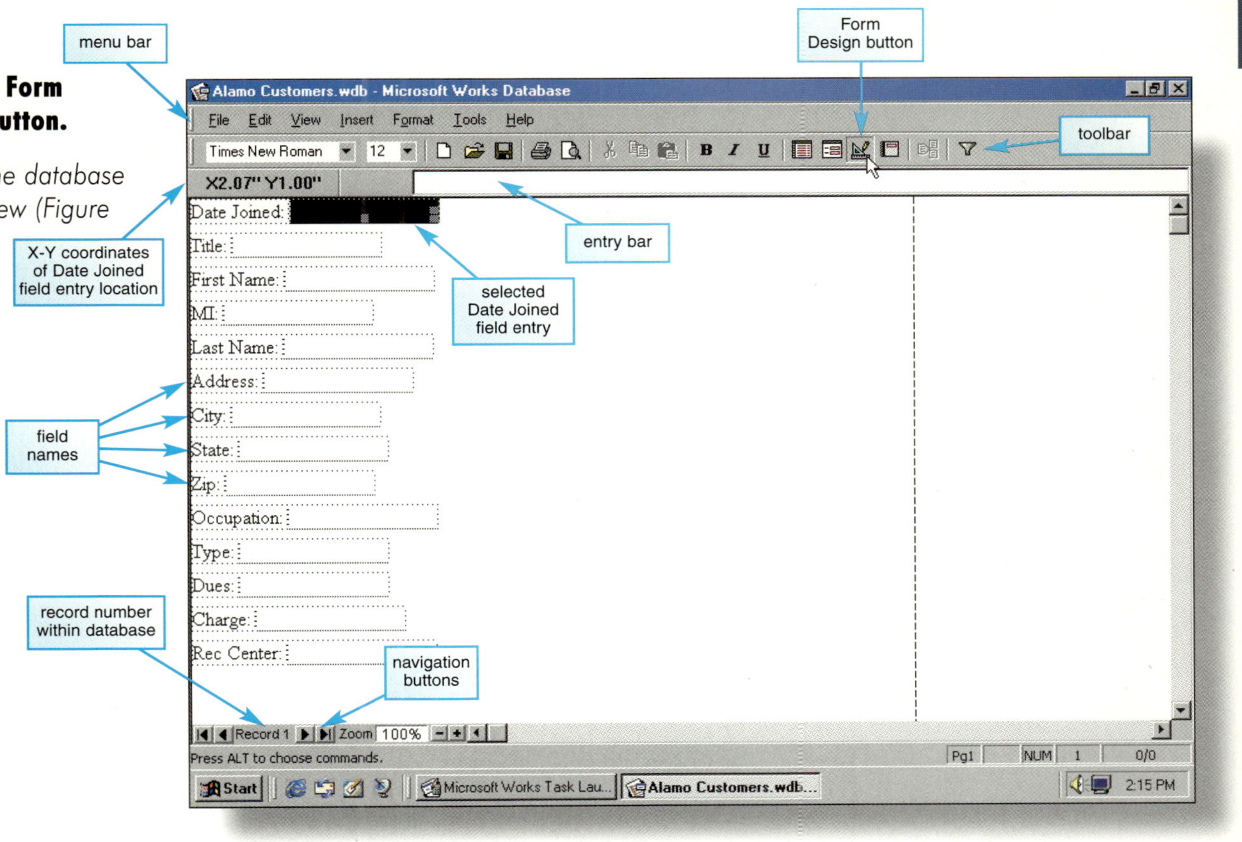

FIGURE 3-13

Other Ways

1. On View menu click Form Design
2. Press CTRL+F9

Although you can see in Figure 3-13 that the Database window displays much the same as the Word Processor and Spreadsheet windows, some important differences are present. These differences are noted below.

MENU BAR The **menu bar** in the Works Database window is the same as the menu bar in the Spreadsheet window. The menu names are File, Edit, View, Insert, Format, Tools, and Help. Most of the Database menus, however, contain additional or different commands from the corresponding Works Spreadsheet menu. These commands are explained as they are used.

TOOLBAR The single **toolbar** contains many of the same buttons as the Word Processor and Spreadsheet toolbars; however, the Database toolbar also contains a number of unique buttons on the right side of the toolbar. These buttons are explained as they are used. In Figure 3-13, the Form Design button is light gray and is recessed, indicating the screen is showing the database in form design view.

ENTRY BAR The Database **entry bar** functions in much the same manner as the Spreadsheet entry bar. When you type an entry into the database, the entry will display in the entry bar. The X and Y values shown in Figure 3-13 indicate the X-Y coordinates of the selected field. The X value specifies the number of inches from the left edge of the form. The Y value specifies the number of inches from the top of the form. In Figure 3-13, the X coordinate is 2.07" and the Y coordinate is 1.00". This means the field entry for Date Joined is located two and seven-hundredths inches from the left edge of the form and one inch from the top of the form.

Toolbars

Normally, the correct Works toolbar automatically will display. If it does not display, click View on the menu bar, and then click Toolbars. The Toolbars is a toggle in Works, meaning it is either on or off.

RIGHT MARGIN MARKER The **right margin marker** is the dashed vertical line down the right side of the screen in Figure 3-14. It marks the right margin on the form. The default margin setting is one and one-quarter inches on the right of the form.

SCROLL BAR The **scroll bar**, in addition to the normal scroll arrows, scroll box, and scroll bar, contains navigation buttons and a Zoom box. You use **navigation buttons** to move from record to record. The function of each of the buttons is described in Figure 3-14. The use of these buttons will be illustrated later.

The Zoom box is located to the right of the navigation buttons. The **Zoom box** controls how much of the record displays at one time in the Database window. Clicking the Zoom box displays a list of available zoom percentages to magnify or reduce your database. You also can use the plus or minus buttons next to the Zoom box to control the display. To magnify your display, click the **plus button**. To reduce your display, click the **minus button**.

More About

Positioning Fields on a Form

When positioning fields on a form consider which fields always are filled and which fields seldom are filled. Entering data is faster and more efficient if the user does not need to press the TAB key to skip over seldomly used fields. Group the most frequently used fields together at the top of the form.

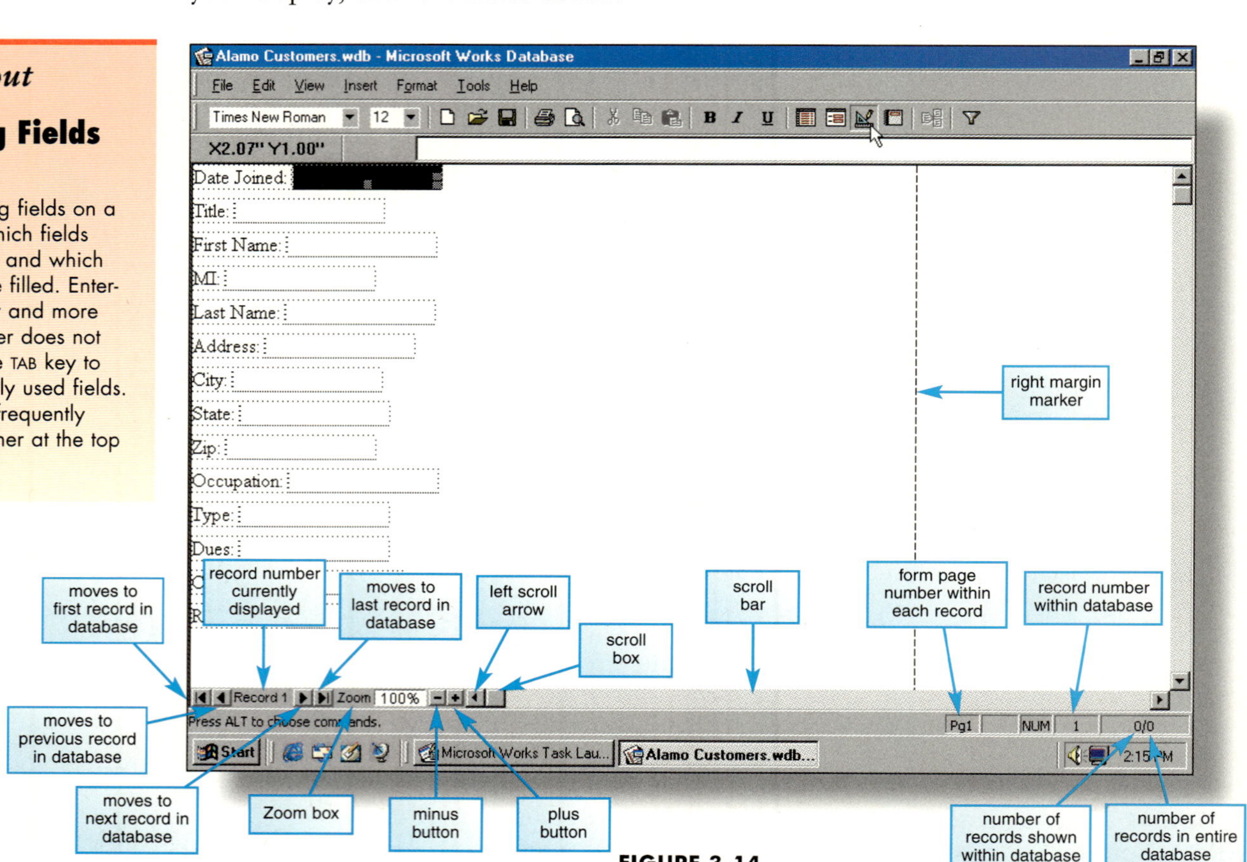

FIGURE 3-14

STATUS BAR The **status bar** contains information regarding the database and the record currently displayed (Figure 3-14). The entry Pg1 indicates that the screen shows page one of the record. In some instances, a record may consist of more than one form page. Works allows a maximum of eight pages to a record. The entry 1 following the NUM indicator indicates that record number one in the database is displayed. The next value, a number 0 (zero) separated from another number 0 (zero) by a slash (0/0), specifies the record number currently displaying in the database and the total number of records stored in the database. Works allows a maximum of 32,000 records in a database.

Changing Form Margins

In this project, you must increase the area into which you will enter data to create the form shown in Figure 3-11 on page W 3.12. This requires setting the left and right margins to one inch. To change the margins on the database form, perform the following steps.

To Change the Margins on the Database Form

1 **Click File on the menu bar and then point to Page Setup (Figure 3-15).**

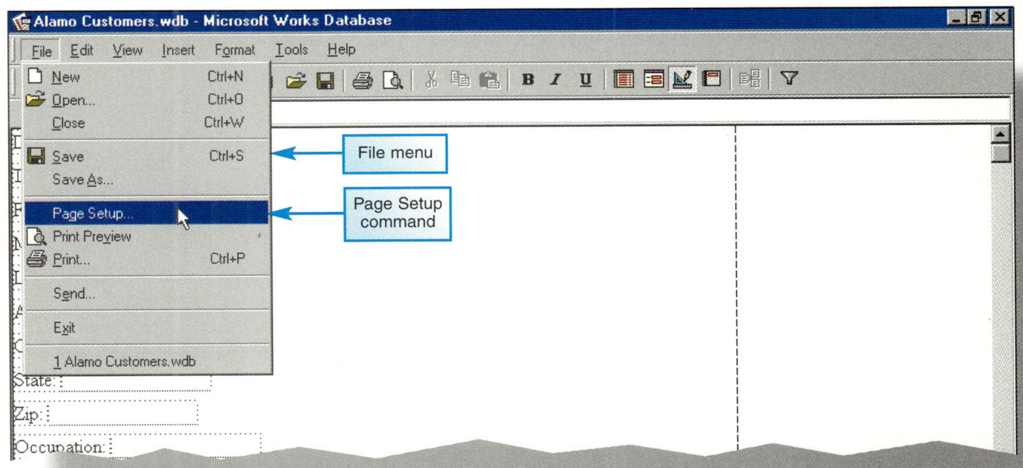

FIGURE 3-15

2 **Click Page Setup. When the Page Setup dialog box displays, ensure that the Margins sheet displays. Double-click the Left Margin text box and then type 1 to set the left margin. Press the TAB key to move to the Right Margin text box and then type 1 to set the right margin. Point to the OK button.**

Works displays the Page Setup dialog box (Figure 3-16). The left and right margins have been changed to one inch.

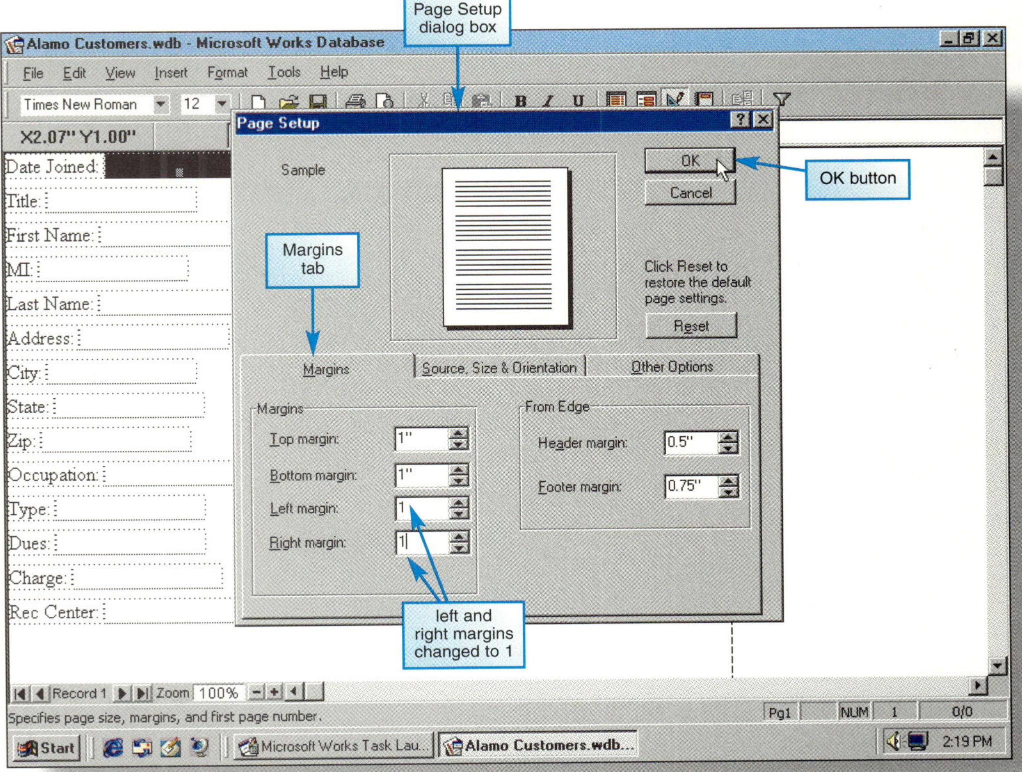

FIGURE 3-16

Click the OK button.

The Works database form design view displays (Figure 3-17). The right margin marker moves to the right because of the change in margins. Works also has moved the default X–Y coordinates of the Date Joined field entry to the new location of X1.82" Y1.00".

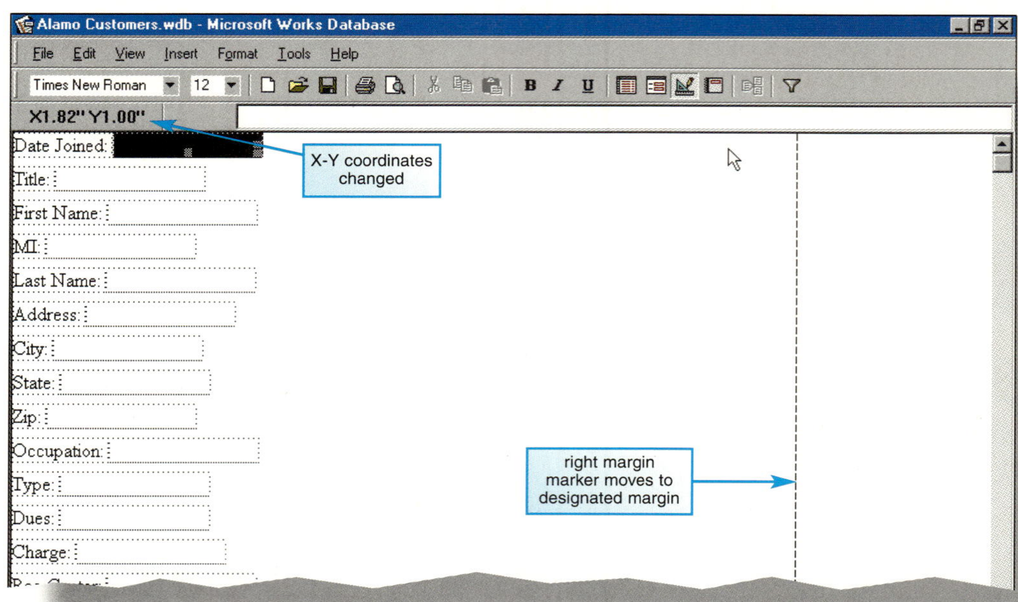

FIGURE 3-17

Setting Field Widths

The next step in formatting the form is to set the field widths for each of the fields in form design view. Table 3-2 on page W 3.13 shows the field widths for the form design view of the database. Perform the following steps to set the field widths.

To Set Field Widths in Form Design View

1 **If necessary, click the Date Joined field entry to select it. Click Format on the menu bar and then point to Field Size.**

The Date Joined field entry is selected and the Format menu displays (Figure 3-18).

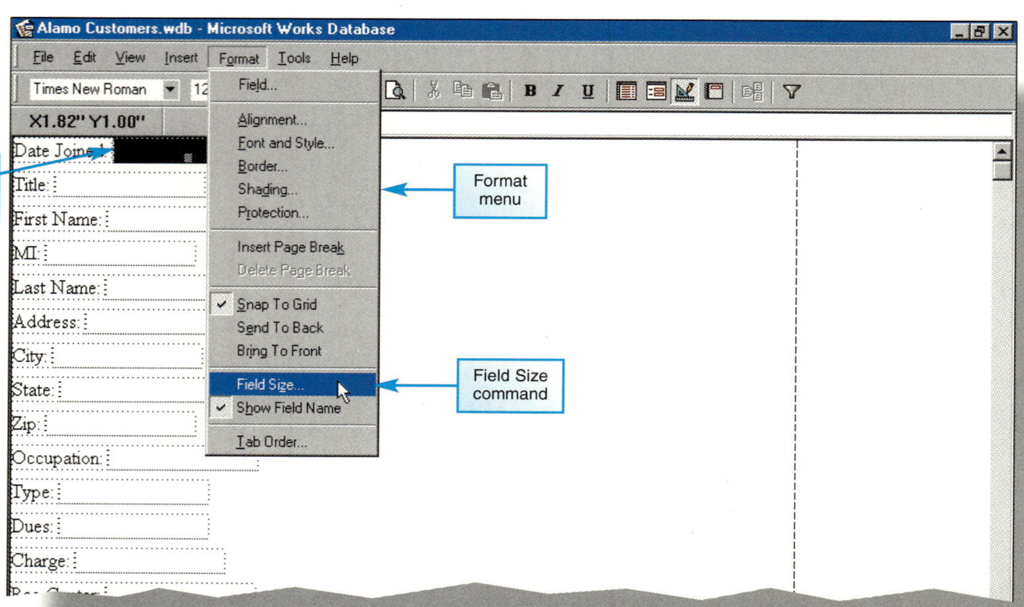

FIGURE 3-18

2 Click Field Size. When the Format Field Size dialog box displays, type 14 **in the Width text box, and then point to the OK button.**

Works displays the Format Field Size dialog box (Figure 3-19). The value 14, which is the new field size, displays in the Width text box.

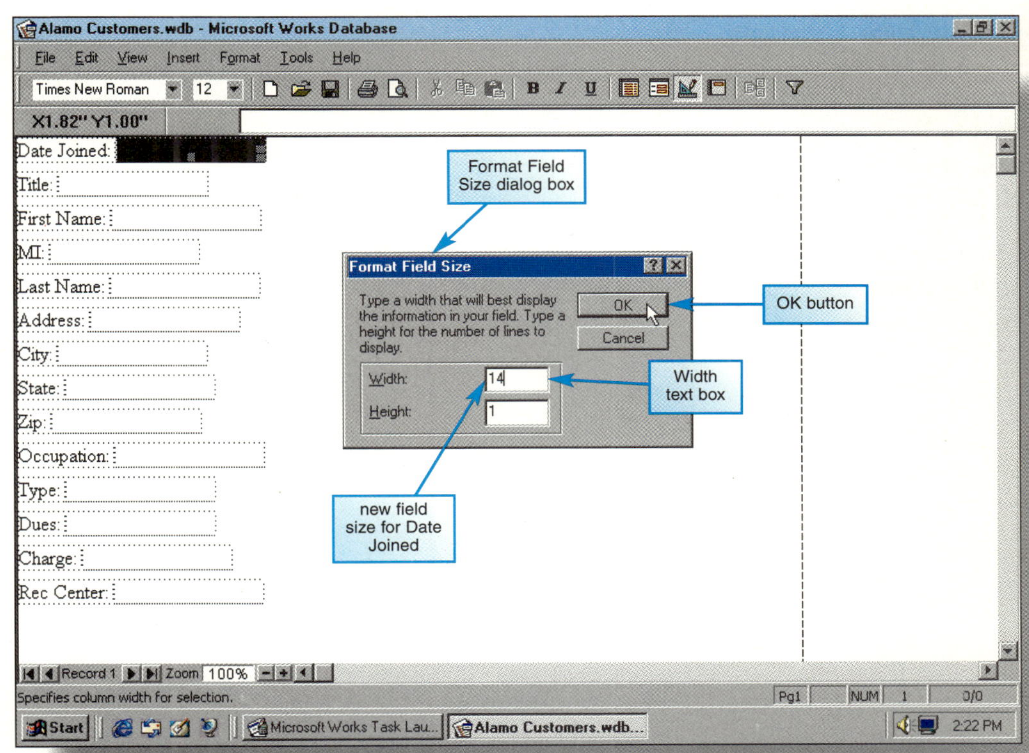

FIGURE 3-19

3 Click the OK button.

Works changes the width of the Date Joined field entry to 14 (Figure 3-20).

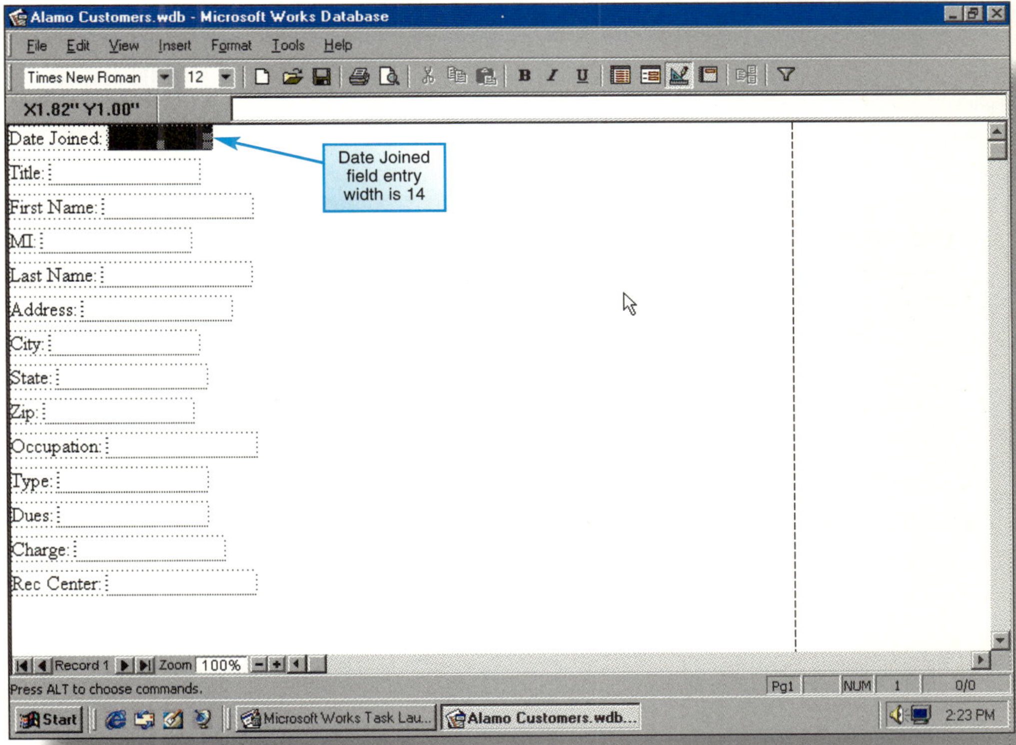

FIGURE 3-20

4 Use Steps 1 through 3 to set the remainder of the field entries to their proper widths as specified in Table 3-2 on page W 3.13.

The field entry widths are set to their new sizes (Figure 3-21).

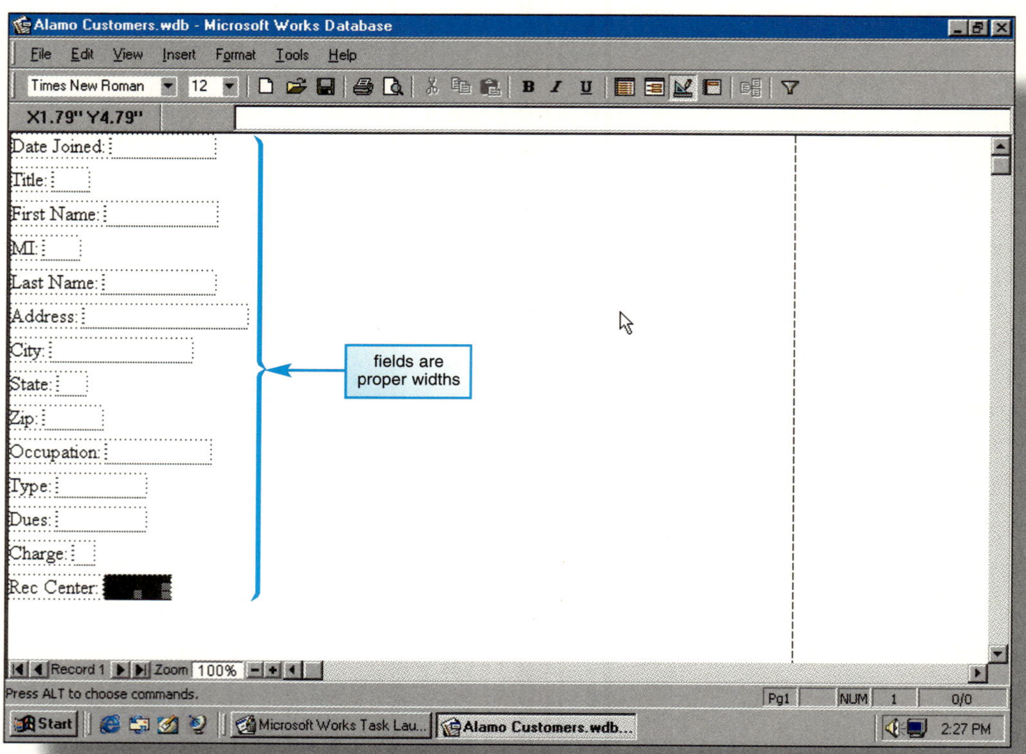

FIGURE 3-21

Other Ways

1. Click field entry, click middle handle and drag to desired width

Positioning Fields on the Form

The first task of positioning the fields in the proper location requires that you determine X-Y coordinates for each of the fields. You can do this by dragging the field names and field entries to various locations until you are satisfied with their placement on the form. The coordinates in Table 3-3 are specified to assist in illustrating the technique of dragging fields in form design view. They were determined after moving the fields into various locations and then finally deciding on the best form layout. These locations can be modified at a later time, as will be seen when the clip art and form title are entered and formatted.

Table 3-3 Field Coordinates

FIELD NAME	X COORDINATE	Y COORDINATE
Date Joined	X1.00″	Y1.00″
Title	X1.00″	Y1.33″
First Name	X2.42″	Y1.33″
M.I.	X4.58″	Y1.33″
Last Name	X5.58″	Y1.33″
Address	X1.00″	Y1.67″
City	X3.50″	Y1.67″
State	X5.58″	Y1.67″
Zip	X6.50″	Y1.67″
Occupation	X5.58″	Y2.00″
Type	X1.00″	Y2.67″
Dues	X1.00″	Y3.00″
Charge	X3.58″	Y2.67″
Rec Center	X3.58″	Y3.00″

Perform the following steps to position the fields on the form.

To Position Fields on the Form

1 Select the Last Name field name by clicking the words, Last Name.

Works selects the Last Name field name with a dark background and the block arrow mouse pointer displays with the word DRAG below it (Figure 3-22). You often will find it easier to move fields out of sequence. The Last Name field is moved in this step because it occupies the rightmost position on the second line of the form.

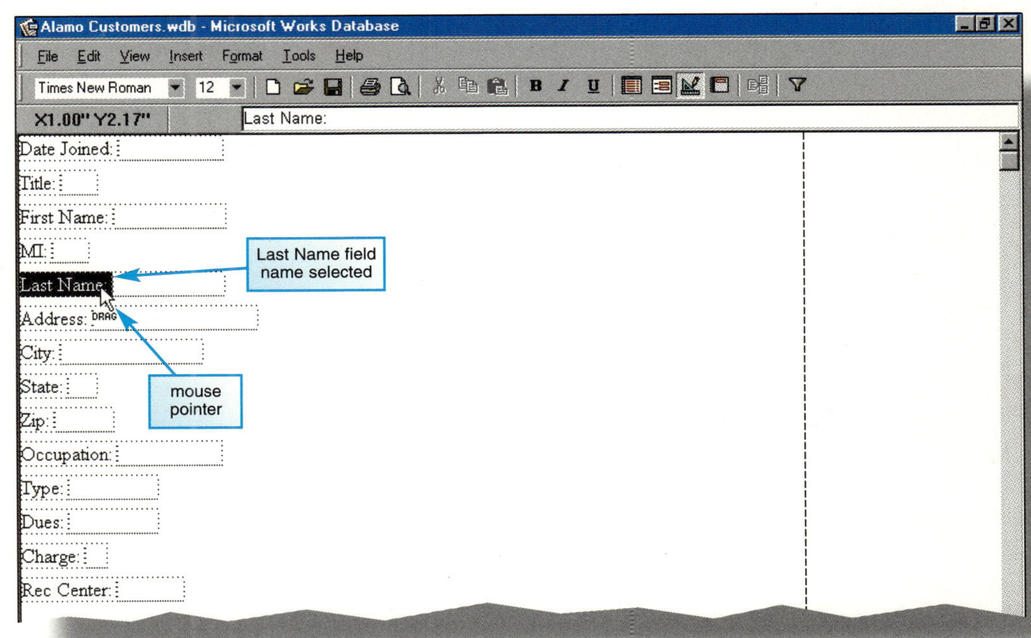

FIGURE 3-22

2 Drag the Last Name field toward its location.

As you drag the field, Works displays a dotted border around both the field name and the field itself (Figure 3-23). The word MOVE displays below the mouse pointer. The coordinates of the border are changed as you drag the border. The field you drag remains selected and does not move while you drag.

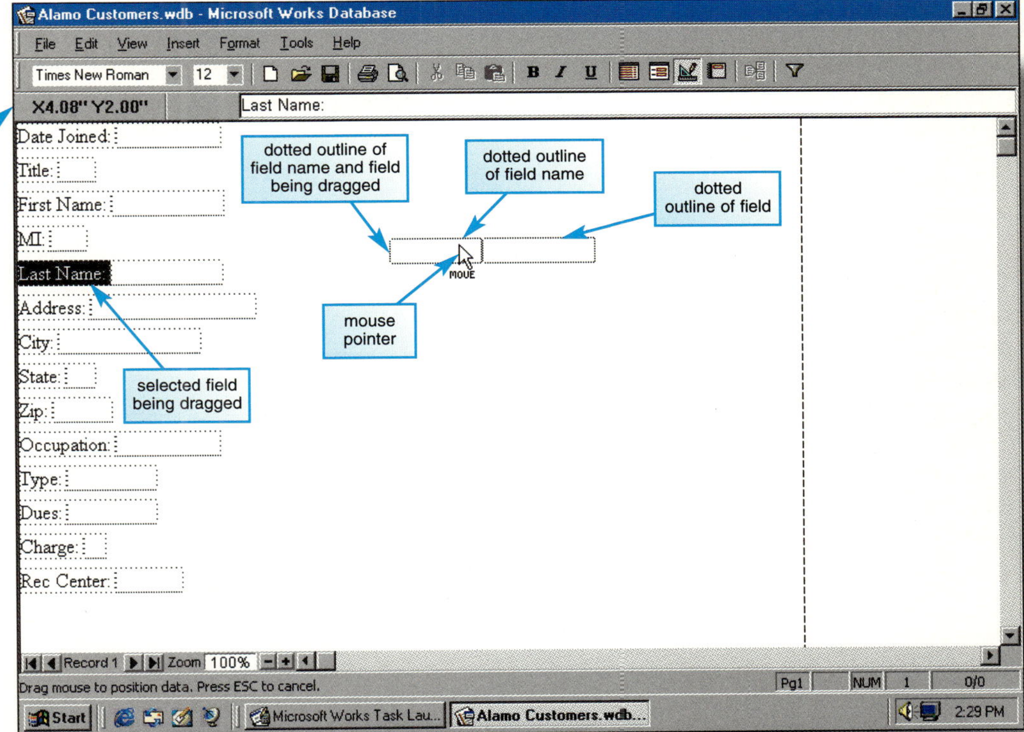

FIGURE 3-23

3 When the dotted border is at the desired location (X5.58″ Y1.33″), release the mouse button.

Works moves the selected field to the location of the dotted border (Figure 3-24). After being moved, the field name remains selected.

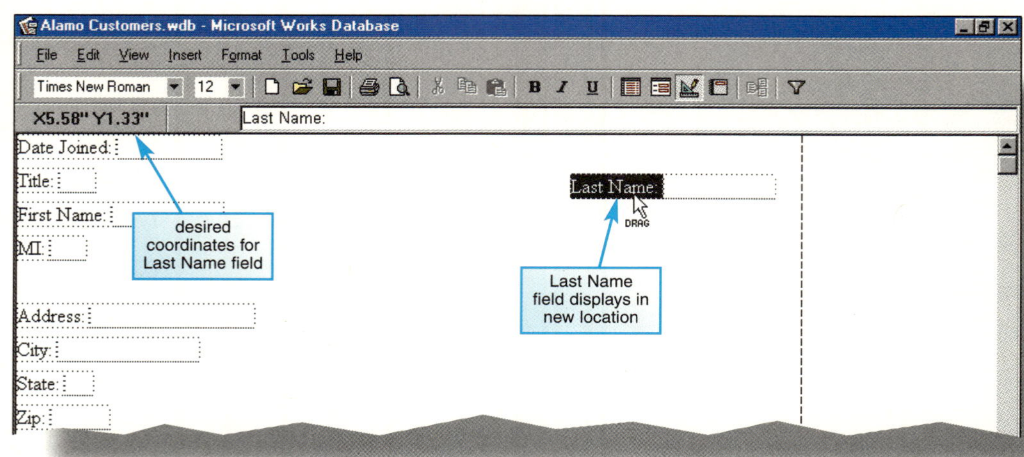

FIGURE 3-24

4 Using the same technique, move the MI field to coordinates X4.58″ Y1.33″, the First Name field to coordinates X2.42″ Y1.33″, and the Title field to coordinates X1.00″ Y1.33″.

The fields are moved to the prescribed locations (Figure 3-25). Each of the fields is on the same line (Y coordinate 1.33″).

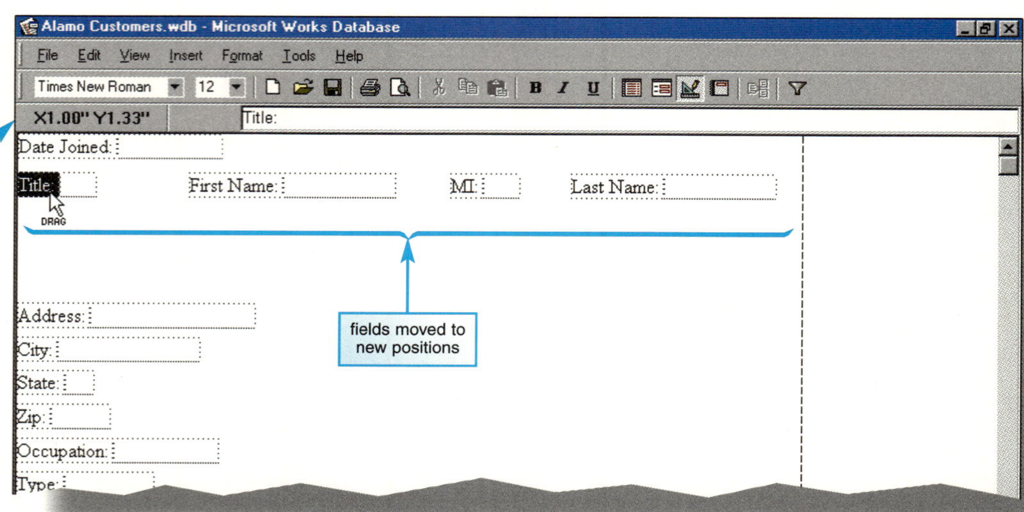

FIGURE 3-25

5 Drag the Zip, State, City, Address, and Occupation fields to their proper locations, as specified in Table 3-3 on page W 3.20.

Each of the fields is positioned in its proper location (Figure 3-26).

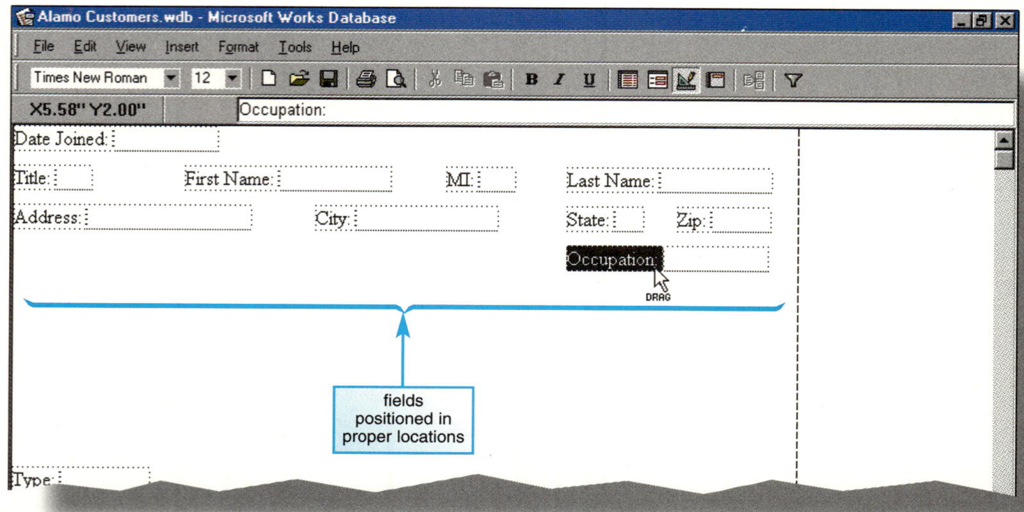

FIGURE 3-26

6 Drag the remaining fields to their proper locations as specified in Table 3-3.

All the fields are positioned in their proper locations (Figure 3-27).

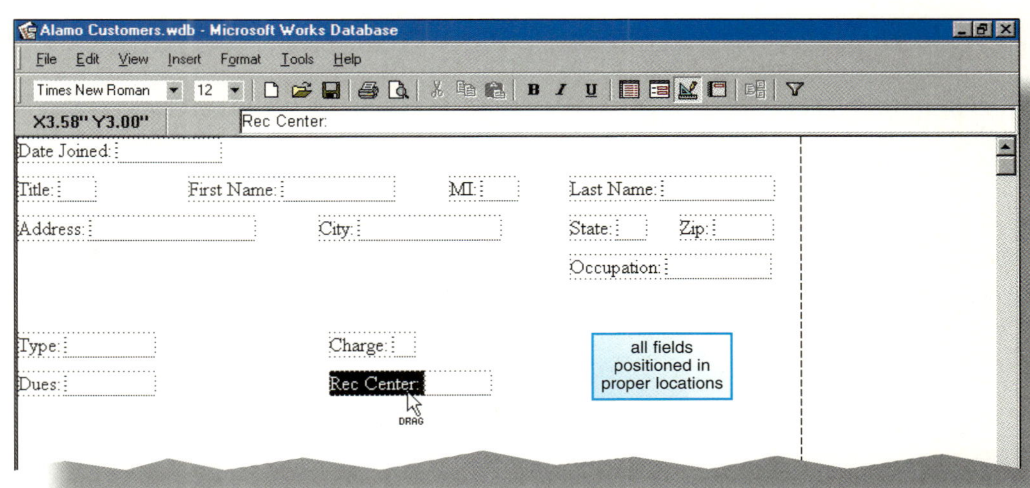

FIGURE 3-27

Other Ways

1. On Edit menu click Position Selection

You should note that even after arranging the fields in the form, you can move the fields at any time to make the form more attractive and easier to read.

Moving the Field Names as a Unit

You must make room at the top of the form because the clip art will be inserted in the upper-left corner of the form, and the title will be entered, increased in size, and formatted using WordArt. The title will occupy an area approximately one inch at the top of the form. Below the title, you also will insert a bar and a text label to identify the information located after the label. To provide for this area at the top of the form, move the field names down approximately one inch. Rather than moving each field name individually, you can move the field names down as a unit on the form, as shown in the following steps.

More About

Selecting Field Names

To select many fields at one time in form view, you can save time by drawing a lasso around the fields. Click at one corner of the block, and then drag to the opposite corner to lasso the block.

To Move Field Names as a Unit

1 Click the Date Joined field name. Hold down the CTRL key and click the Title field name. Continue this process until all fields on the database form are selected. Release the CTRL key.

All fields are selected on the form (Figure 3-28).

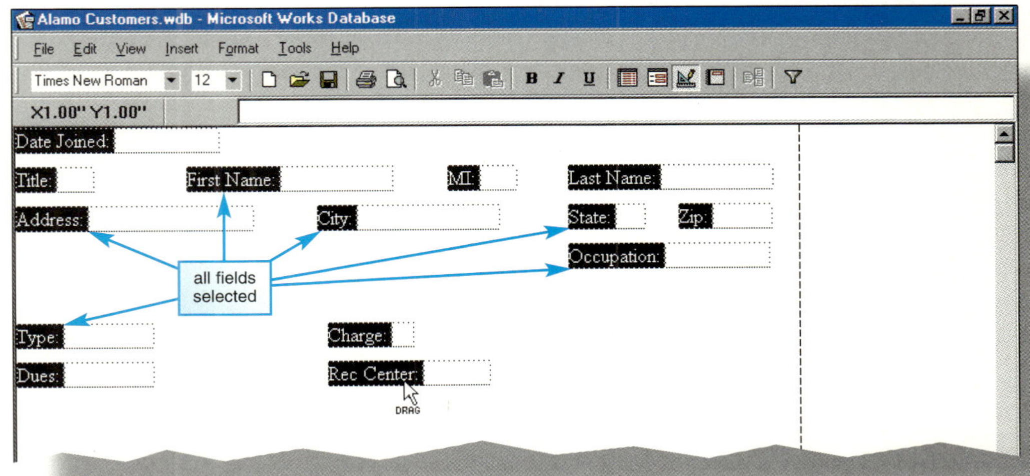

FIGURE 3-28

2 Point to the Date Joined field name and drag all fields down by dragging the Date Joined field down.

After you select all field names, dragging a single field name will drag all field names as a unit (Figure 3-29).

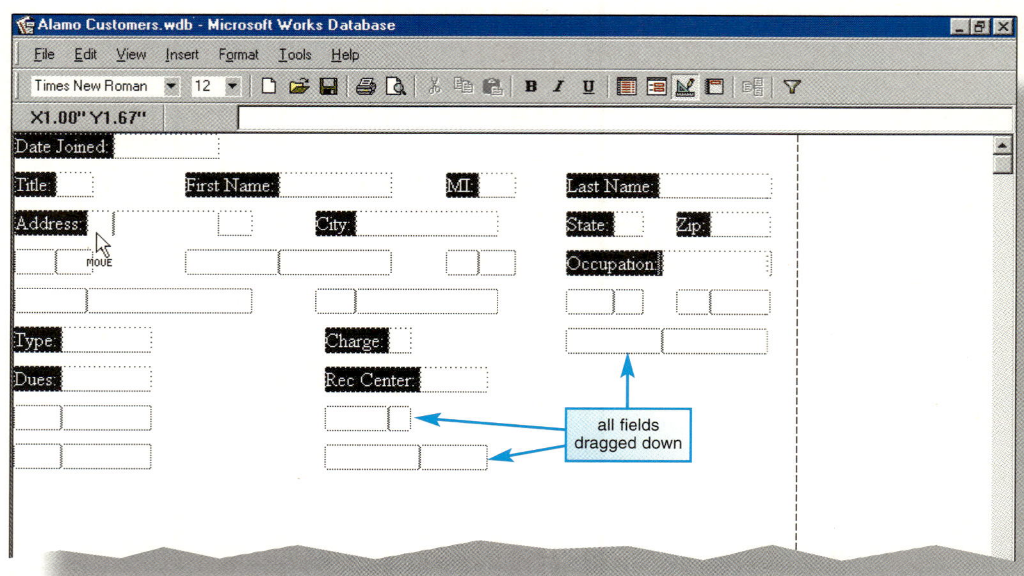

FIGURE 3-29

3 When the coordinates are X1.00" Y2.00", release the mouse button.

The fields are repositioned on the database form (Figure 3-30). The Date Joined field is positioned at coordinates X1.00" Y2.00". The other fields retain their relative positions.

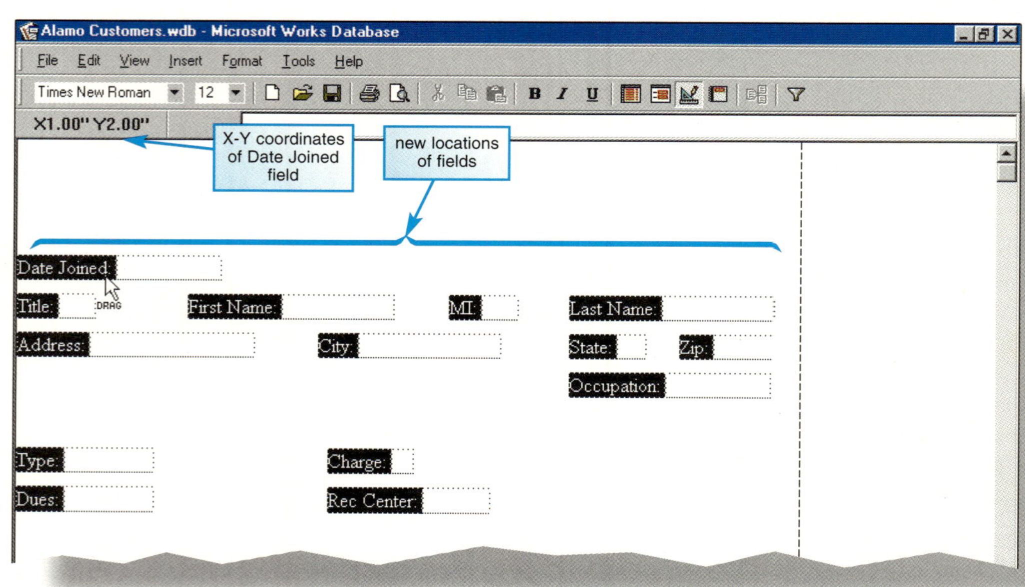

FIGURE 3-30

Inserting Clip Art in a Database Form

In Project 1, you inserted clip art from the Clip Gallery into a word processing document. Works also allows users to insert clip art into a database form. In this project, you will insert a clip art image that will highlight the Alamo Golf and Recreation Centers as a world-class entertainment facility. Perform the following steps to insert a clip art image from the Clip Gallery.

To Insert Clip Art in a Database Form

1 **Click the upper-left corner of the form at the coordinates X1.00" Y1.00". Click Insert on the menu bar and then point to ClipArt.**

The insertion point is positioned in the upper-left corner on the form at the coordinates X1.00" Y1.00", and the Insert menu displays (Figure 3-31).

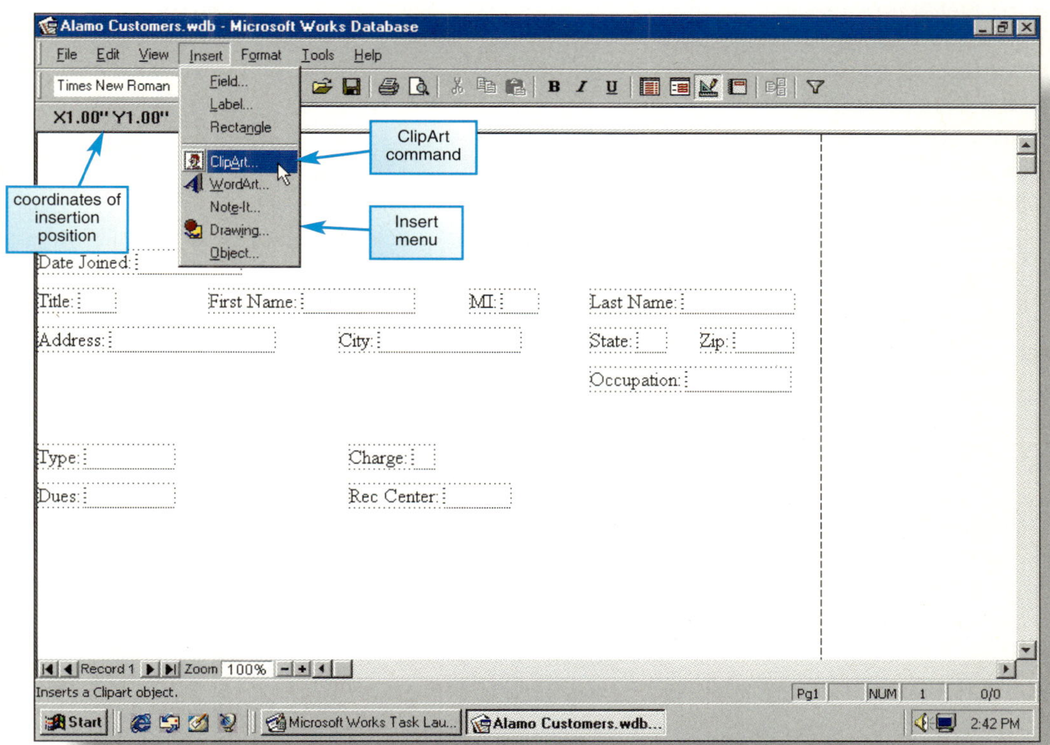

FIGURE 3-31

2 **Click ClipArt. When the Insert Clip Art dialog box displays, if necessary click the Find tab and then type** `world` **in the Type a keyword text box. If necessary, click All pictures (clip art and photographs) in the Select a media type list, and then point to the Search button.**

The Find sheet displays in the Insert Clip Art dialog box (Figure 3-32).

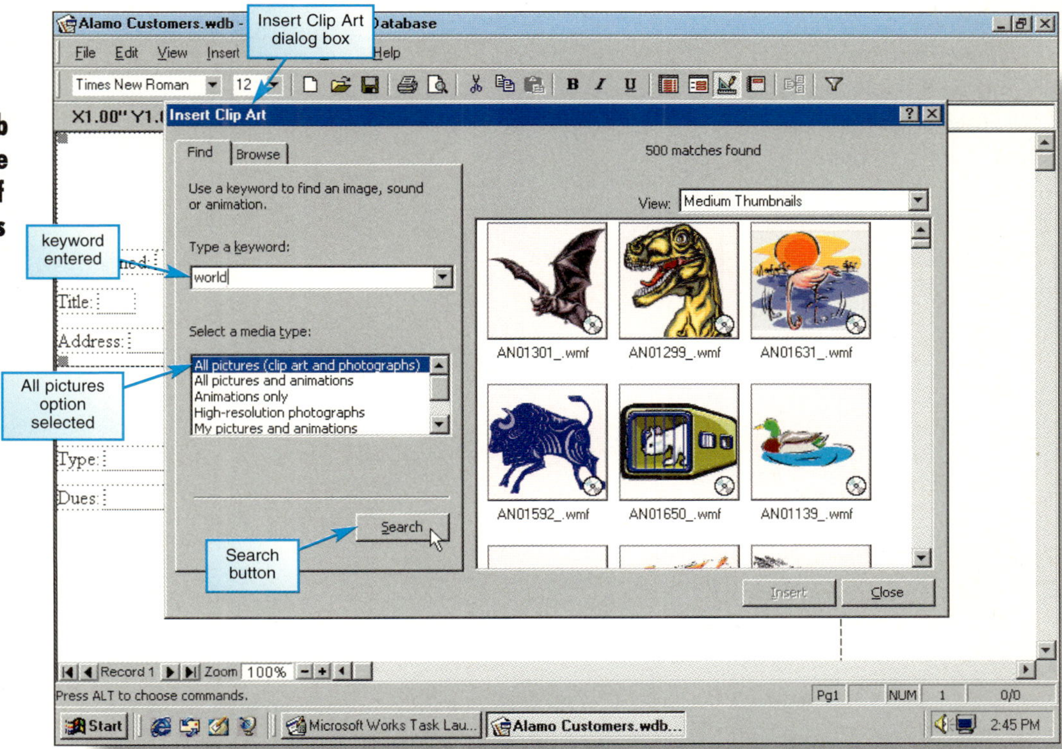

FIGURE 3-32

3 **Click the Search button. When the clip art displays, scroll the list until the clip art illustrating the world within a blue background displays. Click the world image and then point to the Insert button.**

Works displays the requested clip art images and the clip art illustration of the world within a blue background is selected as indicated by the blue border around the image (Figure 3-33).

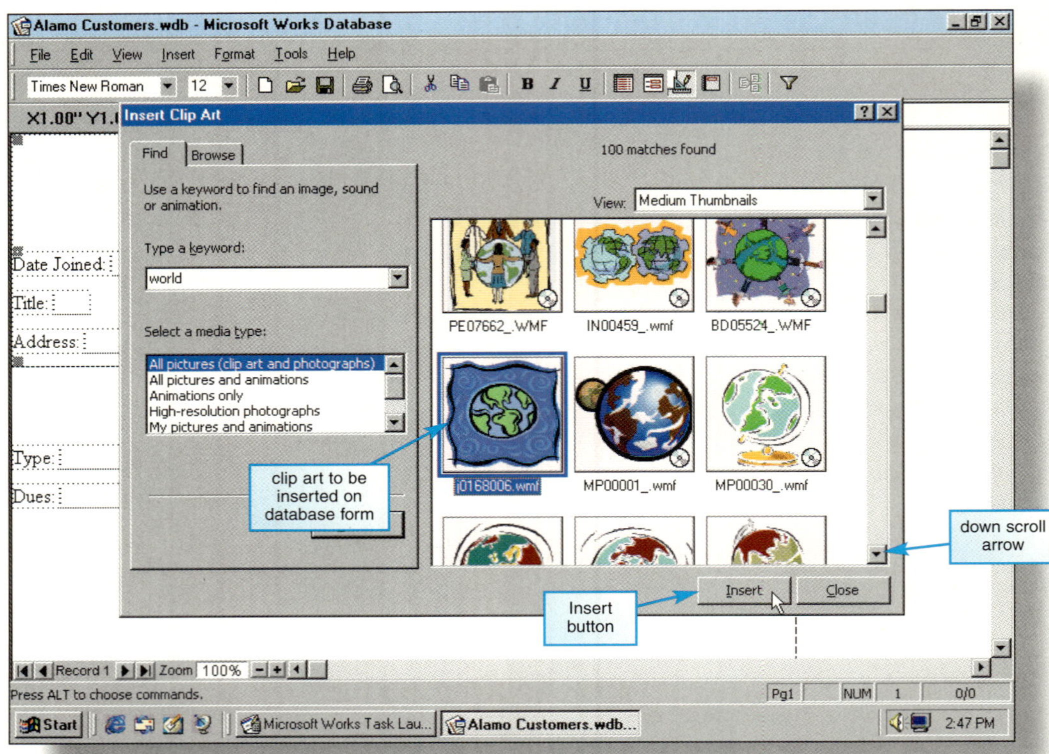

FIGURE 3-33

Click the Insert button.

Works inserts the clip art at the location of the insertion point (Figure 3-34). A rectangular box containing dotted lines and selection handles surrounds the clip art, indicating the clip art is an object and may be moved or resized.

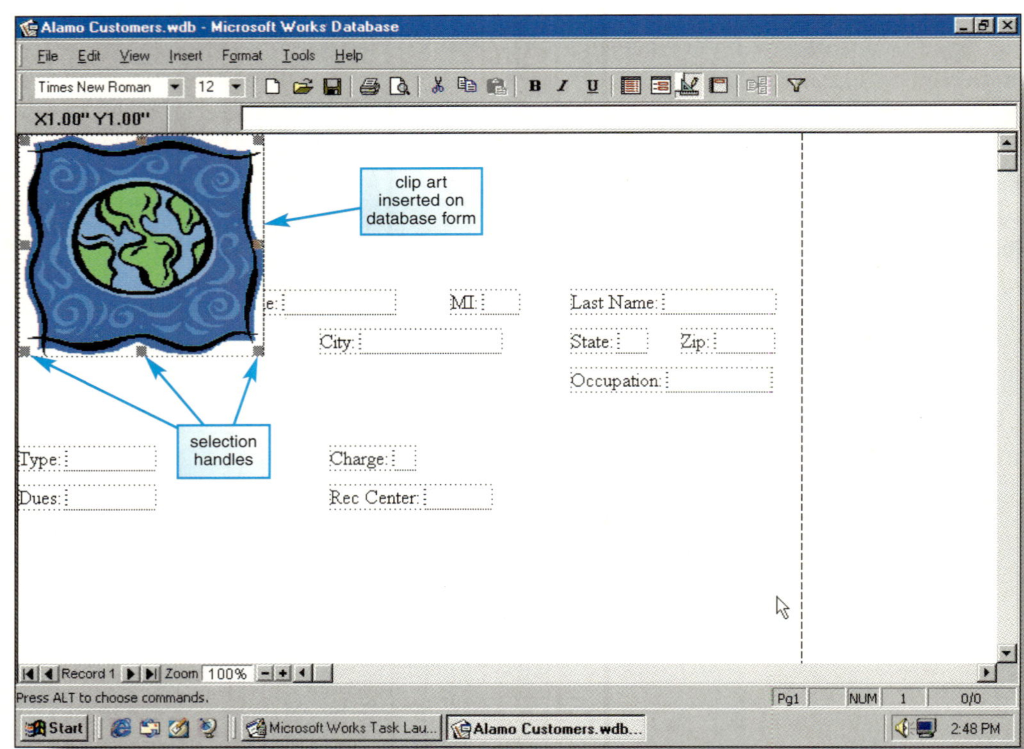

FIGURE 3-34

5 **Right-click the clip art and then point to Format Picture on the shortcut menu.**

The shortcut menu displays (Figure 3-35).

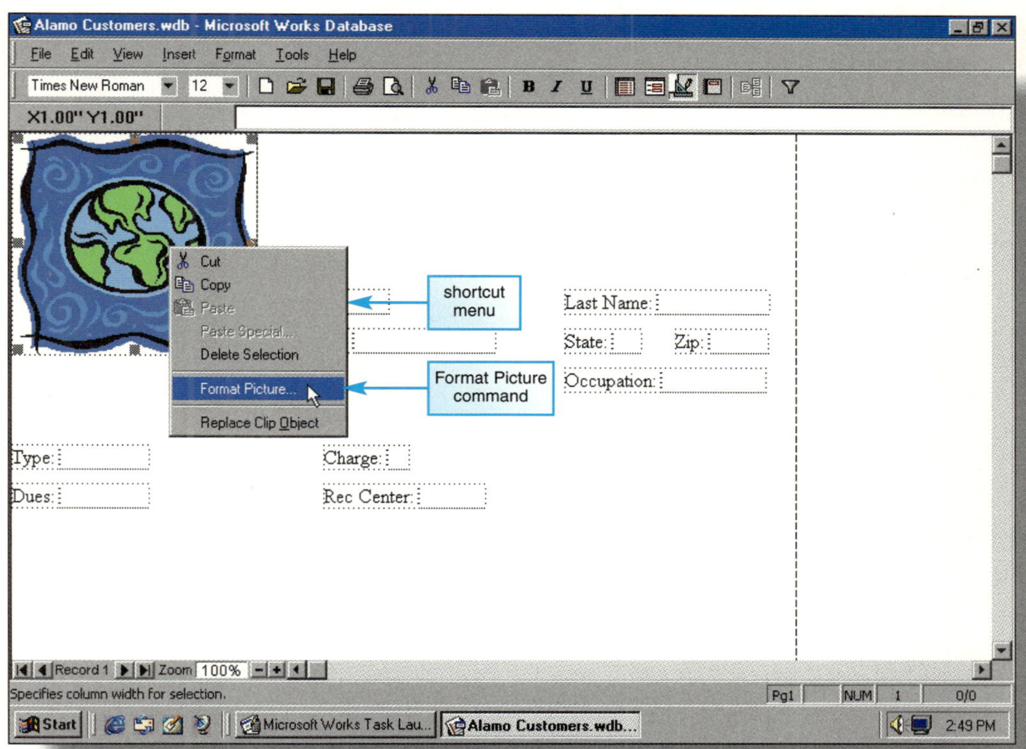

FIGURE 3-35

6 **Click Format Picture. When the Format Picture dialog box displays, in the Size area, type** .67 **in the Width text box and type** .58 **in the Height text box. Point to the OK button.**

The Format Picture dialog box displays with the values you entered, indicating you want the width to be .67 inch and the height to be .58 inch. (Figure 3-36). The Format Picture dialog box allows you to control the size of an object precisely.

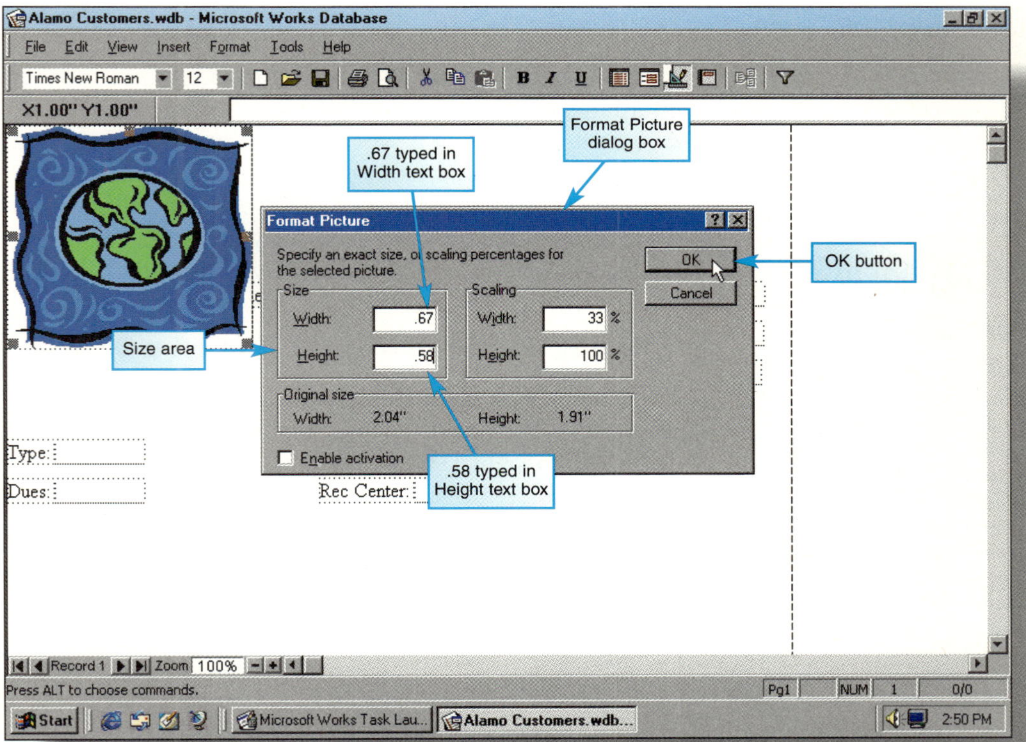

FIGURE 3-36

7 Click the OK button and then click a blank area of the form screen.

The resized clip art displays on the database form (Figure 3-37).

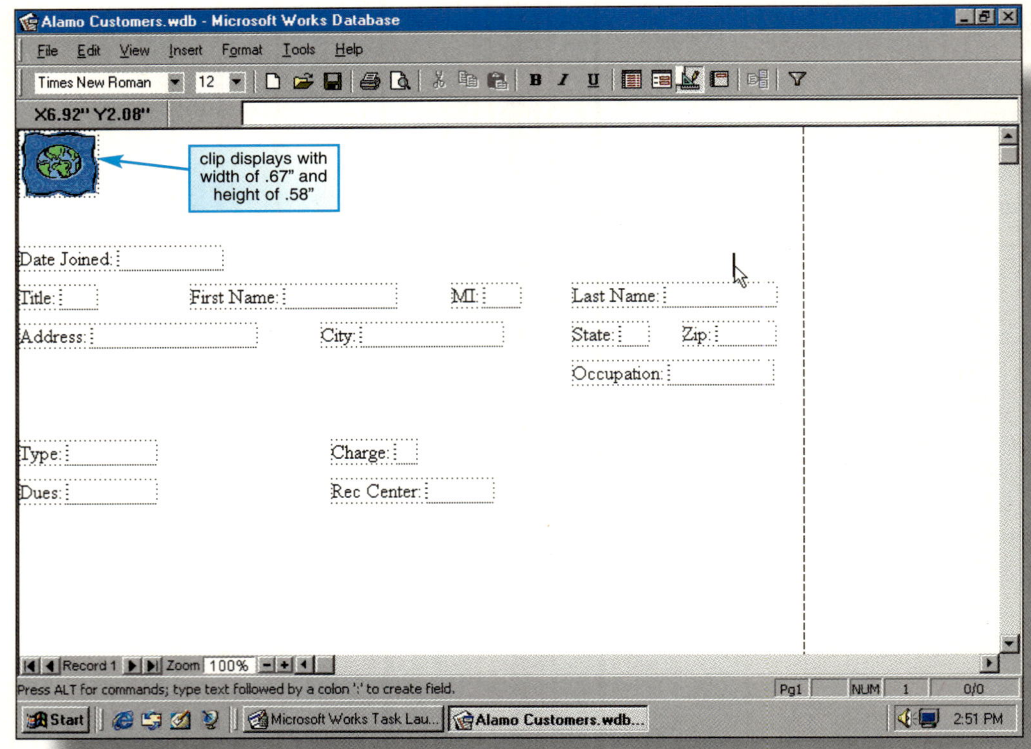

FIGURE 3-37

Using the Format Picture command allows more precise control over the sizing in applications where the exact size is important.

As is possible in a word processing document, you also may insert clip art images downloaded from the Internet. The easiest way to insert downloaded clip art images is to store downloaded clip art and pictures from the Internet in Works Portfolio collections and then copy and paste or drag the clip art from a Portfolio's collection into the database form when needed.

More About

Works 6

You can take advantage of special offers from Microsoft's home-publishing partners. To view a Web site that offers access to Microsoft's library of seasonal design templates and Picture Art, visit the Works 6 More About Web page (www.scsite.com/works6/more.htm) and then click Picture It! Publishing.

Entering and Formatting a Title on a Database Form Using WordArt

The title on the database form, Alamo Golf and Recreation Centers, displays using special effects; that is, the characters in the title display in a wave-like contour from left to right. The characters in the title also display in navy with a silver shadow. To create a title with special effects, Works provides an accessory called **WordArt**. Complete the following steps to enter and format a title using WordArt.

To Enter and Format a Title Using WordArt

1 Position the insertion point at the coordinates X1.75" Y1.00". Click Insert on the menu bar and then point to WordArt.

The Insert menu displays (Figure 3-38). The insertion point is located at the coordinates X1.75" Y1.00". This is the position where Works will insert the title on the database form.

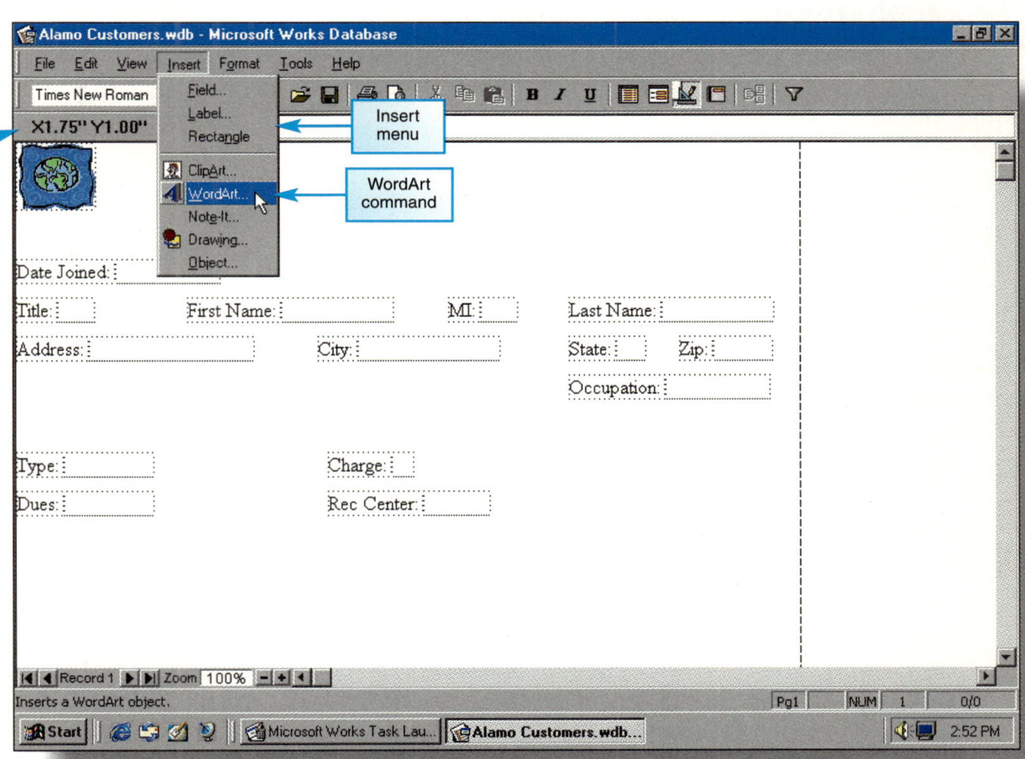

FIGURE 3-38

2 Click WordArt.

The Enter Your Text Here dialog box displays (Figure 3-39). The default text, Your Text Here, is selected in the box. A shaded border area containing the words, Your Text Here, displays on the database form above the dialog box. After you type and display text, the text will display in the shaded border area on the database form. A new menu bar and a WordArt toolbar also display. The ***WordArt toolbar*** *contains a number of buttons unique to WordArt that assist in using WordArt. The buttons used in this project will be explained as needed.*

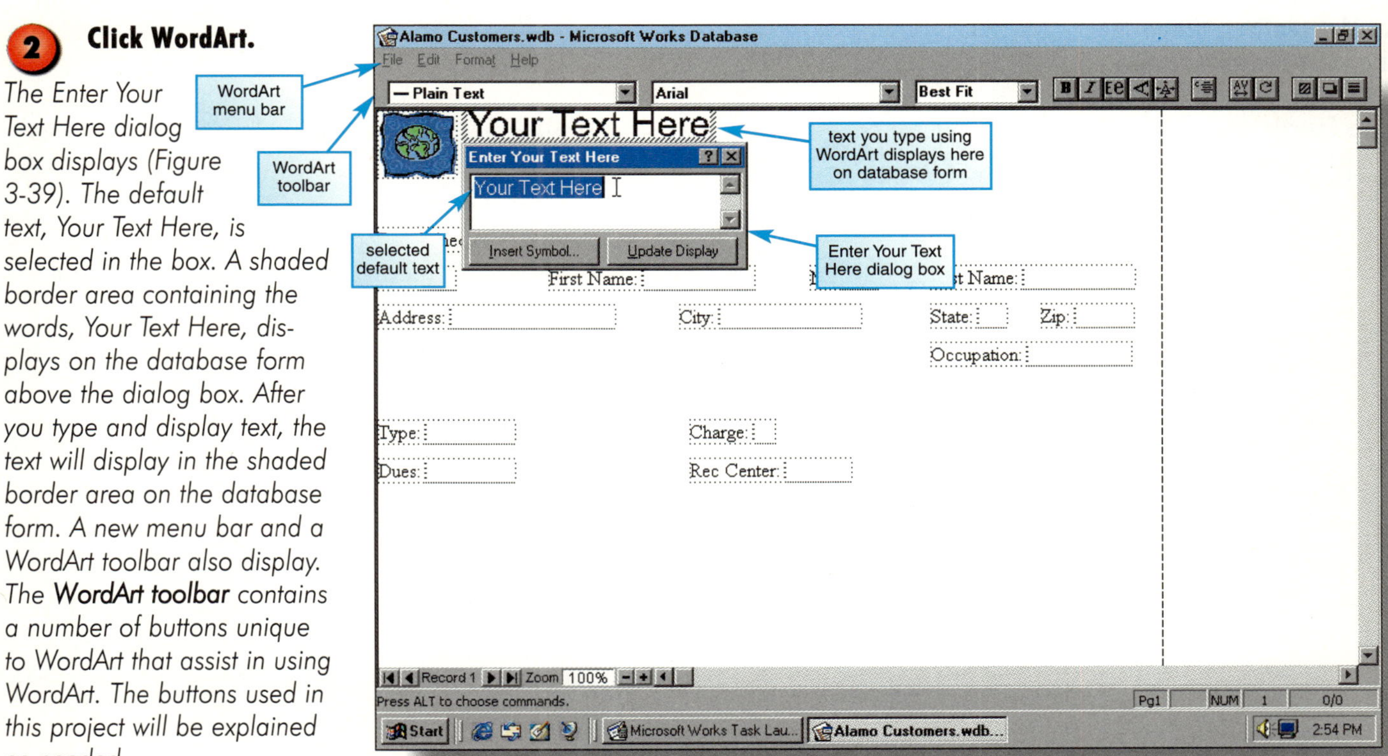

FIGURE 3-39

3 Type `Alamo Golf and Recreation Centers` **in the Enter Your Text Here dialog box and then click the Update Display button.**

Works displays the words, Alamo Golf and Recreation Centers, in the box as you type (Figure 3-40). When you click the Update Display button, the words, Alamo Golf and Recreation Centers, display in the shaded border area on the database form.

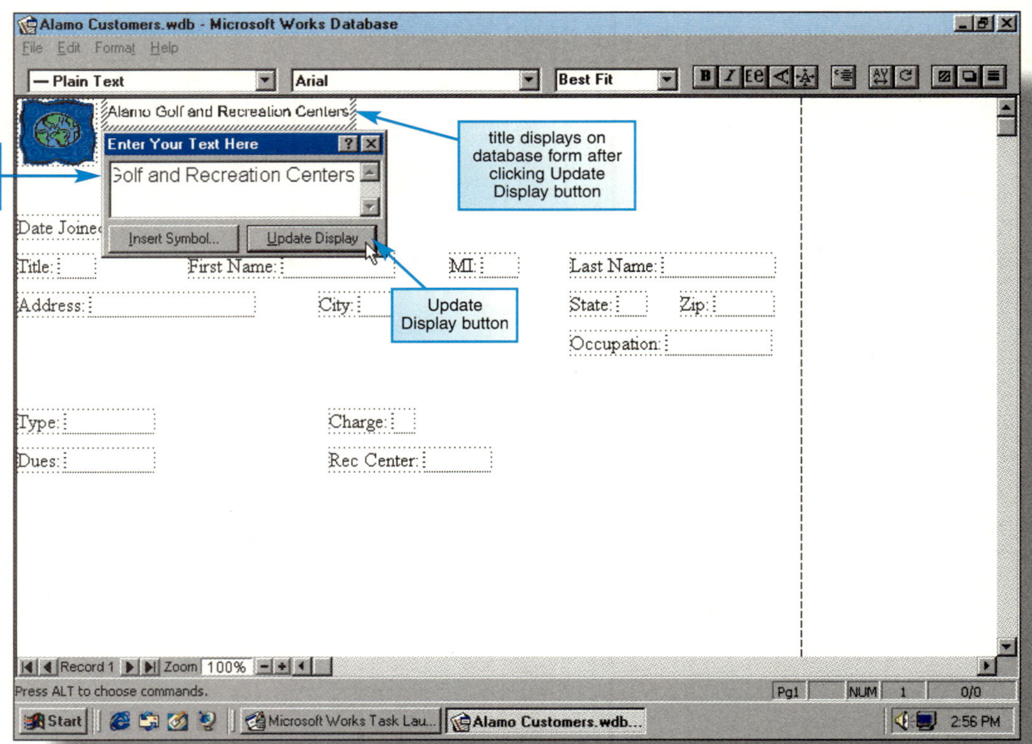

FIGURE 3-40

4 Click the Shape box arrow on the WordArt toolbar. When the Shape list displays, point to the first box on the right in the fourth row.

The Shape list displays and the Wave 2 shape is selected (Figure 3-41).

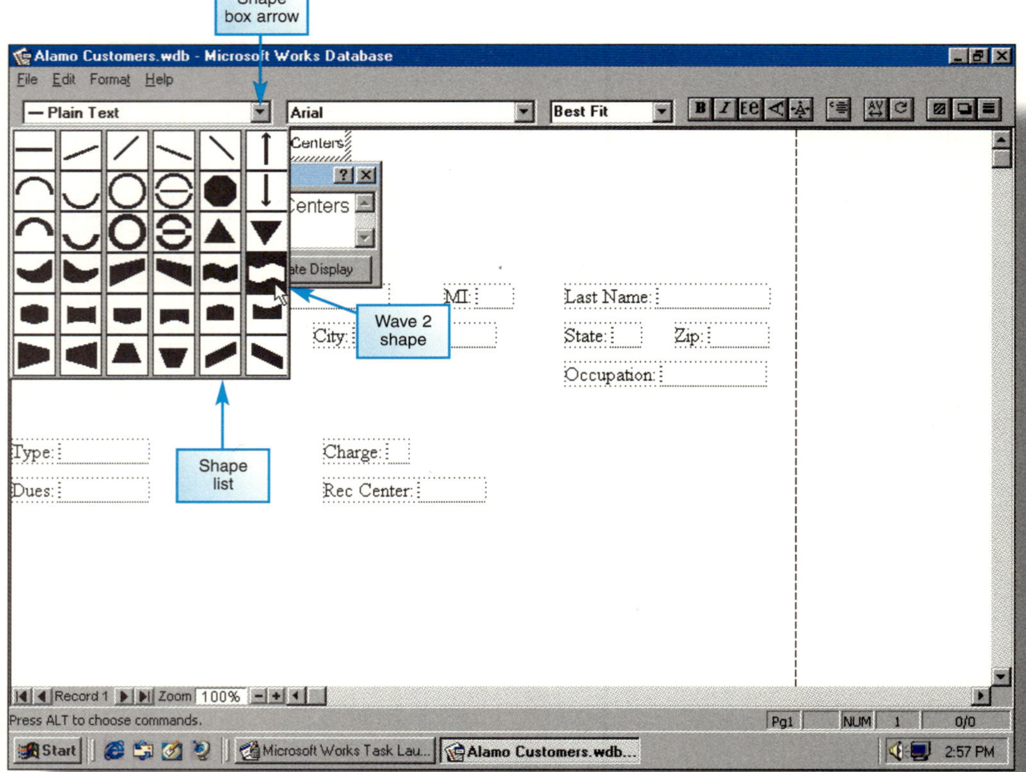

FIGURE 3-41

5 Click Wave 2. Point to the Stretch button on the WordArt toolbar.

The words, Alamo Golf and Recreation Centers, display in the object area on the form in compressed text (Figure 3-42). The shape you clicked, Wave 2, displays in the Shape box.

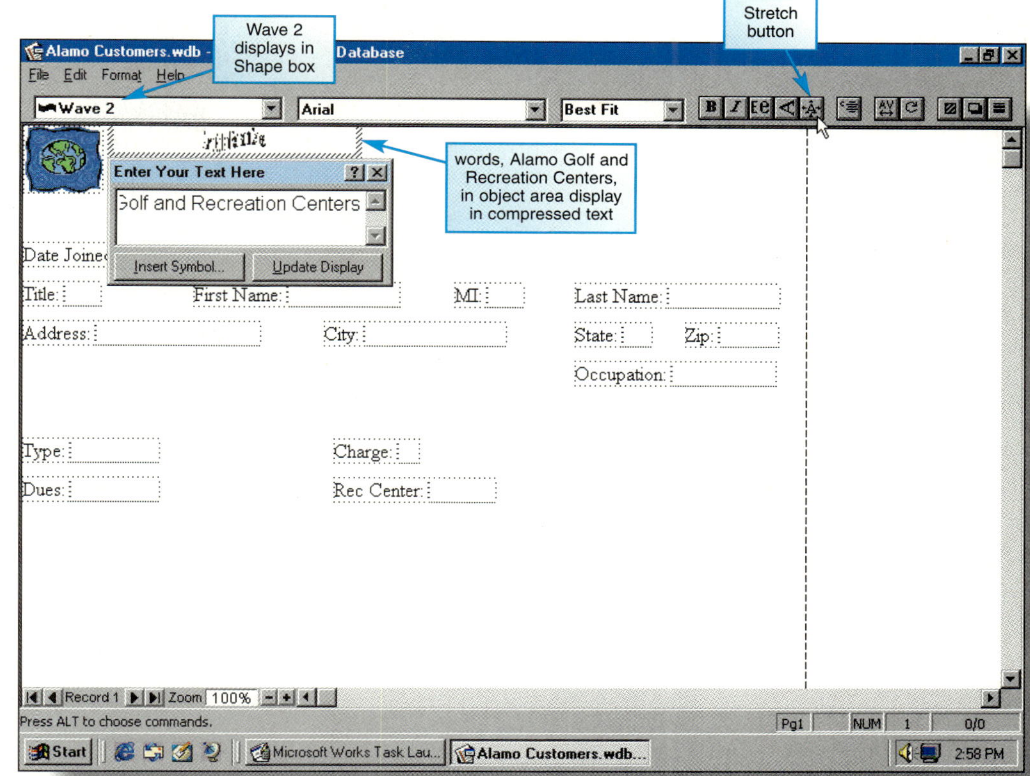

FIGURE 3-42

6 Click the Stretch button and then click the Shadow button on the WordArt toolbar.

WordArt displays the words, Alamo Golf and Recreation Centers, with a Wave 2 effect in the object area on the database form (Figure 3-43). The Shadow dialog box displays. The Choose a Shadow area displays eight special effects for shadows. The Shadow Color box displays Silver as the default color of the shadow.

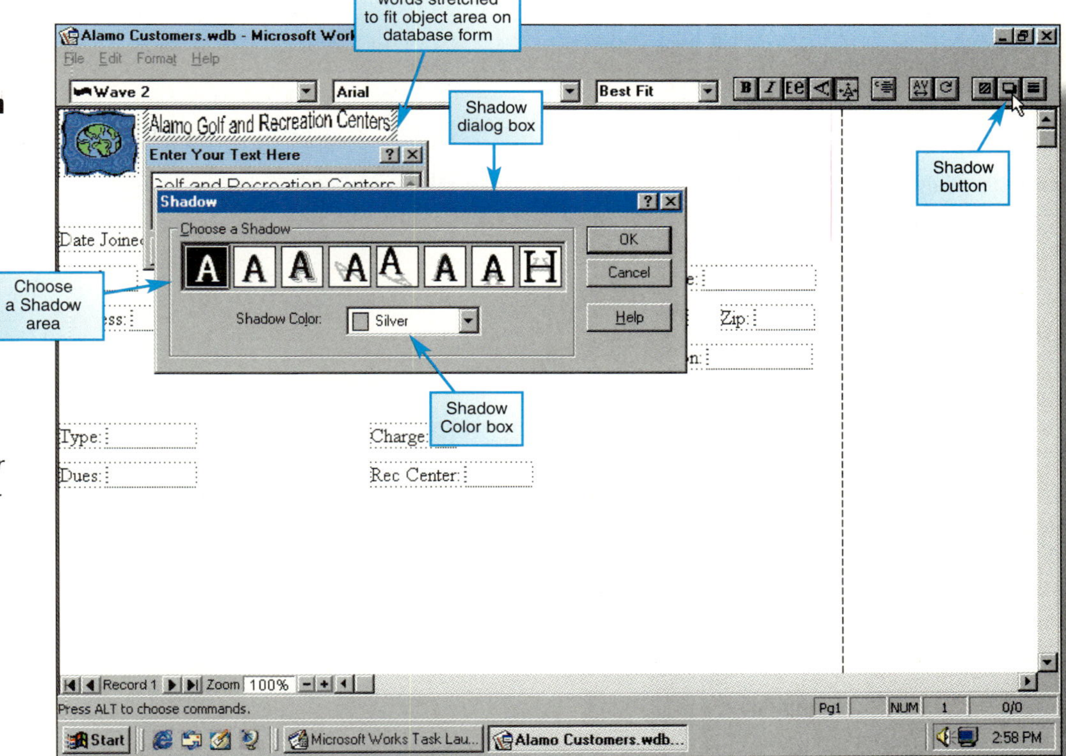

FIGURE 3-43

7 Click the second box on the left in the Choose a Shadow area and then point to the OK button.

WordArt displays the words, Alamo Golf and Recreation Centers, with a silver shadow within the object area on the database form (Figure 3-44).

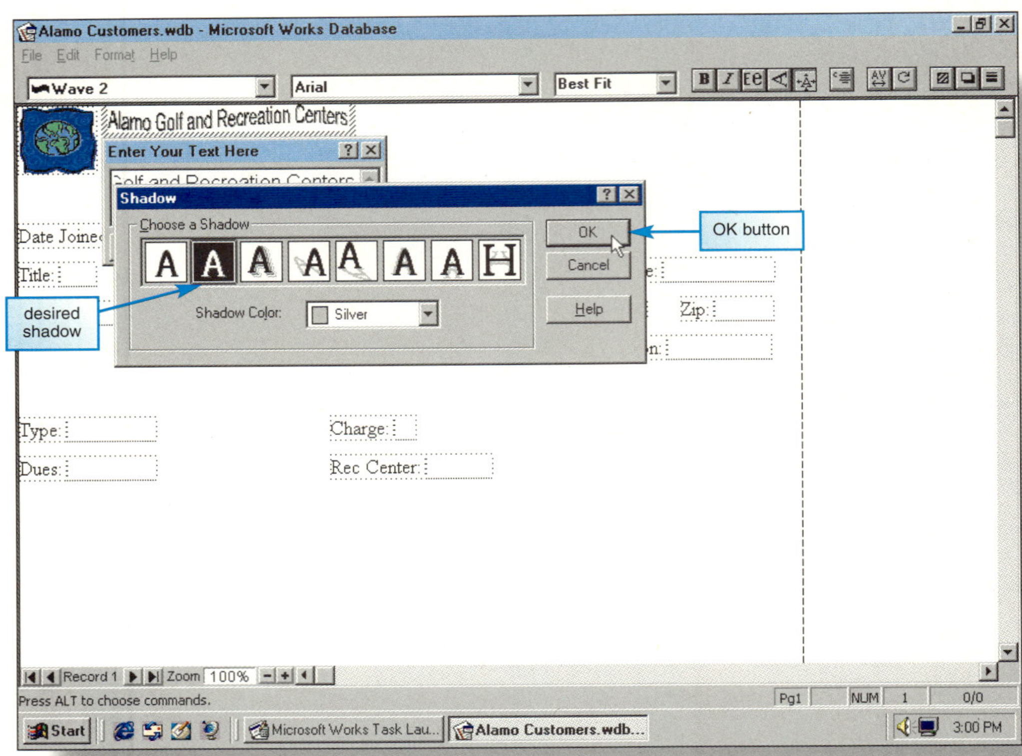

FIGURE 3-44

8 Click the OK button. Click the Shading button on the WordArt toolbar.

The words, Alamo Golf and Recreation Centers, contain a shadow effect, and the Shading dialog box displays (Figure 3-45). In the Style area, 24 fill patterns are provided for the characters in the WordArt object. The Color area contains the foreground and background fill colors.

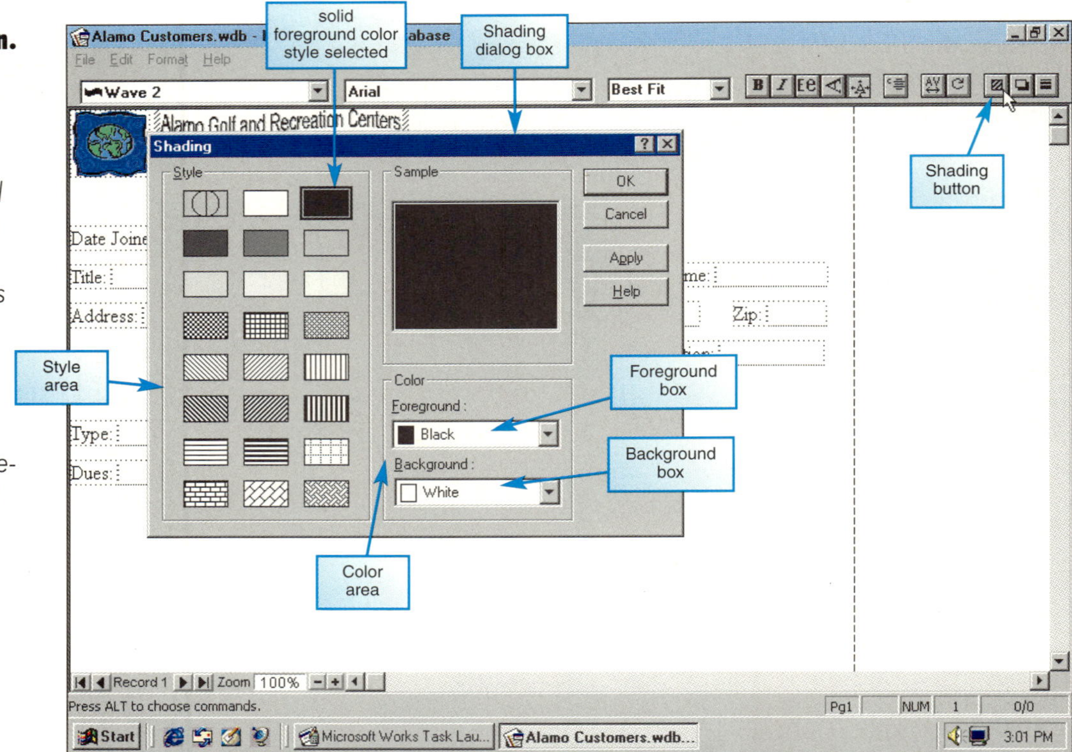

FIGURE 3-45

9 **Click the solid foreground style box in the Style area. Click the Foreground box arrow, scroll through the list until Navy displays, and then click Navy. Point to the OK button.**

The solid foreground style box is selected in the Style area (Figure 3-46). The Foreground list displays Navy. The Sample area displays the solid navy fill pattern to be applied to the text on the database form.

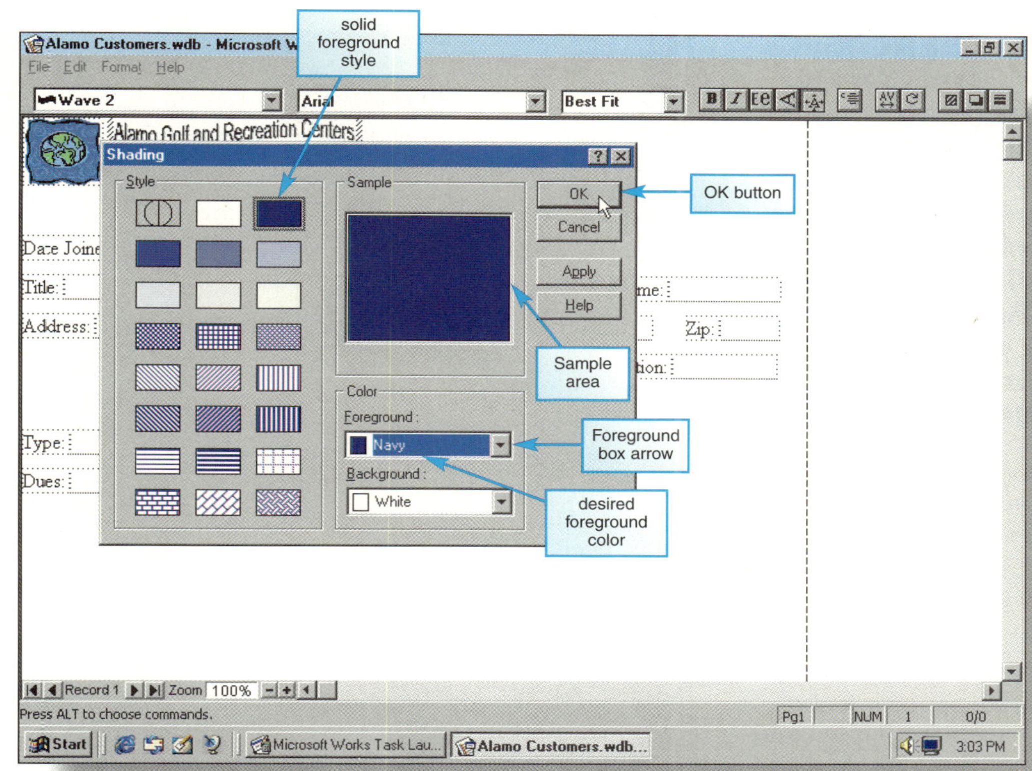

FIGURE 3-46

10 **Click the OK button. Click anywhere outside the Enter Your Text Here dialog box to close it. Point to the bottom center selection handle on the object border.**

The formatted words display (Figure 3-47). The X coordinate is 1.75" and the Y coordinate is 1.00". These coordinates refer to the leftmost and topmost position of the object containing the words, Alamo Golf and Recreation Centers. The mouse pointer displays with a small square box and arrows pointing up and down. The word RESIZE displays below the arrows.

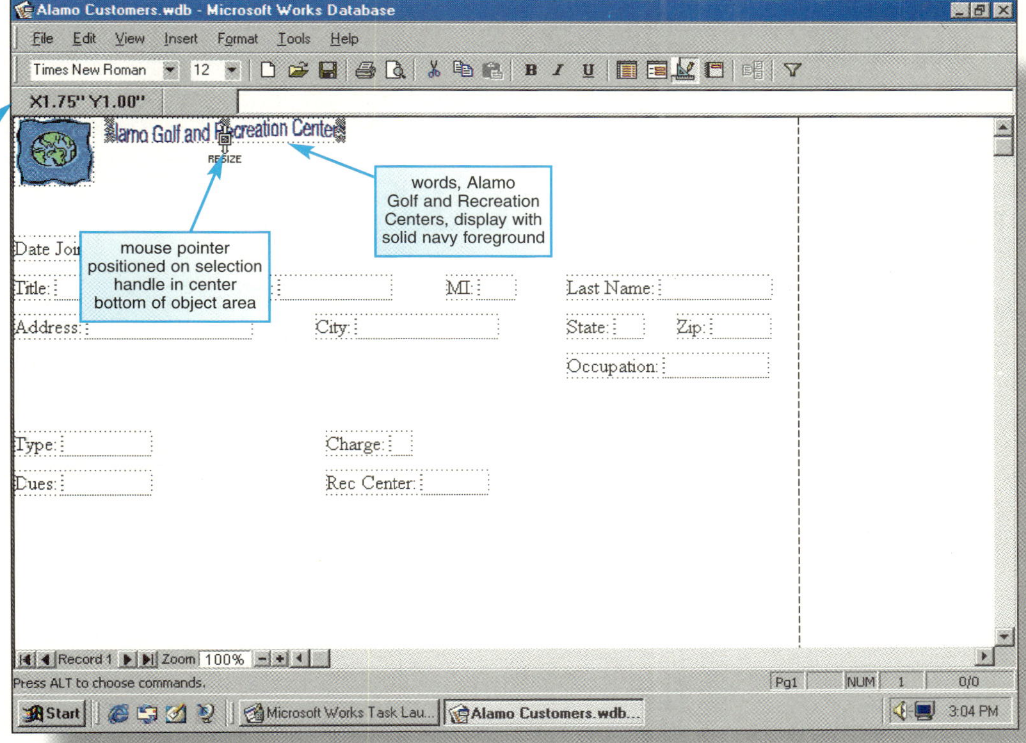

FIGURE 3-47

11 Drag the selection handle down to approximately the bottom of the clip art. With the mouse pointer inside the WordArt object, drag the WordArt object to the left until the object is adjacent to the right border of the clip art object. Place the mouse pointer on the right center selection handle.

As you drag the selection handle down, the object expands vertically (Figure 3-48). The object area moves to the left. Dragging the selection handle in the lower-right corner expands the rectangular box both vertically and horizontally at one time. For some individuals, a two-step approach makes it easier to control the vertical and horizontal expansion.

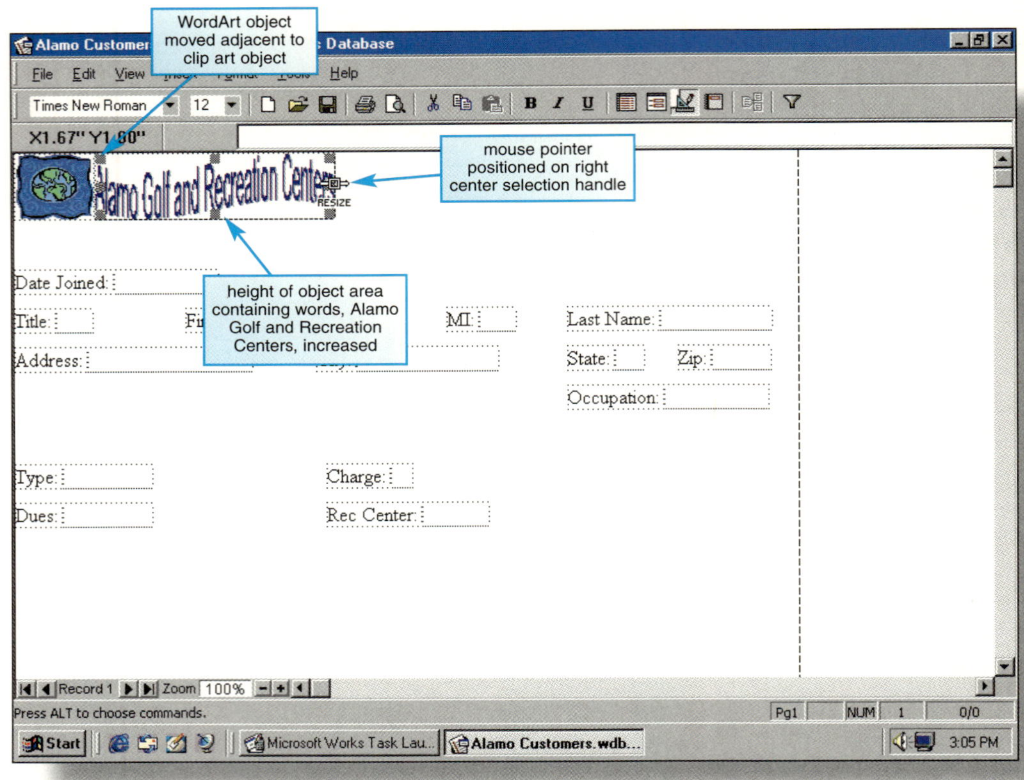

FIGURE 3-48

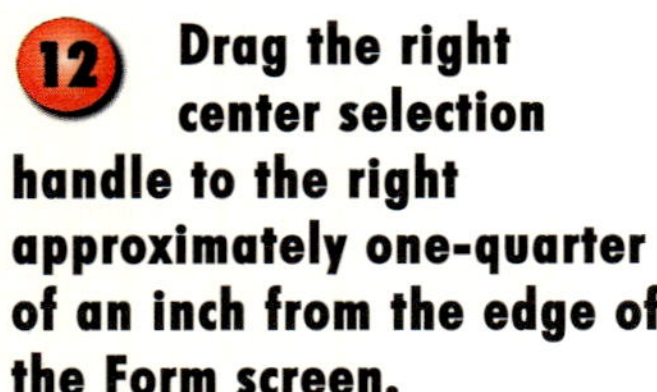

12 Drag the right center selection handle to the right approximately one-quarter of an inch from the edge of the Form screen.

The words, Alamo Golf and Recreation Centers, expand horizontally to fill the object area (Figure 3-49).

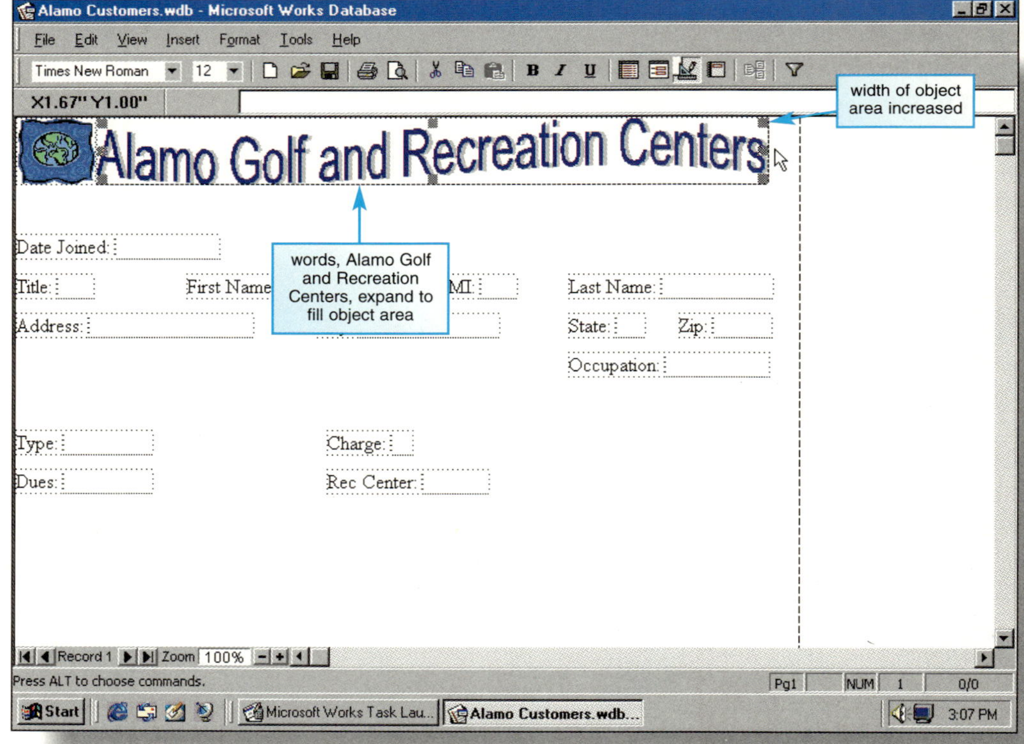

FIGURE 3-49

The words, Alamo Golf and Recreation Centers, have now been formatted as required. WordArt provides many special effects for text when using Microsoft Works. To edit the object, double-click the embedded object to open WordArt and make the desired changes to the object.

Inserting a Rectangular Bar below the Title

To further enhance the title area, the area is to contain a rectangular bar below the clip art and the words, Alamo Golf and Recreation Centers (see Figure 3-11 on page W 3.12). Complete the following steps to insert the bar.

To Insert a Rectangular Bar in the Title Area

1 **Position the insertion point below the clip art object at the coordinates X1.00" Y1.58" and then right-click. Point to Insert Rectangle on the shortcut menu.**

The shortcut menu displays (Figure 3-50).

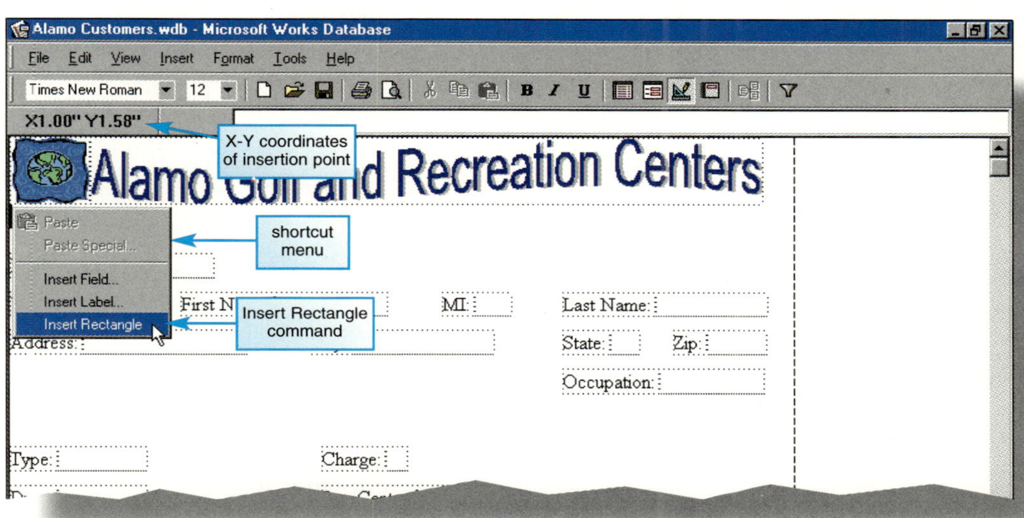

FIGURE 3-50

2 **Click Insert Rectangle. When the rectangle displays, position the mouse pointer on the selection handle in the lower-right corner of the rectangle.**

Works displays a rectangle containing dotted lines and selection handles on the database form (Figure 3-51).

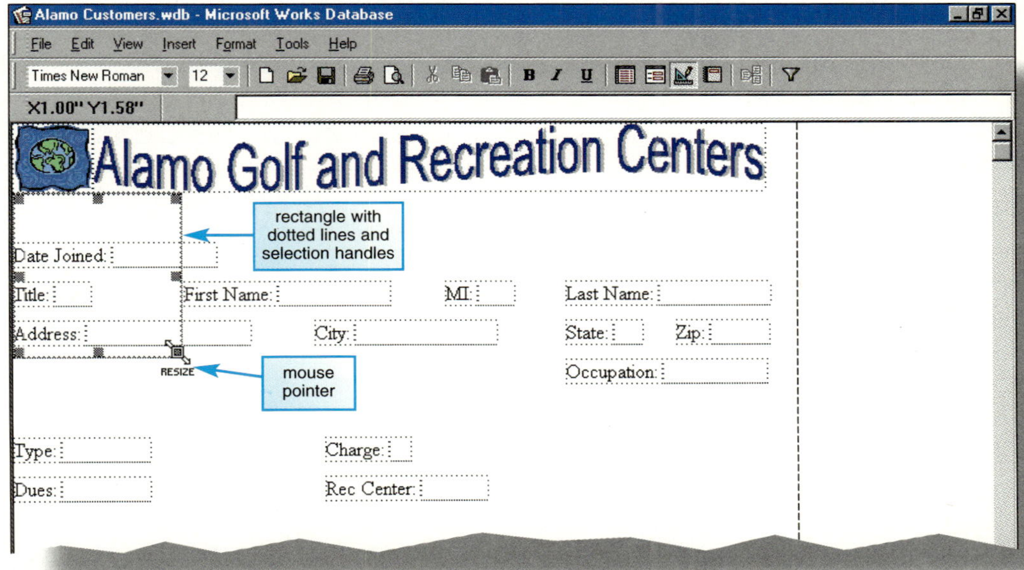

FIGURE 3-51

3 **Drag the selection handle up to the bottom of the clip art and to the right until the rectangle is the same width as the WordArt.**

Works displays the resized rectangle below the clip art and the words, Alamo Golf and Recreation Centers (Figure 3-52).

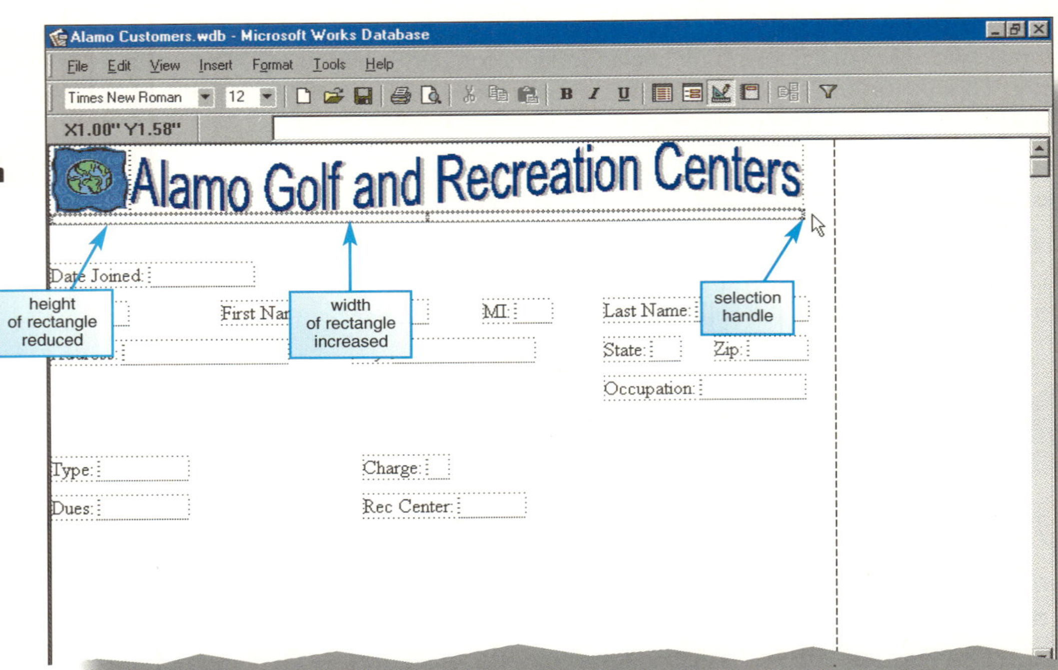

FIGURE 3-52

1. On Insert menu in form design view click Rectangle

Adding Color to the Rectangle

The next step is to add color to the rectangle. Dark blue displays in the rectangular bar below the clip art and the words, Alamo Golf and Recreation Centers. To add color, perform the following steps.

To Add Color to the Rectangular Bar

1 **Right-click the rectangle and then point to Shading on the shortcut menu.**

The rectangle contains selection handles indicating it is selected, and the shortcut menu displays (Figure 3-53).

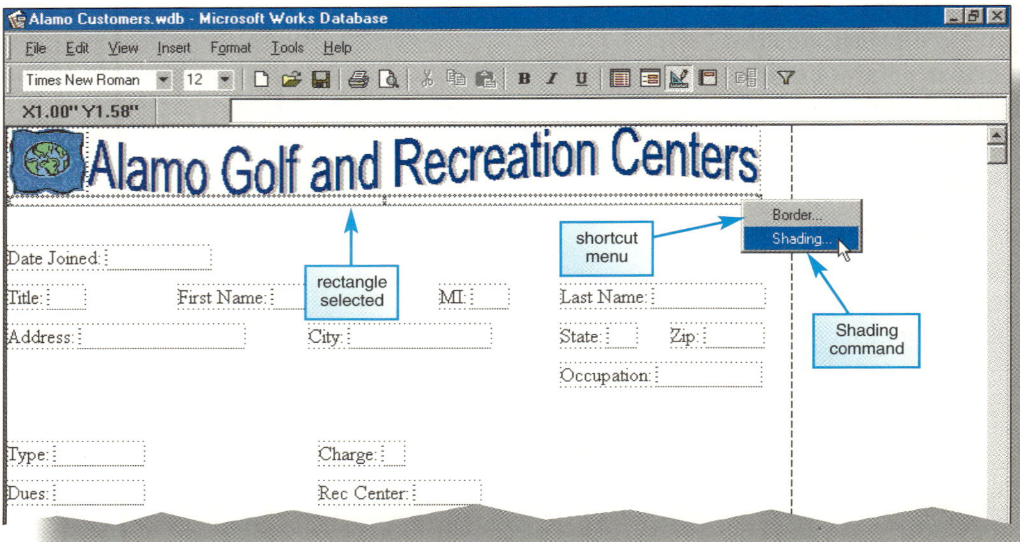

FIGURE 3-53

2 **Click Shading. When the Format dialog box displays, click the solid pattern in the Pattern list on the Shading sheet. Scroll through the Foreground list in the Colors area until Dark Blue displays. Click Dark Blue and then point to the OK button.**

Works displays the Format dialog box (Figure 3-54). The solid pattern is selected in the Pattern list, and Dark Blue is selected in the Foreground list. The Sample area displays a sample of the pattern and color.

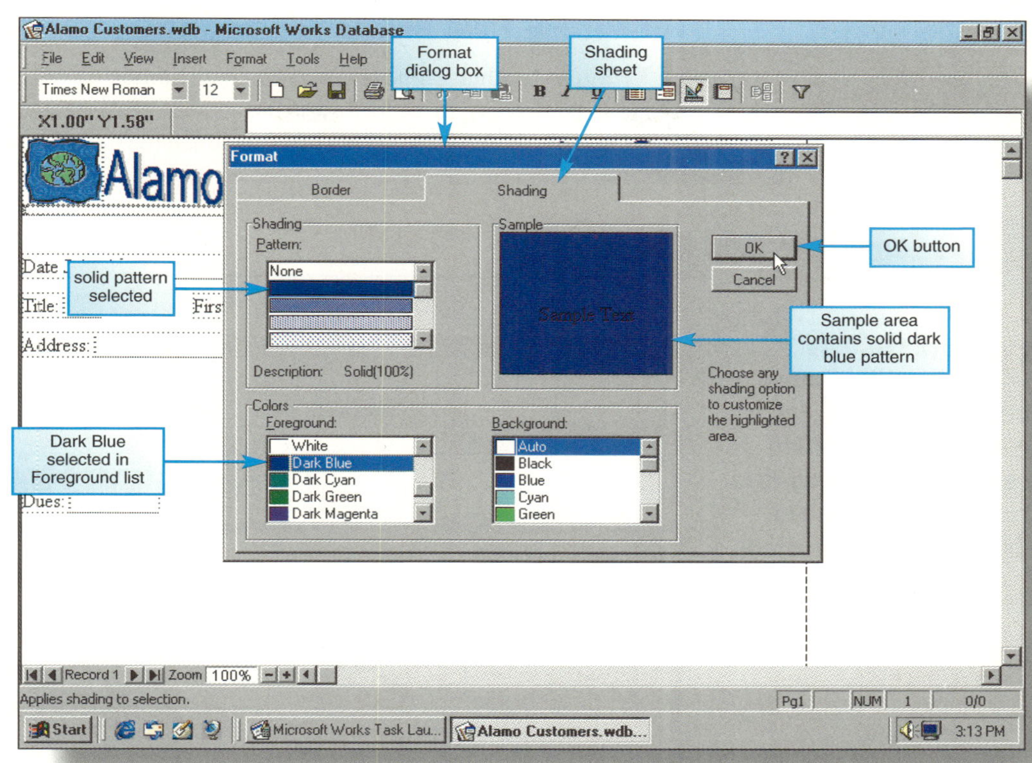

FIGURE 3-54

3 **Click the OK button. Click anywhere on the form to remove the selection.**

Works displays the rectangle with a solid dark blue pattern (Figure 3-55).

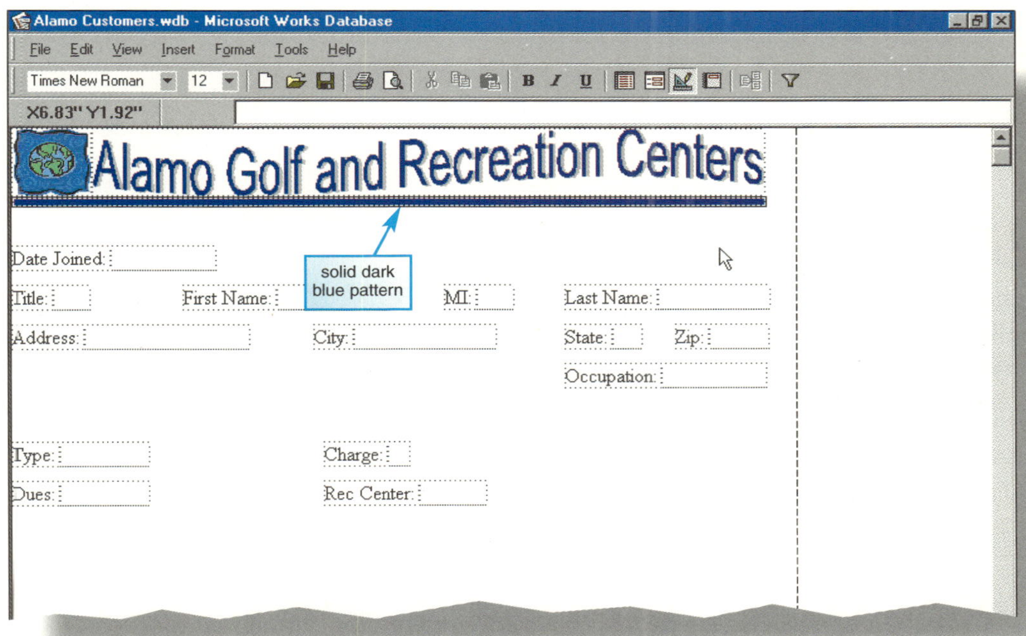

FIGURE 3-55

Most database forms in a modern computing environment use color to enhance the appearance of the form.

Formatting Field Names

To give further emphasis to the field names on the database form, each field name is to display in bold and italics.

The following steps explain how to display the names in bold and italics.

To Format the Field Names

1 **Click the Date Joined field name. While holding down the CTRL key, click each field name on the database form to select it. Point to the Bold button on the toolbar.**

Each field name on the database form is selected (Figure 3-56).

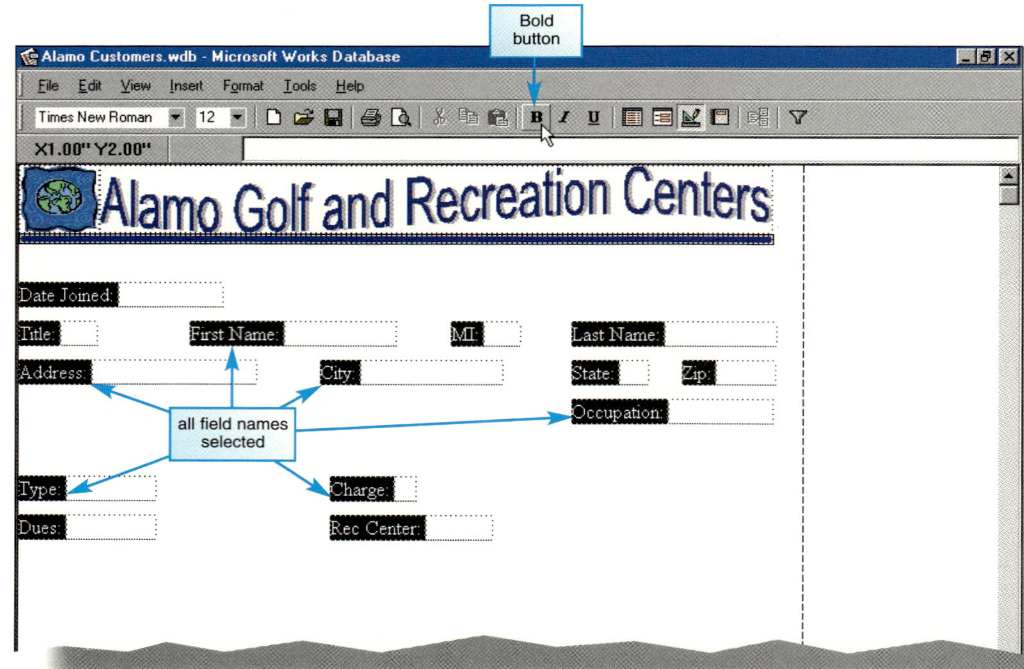

FIGURE 3-56

2 **Click the Bold button. Click the Italic button on the toolbar. Click on the form to remove the selection.**

Each field name on the database form displays in bold and italics (Figure 3-57).

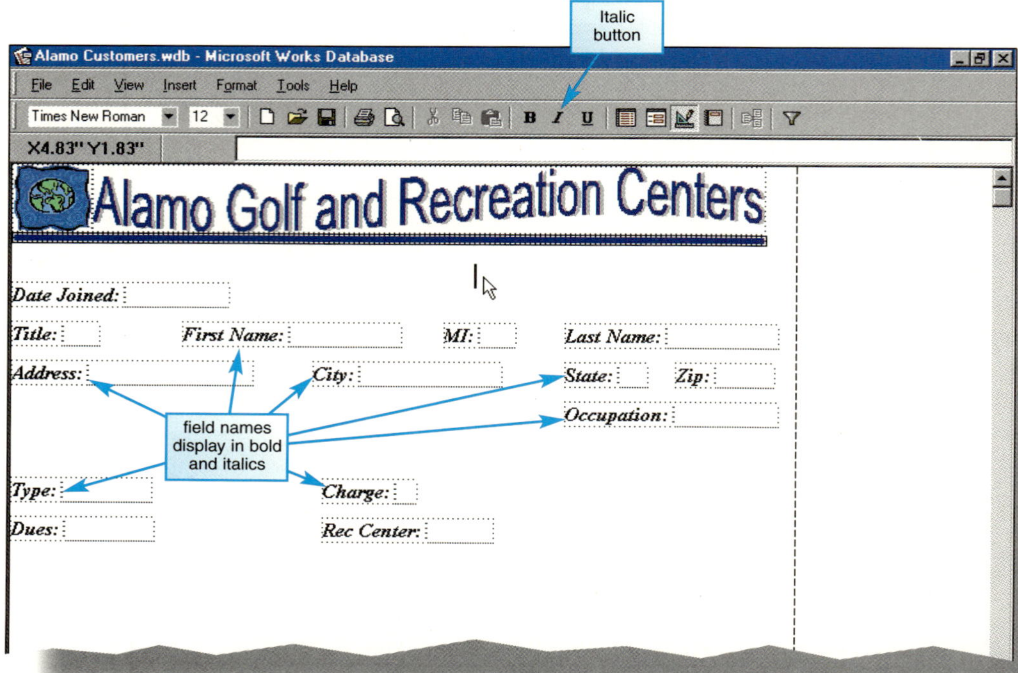

FIGURE 3-57

Adding a Border on Fields

The next step in developing the format of the database form is to add a color border to the fields. This technique precisely defines for the user where data is to display. To accomplish this task, it is recommended that you first remove the field lines and then add the color borders.

Perform the following steps to accomplish this task.

To Remove Field Lines and Add a Border on Fields

1 Click the Date Joined field. While holding down the CTRL key, click each field to select it. Click View on the menu bar and then point to Field Lines.

All fields are selected and the View menu displays (Figure 3-58).

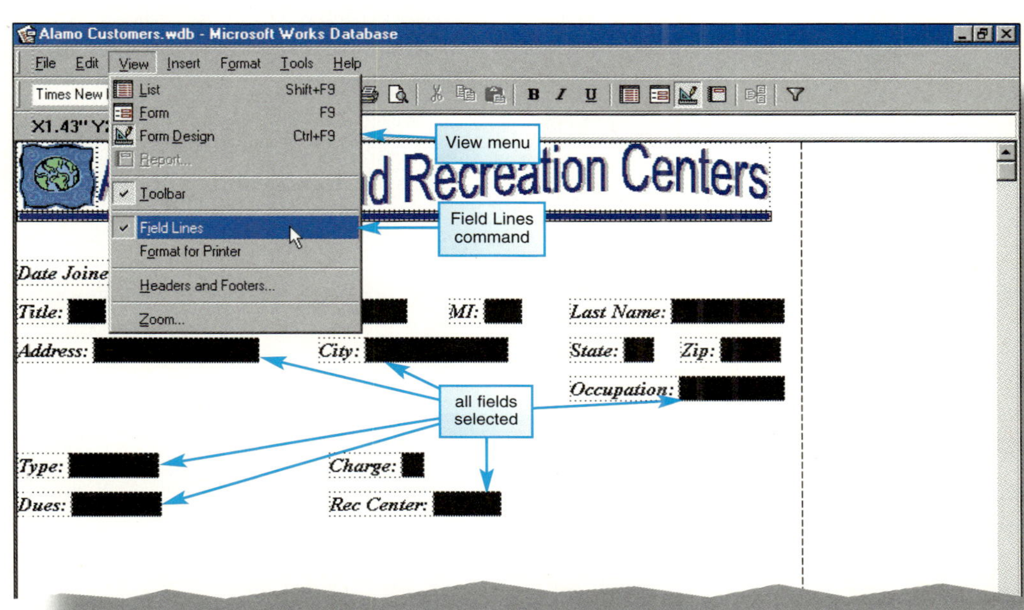

FIGURE 3-58

2 Click Field Lines. Right-click the Date Joined field and then point to Border on the shortcut menu.

The field lines no longer show and the shortcut menu displays (Figure 3-59).

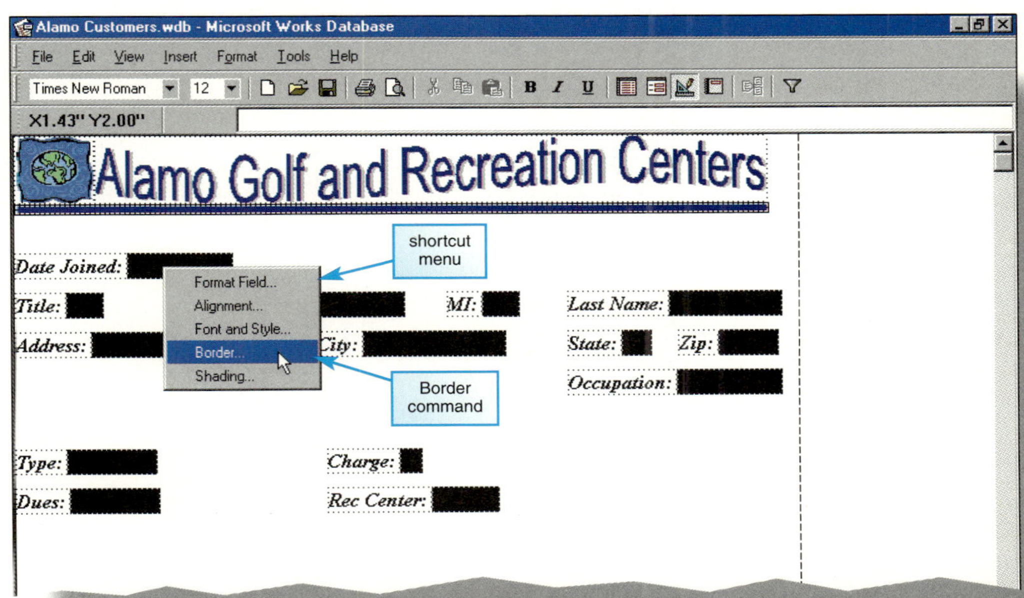

FIGURE 3-59

3 **Click Border. When the Format dialog box displays, click the Outline box in the Border area and scroll through the Color list until Dark Blue displays. Click Dark Blue and then point to the OK button.**

The Format dialog box displays the selected entries (Figure 3-60).

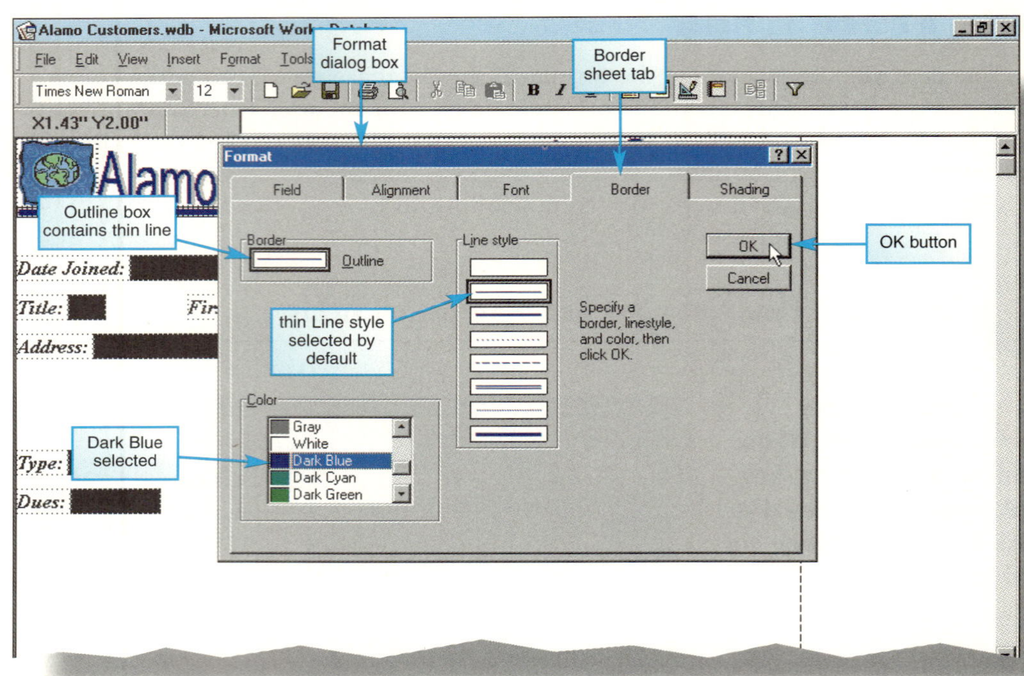

FIGURE 3-60

4 **Click the OK button and then click the form to remove the selection from the fields.**

Works removes the selection from the fields and applies the dark blue border to all fields (Figure 3-61).

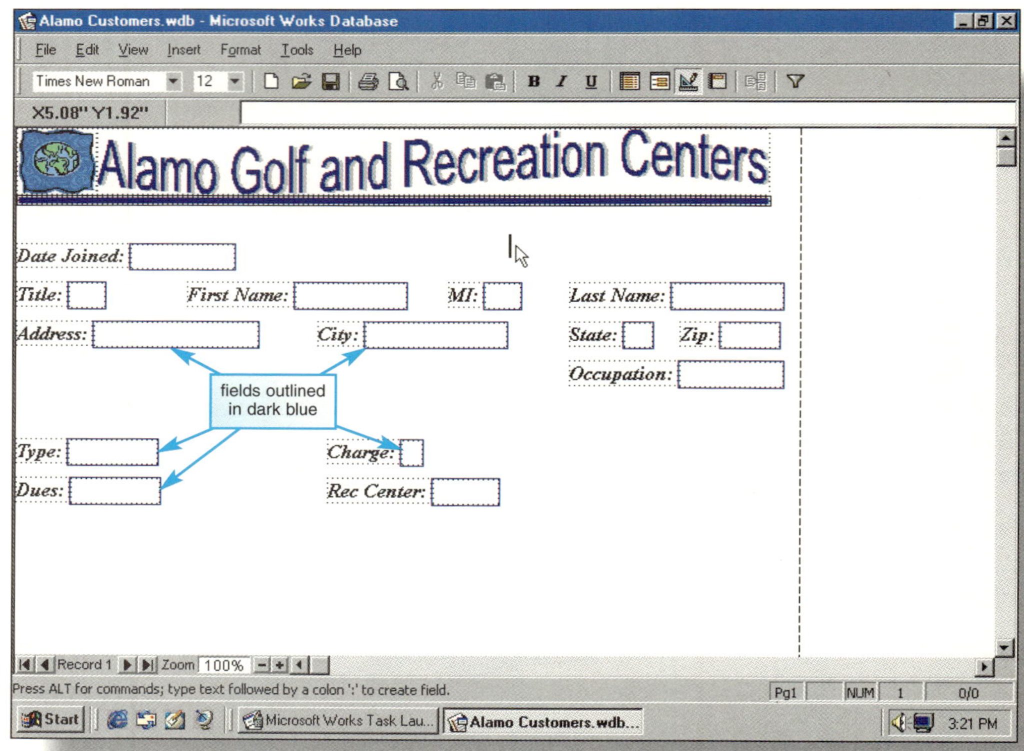

FIGURE 3-61

Other Ways

1. On Format menu in form design view click Border

Adding Text Labels to the Database Form

The next step in formatting the form is to add two text labels to the database form. A **text label** is identifying information placed on a database form. Text labels can be any length and can contain any words or numbers that provide the description or instructions you need. The two text labels that display on the form are CUSTOMER INFORMATION and ACCOUNT INFORMATION as illustrated in Figure 3-11 on page W 3.12. To add the text labels, perform the following steps.

To Add Text Labels to the Database Form

1 Click at the coordinates X1.00" Y1.75".

Works displays the insertion point at the coordinates X1.00" Y1.75" (Figure 3-62).

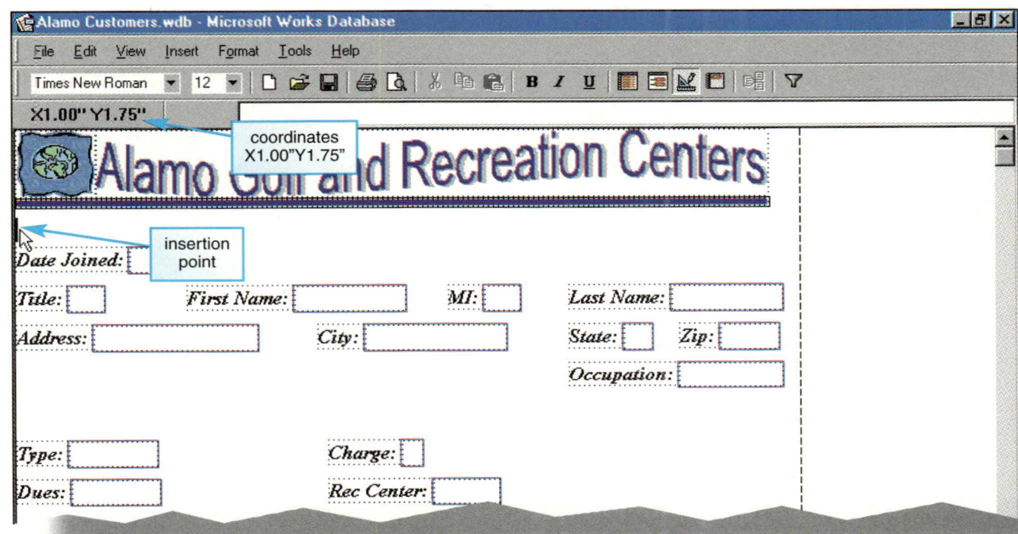

FIGURE 3-62

2 Press the CAPS LOCK key and then type CUSTOMER INFORMATION **as the text label.**

Works displays the label in the entry bar and on the form (Figure 3-63).

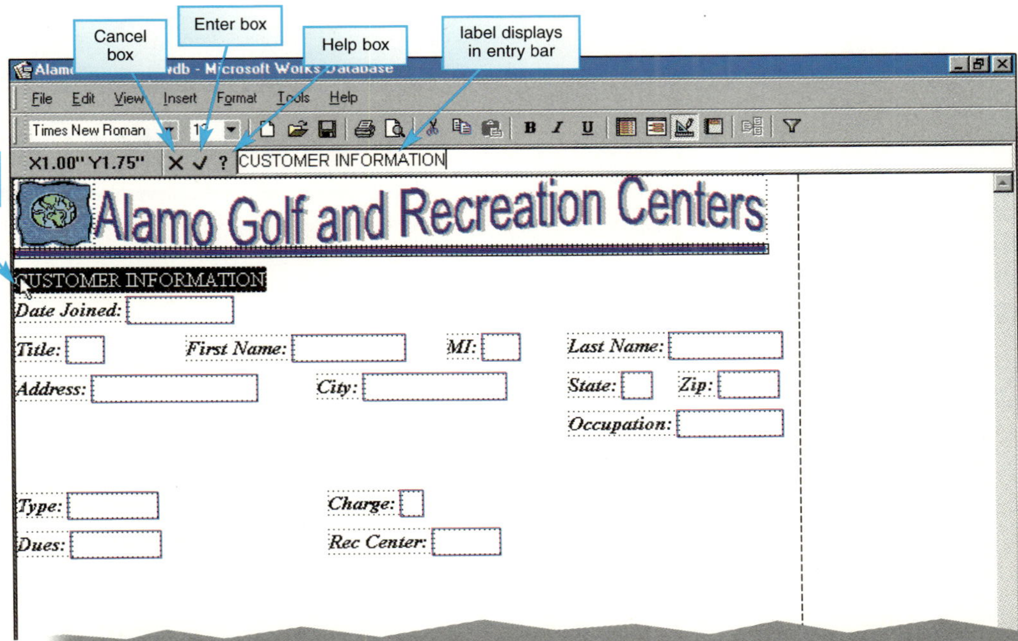

FIGURE 3-63

3 **Click the Enter box or press the ENTER key. Click to position the insertion point at the coordinates X1.00" Y3.33". Type** ACCOUNT INFORMATION **and then click the Enter box or press the ENTER key. Press the CAPS LOCK key.**

Works enters the text labels on the database form at the coordinates X1.00" Y1.75" and X1.00" Y3.33" (Figure 3-64).

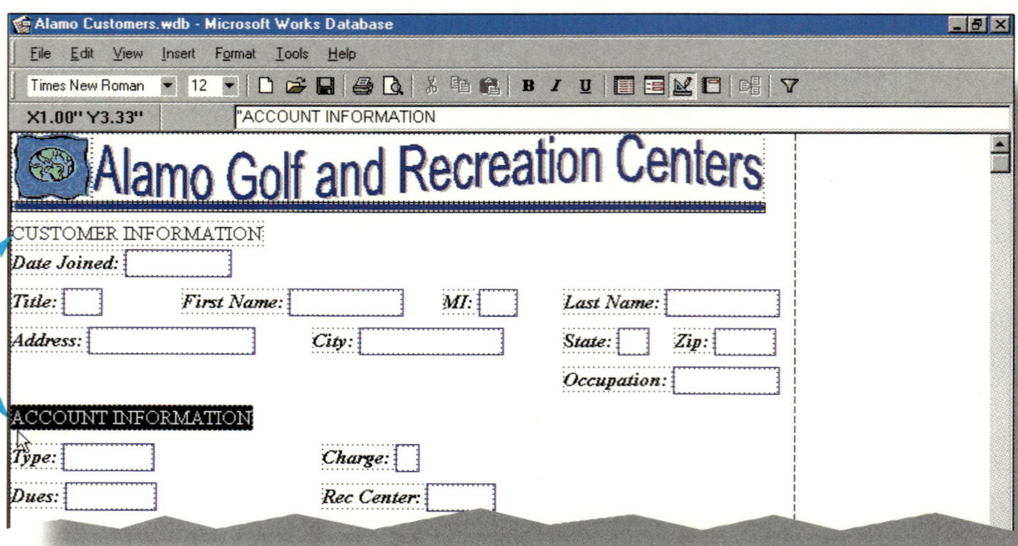

FIGURE 3-64

Other Ways

1. On Insert menu in form design view click Label, type desired text label, click Insert button

Adding an Underline and Bold to the Text Labels

The final task in developing the format of the database form is to add a single underline below the text labels and display the labels in bold. Perform the following step to accomplish this task.

Steps To Underline and Apply Bold to Text Labels

1 **Click the text label, CUSTOMER INFORMATION. Select the text label, ACCOUNT INFORMATION, by holding down the CTRL key and clicking the label. Click the Underline button on the toolbar and then click the Bold button on the toolbar.**

The text labels display with a single underline and bold formatting (Figure 3-65).

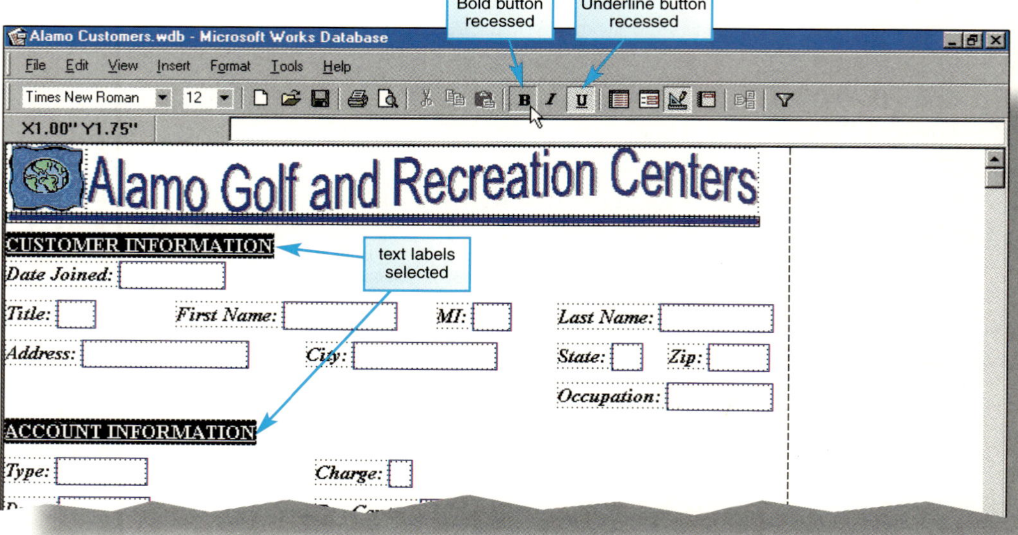

FIGURE 3-65

Other Ways

1. On Format menu in form design view click Font and Style, click Underline, click Bold, click OK button

Saving the Database

The format of the database form now is complete. In most cases, you should save the completed form on disk. To save the database, perform the following step.

TO SAVE THE DATABASE

1. Click the Save button on the toolbar.

The database is saved as specified in the last save process; that is, on drive A with the file name, Alamo Customers.

Entering Data into the Database in Form View

The fields contained within each record of the database constitute the structure of the database. The **structure** defines the fields within the database. The whole purpose of a database is to enter data so the data is available for printing, sorting, filtering, and other uses. Therefore, the next step is to enter data into the database. The data can consist of text, numbers, formulas, and even functions.

More About

Form View

Displaying one record at a time in form view is the easiest way to work with a database. Form view is similar to having a stack of paper forms inside your computer. You can also see titles, graphics, and other enhancements on the form.

Changing to Form View

Thus far, you have viewed the database in form design view. To type information into fields on a form, you use form view. **Form view** allows you to enter information into the database one record at a time. To change to form view, perform the following steps.

To Change to Form View

1. **Point to the Form View button on the toolbar (Figure 3-66).**

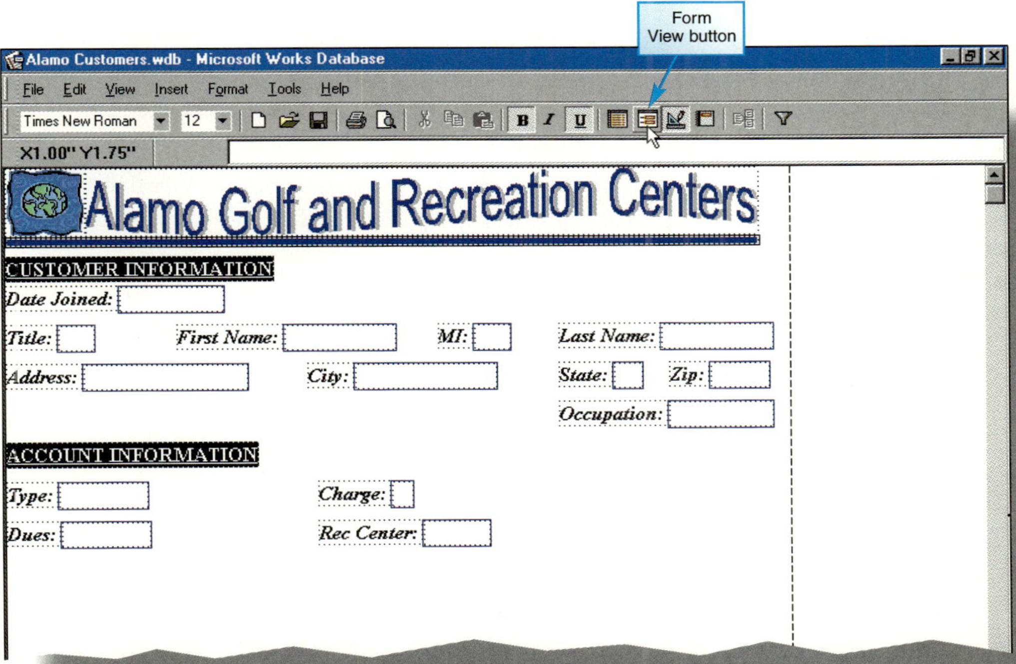

FIGURE 3-66

Click the Form View button.

The database displays in form view (Figure 3-67). Form view resembles form design view except no dotted lines surround the field names, field entries, or the objects on the database form. Works places a black background in the Date Joined field. The coordinates of the fields do not display in form view. The Record menu name replaces the Insert and Format menu names on the menu bar.

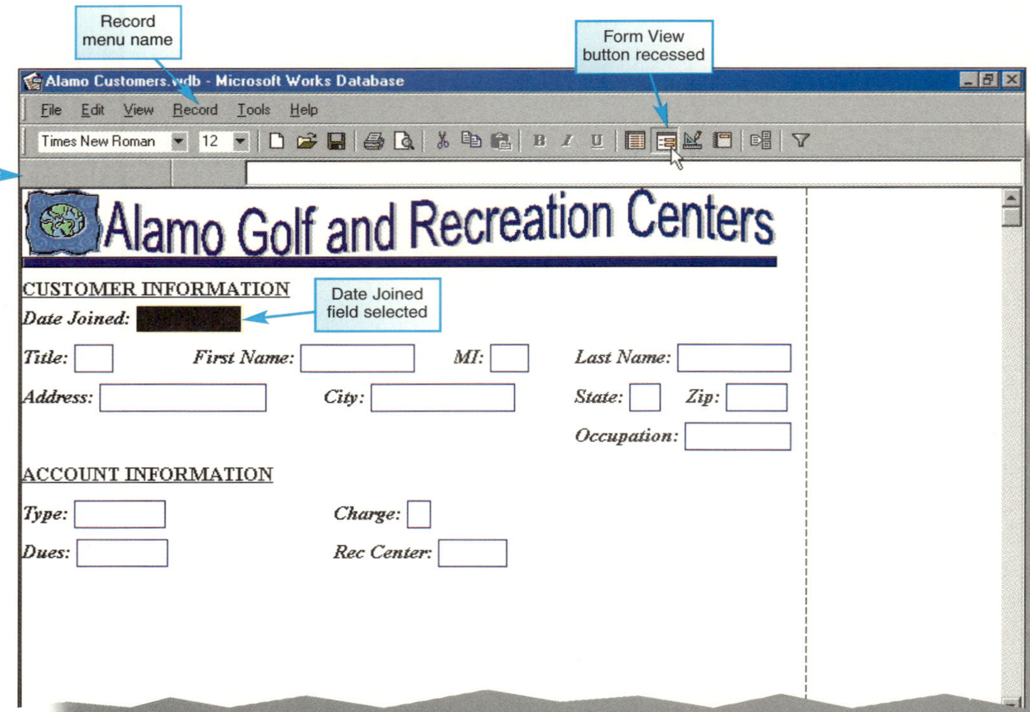

FIGURE 3-67

Other Ways

1. On View menu click Form
2. Press F9

Entering Data into the Database

To enter data, select the field where you want to enter the data and then type the data. To enter the data for the first record in the database, complete the following steps.

To Enter Data into the Database

Ensure the Date Joined field is selected. Type 6/12/01 into the field.

The date joined displays in the entry bar and in the field (Figure 3-68).

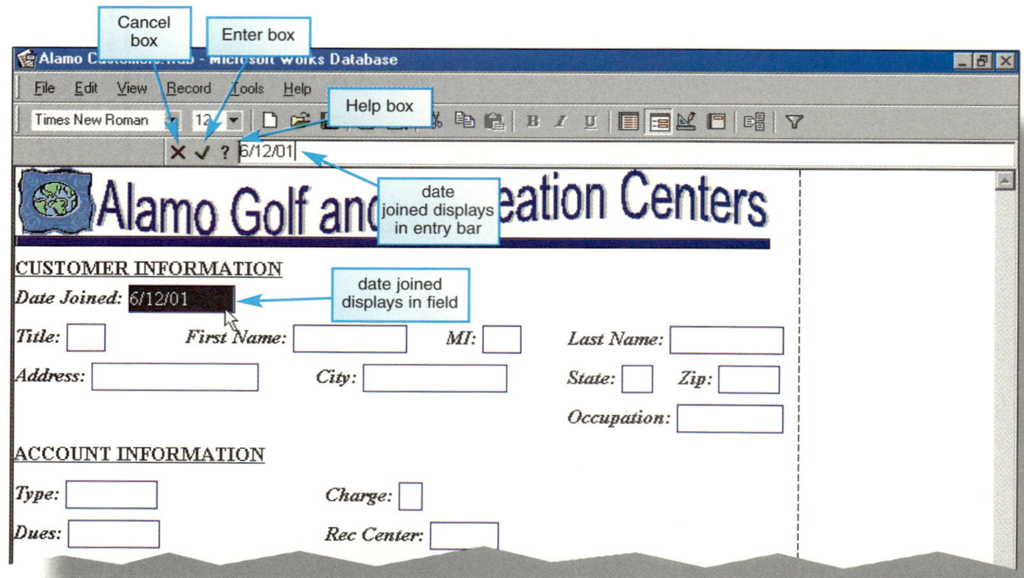

FIGURE 3-68

2 **Press the TAB key.**

Works enters the date as 06/12/01 into the Date Joined field and selects the next field, Title, (Figure 3-69). When you press the TAB key, it causes both the data to be entered and the highlight to be moved from the previous field. If you press the ENTER key or click the Enter box, the data is entered but the highlight is not moved. Pressing the TAB key is the most efficient technique to enter data into a database.

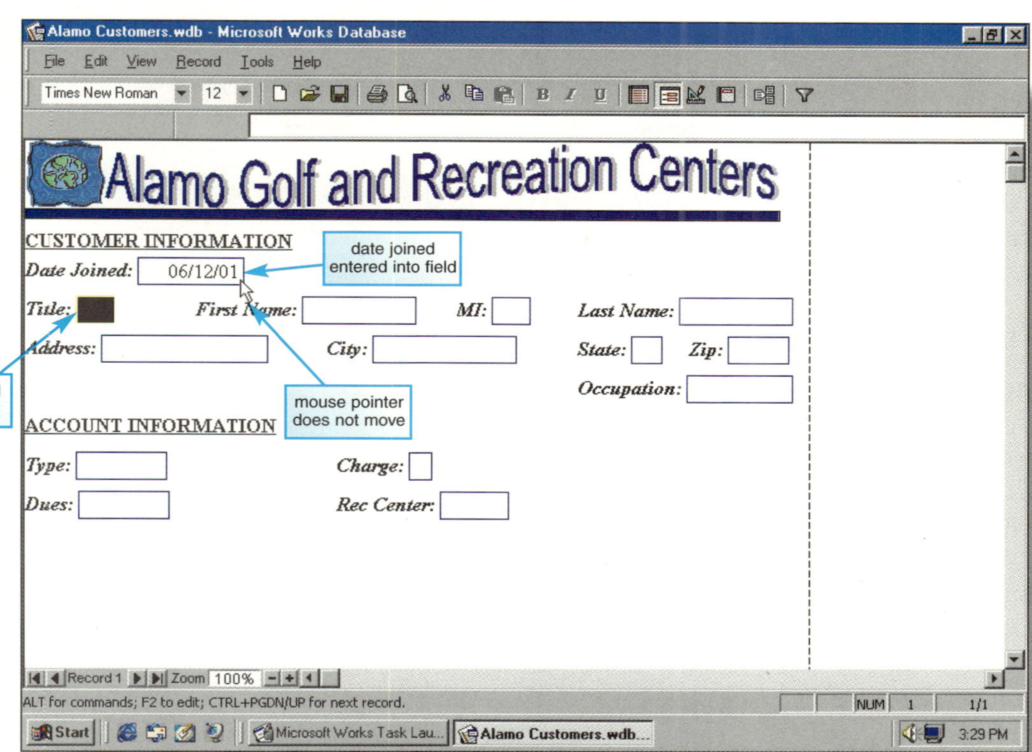

FIGURE 3-69

3 **Type Mr. in the Title field and then press the TAB key.**

Works enters the title, Mr., into the Title field and selects the next field, First Name (Figure 3-70).

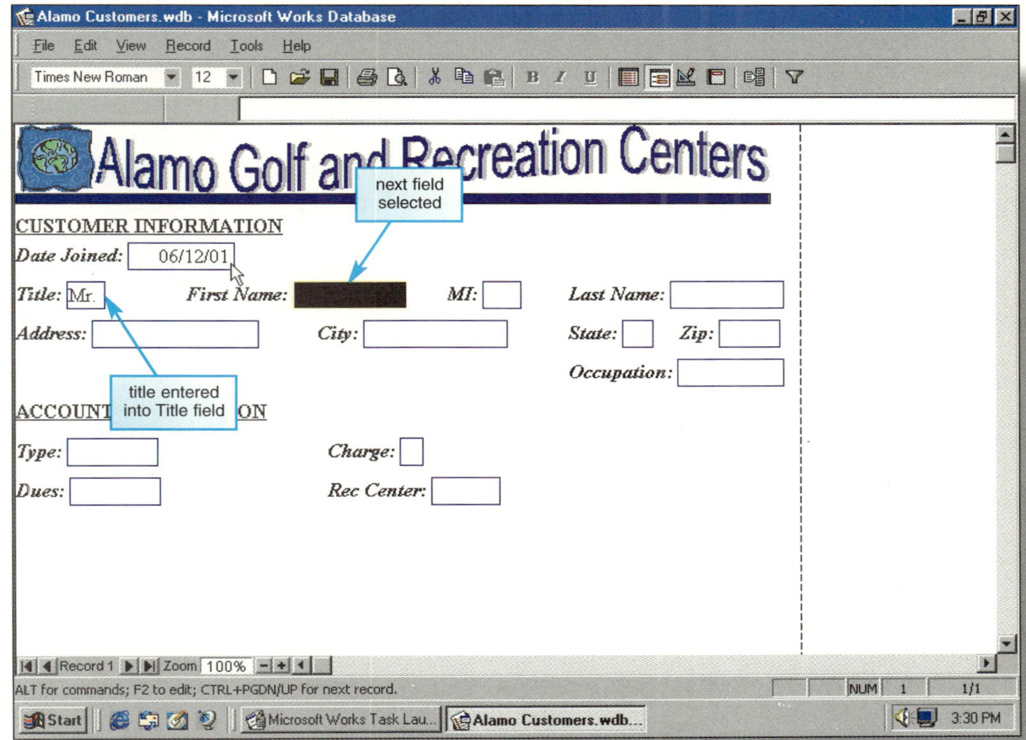

FIGURE 3-70

4 Refer to Figure 3-71 and enter the remaining data for each of the fields in the first record. After entering the Rec Center value, press the ENTER key or click the Enter box.

All the data for the first record is now entered (Figure 3-71). The Rec Center field is selected because you pressed the ENTER key or clicked the Enter box rather than pressing the TAB key. Pressing the TAB key would cause Works to select the Date Joined field in the second record.

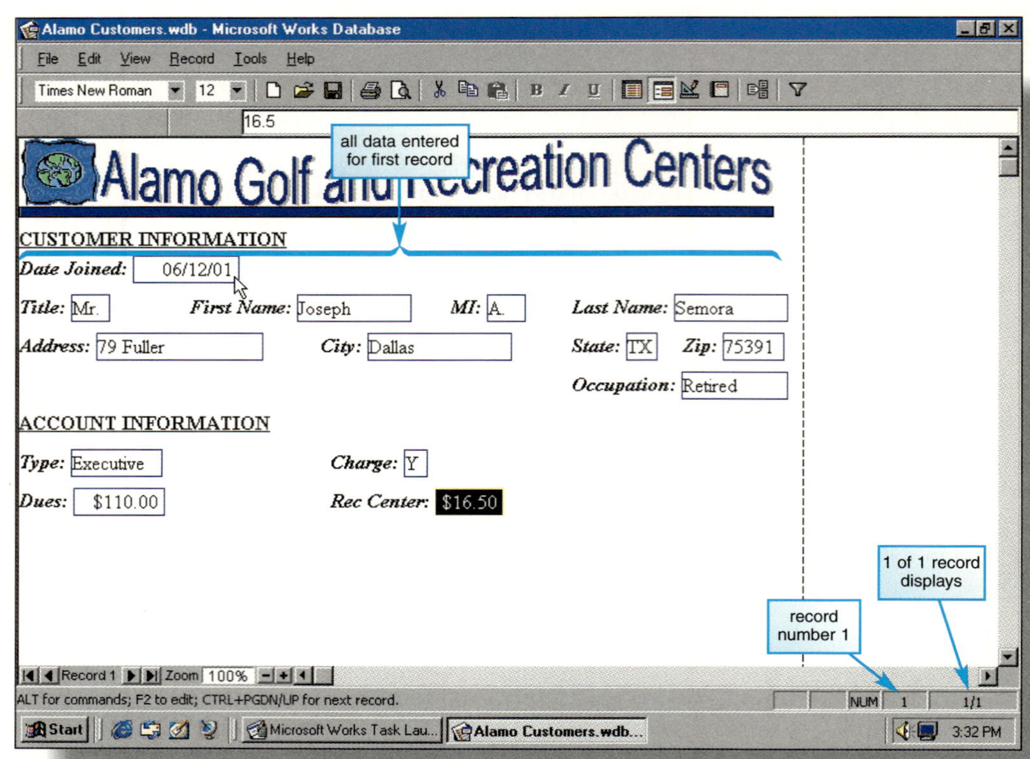

FIGURE 3-71

Notice several important items in the record shown in Figure 3-71. First, Works considers the Date Joined field to be numeric because the field was formatted as a date field. Thus, the date entered is right-aligned in the field. Dues and Rec Center fields also are numeric fields and data is right-aligned in the fields. Second, text fields, such as Title and First Name, are left-aligned in their fields.

If you accidentally enter erroneous data, you can correct the entry by selecting the field containing the error and entering the correct data. Works will replace the erroneous data with the correct data.

To continue entering data into the database, you must display the form for record number 2 as shown in the following step.

To Display the Next Record in Form View

1 **Ensure that the Rec Center field is selected and then press the TAB key.**

Works displays record number 2 (Figure 3-72). Notice that the Date Joined field is selected. When you press the TAB key, Works selects the next field, even if the next field is in the next record in the database. The field names are formatted the same as in record number 1.

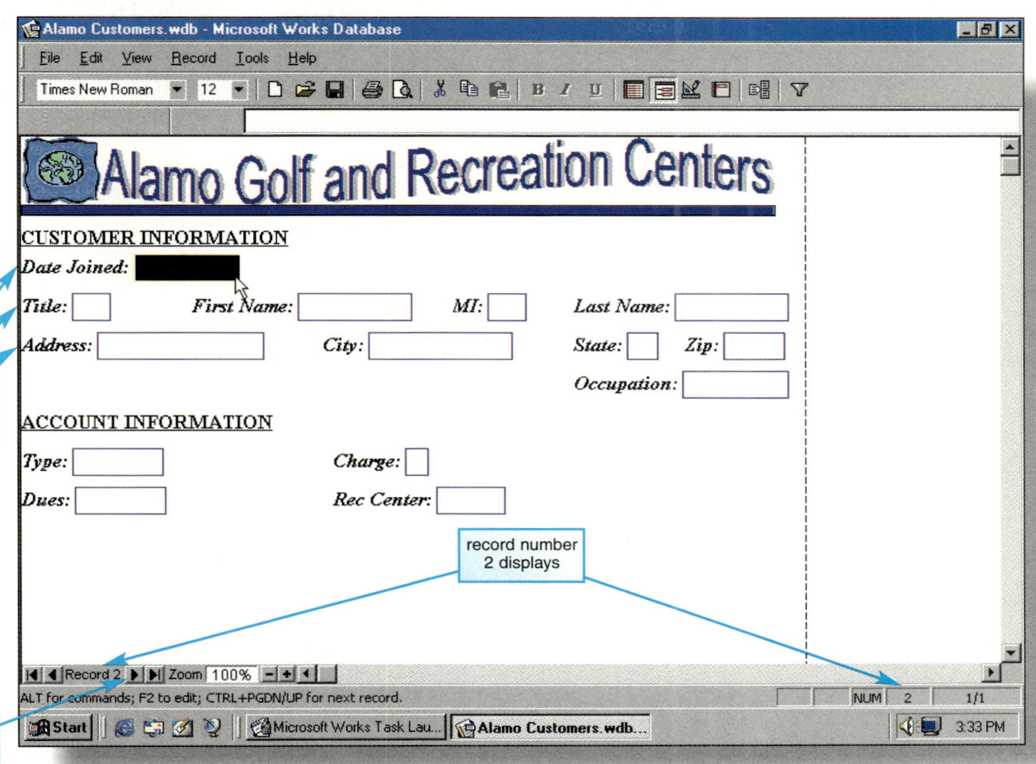

FIGURE 3-72

You also can move from one record to another using the navigation buttons on the scroll bar at the bottom of the screen (Figure 3-72). When record number 1 is displayed and you click the next record navigation button, Works will display record number 2. The field selected, however, is the same field as on record number 1. Therefore, in the sequence from Figure 3-71 to Figure 3-73 on pages W 3.46 through W 3.48, if you click the next record navigation button, record number 2 will display with the Rec Center field selected. When you are entering data into the database, normally you want the first field in the next record selected. Therefore, pressing the TAB key is the preferred way to move from the last field in one record to the first field in the next record.

With record number 2 displayed, complete the steps on the next page to enter the data for record number 2 (Figure 3-73).

More About

Tab Order

In some database programs, when you rearrange the fields on the database form, the tab order, which is the order you move from field to field using the TAB key, does not change. This means when you press the TAB key to move from field to field, the selection moves according to the original order of the fields, not in the order in which they currently appear on the screen. In Works, the tab order automatically changes when you rearrange fields. The tab order always goes from top to bottom, left to right. You can change this default tab order by clicking Tab Order on the Format menu in form design view.

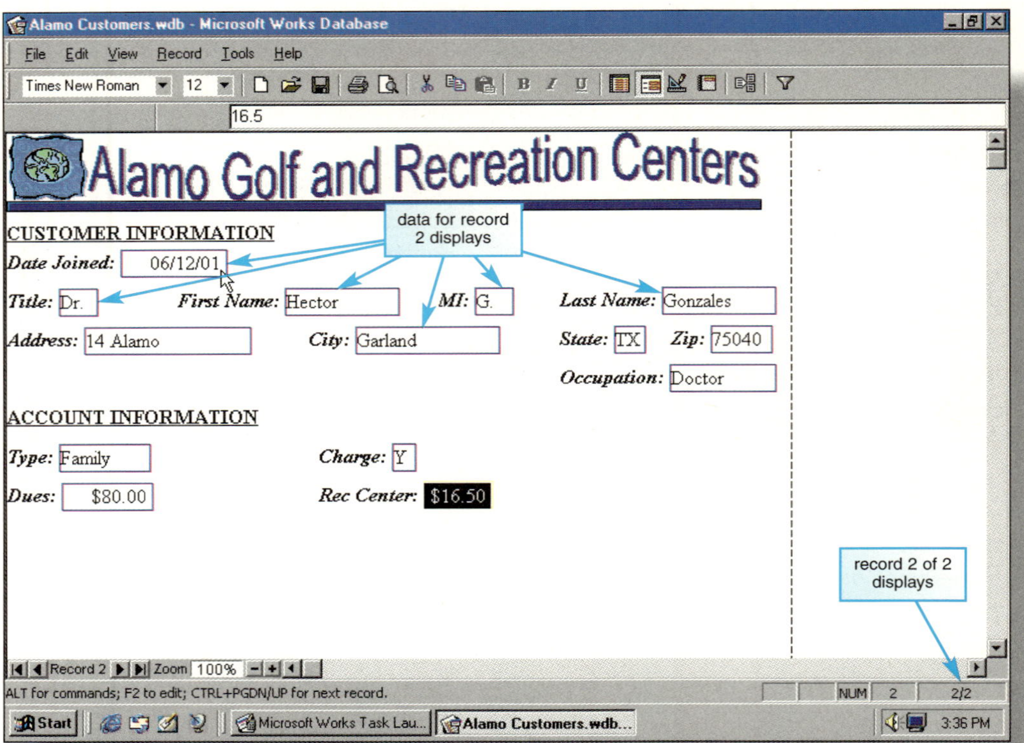

FIGURE 3-73

TO ENTER DATA FOR THE NEXT RECORD

1. Type `6/12/01` in the Date Joined field and then press the TAB key.
2. Type `Dr.` in the Title field and then press the TAB key.
3. Complete the remainder of the record using the data shown in Figure 3-73. When you type `16.50` for the Rec Center, press the ENTER key or click the Enter box to enter the value in the field.

Continue entering data for the remaining records in the database as specified in the following steps.

TO ENTER ALL DATA IN THE DATABASE

1. With the Rec Center field in the second record selected, press the TAB key.
2. Using the table in Figure 3-1 on page W 3.5 for data, enter the data for records 3 through 16. As you enter the data, you should save the database periodically so your work will not be lost in case of a power failure or other mishap. When you enter the data for the Rec Center field for record 16, press the ENTER key or click the Enter box.
3. Click the Save button on the toolbar.

The database contains 16 records. The sixteenth record is shown in Figure 3-74.

After you have entered all records, you may want to display the first record in the database. To accomplish this, perform the following steps.

To Display the First Record in the Database

1. **Point to the first record navigation button on the scroll bar (Figure 3-74).**

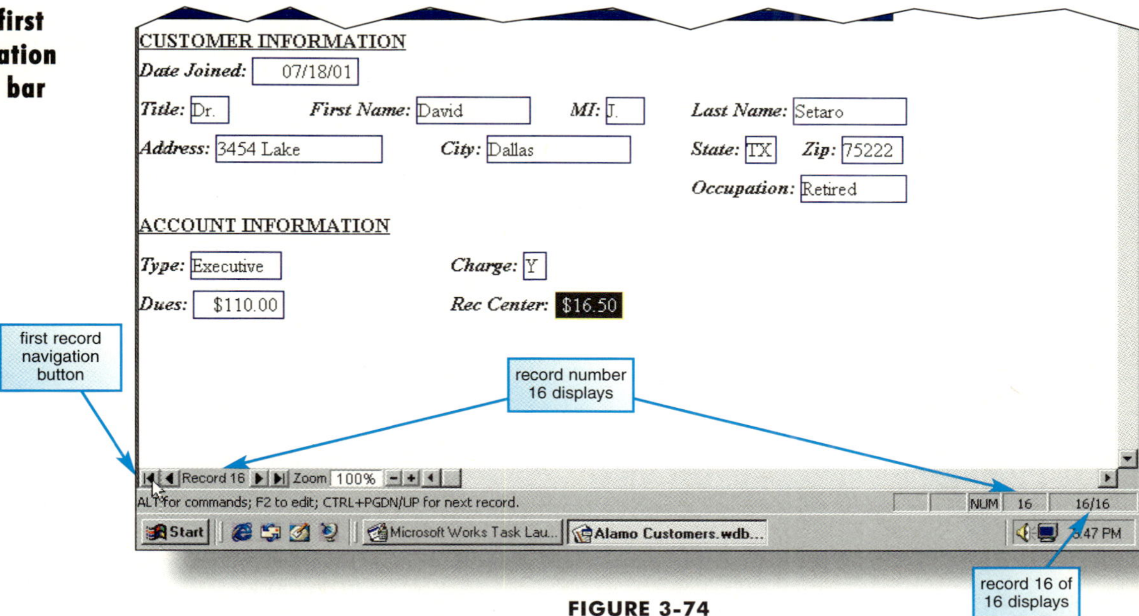

FIGURE 3-74

2. **Click the first record navigation button.**

Works displays the first record in the database (Figure 3-75).

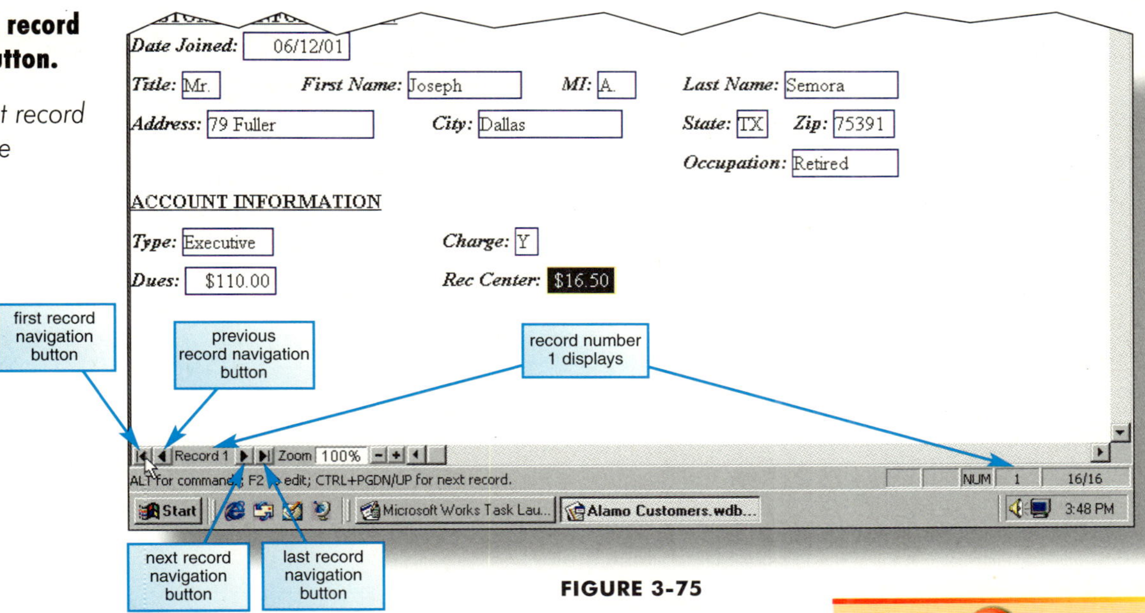

FIGURE 3-75

Other Ways

1. On Edit menu click Go To, type 1 in Go to text box, click OK button
2. Press CTRL+G, type 1 in Go to text box, click OK button
3. Press CTRL+HOME

To move from record to record in the database, you can use the **next record navigation button** or the **previous record navigation button** (Figure 3-75 on the previous page). To move to the last record in the database, click the **last record navigation button**. Works always displays the last record in the database as a blank record. For example, in the database for this project, 16 records have been entered. If you click the last record navigation button, Works will display the seventeenth record, a blank record.

You also can move to a specific record in the database by clicking Edit on the menu bar and then clicking Go To. In the Go to text box in the Go To dialog box, type the record number you want to display and click the OK button. In the Go To dialog box, you also can select a desired field.

List View

Thus far, you have created and formatted the database form in form design view and entered the data into the database one record at a time in form view. Works allows you to view multiple records at the same time using **list view**. To display the database in list view, perform the steps on the next two pages.

Steps To Display the Database in List View

1 Select the Date Joined field. Point to the List View button on the toolbar (Figure 3-76).

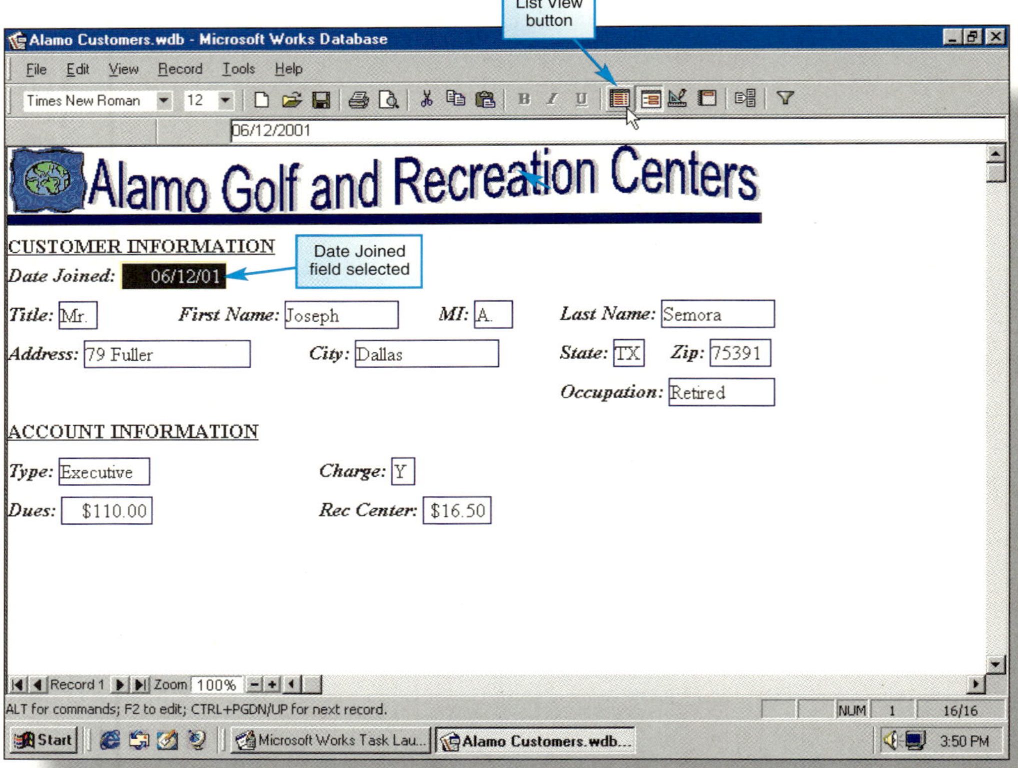

FIGURE 3-76

2 Click the List View button.

Works displays the records in the database in a grid that resembles a spreadsheet (Figure 3-77). In list view, the default font is Arial and the point size is 10. The field names identify each column and the record numbers identify each row. All 16 records in the database are displayed, but not entirely because the records are too long. Works adjusts the width of each column to accommodate the field name entry. For example, the Date Joined column displays with a width of 12; the Title column displays with a width of 10. Field sizes in list view can be different from form view. The field sizes in Figure 3-77 must be adjusted. The Date Joined field for record 1 is selected, designated by a dark border around the field.

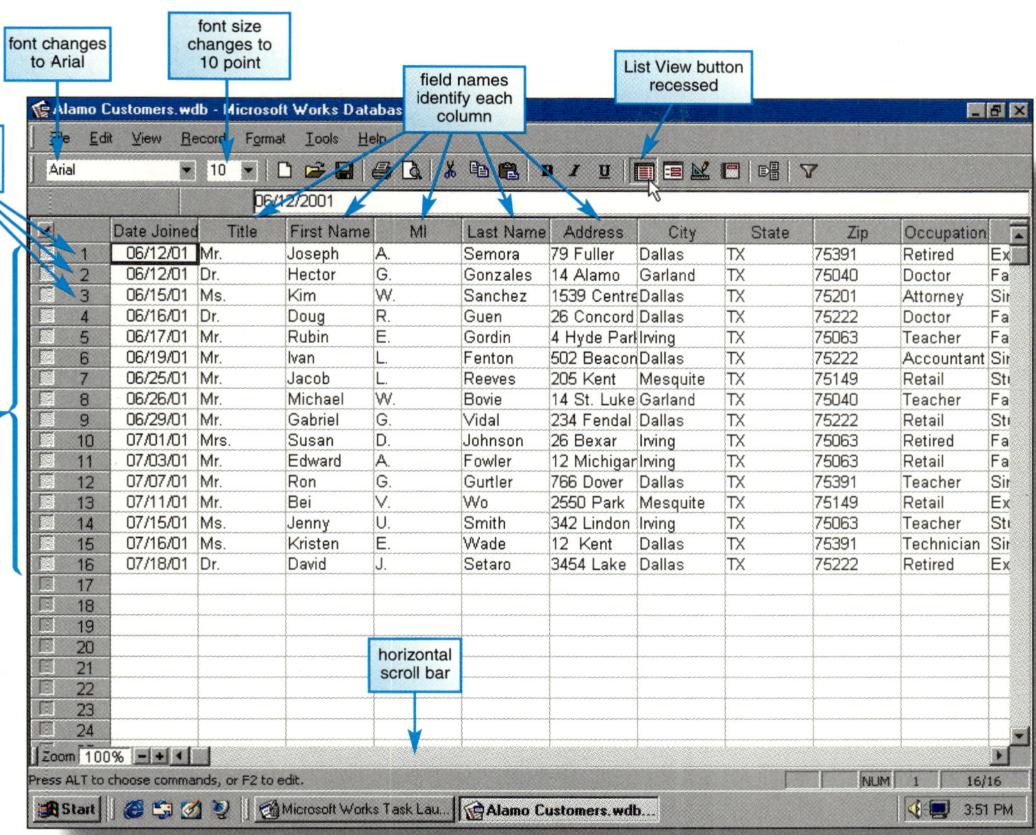

FIGURE 3-77

3 Click the horizontal scroll bar one time to display the remainder of each record.

Works displays the rightmost fields in the database records (Figure 3-78).

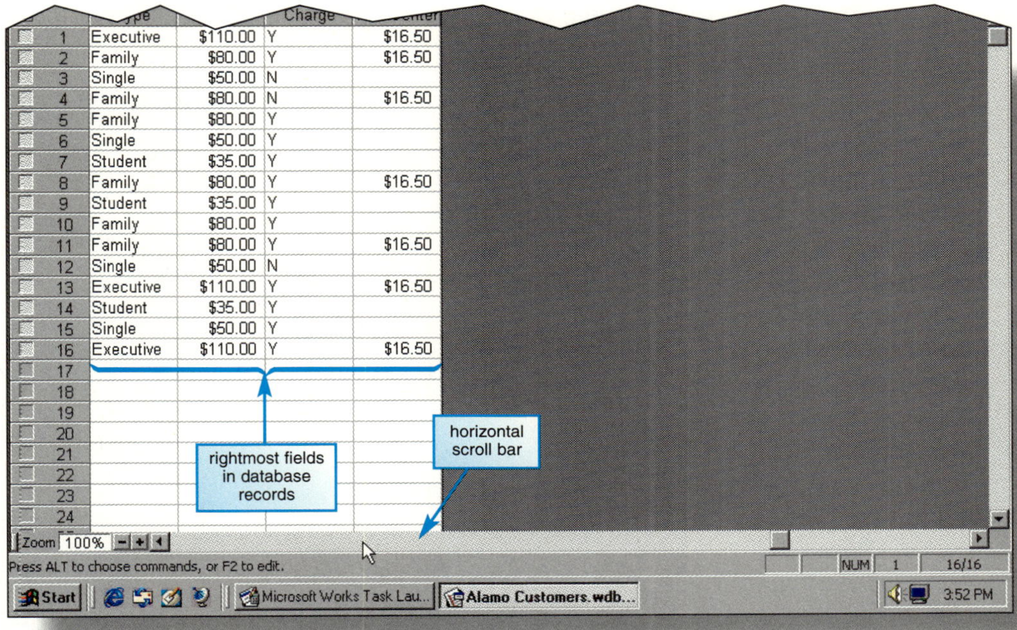

FIGURE 3-78

1. On View menu click List
2. Press SHIFT+F9

Notice several important factors about the list view of the database. First, even though the field widths of the columns are not the same as the field widths in form view, the formatting of the data in each field is the same. For example, in Figure 3-78 on the previous page, the Dues and Rec Center field entries display the values with dollar signs and decimals.

Second, in Figure 3-78, when you clicked the scroll bar, the window display moved to the right one full window. If you click the scroll arrow, the window display moves one column at a time.

Third, when switching from form view to list view, the record and field selected in form view will be the record and field selected in list view. In Figure 3-76 on page W 3.50, the Date Joined field in record 1 is selected. When you change to list view (Figure 3-77 on the previous page), the Date Joined field in record 1 is still selected. This process works in the same manner when switching from list view to form view.

List View

List view looks like a spreadsheet with records in rows and fields in vertical columns. In this view, you can enter data across one record at a time or down one field at a time. Because you can see more than one record at a time, you easily can see whether you have duplicate records.

Formatting the Database in List View

When you format the database in list view, normally you will not change the field entry formats such as Text, Date, or Number. Instead, normally you change the field widths, font sizes, and other factors to accomplish two goals: (1) display all the data in the fields; and (2) if possible, size the list view so an entire record can print on a single page.

To accomplish these goals, you should proceed as follows: (1) change the font size from the default of 10-point to the smaller 8-point size; and (2) arrange the column widths to accomplish the goals. Complete the following steps to format the database in list view.

Steps: To Select the Entire Database and Change Font Size in List View

1 Click the horizontal scroll bar so the first fields in the database display. Click the selection box in the upper-left corner of the grid above the row headings to select the entire database. Click the Font Size box arrow on the toolbar and then point to the number 8 in the Font Size list (Figure 3-79).

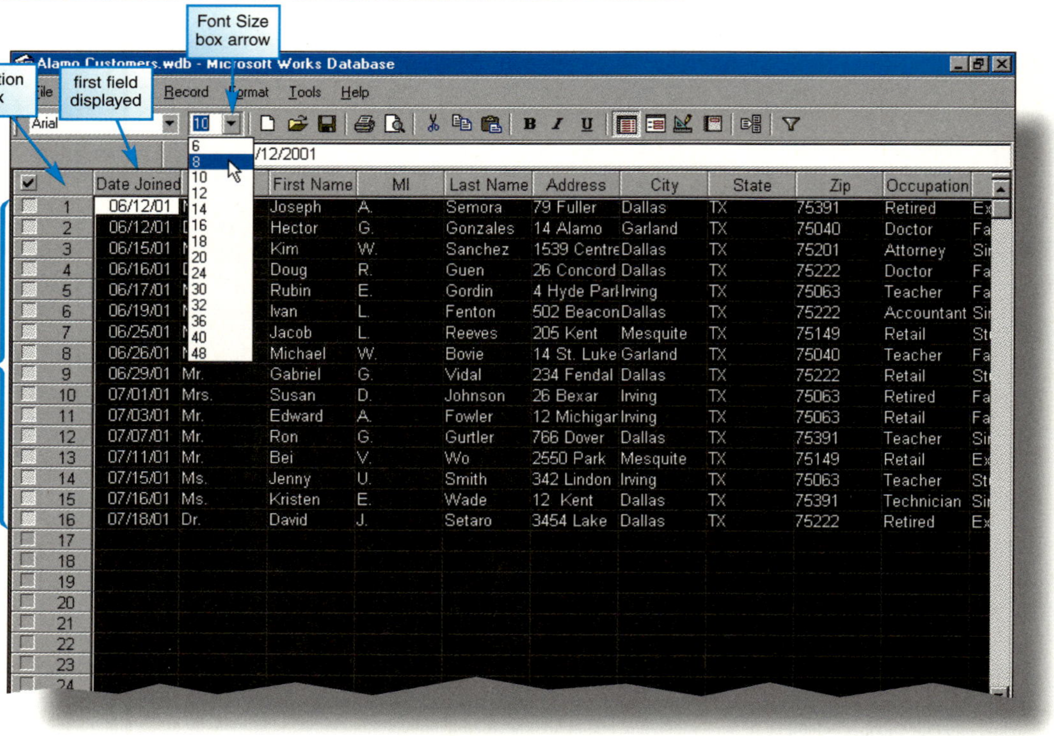

FIGURE 3-79

2 Click 8 and then click anywhere in the database to remove the highlight.

The entire database, including the field names, the record numbers, and the actual data in the database display in 8-point Arial font (Figure 3-80). A font size of 8 point is large enough to be readable but small enough to allow an entire record to print on one page in this project.

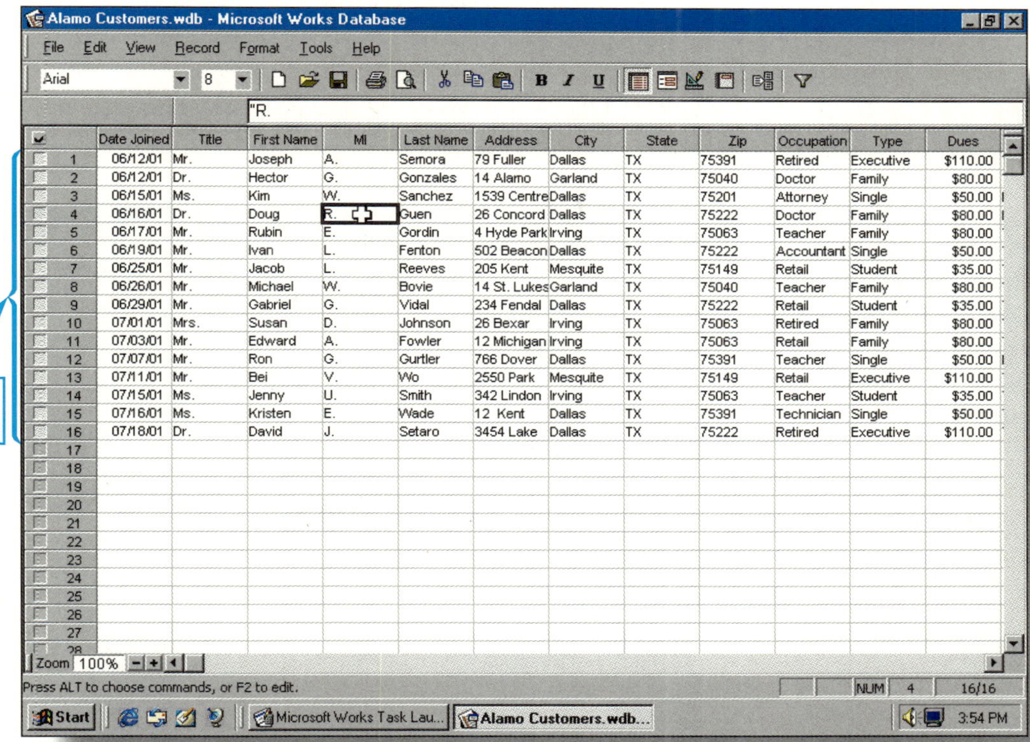

FIGURE 3-80

Setting Field Widths

The next step is to set the field widths for each of the fields in list view. Recall that the field widths set in list view will not necessarily be the same as those in form view, and changing the list view field widths will have no effect on the form view field widths.

Setting field widths in list view may involve some experimentation to determine the proper widths to show the field names and to show data in all records, and yet keep the field widths to a minimum. Table 3-4 shows the field widths for the list view of the database.

Other Ways

1. On Edit menu click Select All, on Format menu click Font and Style, click desired font size in Font Size list box, click OK button
2. Press CTRL+A, on Format menu click Font and Style, click desired font size in Font Size list box, click OK button
3. Press CTRL+SHIFT+F8

Table 3-4 Field Widths

FIELD NAME	FIELD WIDTH	FIELD NAME	FIELD WIDTH
Date Joined	11	State	5
Title	5	Zip	6
First Name	10	Occupation	10
MI	3	Type	8
Last Name	10	Dues	8
Address	11	Charge	7
City	10	Rec Center	11

Perform the following steps to set the field widths of the fields in list view.

To Set Field Widths in List View

1 **Select the Date Joined field in any of the records by clicking the field. Click Format on the menu bar and then point to Field Width (Figure 3-81).**

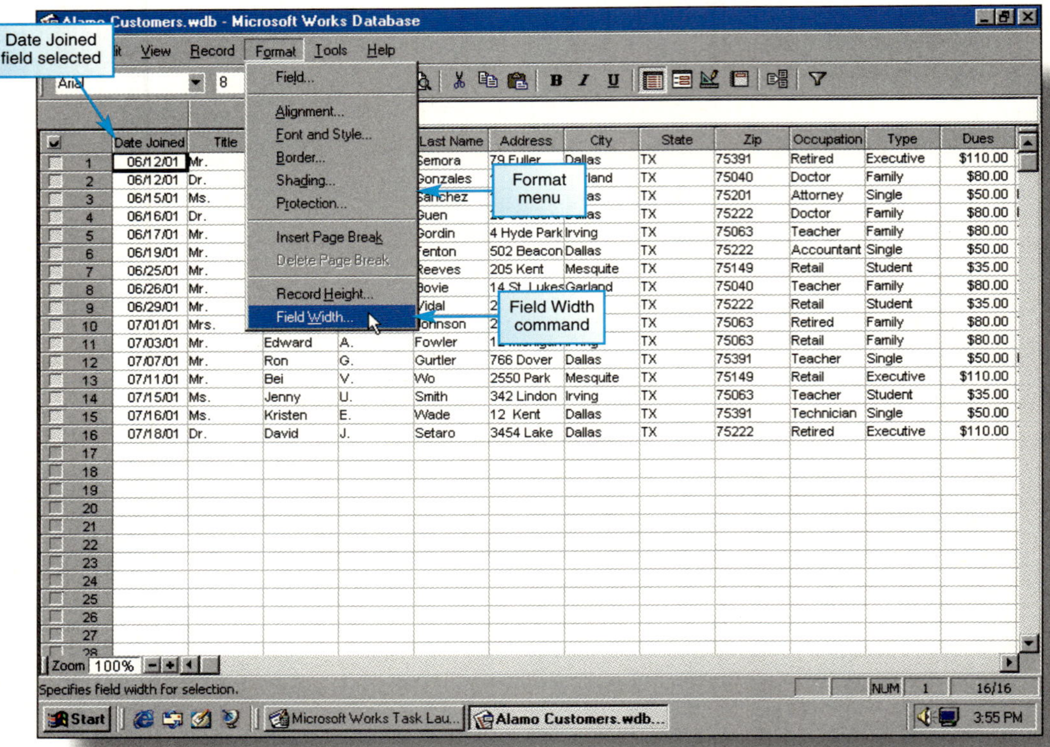

FIGURE 3-81

2 **Click Field Width. Type** 11 **in the Column width text box and then point to the OK button in the Field Width dialog box.**

Works displays the Field Width dialog box (Figure 3-82).

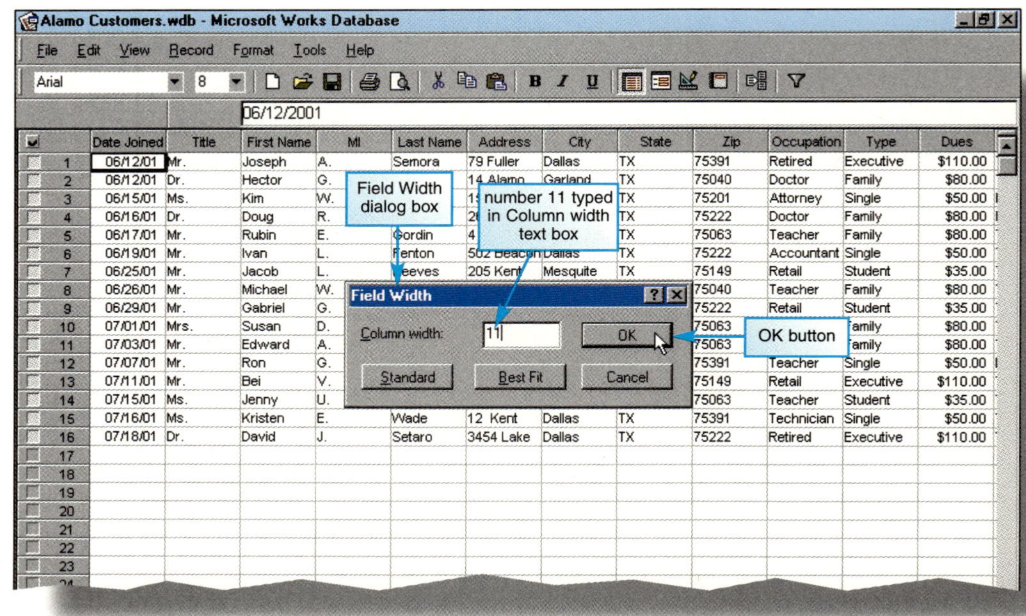

FIGURE 3-82

3 Click the OK button.

Works changes the width of the Date Joined field to 11 (Figure 3-83). All the values fit within the field.

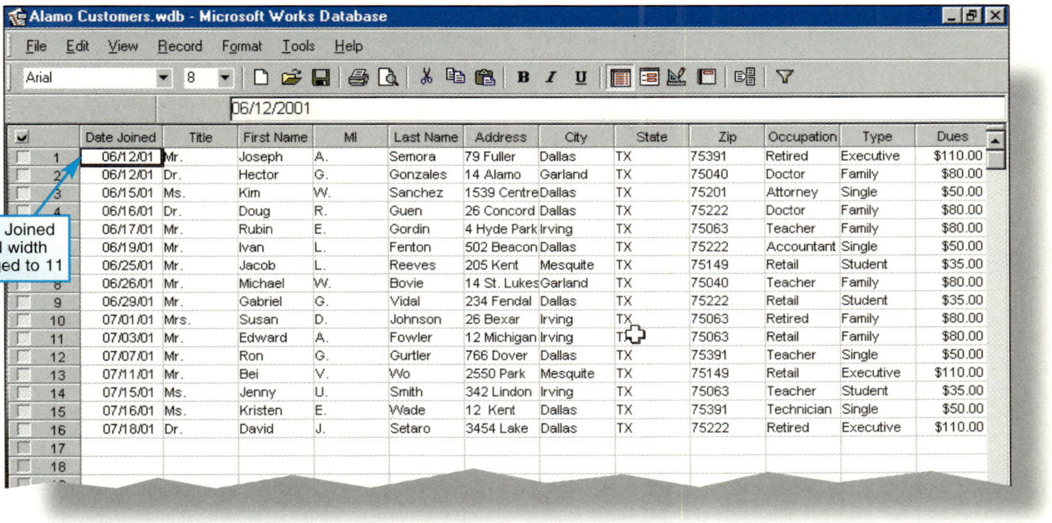

FIGURE 3-83

4 Use the techniques in steps 1 through 3 to set the remainder of the field columns to their proper width as specified in Table 3-4 on page W 3.53.

After setting the field sizes, each of the fields is just wide enough to display both the field name and all the data in each field (Figure 3-84).

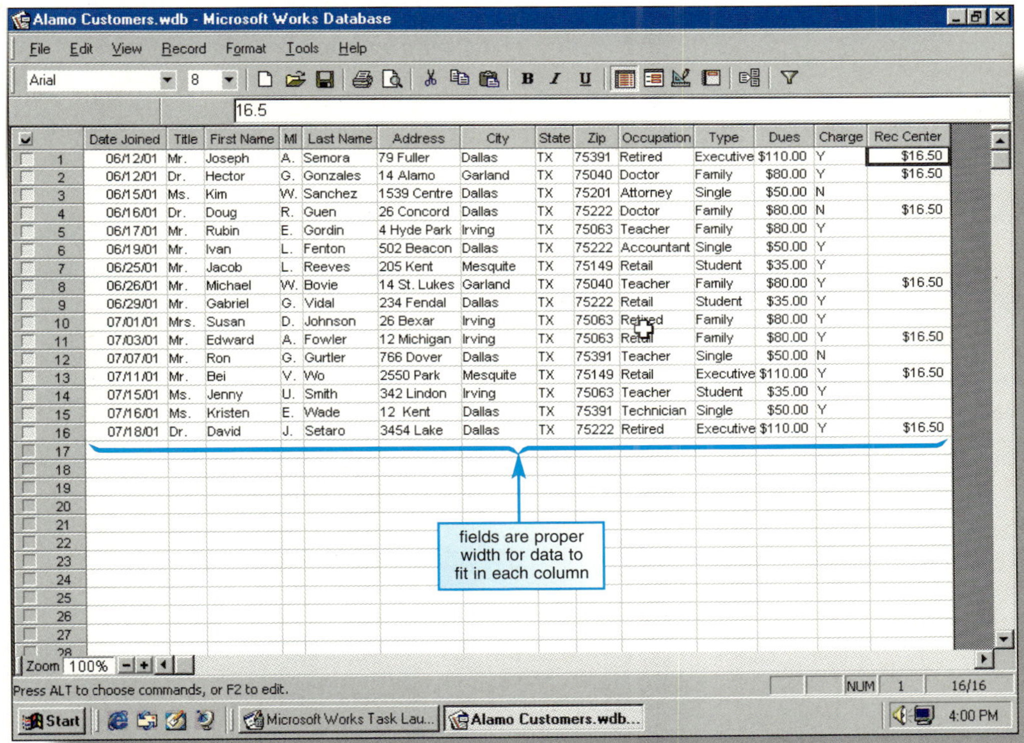

FIGURE 3-84

As previously stated, you also can drag the border to change the field width or use the Best Fit feature of Works. The method you choose when specifying the field width depends on your preference. Using the Field Width command from the Format menu is slower than dragging, but you can specify the exact field width. Dragging allows you to see the actual field width, but because Works does not display the field width, the only way to determine the exact width is by using the Field Width command on the Format menu.

Formatting the database in list view now is complete. Once the database is formatted, you should save it once again, as described in the following step.

TO SAVE THE DATABASE WITH THE SAME FILE NAME

Click the Save button on the toolbar.

> **More About**
>
> **Printing**
>
> When you click the Print button on the toolbar or click Print on the File menu in form design view, Works prints a blank form showing the field names and labels of the database form. You can use this blank form as a paper form to enter data manually.

Printing the Database

The next step is to print the database. You can print the database from either form view or list view. When you print from form view, normally you will see one record per page, with the record appearing in the same format as it displays. When you print from list view, you can view up to 26 entire records per page, assuming the record is not too long to fit on one page. The next section of this project describes the steps to print the database from both form view and list view.

Printing the Database in Form View

To print in form view, first you must display the database in form view. Then, after setting some options for how the database should print, click the Print button on the toolbar. The steps to perform these tasks follow.

To Print the Database in Form View

1 **With the database displayed in list view, point to the Form View button on the toolbar (Figure 3-85).**

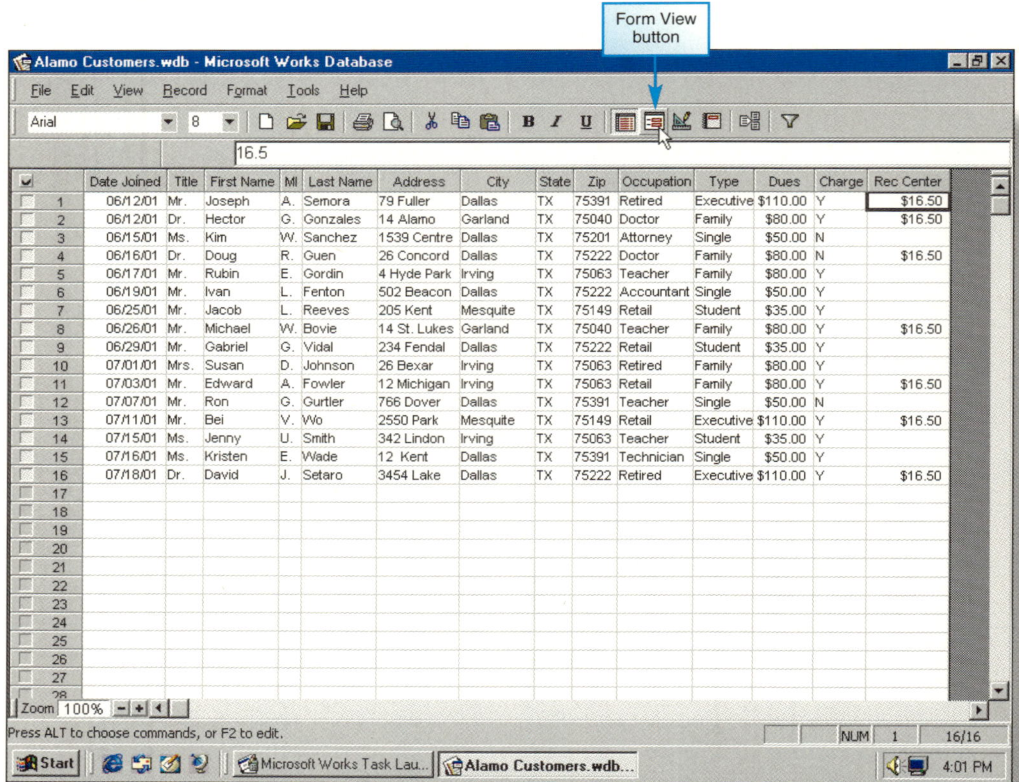

	Date Joined	Title	First Name	MI	Last Name	Address	City	State	Zip	Occupation	Type	Dues	Charge	Rec Center
1	06/12/01	Mr.	Joseph	A.	Semora	79 Fuller	Dallas	TX	75391	Retired	Executive	$110.00	Y	$16.50
2	06/12/01	Dr.	Hector	G.	Gonzales	14 Alamo	Garland	TX	75040	Doctor	Family	$80.00	Y	$16.50
3	06/15/01	Ms.	Kim	W.	Sanchez	1539 Centre	Dallas	TX	75201	Attorney	Single	$50.00	N	
4	06/16/01	Dr.	Doug	R.	Guen	26 Concord	Dallas	TX	75222	Doctor	Family	$80.00	N	$16.50
5	06/17/01	Mr.	Rubin	E.	Gordin	4 Hyde Park	Irving	TX	75063	Teacher	Family	$80.00	Y	
6	06/19/01	Mr.	Ivan	L.	Fenton	502 Beacon	Dallas	TX	75222	Accountant	Single	$50.00	Y	
7	06/25/01	Mr.	Jacob	L.	Reeves	205 Kent	Mesquite	TX	75149	Retail	Student	$35.00	Y	
8	06/26/01	Mr.	Michael	W.	Bovie	14 St. Lukes	Garland	TX	75040	Teacher	Family	$80.00	Y	$16.50
9	06/29/01	Mr.	Gabriel	G.	Vidal	234 Fendal	Dallas	TX	75222	Retail	Student	$35.00	Y	
10	07/01/01	Mrs.	Susan	D.	Johnson	26 Bexar	Irving	TX	75063	Retired	Family	$80.00	Y	
11	07/03/01	Mr.	Edward	A.	Fowler	12 Michigan	Irving	TX	75063	Retail	Family	$80.00	Y	$16.50
12	07/07/01	Mr.	Ron	G.	Gurtler	766 Dover	Dallas	TX	75391	Teacher	Single	$50.00	N	
13	07/11/01	Mr.	Bei	V.	Wo	2550 Park	Mesquite	TX	75149	Retail	Executive	$110.00	Y	$16.50
14	07/15/01	Ms.	Jenny	U.	Smith	342 Lindon	Irving	TX	75063	Teacher	Student	$35.00	Y	
15	07/16/01	Ms.	Kristen	E.	Wade	12 Kent	Dallas	TX	75391	Technician	Single	$50.00	Y	
16	07/18/01	Dr.	David	J.	Setaro	3454 Lake	Dallas	TX	75222	Retired	Executive	$110.00	Y	$16.50

FIGURE 3-85

2 Click the Form View button. Click File on the menu bar and then point to Print.

Works displays the database in form view, and the File menu displays (Figure 3-86). The record number displayed and the field selected will be the same as when the database was displayed in list view unless another field is selected.

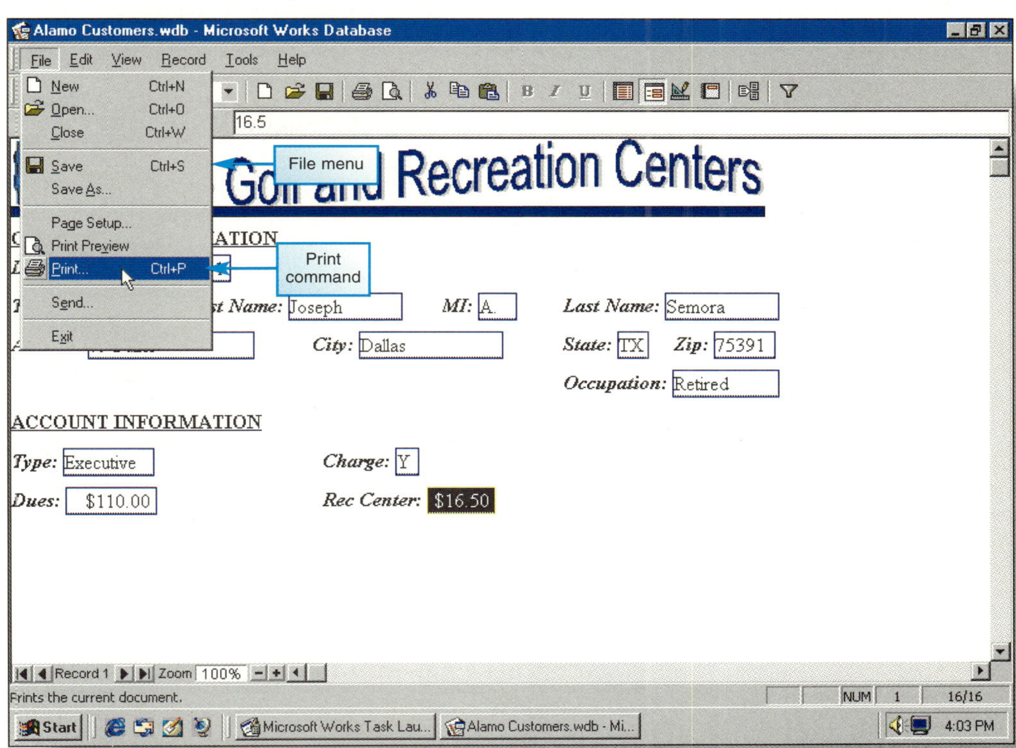

FIGURE 3-86

3 Click Print. Make the appropriate entries in the Print dialog box, and then point to the OK button.

Works displays the Print dialog box (Figure 3-87). Make sure the All records option button is selected.

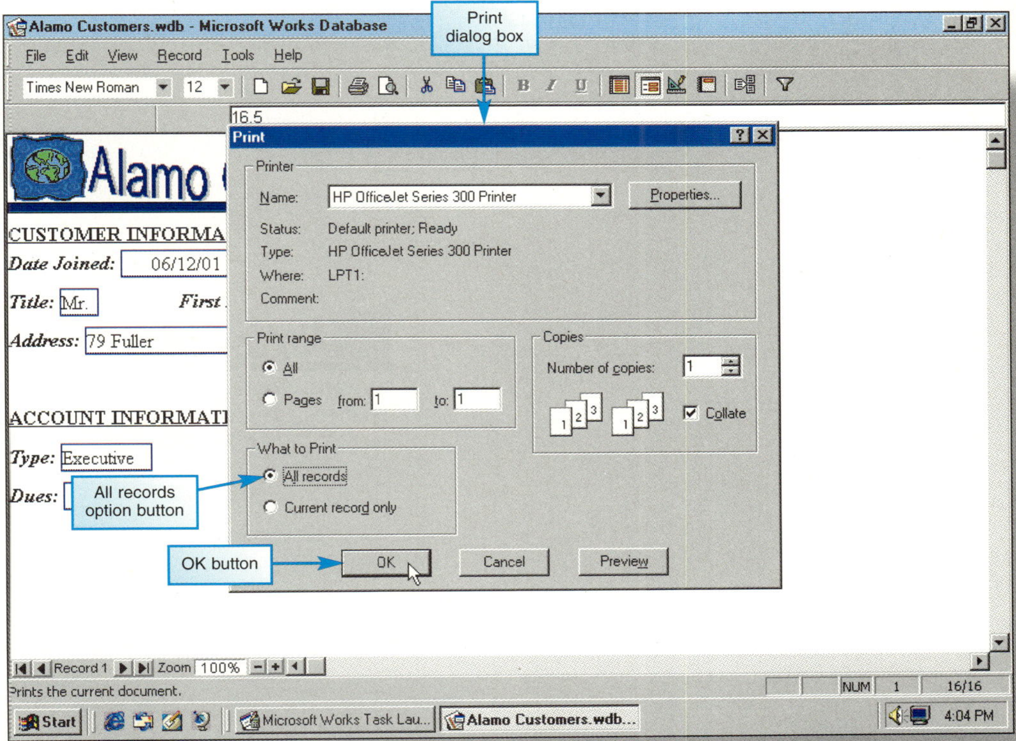

FIGURE 3-87

Click the OK button.

The form view records print (Figure 3-88).

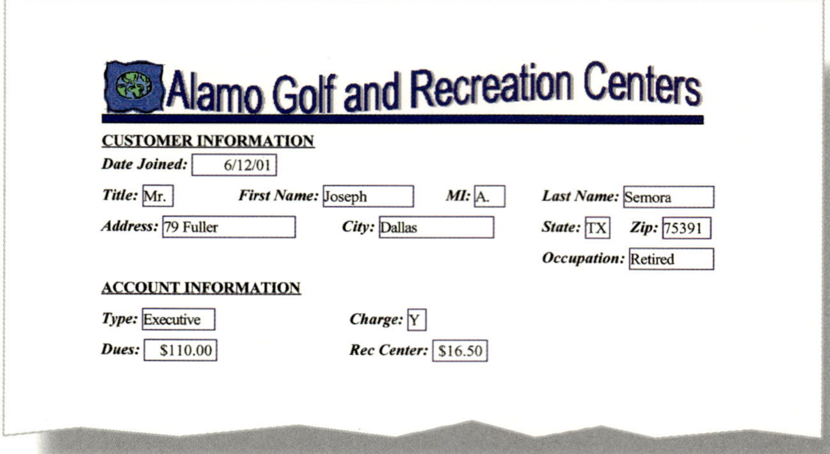

Alamo Golf and Recreation Centers

CUSTOMER INFORMATION

Date Joined: 6/12/01

Title: Mr. First Name: Joseph MI: A. Last Name: Semora

Address: 79 Fuller City: Dallas State: TX Zip: 75391

Occupation: Retired

ACCOUNT INFORMATION

Type: Executive Charge: Y

Dues: $110.00 Rec Center: $16.50

(a) Record One

Alamo Golf and Recreation Centers

CUSTOMER INFORMATION

Date Joined: 6/12/01

Title: Dr. First Name: Hector M.I.: G. Last Name: Gonzales

Address: 14 Alamo City: Garland State: TX Zip: 75040

Occupation: Doctor

ACCOUNT INFORMATION

Type: Family Charge: Y

Dues: $80.00 Rec Center: $16.50

(b) Record Two

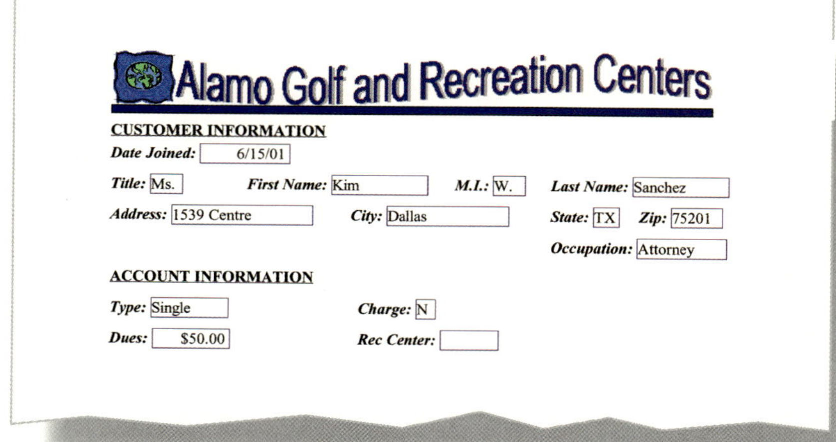

Alamo Golf and Recreation Centers

CUSTOMER INFORMATION

Date Joined: 6/15/01

Title: Ms. First Name: Kim M.I.: W. Last Name: Sanchez

Address: 1539 Centre City: Dallas State: TX Zip: 75201

Occupation: Attorney

ACCOUNT INFORMATION

Type: Single Charge: N

Dues: $50.00 Rec Center:

(c) Record Three

FIGURE 3-88

Other Ways

1. Click Print button on toolbar in form view
2. Press CTRL+P

Printing a Single Record in Form View

When working in form view, you may want to print a single record. To print a single record, such as record eight, perform the following steps.

To Print a Single Record in Form View

1 Click Edit on the menu bar and then point to Go To (Figure 3-89).

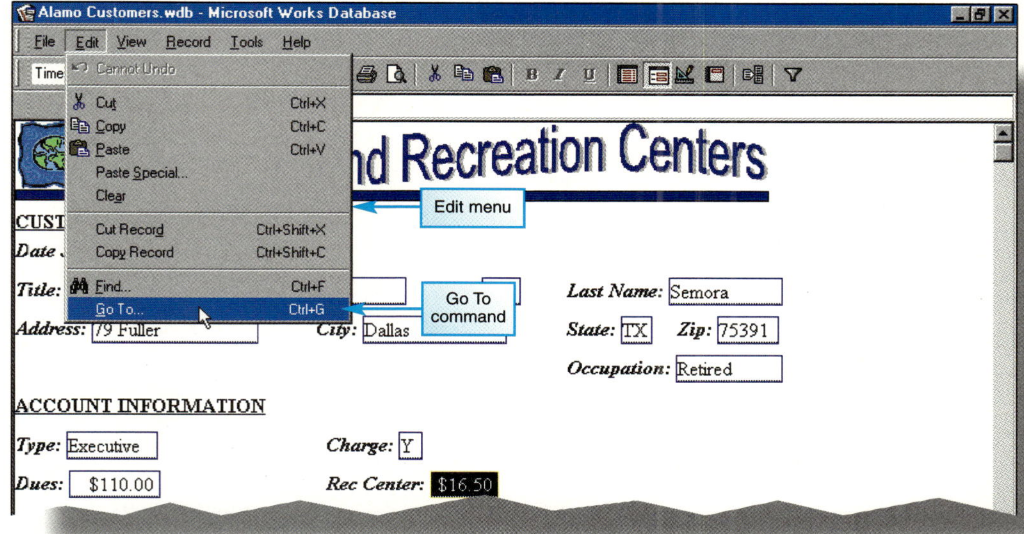

FIGURE 3-89

2 Click Go To. When the Go To dialog box displays, type 8 **in the Go to text box, and then point to the OK button.**

The Go To dialog box displays (Figure 3-90).

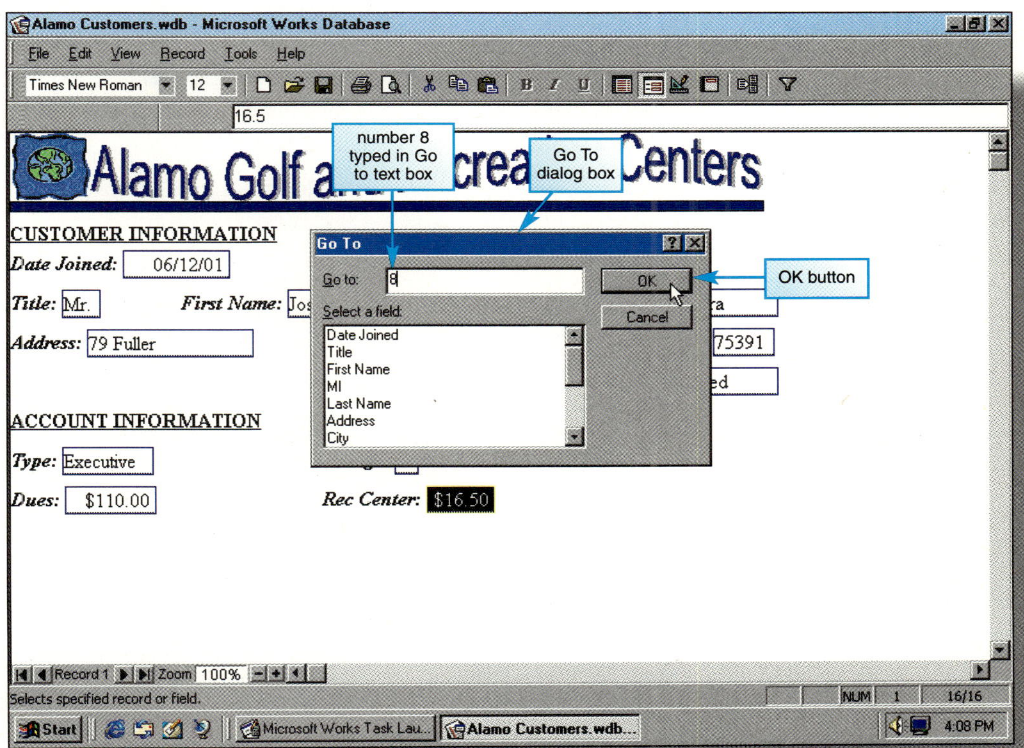

FIGURE 3-90

3 Click the OK button. Click File on the menu bar and then point to Print.

Works displays record 8 in form view, and the File menu displays (Figure 3-91).

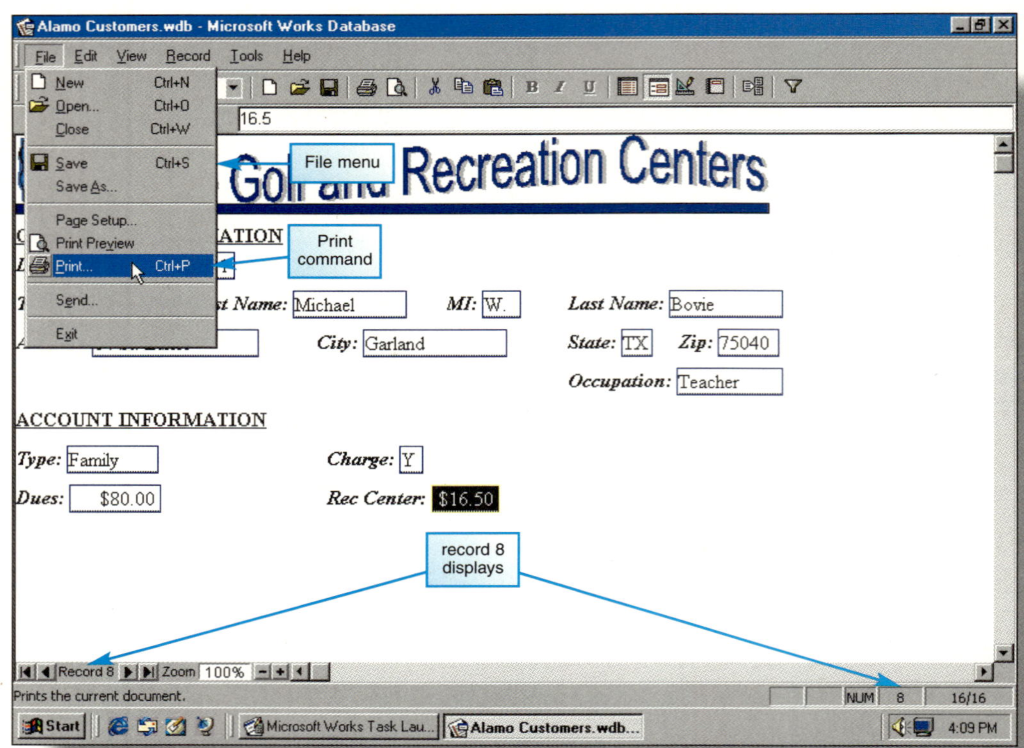

FIGURE 3-91

4 Click Print. When the Print dialog box displays, click Current record only in the What to Print area, and then point to the OK button.

The Print dialog box displays (Figure 3-92). The Current record only option button is selected.

Click the OK button.

Record 8 in form view will print on the printer.

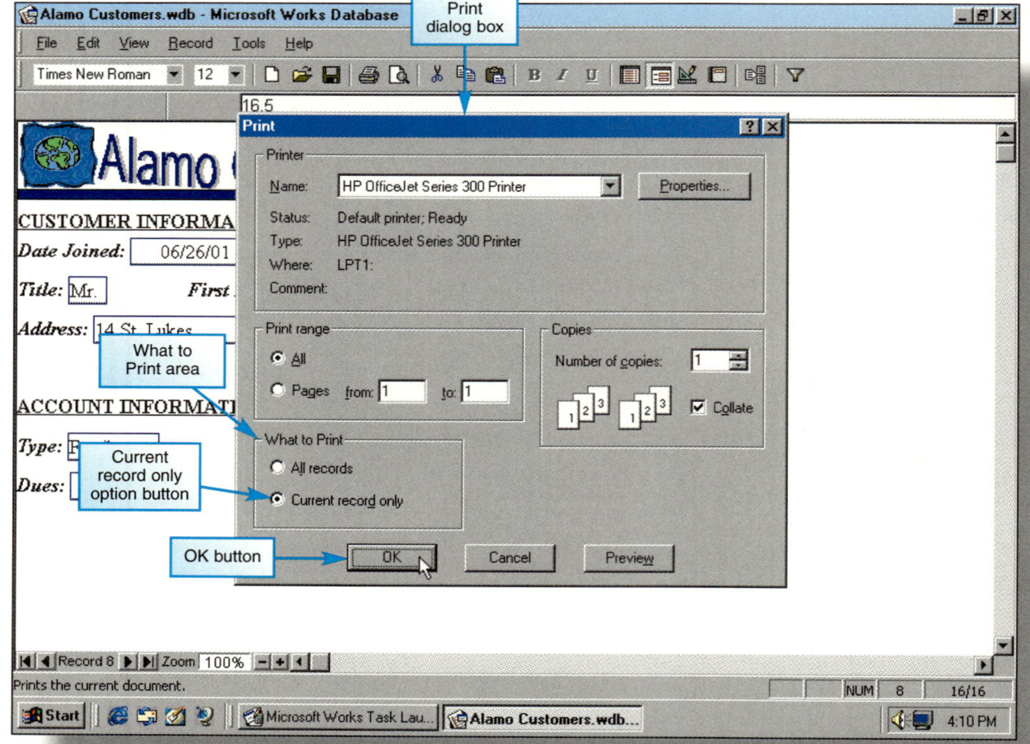

FIGURE 3-92

You have additional control over how form view records print by using the Page Setup command on the File menu. The dialog box that displays when using this command contains settings that allow you to control the printing of Field Lines and Field Entries. You also can control printing more than one record on a page.

It also is possible to print records in list view. The method to do this is explained in the following paragraphs.

Printing the Database in List View

Printing the database in list view allows you to print multiple records on one page. One of the concerns when printing in list view is to ensure the entire record fits on a single page. You can use the Print Preview feature of Works to determine if the record fits on one page. In this project, you must print the database using Landscape orientation in order to fit the entire record on a single page. To print using Landscape orientation, click Landscape in the Page Setup dialog box.

To use Print Preview and then print the list view of the database using Landscape orientation, perform the following steps.

To Print the Database in List View

1 If the database is not displayed in list view, display it in list view by clicking the List View button on the toolbar. Click the Date Joined field for record 1, click File on the menu bar, and then point to Page Setup.

Works displays the database in list view, and the File menu displays (Figure 3-93).

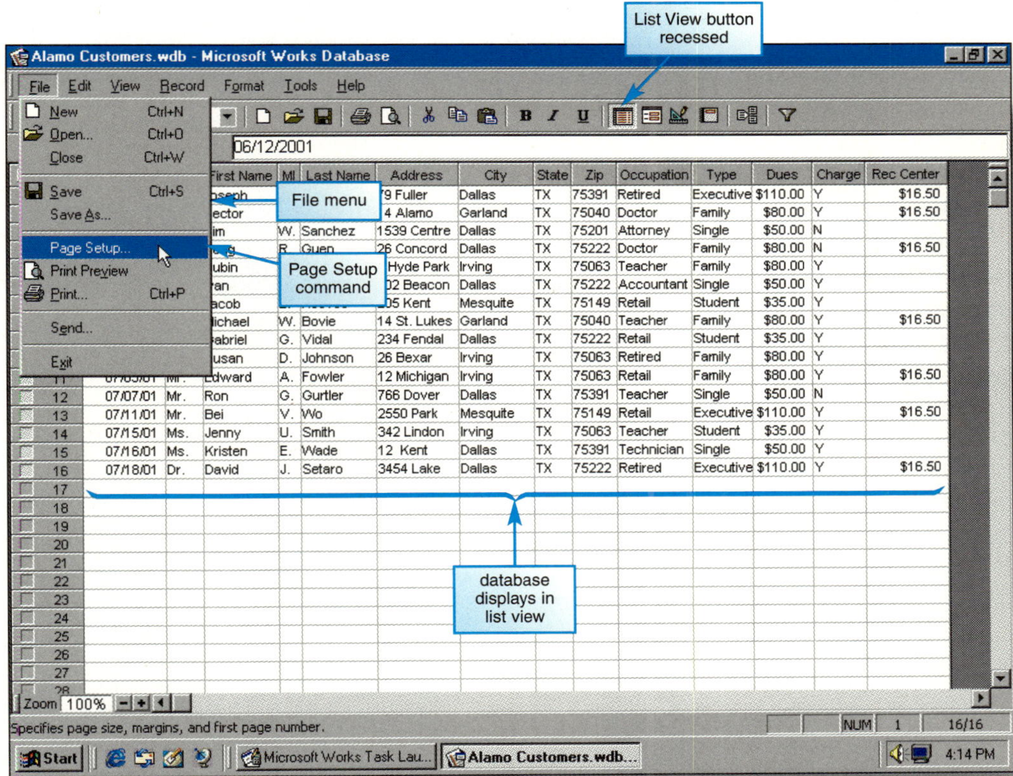

FIGURE 3-93

2 Click Page Setup. When the Page Setup dialog box displays, click the Source, Size & Orientation tab. Click Landscape in the Orientation area and then point to the Other Options tab.

The Page Setup dialog box displays (Figure 3-94). Works automatically enters 11" in the Width text box and 8.5" in the Height text box when the Landscape option button is selected. The Sample area illustrates Landscape orientation.

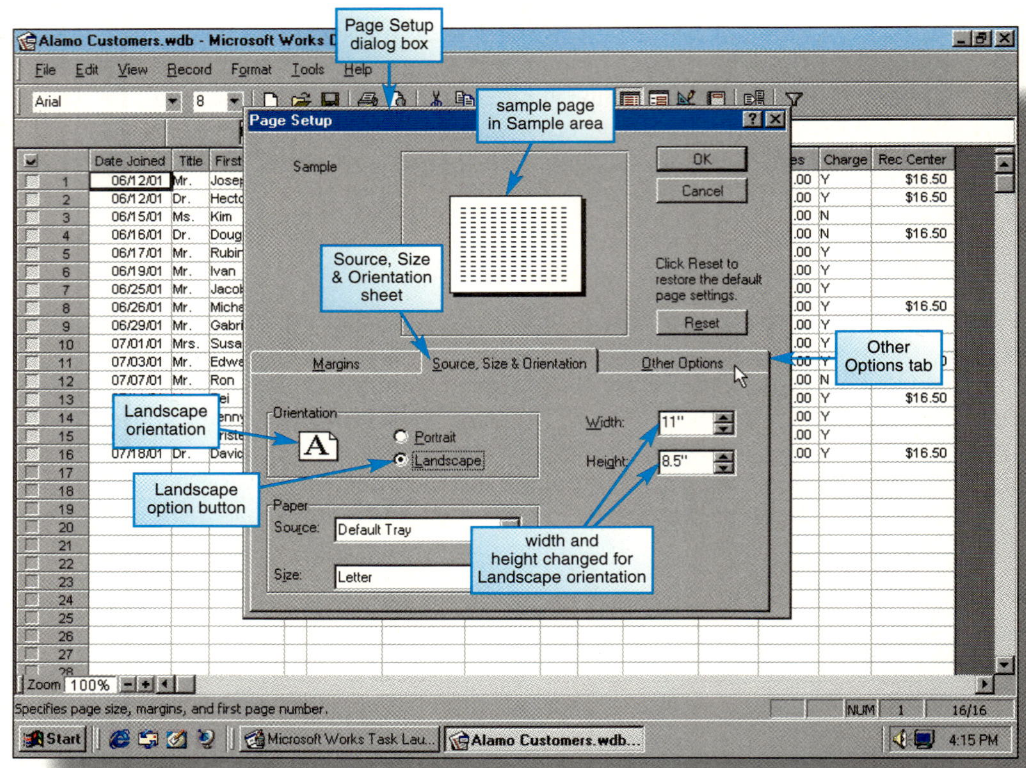

FIGURE 3-94

3 Click the Other Options tab. When the Other Options sheet displays, click Print record and field labels, and then point to the OK button.

The Other Options sheet displays (Figure 3-95). The Print record and field labels check box is selected, which means both the record numbers and the field labels will print. If you leave this box unselected, only the field entries will print.

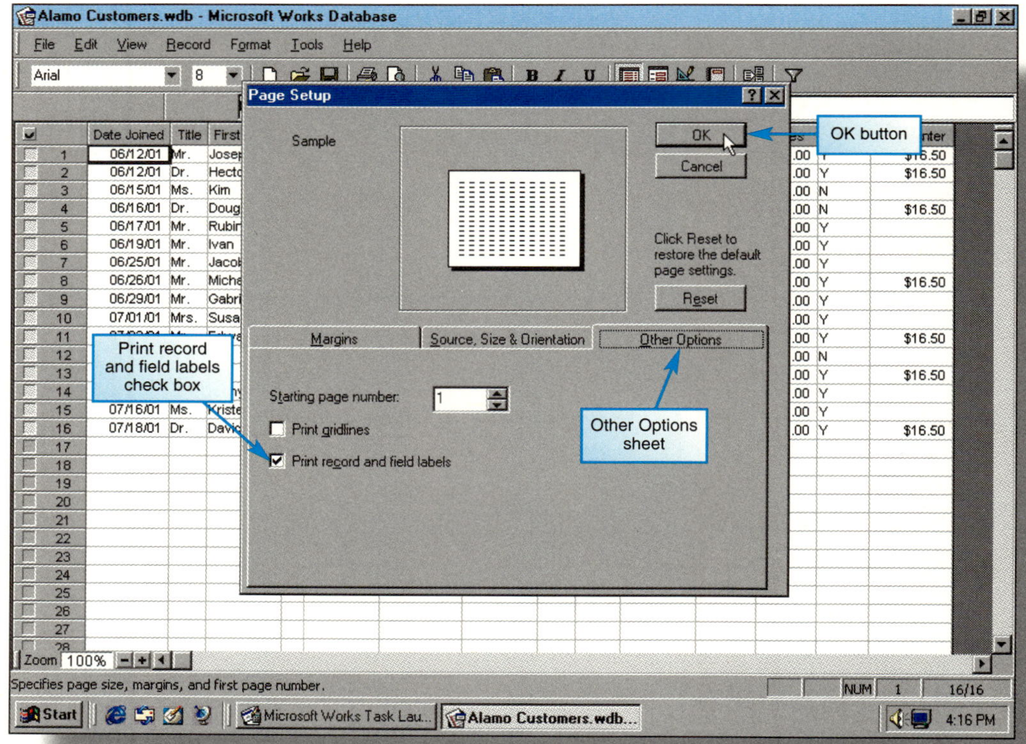

FIGURE 3-95

4 **Click the OK button. Point to the Print Preview button on the toolbar (Figure 3-96).**

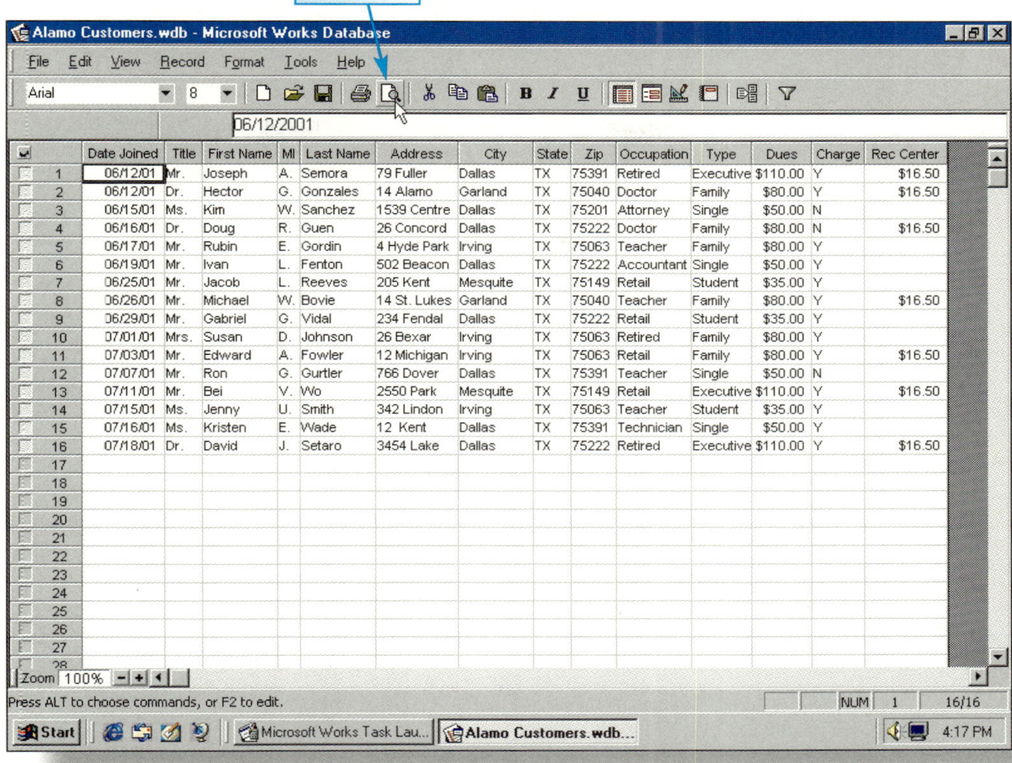

FIGURE 3-96

5 **Click the Print Preview button. When the Print Preview window displays, click the report twice to magnify the view of the database. Scroll left and right to ensure the database displays properly and then point to the Print button.**

Works magnifies the report to approximately the same size as the list view display (Figure 3-97). You can see the Rec Center field fits on the page. Because the Rec Center field is the rightmost field in the list view of the database and all the other fields are to the left, the entire record fits on one page.

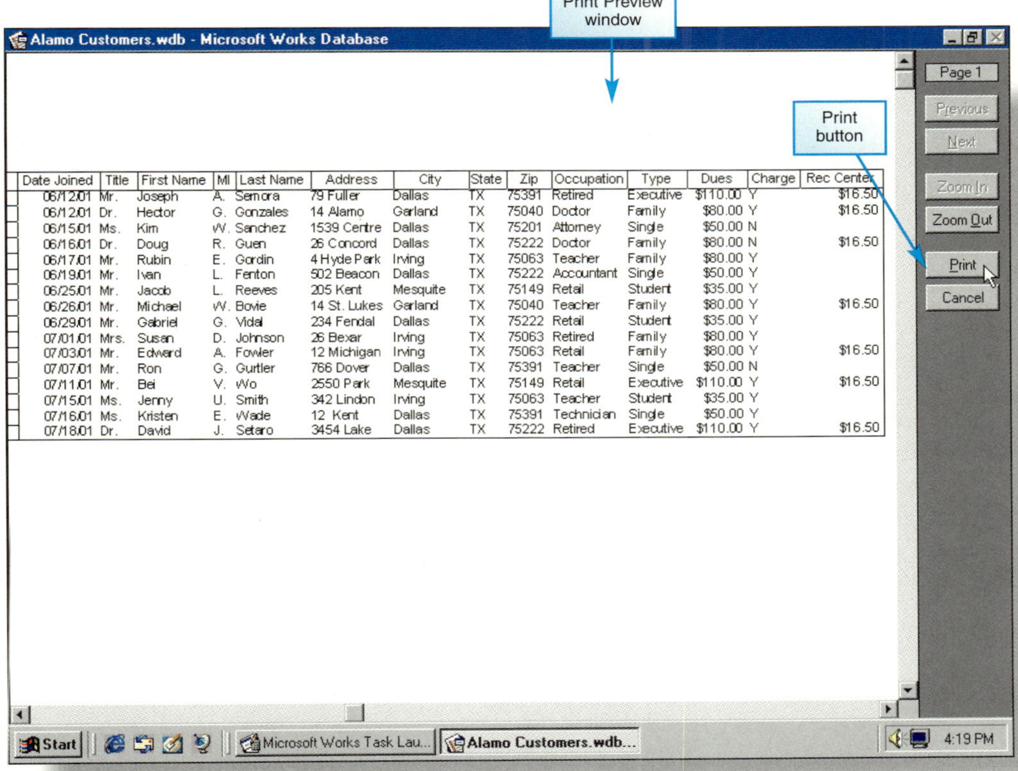

FIGURE 3-97

Click the Print button.

Works momentarily displays the Printing dialog box, and then prints the report (Figure 3-98). Notice the entire database fits on one page in landscape orientation.

	Date Joined	Title	First Name	M.I.	Last Name	Address	City	State	Zip	Occupation	Type	Dues	Charge	Rec Center
1	6/12/01	Mr.	Joseph	A.	Semora	79 Fuller	Dallas	TX	75391	Retired	Executive	$110.00	Y	$16.50
2	6/12/01	Dr.	Hector	G.	Gonzales	14 Alamo	Garland	TX	75040	Doctor	Family	$80.00	Y	$16.50
3	6/15/01	Ms.	Kim	W.	Sanchez	1539 Centre	Dallas	TX	75201	Attorney	Single	$50.00	N	
4	6/16/01	Dr.	Doug	R.	Guen	26 Concord	Dallas	TX	75222	Doctor	Family	$80.00	N	$16.50
5	6/17/01	Mr.	Rubin	E.	Gordin	4 Hyde Park	Irving	TX	75063	Teacher	Family	$80.00	Y	
6	6/19/01	Mr.	Ivan	L.	Fenton	502 Beacon	Dallas	TX	75222	Accountant	Single	$50.00	Y	
7	6/25/01	Mr.	Jacob	L.	Reeves	205 Kent	Mesquite	TX	75149	Retail	Student	$35.00	Y	
8	6/26/01	Mr.	Michael	W.	Bovie	14 St. Lukes	Garland	TX	75040	Teacher	Family	$80.00	Y	$16.50
9	6/29/01	Mr.	Gabriel	G.	Vidal	234 Fendal	Dallas	TX	75222	Retail	Student	$35.00	Y	
10	7/1/01	Mrs.	Susan	D.	Johnson	26 Bexar	Irving	TX	75063	Retired	Family	$80.00	Y	
11	7/3/01	Mr.	Edward	A.	Fowler	12 Michigan	Irving	TX	75063	Retail	Family	$80.00	Y	$16.50
12	7/7/01	Mr.	Ron	G.	Gurtler	766 Dover	Dallas	TX	75391	Teacher	Single	$50.00	N	
13	7/11/01	Mr.	Bei	V.	Wo	2550 Park	Mesquite	TX	75149	Retail	Executive	$110.00	Y	$16.50
14	7/15/01	Ms.	Jenny	U.	Smith	342 Lindon	Irving	TX	75063	Teacher	Student	$35.00	Y	
15	7/16/01	Ms.	Kristen	E.	Wade	12 Kent	Dallas	TX	75391	Technician	Single	$50.00	Y	
16	7/18/01	Dr.	David	J.	Setaro	3454 Lake	Dallas	TX	75222	Retired	Executive	$110.00	Y	$16.50

FIGURE 3-98

Quitting Works

After you have completed your work on the database, you should close the database file and quit Works, as shown in the following steps.

TO CLOSE THE DATABASE AND QUIT WORKS

1. Click the Close button in the upper-right corner of the database window.
2. Click the Close button in the upper-right corner of the Microsoft Works Task Launcher window.

The database file closes and the Windows desktop displays.

Project Summary

In this project, you learned to define the structure of a database using the Works Database tool. You inserted clip art from the Clip Gallery. Using WordArt, you entered the database title. In form design view, you moved the fields to an appropriate location and formatted the field names. You inserted a title using WordArt, inserted a rectanglar bar, and added color. Using the techniques you learned in an earlier project, you saved the database on disk. Then you entered data into the database in form view. Switching to the list view of the database, you specified the field widths for the fields. Finally, you printed the database using both form view and list view.

What You Should Know

Having completed this project, you should now be able to perform the following tasks:

- Add Color to the Rectangular Bar *(W 3.36)*
- Add Text Labels to the Database Form *(W 3.41)*
- Change the Margins on the Database Form *(W 3.17)*
- Change to Form View *(W 3.43)*
- Close the Database and Quit Works *(W 3.64)*
- Create a Database *(W 3.7)*
- Display the Database in Form Design View *(W 3.14)*
- Display the Database in List View *(W 3.50)*
- Display the First Record in the Database *(W 3.49)*
- Display the Next Record in Form View *(W 3.47)*
- Enter All Data in the Database *(W 3.48)*
- Enter and Format a Title Using WordArt *(W 3.29)*
- Enter Data for the Next Record *(W 3.48)*
- Enter Data into the Database *(W 3.44)*
- Format the Field Names *(W 3.38)*
- Insert a Rectangular Bar in the Title Area *(W 3.35)*
- Insert Clip Art in a Database Form *(W 3.25)*
- Move Field Names as a Unit *(W 3.23)*
- Position Fields on the Form *(W 3.21)*
- Print a Single Record in Form View *(W 3.59)*
- Print the Database in Form View *(W 3.56)*
- Print the Database in List View *(W 3.61)*
- Remove Field Lines and Add a Border on Fields *(W 3.39)*
- Save the Database (*W 3.12, W 3.43)*
- Save the Database with the Same File Name *(W 3.56)*
- Select the Entire Database and Change Font Size in List View *(W 3.52)*
- Set Field Widths in Form Design View *(W 3.18)*
- Set Field Widths in List View *(W 3.54)*
- Start Microsoft Works (*W 3.6)*
- Underline and Apply Bold to Text Labels *(W 3.42)*

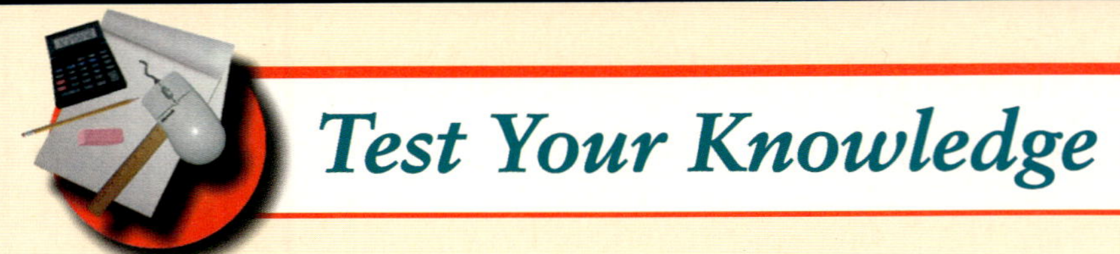

Test Your Knowledge

1 True/False

Instructions: Circle T if the statement is true or F if the statement is false.

T F 1. A database is defined as a collection of information organized in a manner that allows use of that information through access and retrieval.

T F 2. The default formatting for a field is Text.

T F 3. A field entry is the name you assign to the field.

T F 4. In form design view, dotted lines display around all elements, indicating you can select the elements for editing or change their locations on the form.

T F 5. A text label is descriptive information, such as a title, that you can add to a database form.

T F 6. You can specify a maximum of 25 fields in a database.

T F 7. List view displays your database one record at a time on the screen.

T F 8. You use form view to position the fields and set field widths on the database form.

T F 9. A record consists of one or more fields.

T F 10. When you create a new database, you must enter a field name and a field format for each field in the database.

2 Multiple Choice

Instructions: Circle the correct response.

1. The Works database tool allows you to __________ data.
   a. create
   b. save
   c. access
   d. all of the above
2. A record consists of a series of __________.
   a. data
   b. fields
   c. information
   d. numbers
3. In form design view, to select multiple fields hold down the __________ key and click each field to be selected.
   a. SHIFT
   b. TAB
   c. CTRL
   d. ALT
4. When you print a database in list view, __________.
   a. you can choose to print gridlines and record and field labels
   b. you can choose to print the records in landscape orientation
   c. you can use Print Preview to ensure all fields in the database will print
   d. all of the above

Test Your Knowledge

5. If a field is formatted to receive numeric data in a database, Works will enter the data ____________.
   a. left-aligned in the field
   b. right-aligned in the field
   c. center-aligned in the field
   d. evenly across the field
6. When you print a database in form view, __________.
   a. you can print all records in the database on one page
   b. you can print only the record displayed on the screen
   c. you must print all records
   d. you can print all records or any single record
7. In form view, to move from the last record of the database to the first record of the database, __________.
   a. click the first record navigation button
   b. click the last record navigation button
   c. press the TAB key
   d. click the List View button on the toolbar
8. To set the field widths for a field in list view, click __________ on the Format menu.
   a. Field
   b. Border
   c. Field Width
   d. Field Size
9. Works displays multiple records at a time in __________.
   a. form view
   b. list view
   c. form design view
   d. print preview
10. To move from one field to the next in form view of the database, __________.
    a. click the first record navigation button
    b. press the TAB key
    c. click the List View button on the toolbar
    d. press the SHIFT+TAB keys

3 Understanding Form Design View

Instructions: In Figure 3-99 on the next page, arrows point to the toolbar and major parts of a record displayed in form design view. Identify the elements in the spaces provided.

(continued)

Understanding Form Design View *(continued)*

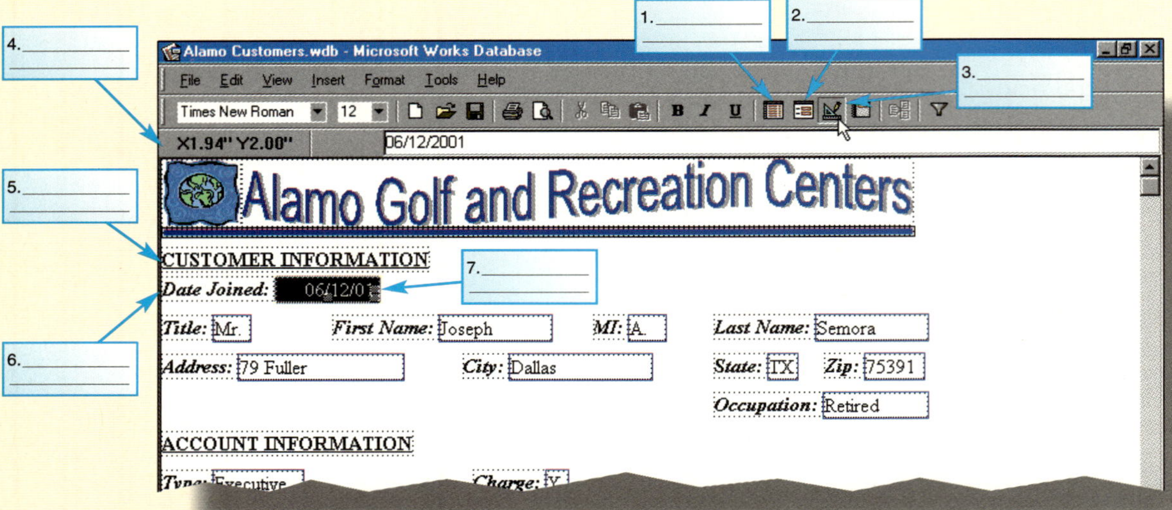

FIGURE 3-99

4 Working with Database Views

Instructions: In Figure 3-100, arrows point to the major components of a database displayed in list view. Identify the elements in the spaces provided.

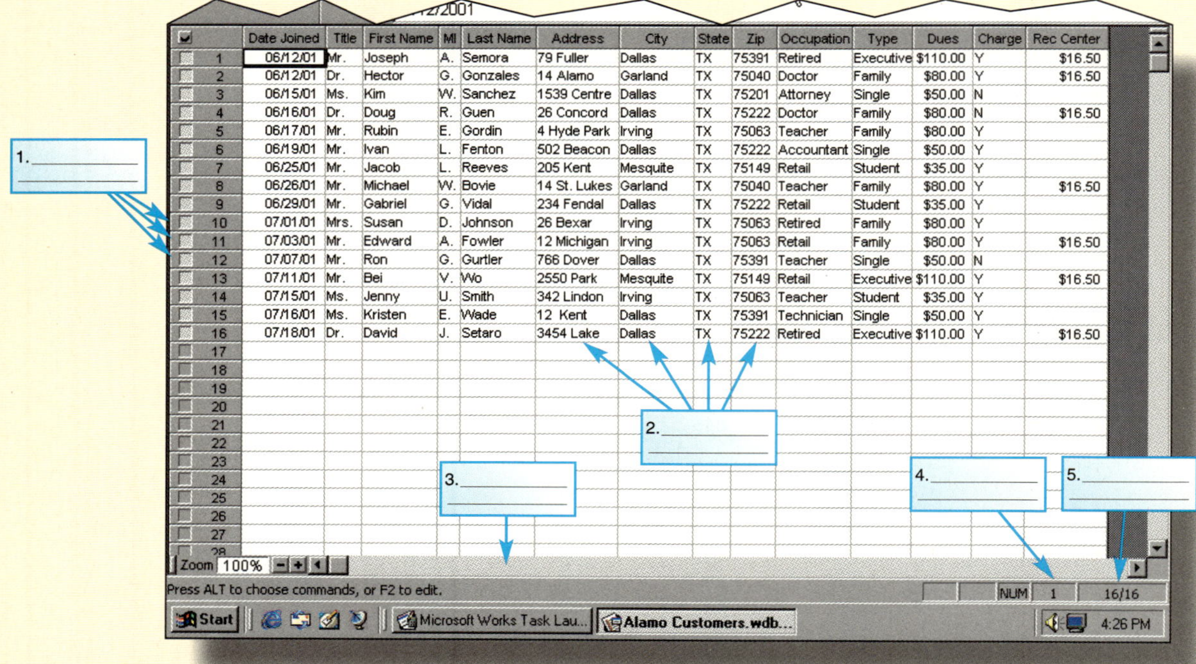

FIGURE 3-100

Use Help

1 Reviewing Project Activities

Instructions: Use your computer to perform the following tasks to obtain experience using Help.

1. Start Microsoft Works Task Launcher and then click the History tab.
2. Click the Alamo Customers database link to open the database file you created in this project from your floppy disk.
3. If necessary, click Works Help on the Help menu to display the Help pane to the right of the Database window.
4. Click the topic Create a new blank database on the Start using the Database Menu. When the Create a new blank database topic displays in the Help pane, read and print the numbered information on the topic.
5. Click About creating a database. When the About creating a database topic displays in the Help pane, read the information on the topic and then click Database Essentials. View the Quick Tour on Database Essentials. Click the Close button.
6. Click the Contents button located in the Help toolbar to view the Database Table of Contents. Click the Final Checklist Before Printing topic, and then click the Preview a Database Before Printing topic. Click the Preview a document before printing link.
7. When the Preview a document before printing topic displays in the Help pane, read the numbered information on the topic.
8. Close the Works Help pane.
9. Quit Microsoft Works.

2 Expanding on the Basics

Instructions: Use Works Help to better understand the topics listed below. Print the topic or topics that substantiate your answer.

1. Start Microsoft Works.
2. When the Microsoft Works Task Launcher dialog box displays, click the Works Database link and then click Start a blank database. If the First-time Help dialog box displays, click the OK button. When the Create Database dialog box displays, use the question mark button in the upper-right corner to answer the following questions.
   a. What are the rules for typing a field name in the Field name text box in the Create Database dialog box?
   b. What button changes names depending upon the status of the Create Database dialog box?
   c. What is the purpose of the Serialized option in the Format area?
   d. What format is best for a field that contains numbers with special characters such as a hyphen or a telephone number?
3. Click the Close button in the Create Database dialog box.
4. Quit Microsoft Works.

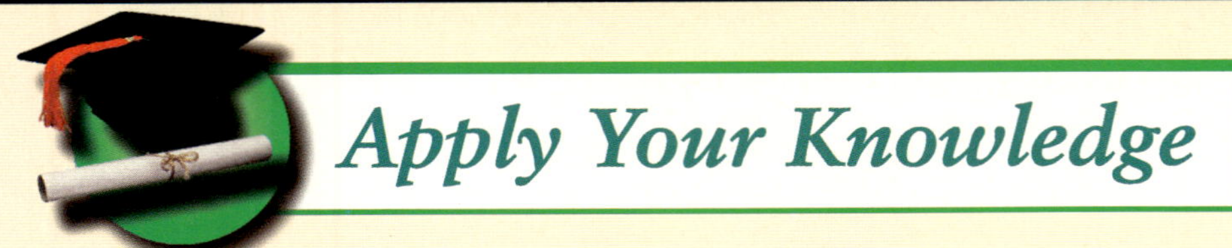

Apply Your Knowledge

1 Understanding Form Design View and Form Formatting

Instructions: Start Works. Open the file named, Office Inventory, on the Data Disk. If you did not download the Data Disk, see the inside back cover of this book for instructions for downloading or see your instructor. This file contains the form design view of the database before positioning and formatting the fields. Format the form as illustrated in Figure 3-101. Choose the illustration shown in Figure 3-101 from the Clip Gallery (search using the keyword, pen). After formatting, print the form and turn in the form to your instructor. Save the database with the file name, Modified Office Inventory.

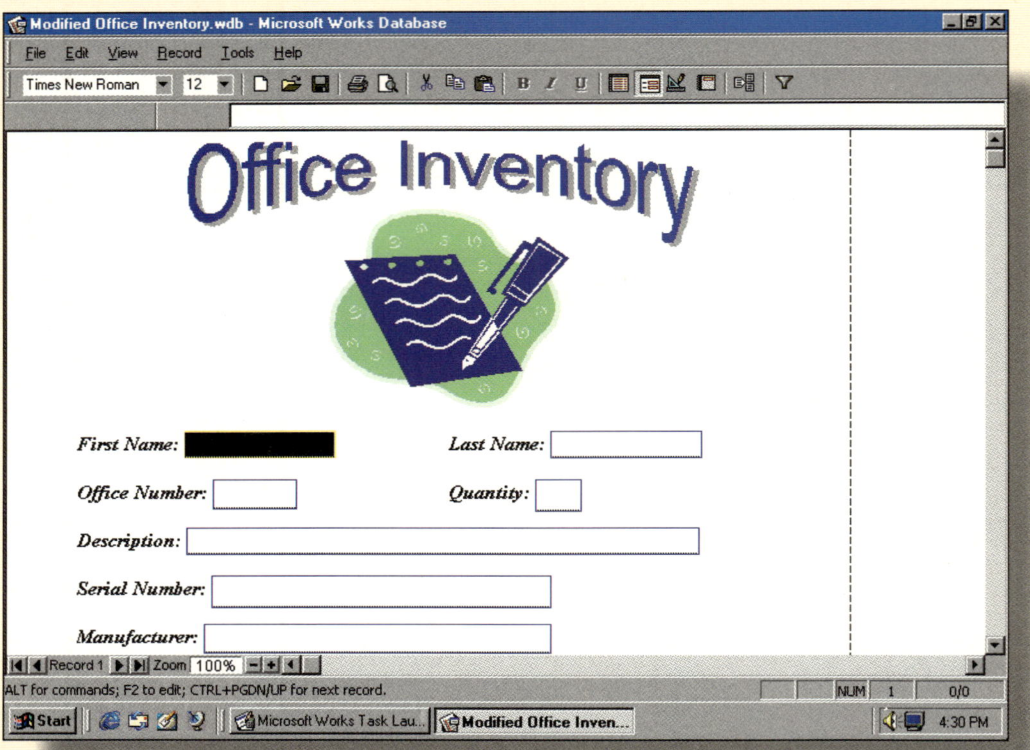

FIGURE 3-101

1 Creating and Formatting the Business Partners and Mentors Database

Problem: Create a database that contains information regarding individuals who have agreed to be business partners and mentors to local high school teachers and students. The contents of the database are shown in Table 3-5.

Table 3-5 Business Partners and Mentors Database

COMPANY	TITLE	FIRST NAME	LAST NAME	POSITION	START DATE	PERSON	HIGH SCHOOL
CYM Software	Ms.	Rae	Holton	Designer	07/21/99	Linda Freeman	Madison
HighTech	Mr.	Arnie	Garland	Network Specialist	09/18/99	Andy Holdman	Lyman
EZ Systems	Ms.	Donna	Emery	President	03/11/00	Andrea Simpson	Eighth Street
New Horizon	Mr.	Mason	Culp	Web Master	02/16/00	John Lucas	Eighth Street
New Horizon	Mrs.	Dorothy	Graham	Database Specialist	11/19/99	Shakeitha Reynolds	Lyman
CYM Software	Mr.	James	Peach	CEO	08/24/99	Frank Stern	Madison
CYM Software	Mr.	Vincent	Lopez	Designer	09/13/99	Jason Culvert	Madison
EZ Systems	Ms.	Lillith	Bjorlie	Tech Support	03/11/00	Regina Smith	Lyman
HighTech	Miss	Lucy	Osborn	Network Specialist	09/18/99	Rose Manoff	Eighth Street
HighTech	Mr.	Mark	Deric	Manager	02/29/00	Barney Knight	Lyman

Instructions: Perform the following tasks:

1. Create the database in the format shown in Figure 3-102 on the next page. Choose the illustration shown in Figure 3-102 from the Clip Gallery (search using the keyword, money). Experiment with the clip art size, title size, text label, and field positions to obtain the desired format.
2. Format the field names as shown in Figure 3-102.
3. Enter the data from the table into the database.
4. Determine the proper field widths so that in list view the entire record in the database prints on a single page.
5. Save the database on a floppy disk. Use the file name, Business Partners.
6. Print the database in both form view and list view.
7. Follow the directions from your instructor for turning in this assignment.

(continued)

Creating and Formatting the Business Partners and Mentors Database *(continued)*

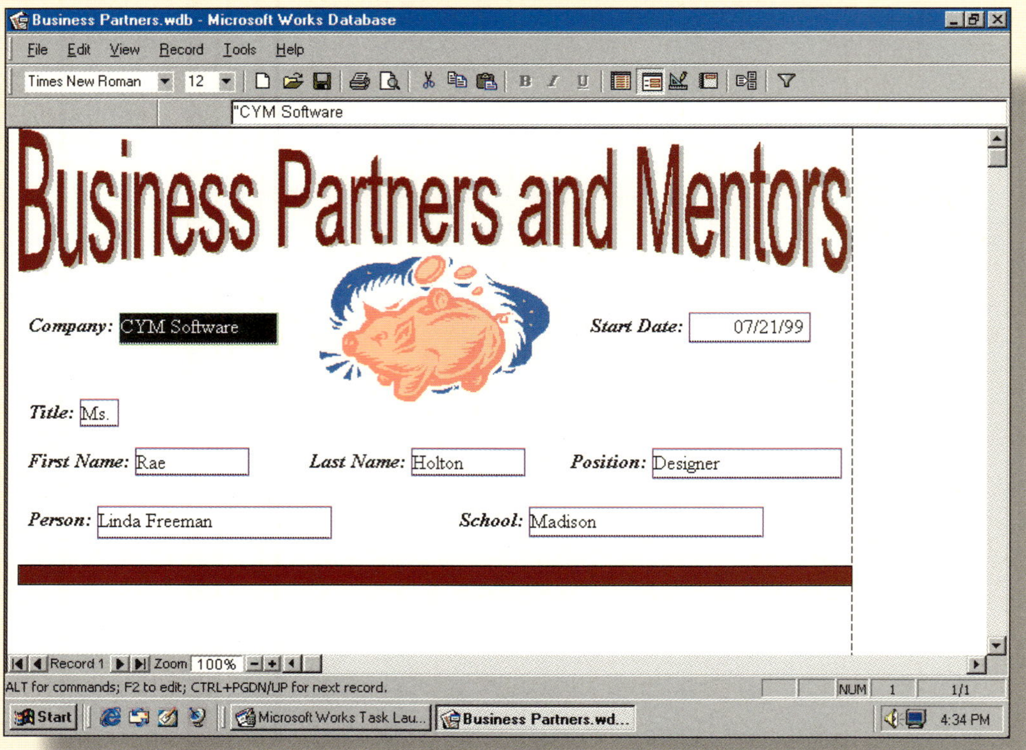

FIGURE 3-102

2 Creating and Formatting the Personal Shopper Customer Database

Problem: Create a database that contains information regarding Personal Shopper customers. The contents of the database are shown in Table 3-6.

Table 3-6 Personal Shopper Customers

FIRST NAME	LAST NAME	DRESS SIZE	PANT SIZE	SHIRT SIZE	AVERAGE SPENT	PROFESSION	LAST CONTACT
Athena	Alveraz	10	10	M	$300	Lawyer	04/13/99
Adam	Rubin		34/32	16	$500	Accountant	12/26/99
Denzal	Rogers		36/34	17	$800	CEO	01/14/00
Abdul	Rahamad		32/32	15	$450	Professor	11/15/99
Sarah	Johnson	8P	8P	S	$500	Doctor	03/01/00
Juan	Ortega		36/32	16	$350	Lawyer	01/07/00
John	Ecklund		34/34	16	$750	Congressman	08/03/99
Joy	Marcks	12	14	L	$600	Dentist	09/24/99
Michelle	Owen	6	6	S	$250	Homemaker	01/15/00
Donna	DeLucas	4P	2	XS	$400	Teacher	03/14/00

In the Lab

Instructions: Perform the following tasks:

1. Create the database in the format shown in Figure 3-103. Choose the illustration shown in Figure 3-103 from the Clip Gallery (search using the keyword, money). Experiment with the clip art size, title size, and field positions to obtain the desired format.
2. Format the field names as shown in Figure 3-103.
3. Enter the data from the table into the database.
4. Determine the proper field widths so that in list view the entire record in the database prints on a single page.
5. Save the database on a floppy disk. Use the file name, Personal Shopper.
6. Print the database in both form view and list view.
7. Follow the directions from your instructor for turning in this assignment.

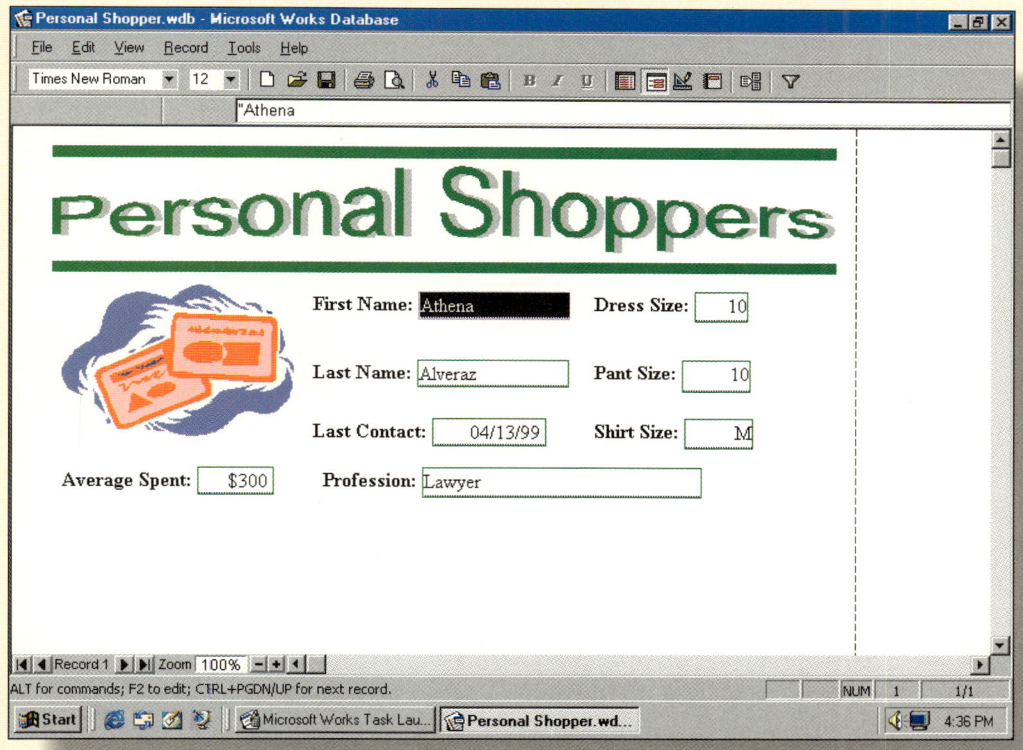

FIGURE 3-103

3 Creating and Formatting the Adventure Travel Members Database

Problem: Create a database that contains information regarding members of Adventure Travel. The contents of the database are shown in Table 3-7.

Table 3-7 Adventure Travel Members Database

DATE JOINED	TITLE	FIRST NAME	LAST NAME	ADDRESS	CITY	STATE	ZIP	MEMBERSHIP	AGE	NUMBER OF TRIPS
01/12/95	Ms.	Susan	Messer	12362 Grand	Austin	TX	73301	Family	35	5
03/15/00	Mr.	Roger	Krantz	1200 Bathe	Ellis	TX	78701	Individual	20	1
09/25/90	Dr.	Edna	Cruz	18021 Cove	Bexar	TX	78989	Individual	42	15
01/26/00	Dr.	Janie	Katz	323 Raintree	Ellis	TX	78701	Family	35	1
12/27/80	Mr.	Philip	Scott	125 Terrell	Bexar	TX	78989	Family	60	30
02/02/85	Dr.	Ester	Clifton	535 Escambi	Austin	TX	73301	Individual	55	7
01/03/00	Mr.	Frank	Mulson	448 Canal	Austin	TX	73301	Individual	69	1
07/05/97	Mr.	Essey	Meshi	555 Shafer	Ellis	TX	78701	Individual	30	5
10/09/98	Dr.	Rico	Bacani	299 Lake Sue	Bexar	TX	78989	Family	29	3
02/11/00	Ms.	Ruth	Zona	352 Portola	Ellis	TX	78701	Family	25	1

Instructions: Perform the following tasks:

1. Create the database in the format shown in Figure 3-104. Choose the illustration shown in Figure 3-104 from the Clip Gallery (search using the keyword, vacation). Experiment with the clip art size, title size, and field positions to obtain the desired format.
2. Format the field names as shown in Figure 3-104.
3. Enter the data from the table into the database.
4. Determine the proper field widths so that in list view the entire record in the database prints on a single page.
5. Save the database on a floppy disk. Use the filename, Adventure Travel.
6. Print the database in both form view and list view.
7. Follow the directions from your instructor for turning in this assignment.

In the Lab

Adventure Travel.wdb - Microsoft Works Database
File Edit View Record Tools Help
Times New Roman 12
"Ms.
Adventure Travel
Member Information
Title: Ms.
First Name: Susan
Last Name: Messer
Age: 35
Membership: Family
Date Joined: 01/12/95
Number of Trips: 05
Address: 12362 Grand
City: Austin
State: TX
Zip: 73301
Record 1
Zoom 100%
ALT for commands; F2 to edit; CTRL+PGDN/UP for next record.
NUM 1 1/1
Start
Microsoft Works Task Lau...
Adventure Travel.wd...
4:38 PM

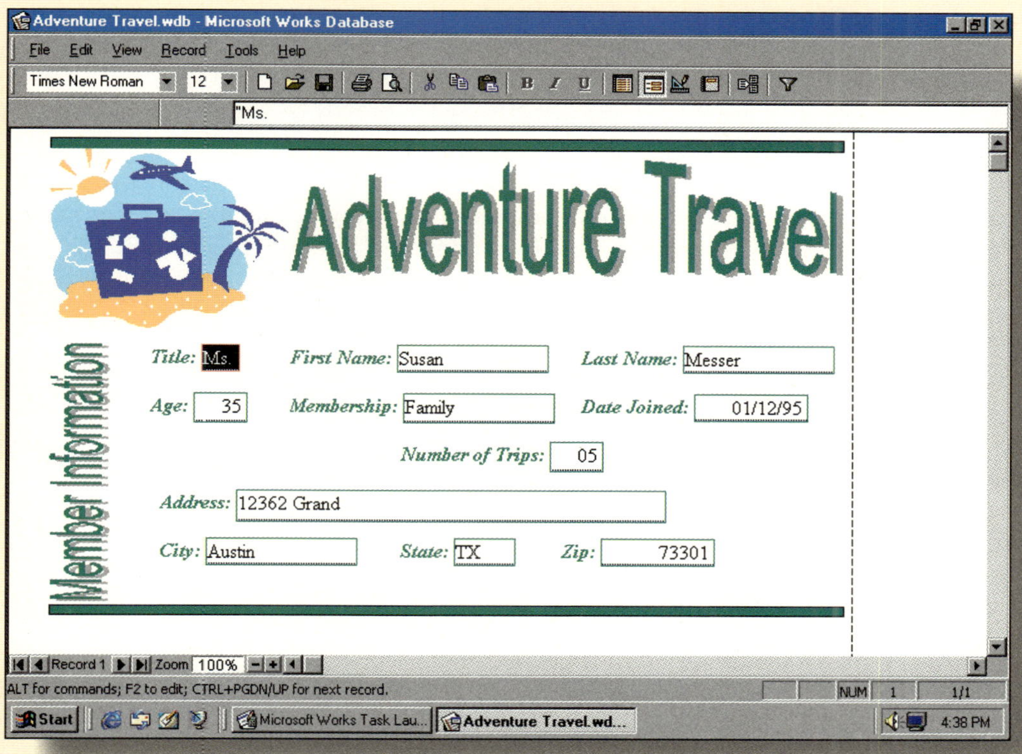

FIGURE 3-104

Cases and Places

The difficulty of these case studies varies:
▶ are the least difficult; ▶▶ are more difficult; and ▶▶▶ are the most difficult.

1 ▶ Your parents want to purchase you a wireless phone because you will be starting college in the fall. They have asked you to gather information on companies that service the area and compare their rate plans and per minute charges. You compile the information in Table 3-8 to help you and your parents decide which plan will best meet your needs.

Create a database that contains these records, and enter the data from Table 3-8. Design the form using illustrations from the Clip Gallery and WordArt. Use rectangles to set off areas of the form.

Table 3-8 Wireless Phone Rate Information

DEALER	RATE	MINUTES	ADDITIONAL MINUTES	RATE	MINUTES	ADDITIONAL MINUTES
Aerial	$19.95	80	$.29	$34.95	300	$.27
BellSouth	$25.00	100	$.35	$35.00	250	$.30
AT&T	$24.99	100	$.32	$39.99	300	$.29
Sprint	$16.99	15	$.39	$29.99	180	$.35

2 ▶ The students at your school have complained about the inequities of the book buy-back policy. Student government finally has decided to do something about it by organizing a used textbook cooperative. As a member of student government, you create a system whereby students can locate other students who have used a particular book in a previous semester and want to sell it to another student. Student government advertised the plan on its Web page and received the responses shown in Table 3-9.

Create a database that contains this information and enter the data from Table 3-9. Design the form using clip art from the Clip Gallery and WordArt.

Table 3-9 Text Book Information

BOOK TITLE	AUTHOR	COURSE	SELLER'S PRICE	NAME	PHONE	CONDITION
Sociology Today	Munroe	Soc 101	$24	Joe Van	555-7632	Good
Creative Writing	Swan & Shell	Eng 150	$28	Mary North	555-9421	Excellent
Reach for the Stars	Alvarez	Ast 210	$33	John Mott	555-9981	Excellent
Creative Writing	Swan & Shell	Eng 150	$23	Peter Rudd	555-9156	Excellent
Sociology Today	Munroe	Soc 101	$28	Daniel Lewis	555-0873	Excellent
Understanding Psychology	Navarone	Psy 101	$22	Karen Sing	555-9802	Poor
Electronic Circuitry	Carlson	Eng 255	$43	Karen Sing	555-9802	Good
Nutrition for Our Souls	Francis	Nrs 330	$28	Dave Corsi	555-2384	Excellent
Geriatric Nursing	Dyer	Nrs 265	$36	Mary Healy	555-9932	Excellent

Cases and Places

3 ▶▶ Whale-watching expeditions have been growing in popularity. You are planning such a trip to see the humpback or orca whales as a graduation present to yourself. After visiting several travel agencies and calling environmental organizations for details, you have learned that humpback whales can be seen during the summer in Antarctica and Massachusetts. They are best viewed from a boat. Humpback whales also can be seen in the Dominican Republic during the winter season both from a boat and from the shore and in Mexico all year long from a boat and the shore. To view orca whales, you can go to British Columbia or Norway during the summer and view them from a boat. In Argentina, you can view orca whales during the summer and fall from a boat, or you can go to South Africa to view orca whales during fall from the shore. Finally, you can see orca whales in New Zealand all year long from the shore. Using this information, together with the techniques presented in this project, create a database showing the destination, whale species, watching season, and access.

4 ▶▶ You are the assistant director of activities at an assisted living facility and you have decided to create an inventory of movies on DVD that are available to the residents. You list each movie by name, leading actors, year produced, and running time. You also assign a rating system of one to four stars. You create the following list: *The Little Princess*, starring Shirley Temple and Richard Greene, 1939, 94 minutes, three stars; *North by Northwest*, Cary Grant and Eva Marie Saint, 1959, 136 minutes, four stars; *And Then There Was None*, Walter Houston and Judith Anderson, 1945, 97 minutes, four stars; *The Maltese Falcon*, Humphrey Bogart and Mary Astor, 1941, 101 minutes, three stars; *The Quiet Man*, John Wayne and Maureen O'Hara, 1952, 129 minutes, four stars; *On the Waterfront*, Marlon Brando and Eva Marie Saint, 1954, 108 minutes, four stars; *Pardon My Sarong*, Bud Abbott and Lou Costello, 1942, 84 minutes, three stars; *Ride 'em Cowboy*, Bud Abbott and Lou Costello, 1942, 82 minutes, two stars; *You Can't Take It With You*, Jean Arthur and Lionel Barrymore, 1938, 127 minutes, three stars; *The Undefeated*, John Wayne and Rock Hudson, 1969, 119 minutes, two stars; and *Operation Pacific*, John Wayne and Patricia Neal, 1951, 109 minutes, three stars. Using this information, together with the techniques presented in this project, create a database showing the movie title, leading actors, year produced, running time, and rating.

5 ▶▶▶ You work for the classified ad section of your local newspaper. Your editors have decided to introduce a new service where readers can call the office and inquire if a particular car is being advertised. The editors have assigned this task to you. Begin by creating a database with fields for car manufacturer, model, year, price, transmission (automatic or manual), mileage, and engine size. Then enter data for 20 ads in today's newspaper. If any information is missing, enter the letters NA (not available).

Cases and Places

6 ▶▶▶ Food manufacturers claim that consumers can eat more nutritionally by purchasing specific items. For example, an ice cream manufacturer will label its products as low calorie (the product has 40 or fewer calories per serving), light calorie (1/3 fewer calories than the referenced product), or calorie free (fewer than 5 calories per serving). Visit a grocery store and examine the labels of five specific products claiming to be low, light, or calorie free. Then compare these five products to the referenced products. Using this information, together with the techniques presented in this project, create a database showing the name of the reduced-calorie product, the name of the referenced product, the serving size of each, and the number of calories per serving.

7 ▶▶▶ You have managed to save $5,000 and want to invest this money in a six-month certificate of deposit (CD). Visit a local bank, credit union, and savings and loan association and make a list of the current interest rates, minimum investment amounts, total amounts earned in six months, penalties for early withdrawal, and other restrictions. Using this information, together with the techniques presented in this project, create a database showing the name of the financial institution, its address and telephone number, the interest rate, the total value of the CD in six months, the amount of interest earned, the amount you would be penalized if you withdrew the money in two months and in four months, and any other restrictions.

Index

A few of the exercises in this book require that you begin by opening a data file from a Data Disk. Choose one of the following to obtain a copy of the Data Disk.

Instructors

- ☛ A copy of the Data Disk is on the Teaching Tools CD-ROM under the category Student Data Files, which you can copy to your school's network for student use
- ☛ Download the Data Disk via the World Wide Web by following the instructions below
- ☛ Contact us via e-mail at reply@course.com
- ☛ Call Course Technology's Customer Service department for fast and efficient delivery of the Data Disk

Students

- ☛ Check with your instructor to determine the best way to obtain a copy of the Data Disk

Instructions for Downloading the Data Disk from the World Wide Web

1. Insert a formatted floppy disk in drive A. Start your browser and then enter the URL www.scsite.com.
2. When the SCSITE.COM page displays, perform <u>one</u> of the following procedures: (a) ***Browse by Subject area:*** Click the subject category to which your book belongs. When the category list expands, click the title of your textbook. When the Textbook page displays, scroll down to the Data Disk Files area and then click From FTP Site. Follow the instructions beginning with step 3 below. (b) ***Support area:*** Click Download Instructions. Follow the instructions on the screen.
3. If the Save As dialog box displays, go to step 4. If the File Download dialog box displays, make sure the Save this program to disk option button is selected, and then click the OK button.
4. When the Save As dialog box displays, select a folder on your hard disk to download the file to. Write down the folder name listed in the Save in box and the file name listed in the File name box for use in step 6, and then click the Save button.
5. When a dialog box displays indicating the download is complete, click the OK button. Close your browser.
6. Open Windows Explorer and display the contents of the folder to which you downloaded the file. Double-click the downloaded file name on the right side of the Windows Explorer window.
7. When the WinZip Self-Extractor dialog box displays, type a: in the Unzip To Folder text box, and then click the Unzip button.
8. When the WinZip Self-Extractor displays the number of files unzipped, click the OK button. Click the Close button in the WinZip Self-Extractor dialog box. Close Windows Explorer.
9. Remove the floppy disk from drive A and label it Shelly Cashman Data Disk. You now are ready to insert the Data Disk and open the required files.

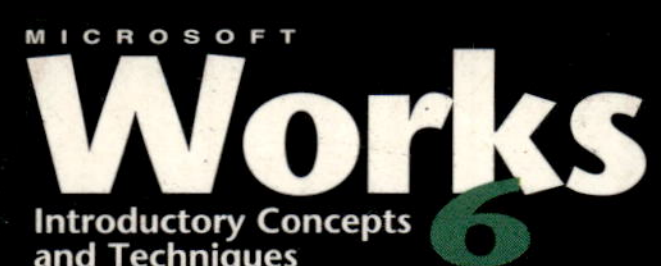

INTRODUCTORY

For the past three decades, the Shelly Cashman Series® has successfully introduced computers to millions of students — consistently providing the highest quality, most up-to-date, innovative materials in computer education.

The Shelly Cashman Series® includes a wide range of titles, from computer concepts to applications, programming, systems analysis and design, networking, and the Internet. These books are available separately or can be bundled together, or bound in any combination into a single volume using the Shelly Cashman Series® Custom Edition® program.

The Shelly Cashman Series® *Microsoft Works* books present material using a pedagogy that combines a project-oriented, step-by-step approach with corresponding screens and numerous exercises at the end of each project.

Features of these books include:

- Project orientation
- Step-by-step instructions with full-color screens showing the results of each step
- A methodology suitable for either a lecture or tutorial approach
- Clear and precise presentation of material
- A wealth of written and computer laboratory exercises at the end of each project, including the unique Cases and Places
- Emphasis on Works Help
- More About feature that provides background and interesting information about a myriad of subjects
- Other Ways feature that shows students all the ways operations can be performed in Works
- Project opening pages that provide depth and perspective for each project
- A writing style that makes the concepts and techniques presented easy to understand

You Can Rely on the Shelly Cashman Series®
The Educators' Choice

The Shelly Cashman Series® *Microsoft Works 6* titles include:

COMPLETE

Thirteen projects on Windows and the Works tools. Includes three projects on the Word Processor tool, three projects on the Spreadsheet tool, three projects on the Database tool, and one project on integration. Contains material for a beginning course that teaches how to use Windows and the Works tools.
ISBN 0-7895-6307-X

INTRODUCTORY

Three projects that introduce students to the Word Processor tool, the Spreadsheet tool, and the Database tool. Includes enough material for a three-to-five week portion of a course that teaches primarily computer concepts with less emphasis on applications.
ISBN 0-7895-6306-1

COURSE.com

for you
www

Course Technology is part of the Thomson Learning family of companies – dedicated to lifelong learning. Thomson is learning.